North Korea
a country study

Federal Research Division
Library of Congress
Edited by
Andrea Matles Savada
Research Completed
June 1993

On the cover: The Tower of Chuch'e Idea on the bank of the
Taedong River, P'yŏngyang, and statuary of the worker,
peasant, and working intellectual in front of its base. The
tower symbolizes the immortality of *chuch'e*—the political
ideology promulgated by President Kim Il Sung—and was
completed in 1982 in honor of Kim's seventieth birthday.

Fourth Edition, First Printing, 1994.

Library of Congress Cataloging-in-Publication Data

North Korea : a country study / Federal Research Division, Library of
Congress ; edited by Andrea Matles Savada. — 4th ed.
     p. cm. — (Area handbook series, ISSN 1057-5294)
(DA pam ; 550-81)
     "Supersedes the 1981 edition of North Korea : a country study,
edited by Frederica M. Bunge"—T.p. verso.
     "Research completed June 1993."
     Includes bibliographical references (pp. 291–321) and index.
     ISBN 0-8444-0794-1
     1. Korea (North)   I. Savada, Andrea Matles, 1950–
II. Library of Congress. Federal Research Division. III. Series.
IV. Series : DA Pam ; 550-81.
DS932.N662   1994   93-48469
951.93—dc20   CIP

Headquarters, Department of the Army
DA Pam 550-81

For sale by the Superintendent of Documents, U.S. Government Printing Office
Washington, D.C. 20402

Foreword

This volume is one in a continuing series of books prepared by the Federal Research Division of the Library of Congress under the Country Studies/Area Handbook Program sponsored by the Department of the Army. The last page of this book lists the other published studies.

Most books in the series deal with a particular foreign country, describing and analyzing its political, economic, social, and national security systems and institutions, and examining the interrelationships of those systems and the ways they are shaped by cultural factors. Each study is written by a multidisciplinary team of social scientists. The authors seek to provide a basic understanding of the observed society, striving for a dynamic rather than a static portrayal. Particular attention is devoted to the people who make up the society, their origins, dominant beliefs and values, their common interests and the issues on which they are divided, the nature and extent of their involvement with national institutions, and their attitudes toward each other and toward their social system and political order.

The books represent the analysis of the authors and should not be construed as an expression of an official United States government position, policy, or decision. The authors have sought to adhere to accepted standards of scholarly objectivity. Corrections, additions, and suggestions for changes from readers will be welcomed for use in future editions.

Louis R. Mortimer
Chief
Federal Research Division
Library of Congress
Washington, D.C. 20540

Acknowledgments

This edition supersedes *North Korea: A Country Study,* published in 1981. The authors wish to acknowledge their use of portions of that edition in the preparation of the current book.

Various members of the staff of the Federal Research Division of the Library of Congress assisted in the preparation of the book. Sandra W. Meditz made helpful suggestions during her review of all parts of the book. Robert L. Worden also reviewed parts of the book and made numerous suggestions and points of clarification. Tim Merrill checked the contents of all the maps and reviewed the sections on geography and telecommunications. Rodney P. Katz assisted with the compilation of several of the maps and also helped to collect research materials. Thanks also go to David P. Cabitto, who provided graphics support; Marilyn L. Majeska, who managed editing and production and edited portions of the manuscript; Andrea T. Merrill, who provided invaluable assistance with regard to tables and figures; and Barbara Edgerton, Alberta Jones King, and Izella Watson, who performed word processing. Alberta Jones King also assisted with the Bibliography.

The authors also are grateful to individuals in various United States government agencies who gave their time and special knowledge to provide information and perspective. These individuals include Ralph K. Benesch, who oversees the Country Studies/ Area Handbook Program for the Department of the Army; Cho Sung Yoon, Far Eastern Law Division, Library of Congress, who reviewed parts of the text and answered queries pertaining to the judicial and the legal systems; and C. Kenneth Quinones of the Department of State who reviewed the text and also offered many valuable suggestions and points of clarification. Inkyong Ahn, Yeonmi Ahn, Paul Dukyong Park, and Key P. Yang of the Library of Congress Korean Section all provided invaluable assistance in researching queries. The editor also wishes to thank the staff of the Democratic People's Republic of Korea Mission to the United Nations for their assistance.

Others who contributed were Ly Burnham, who reviewed the portions of the text on demography; Harriett R. Blood and the firm of Greenhorne and O'Mara, who assisted in the preparation of maps and charts; Teresa E. Kemp, who designed the illustration for the cover of the book and the illustration for the title page of Chapter 4; Deborah A. Clement, who designed the illustrations for the other chapter title pages; Debra Soled, who edited portions of the manuscripts; Cissie Coy, who performed the final prepublication editorial review; and Joan C. Cook, who prepared the Index. Linda Peterson of the Library of Congress Composing Unit prepared camera-ready copy, under the direction of Peggy Pixley. Most of the photographs were provided by Tracy Woodward. The editor is extremely grateful for his help, especially given the difficulty of locating current photographs of North Korea.

Contents

Chapter 5. National Security 209
Guy R. Arrigoni

Appendix. Tables 279

Bibliography 291

List of Figures

Preface

This edition of *North Korea: A Country Study* replaces the previous edition, published in 1981. Like its predecessor, this study attempts to review the history and treat in a concise manner the dominant social, political, economic, and military aspects of contemporary North Korea. Sources of information included books, scholarly journals, foreign and domestic newspapers, official reports of governments and international organizations, and numerous periodicals on Korean and East Asian affairs. A word of caution is necessary, however. The government of a closed communist society such as that of North Korea controls information for internal and external consumption, limiting both the scope of coverage and its dissemination. For instance, data from North Korea are, on the whole, dated, limited, and couched in vagaries—and are often provided as percentages of increases over previous years rather than as hard numbers. In addition, information coming from the outside is subject to the political bent of its originator. Data from South Korea, for example, seek, by and large, to show the superiority of that country's economic and political system. North Korea's 1991 admission to the United Nations, however, may result in the release of more statistics.

Chapter bibliographies appear at the end of the book, and brief comments on some of the more valuable sources recommended for further reading appear at the end of each chapter. A glossary also is included.

Spellings of place-names used in the book are in most cases those approved by the United States Board on Geographic Names (BGN); the spelling of some of the names, however, cannot be verified, as the BGN itself notes. The generic parts appended to some geographic names have been dropped and their English equivalents substituted: for example, Mayang Island, not Mayang-do, and South P'yŏngan Province, not P'yŏngan-namdo. The name North Korea has been used where appropriate in place of the official name, Democratic People's Republic of Korea. The McCune-Reischauer system of transliteration has been employed except for the names of some prominent national figures and internationally recognized corporations where the more familiar journalistic equivalent is used. The names of Korean authors writing in English are spelled as given.

Measurements are given in the metric system. A conversion table is provided to assist those readers who are unfamiliar with metric measurements (see table 1, Appendix).

The body of the text reflects information available as of June 30, 1993. Certain other portions of the text, however, have been updated: the Introduction discusses significant events that have occurred since the completion of research, the Country Profile includes updated information as available, and the Bibliography lists recently published sources thought to be particularly helpful to the reader.

Country Profile

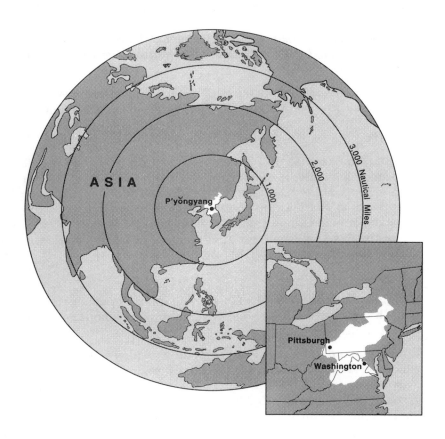

Country

Formal Name: Democratic People's Republic of Korea.

Short Form: North Korea.

Term for Nationals: North Koreans.

Capital: P'yŏngyang.

Geography

Size: North Korea occupies about 55 percent of total land area

NOTE—The Country Profile contains updated information as available.

of the Korean Peninsula, or approximately 120,410 square kilometers of land area; it is about the size of the state of New York or Louisiana.

Topography: Approximately 80 percent of land area mountain ranges and uplands. All mountains on peninsula over 2,000 meters high are in North Korea.

Climate: Long, cold, dry winters; short, hot, humid summers. Approximately 60 percent of rainfall falls in June through September.

Society

Population: Estimated 21.8 million as of July 1991; 177 people per square kilometer in 1989. Annual growth rate 1.8 percent for 1985–89, per United Nations (UN) estimate, and approximately 1.9 percent in 1991. Life expectancy at birth approximately sixty-six years for males, almost seventy-three years for females in 1991. UN estimates 33 percent rural, 67 percent urban population in 1990. Ethnic homogeneity; 100 percent Koreans.

Language: Korean.

Religion: Buddhism, Confucianism, and some Christians and native Ch'ŏndogyo religious adherents, although religious activities almost nonexistent.

Education and Literacy: Free, compulsory, universal (technical) education for eleven years, ages four to fifteen. Literacy estimated over 90 percent. In 1987 pre-first level (nursery schools, kindergartens) 16,964 schools, 35,000 teachers, and 728,000 pupils; first level (elementary/primary schools) 4,813 schools, 59,000 teachers, 1,543,000 pupils; second level (vocational/technical, middle/ secondary, high school, teacher training schools) no figures available; and third level (universities and equivalent institutions) 39,000 students—34 percent female, 27,000 teachers—19 percent female. Several new universities reported founded in 1992, for a total of 270 universities and colleges.

Health: National medical service and health insurance system. In 1989 consumption of estimated 2,823 calories per day to meet all requirements. No acquired immune deficiency syndrome (AIDS) cases reported as of 1990. Infant mortality rate thirty deaths per 1,000 live births in 1992.

Economy

Character and Structure: Socialized, centralized, planned, and primarily industrialized command economy. Principal means of production owned by state through state-run enterprises or cooperative farms. Prices, wages, trade, budget, and banking under strict government control. Growth rate 1984–90 averaged about 3 percent annually. Poor domestic economic performance; gross national product (GNP) down 3.7 percent in 1990 and down 5.2 percent in 1991. Total 1991 GNP US$22.9 billion, or US$1,038 per capita. Withdrawal of Soviet aid in 1991 negatively affected economy.

Agriculture, Forestry, and Fisheries: Traditional source of employment and income but, under party rule, secondary to industry. Completely collectivized by 1958. Estimated 18 percent land, agricultural use; approximately 25 percent GNP. Principal crops: rice, corn, potatoes, soybeans, and pulses. Largely self-sufficient in food production, but reported food shortages. Growth in agriculture, forestry, and fisheries sector 2.8 percent in 1991; increase in rice and other crops offset decrease in fish products.

Industry: Machine building, military products, electric power, chemicals, mining, metallurgy, textiles, and food processing. Manufacturing concentrates on heavy industry; ratio of heavy to light industry in 1990 was 8:2. In 1991 oil imports fell 25 percent; coal production, 6.5 percent; and electricity generation, 5.2 percent. Shortages in oil, coal, and electricity in 1991 led to idled plants and 13.4 percent decrease in manufacturing output.

Labor: Labor force estimated at about 11.2 million in mid-1990; approximately 33.5 percent agricultural, down from about 43 percent agricultural in mid-1980. Shortage of skilled and unskilled labor.

Currency and Exchange Rate: 1 wŏn = 100 chon. As of December 1991, US$1 = 97.1 chon.

Foreign Trade: Major exports: minerals, metallurgical products, agricultural products, and manufactures, for a total of US$1.95 billion (free on board, 1989). Trade statistics according to North Korean source: imports US$2.28 billion, exports US$1.24 billion, and deficit US$1.04 billion in 1991. Estimated 1991 trade decreased by approximately 25 percent, especially affected by withdrawal of Soviet trade concessions beginning January 1991—almost 40 percent—but trade with China up about 17 percent and increased trade with South Korea. Major imports: petroleum, machinery and transport equipment, coking coal, and grain, for a total of US$2.85 billion (free on board, 1989). Major trading partners: Russia, China, and Japan; to a lesser degree, Hong Kong, Germany, India,

Canada, and Singapore. Trade with South Korea classified as internal, not international; major hard-currency source. Lack of foreign investors. Joint Venture Law enacted in 1984, but few projects to mid-1993 and mostly Ch'ochongryŏn (General Association of Korean Residents in Japan) firms. Foreign investment, contractual joint venture, and foreign enterprise laws enacted October 1992 to induce investment.

Transportation and Telecommunications

Transportation: Reconstruction of system destroyed during Korean War complete, but lags behind economic needs.

Railroads: Total railroad network as of 1990 approximately 5,000 kilometers (8,500 kilometers claimed), primarily along east and west coasts. Almost 3,200 kilometers electrified; more being electrified and built.

Roads: Road network estimated between 23,000 and 30,000 kilometers (75,500 kilometers claimed) in 1990, almost all gravel, crushed stone, or dirt; remainder paved.

Ports: Port facilities at Ch'ŏngjin, Haeju, Hamhŭng, Hŭngnam, Najin, Namp'o, Sonbong, Songnim, and Wŏnsan.

Civil Aviation: Approximately fifty-five airports, all usable; about thirty permanent surface runways; less than five runways over 3,659 meters. International airport at Sunan, north of P'yŏngyang.

Telecommunications: Domestic and international communications controlled through Propaganda and Agitation Department of Korean Workers' Party. Radio service from approximately two dozen AM and ten FM government-controlled stations in 1993; nearly all households have access to broadcasts from radios or public loudspeakers. Television transmission widespread; eleven television stations. Wide range of official publications.

Government and Politics

Political System: Communist state under leadership of Kim Il Sung, general secretary of ruling Korean Workers' Party (KWP) and president of state, elected May 1990. Power centralized in hands of Kim Il Sung (''great leader''), son Kim Jong Il (''dear leader''), and select few holding positions on three-member Standing Committee of twenty-member Political Bureau (elected to five-year terms under 1992 revision of 1972 constitution; as of September

1992, thirteen full members; seven candidate members), inner council of 303-member KWP Central Committee (as of September 1992, 160 full members, 143 alternate members). Preeminence of party control (estimated 3 million members) unchallenged and as of mid-1993 no discernible signs of internal opposition to Kim Il Sung's absolute authority. Members of Supreme People's Assembly, unicameral legislature, also elected to five-year terms (as revision to 1972 constitution) in May 1990, with power to elect and recall authority of chairman, National Defense Commission, on president's recommendation; universal suffrage age seventeen. Constitution revised April 1992 at Supreme People's Assembly; text released in November 1992 by South Korean press. Nominally Marxist-Leninist in doctrine, but since mid-1970s, *chuch'e,* indigenous doctrine, promotes ideology of national self-reliance.

Administrative Divisions: 1972 constitution provides a two-tier system: nine provinces and three provincial-level special cities under direct central control; seventeen ordinary cities under provincial control.

Judicial System: Three-level judicial system patterned after Soviet model: Central Court at top, provincial courts at intermediate level, and people's courts at lowest level. Prosecutors grouped under separate, parallel chain of command topped by Central Procurator's Office, which supervises local procurators' offices at provincial and county levels.

Foreign Affairs: End of Cold War, break-up of Soviet Union, and changes in international political scene affected traditional alliances with China and Soviet Union.

Inter-Korean Relations: Agreement on Reconciliation, Non-aggression, Exchanges, and Cooperation signed 1991 defines basic relations between the two Koreas in transition period to peaceful unification. Declaration on the Denuclearization of the Korean Peninsula effective 1992 under the North-South Joint Nuclear Control Committee allows for mutual inspection of nuclear facilities.

International Memberships: Admitted to United Nations in 1991; maintains permanent mission in New York and participates in activities of many of its specialized agencies as well as those of other international organizations. Observer status at International Monetary Fund.

National Security

Armed Forces: Armed forces known collectively as Korean People's Army (KPA); total about 1.13 million 1993. Components (army, approximately 1 million; navy, 40,000 to 60,000; and air force, 70,000 to 92,000) under direction and control of President Kim Il Sung, generalissimo and grand marshal, with political controls parallel to party lines. Kim Jong Il commander in chief. Special operations forces, 60,000 to 100,000. KWP Military Affairs Committee and state National Defense Commission hold coordinated authority of armed forces. Marshal Kim Jong Il supreme commander of the army and chairman of National Defense Commission, as of April 1993. Heavily militarized state; fifth largest population under arms. Active military structure supported by reserves (army, 500,000; air force, unknown; and navy, 40,000) and militia of Worker-Peasant Red Guards and Red Guard Youth numbering over 3.8 million. Estimated 20 to 25 percent of GNP in 1991 for defense expenditures, although officially announced figure was 6 percent; 11.4 percent in 1992; and 11.6 percent in 1993. Conscription ages twenty to twenty-five, with three years for army service and four years for navy and air force service (other sources cite five to eight years for army service and three to four years for navy and air force service). All soldiers serve in reserves—estimated at 1.2 million in 1993—up to age forty, Worker-Peasant Red Guards to age sixty, Red Guard Youth, and College Training Units.

Paramilitary Forces: Under Ministry of Public Security, 115,000 personnel, including Border Guards.

Police and Internal Security: Internal security and maintenance of law and order centered in Ministry of Public Security and State Security Department, two government organs controlled by KWP through Justice and Security Commission and penetration of party apparatus at all levels. Ministry of Public Security responsible for internal security, social control, and basic police duties; estimated 144,000 personnel in 1991. Public security bureaus in each province, county, city, and some city substations; each village has police force. Conventional and secret police apparatus tightly controlled by KWP. Movement also controlled.

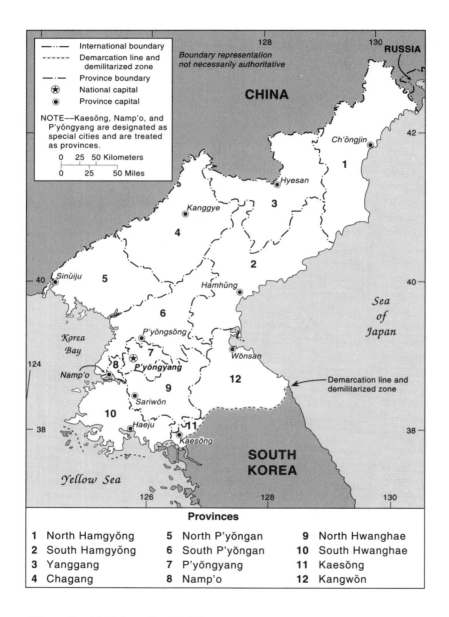

- -··- International boundary
- ------ Demarcation line and
  demilitarized zone
- ---- Province boundary
- ⊛ National capital
- ⊙ Province capital

NOTE—Kaesŏng, Namp'o, and
P'yŏngyang are designated as
special cities and are treated
as provinces.

0   25   50 Kilometers

0   25   50 Miles

CHINA

RUSSIA

Ch'ŏngjin

1

Hyesan

Kanggye

3

4

2

Sinŭiju

5

Hamhŭng

6

Sea
of
Japan

Korea
Bay

P'yŏngsŏng

7

Wŏnsan

8   P'yŏngyang

Namp'o

9

12

Demarcation line and
demilitarized zone

Sariwŏn

10

Haeju

11

Kaesŏng

SOUTH
KOREA

Yellow Sea

Provinces		
1 North Hamgyŏng	5 North P'yŏngan	9 North Hwanghae
2 South Hamgyŏng	6 South P'yŏngan	10 South Hwanghae
3 Yanggang	7 P'yŏngyang	11 Kaesŏng
4 Chagang	8 Namp'o	12 Kangwŏn

Figure 1. Administrative Divisions of North Korea, 1993

xxii

Introduction

IN THE EARLY 1990s, the Democratic People's Republic of Korea (DRPK, or North Korea) remained a vestige of the Cold War era. An isolated, closed, and tightly controlled communist society, North Korea was governed by a leadership that was only gradually opening the country to the outside world—and was doing so, in large part, only because its dire economic circumstances were forcing the issue. Although China, the former Soviet Union, and East European communist countries had undergone some degree of political and economic change, North Korea remained virtually the same as it had been for the more than four decades of its existence.

Korea's division in 1945 along the thirty-eighth parallel was originally intended as a temporary partition to facilitate the surrender of Japanese forces on the Korean Peninsula at the end of World War II. Superpower rivalry between the United States and the Soviet Union, and continued occupation of the peninsula, gave rise to the establishment of two hostile, competitive nations. North Korea was formed under Soviet sponsorship in the northern half of the peninsula. With the assistance of the United States, the Republic of Korea (ROK, or South Korea) emerged in the southern half. North Korea comprises approximately 55 percent of the total land mass of the Korean Peninsula. Some 22 million people live in the north, compared with about twice that number in the south.

North Korea's attempt at reunification by military action in 1950 led to the Korean War (1950–53), known in North Korea as the Fatherland Liberation War. Although North Korean troops initially were successful on the battlefield, only the massive introduction of the Chinese People's Volunteers into the conflict halted the almost total destruction of North Korean forces by the United States led-United Nations (UN) Command forces. The commanders of the Chinese, North Korean, and UN Command troops signed an armistice agreement in July 1953. Neither the United States nor South Korea signed the agreement, but both countries have adhered to it, and the armistice remained in force as of late 1993.

North Korean society revolves around the "religion of Kim Il Sungism" and his *chuch'e* (see Glossary) ideology, North Korea's own brand of Marxism-Leninism, national identity, and self-reliance. Kim's "religion" and *chuch'e* have supplanted Confucianism and other religious and philosophical beliefs such as Daoism,

Buddhism, Christianity, and Ch'ŏndogyo (see Glossary). Interestingly, some observers have suggested a possible connection between Confucian strictures and the transformation of North Korea into a society demanding loyalty to Kim Il Sung, the country's paramount leader.

North Korea's social services are similar to those of other socialist countries. Education is universal, free, and compulsory for eleven years. Health care is provided by a national medical service, and the country has a national health insurance system. Both the education system and the centrally controlled media stress social harmony. Contemporary cultural expression is also driven—and controlled—by the Korean Workers' Party (KWP) and the state.

In the beginning of its regime, North Korea was distinguished by its successes in agricultural growth rates and yields. This record, however, has not been duplicated in terms of growth and yield since then. There were reports of food shortages (leading to rioting and the imposition of food rationing) in the early 1990s, but the shortfalls were as much attributable to poor weather conditions and distribution problems as inherent problems in the agricultural sector.

North Korea's efforts at industrialization have not been very successful. Although the country initially achieved some success in industrialization, the overall record is grim. A portrait emerges of a centrally controlled economy in decline: resources are inequitably allocated, production is hindered by lack of energy and modern technology, shortages of energy and oil have resulted in production declines, and labor productivity is low. Low productivity stems, in part, from obsolescent plants fitted with broken-down equipment, few spare parts, and lack of the technical expertise needed to fix equipment. Further complicating matters, heavy demands for electricity necessitate its production on a staggered schedule in order to maximize its effective use. In addition, the development of key industries is linked to increased electrical production and the construction of power plants. Calls for greater electric power production are common (plants are idled because of cutbacks in power).

In the early years of the regime, the government stressed heavy industry and accorded consumer goods and light industries second priority. Since the late 1970s, however, economic planners have paid more attention to light industry. And, in the early 1990s, some planners even advised operating light industry plants on a full schedule, thereby increasing the production of people's daily necessities. Nonetheless, heavy industry—particularly defense needs—has remained a focus of central planning and a drain on the economy. The military's hold on scarce resources—and the priority of the military over other sectors—adds to the large demand for resources and has further undermined economic efficiency. North Korea has repeatedly failed to achieve economic goals and production schedules. In the past, Soviet and Chinese aid permitted some production targets to be met within specified time allotments, but others had to be sacrificed.

North Korea's poor record of debt repayment and its bad credit rating severely limit its ability to engage in international trade. Further, it has little to sell abroad. The demands made by China and Russia that North Korea pay hard currency for purchases exacerbate the situation. The country's trade problems are also compounded by the layers of economic sanctions the United States has placed on North Korea.

North Korea is not known for releasing statistical (or other) information, and its revelations about its economy are offered in vague terms. For example, at the fifth session of the Ninth Supreme People's Assembly held in April 1993, the Third Seven-Year Plan (1987–93) was not even mentioned in discussions on the state budget. North Korea usually does not discuss increases and decreases in terms of real figures, but provides them as percentages.

In early 1993, a spate of articles from Russian sources, published in the South Korean and Japanese press, detailed North Korea's economic woes. In March 1993, East European and Russian diplomats stationed in P'yŏngyang, North Korea's capital, revealed that North Korea's gross national product (GNP—see Glossary) may have declined as much as 7 to 10 percent. Russians and East European observers attributed the economic decline to failures in the mining industry, which accounts for approximately 40 percent of GNP. Estimated declines in the production of iron, steel, and cement and in oil refining also are significant. Agriculture presents a mixed picture: rice production has continued a decline that began in 1990, but corn and cabbage production apparently has increased. Meanwhile, critical shortages of raw materials and fuel mean that factories operate at far less than capacity. The garment industry is the only area of increased economic activity.

Some analysts have theorized that North Korea's economic problems will ultimately force it to open somewhat to the outside world. Some observers viewed the leadership changes announced at a December 1992 session of the Supreme People's Assembly as aimed at promoting advocates of economic reform and an opening to the outside world. Others argue, however, that the leaders of North Korea fear that economic reform and an opening to the outside world could erode the foundation of the totalitarian state. Political unrest and disarray similar to that experienced in the former communist nations could lead to the collapse of the regime in P'yŏngyang.

Survival of the current regime remains North Korea's foremost priority. Since its founding, the country has been ruled by a single person, Kim Il Sung, in an extremely rigid system. A guerrilla leader active in the resistance against Japan before World War II, Kim became head of state in September 1948. Over the years, a cult of personality has grown up around him. In 1993, at age eighty-one, he continued to dominate the political scene and was the long-standing general secretary of the KWP Secretariat and president of the government. He turned over the chairmanship of the National Defense Commission to his son and designated successor, Kim Jong Il, in April 1993 as part of the process of grooming and positioning his political heir. In his position as president, Kim Il Sung had also previously controlled the military; he appointed his son supreme commander, or *wŏnsu,* of the army in 1992. Like Kim Il Sung, key leaders hold multiple offices: party, state, and military. The death of the elder Kim may destabilize the political situation as contending forces vie for power and Kim Jong Il attempts to assert control.

Chuch'e ideology is also a dominant force in North Korea. On November 23, 1993, the South Korean government released the text of the revised 1972 North Korean constitution, which had been approved, but had not been made public, by the Ninth Supreme People's Assembly on April 9, 1992. The revised constitution substitutes *chuch'e* for Marxism-Leninism as a guiding principle of politics; changes the term of office for members of the Supreme People's Assembly and its Standing Committee from four years to five; and extends by a year the terms of office for the president, Central People's Committee, National Defense Commission, Central Court, and Central Procurator's Office.

The end of the Cold War and the resulting changes in the communist world—the breakup of the former Soviet Union and the East European communist countries—have presented challenges both to P'yŏngyang and to its allies. Not the least of these challenges has been their dealings with and diplomatic recognition of South Korea. The Soviet Union and South Korea established diplomatic relations in September 1990; China and South Korea opened trade offices (with consular functions) in 1991 and established diplomatic relations in August 1992. The success of South Korea's Nordpolitik (see Glossary) further contributed to the isolation of North Korea. In particular, Seoul's establishment of diplomatic relations with Moscow and its considerable trade with Beijing—more important than its trade with P'yŏngyang—have meant that North

Korea has lost the ability to play the two giants off against one another. For China and Russia, the economic advantages of a relationship with South Korea mitigate the effects of a lesser relationship with North Korea.

Normalization of relations with Japan remains a contentious issue. North Korea expects compensation for the period of colonial rule and wants hard currency, investment capital, and technology. North Korea also wants Japan to respect the three-party joint declaration issued by Japan's Liberal Democratic Party and Social Democratic Party and by North Korea's KWP. In addition, it wants Japan to respect North Korea's independent position and apologize for its past deeds. Japan's pressure on the nuclear issue will likely deter an early resumption of negotiations.

Although North Korea has sought reunification of the peninsula on its own terms through the judicious use of force, subversion, or even peaceful political means, efforts at inter-Korean reconciliation through dialogue began in the early 1970s and continued in the early 1990s. The admission of the two Koreas into the UN in September 1991 marked a turning point in P'yŏngyang's inter-Korean policy, despite the fact that the two countries remain committed to unification according to their own programs. Although seated alongside South Korea, North Korea has said it would continue to pursue a "one-Korea policy." Both sides continue their political maneuvering. The signing of the historic December 13, 1991, Agreement on Reconciliation, Nonaggression, Exchanges, and Cooperation, and the Declaration on the Denuclearization of the Korean Peninsula, both of which became effective in February 1992, marked another turning point in inter-Korean relations. The former agreement is sometimes referred to as the North-South Basic Agreement, the latter as the Joint Denuclearization Declaration.

On February 28, 1993, North Korea issued another three-part memorandum on reunification. Three conditions were cited in order for "peace . . . to be guaranteed and the reunification process [to] be continuously promoted on the Korean peninsula." First, the United States and South Korea must end their annual Team Spirit exercises. Second, South Korea must "take the road of national reunification on the principle of national independence." Third, the United States must renounce its Korean policy, which originated during the Cold War.

North Korea's Ten-Point Program of Great Unity of the Whole Nation for Reunification of the Country was presented at the April 1993 session of the Supreme People's Assembly. This program, adopted with the approval of all Supreme People's Assembly deputies, urged an "end to the national division."

North Korea also affirmed its continued interest in holding dialogue with South Korea and somewhat softened its standard demands. For example, the usual demand for the withdrawal of United States troops from the Korean Peninsula was recast and now echoed South Korea's expression of a "will to have US forces withdrawn from South Korea."

In May 1993, Kang Song-san, premier of the State Administration Council, sent a proposal to South Korea that the two sides exchange special envoys—"deputy prime minister-level officials fully in charge of reunification affairs, and the sooner the exchange of their visits, the better." Kang viewed this exchange as opening a new phase in implementing the North–South Basic Agreement and the Joint Denuclearization Declaration and as a way to move forward on the issue of reunification. Kang appealed to South Korea to recognize the importance of "national interest" and to grasp "the opportunity for the North and South to jointly open a bright future for the nation."

The legacy of mutual suspicion continues, however. North Korea maintains that inter-Korean barriers could be dismantled and mutual cooperation ensured once both sides end their arms race and bring about mutual and balanced force reduction. South Korea insists that dialogue should address nonpolitical questions until the two countries have developed mutual trust. Political issues influence all aspects of contact, however.

North Korea's apparent program to develop the ability to produce nuclear weapons has greatly complicated its relations with all nations. In December 1991, after years of secretly working to develop the means to produce plutonium, North Korea and South Korea signed the Joint Denuclearization Declaration. In this document, North Korea publicly pledged it would not develop, purchase, or otherwise seek to obtain nuclear weapons, nor the means to reprocess plutonium. In early 1992, North Korea finally signed a nuclear safeguards agreement with the International Atomic Energy Agency (IAEA). This agreement enabled the IAEA to inspect the major facilities at North Korea's main nuclear installation, Yŏngbyŏn.

IAEA inspections revealed discrepancies between North Korea's claims about the amount of plutonium it had produced and the amount suggested by technical data developed during the inspections. To resolve these discrepancies, the IAEA sought to collect samples at two nuclear waste sites, which North Korea had tried to mask as rice paddies. When repeated diplomatic efforts failed to gain the desired access, the IAEA director general made a call for "special" inspections as provided for in the safeguards agreement between the IAEA and North Korea.

Parallel to these developments, North Korea's eighteen-month-long dialogue with Seoul ground to a halt in the winter of 1992. The first signs of renewed friction had appeared in October 1992, when Seoul's internal security agency, the National Security Planning Agency, announced that it had uncovered an extensive North Korean spy ring. Also in October 1992, at the annual United States-South Korea Security Consultative Meeting, it was decided to resume preparations for Team Spirit, the two countries' annual joint defensive exercise that had been suspended in early 1992 in recognition of North Korea's signing of the Joint Denuclearization Declaration. It was noted, however, that the 1993 exercise would not be held if there were significant progress in the South–North dialogue, particularly concerning formulation of a South–North nuclear inspection regime. North Korea pointed to these developments as it disengaged from all meetings with Seoul except for those focused on implemention of the denuclearization accord in the Joint Nuclear Control Committee (JNCC). But JNCC talks were discontinued in late January 1993 when the United States and South Korea announced they would conduct Team Spirit 1993.

By February 1993, all South–North dialogue had stalled, Team Spirit 1993 was about to begin, and the IAEA had yet to gain access to the two suspected North Korean nuclear waste sites at Yŏngbyŏn. The IAEA Board of Governors served notice to North Korea on February 25 that if it did not cooperate with the IAEA's director general and allow access to the suspected sites, the board would find North Korea in noncompliance with its obligations under its safeguards agreement with the IAEA and would report the situation to the UN Security Council.

North Korea reacted on March 12 by announcing its intention to withdraw from the Nuclear Nonproliferation Treaty (NPT); it would be the first nation ever to do so. A ninety-day grace period would have to run its course before the withdrawal became effective.

There was an immediate, worldwide outcry. The more than 100 members of the NPT urged North Korea to reconsider its decision to withdraw. The IAEA Board of Governors passed a resolution at the end of March that found North Korea in noncompliance with its safeguards obligations and referred the matter to the UN Security Council. The global condemnation of North Korea climaxed on May 11 when the Security Council passed, with China and Pakistan abstaining, Resolution S/25768, which urged North Korea to comply with the IAEA director general's requests for "special" inspections at the two suspected nuclear waste sites. The resolution expressed full support for the IAEA, asked that North Korea remain a member of the NPT, and called on UN members to assist in seeking a solution to the impasse.

The United States subsequently agreed to engage North Korea in the first ever bilateral talks. At the first round of talks held in New York in June, the two countries issued a joint statement in which they noted that "the two sides discussed policy-related issues raised for fundamentally resolving the nuclear issue of the Korean Peninsula, and expressed support of the Declaration on the Denuclearization of the Korean Peninsula in accordance with the purpose for preventing nuclear proliferation." North Korea stated that it had "decided to unilaterally and temporarily suspend the effectuation of the withdrawal from the NPT as long as it considers necessary." A second round of talks in Geneva produced some additional progress toward a resolution of the nuclear issue. The United States promised that as part of a final resolution of the nuclear issue, it would be willing to consider assisting North Korea in its desire to acquire light-water reactor technology.

P'yŏngyang promised that it would maintain continuity of safeguards, which requires IAEA inspection of its nuclear facilities, and indicated that it would consult with the IAEA about outstanding safeguards issues and resume serious dialogue with Seoul prior to a third round of talks with Washington.

As of late 1993, however, North Korea remained reluctant to allow the scope of inspection that the IAEA deems necessary to maintain the continuity of safeguards. Further, North Korea had yet to agree to resume its dialogue with South Korea. Consequently, the United States was refusing to agree to a third round of talks with North Korea. In short, the talks appeared close to being broken off, despite the willingness of the United States to suspend Team Spirit 1994 and ultimately to consider improving diplomatic and economic ties with P'yŏngyang in exchange for its remaining a member of the NPT, complying fully with the IAEA, and agreeing to the implementation of the Joint Denuclearization Declaration.

The future of the Korean Peninsula is far from resolved. Although there has been progress in inter-Korean relations, much remains to be worked out. The costs of reunification are high, both economically and politically. Analysts have noted that some South Korean government officials believe that North Korea has designated 1995 as the year for reunification and is accelerating its war preparations. Much of the current increased posturing by North Korea—particularly its nuclear stance—may be related to this issue. The only certainty is that the situation is far from closure.

December 16, 1993

The chronology of events since the Introduction was written shows little progress in inter-Korean relations, United States-North Korean relations, or full compliance by North Korea with IAEA nuclear inspection. The situation remains uncertain. Desirous of diplomatic recognition and economic aid from the United States—the latter also from its neighbors—P'yŏngyang, in the view of some observers, has used the "nuclear card" as a strategy to exact concessions from Washington but is also determined to continue its military program and develop a powerful nuclear arsenal. The United States Central Intelligence Agency suspects that North Korea already possesses two nuclear bombs and may have the potential to develop four to five more weapons.

In March 1994, almost one year after nuclear inspections were halted in North Korea, visas were issued to two teams of IAEA inspectors for access to seven of the nine nuclear facilities they sought to examine as part of the inspection process. Subsequently, the United States announced that a third round of high-level talks with North Korea on diplomatic and economic matters would be resumed in Geneva on March 21. The United States and South Korea agreed to conditionally suspend—pending North Korea's holding of nuclear inspections—their annual Team Spirit exercise scheduled for late March. For its part, North Korea also agreed to resume talks with South Korea. In early March, a broken seal was discovered at the Yŏngbyŏn nuclear reprocessing facility, a site where the surveillance cameras have been without operating batteries since October 1993. On March 16, the third round of talks between the United States and North Korea was canceled because of P'yŏngyang's refusal to allow a complete IAEA inspection. On March 21, President William Clinton ordered a battalion of Patriot missile interceptors shipped to South Korea. That same day, the nine-member IAEA Board of Governors (with China abstaining) passed a resolution asking North Korea "immediately to allow the IAEA to complete all requested inspection activities" and to "comply fully with its safeguards agreement."

On March 31, 1994, the UN Security Council issued a formal statement calling on North Korea to allow the IAEA full and complete inspection of all North Korean nuclear sites. (The United States, with the support of Britain, France, and Russia, had wanted to issue a UN resolution—which carries the weight of international law—on the matter, but China opposed such a stance.) The statement proposed a six-week deadline for the IAEA to report on whether or not inspections had been completed and whether or not North Korea was in compliance with international nuclear safeguards. A few days later, North Korea rejected the demand to comply with full inspections as "unjustifiable."

The stalemate continued in April. By mid-April Kim Il Sung had announced that the United States must abide by its pledge to proceed with high-level talks without preconditions. Moreover, Kim denied that North Korea has been—or is—developing nuclear weapons. On April 18, United States Navy ships began offloading Patriot missiles in South Korea.

There was no resolution to the situation in May. On May 19, the IAEA condemned North Korea for "serious violation" of the nuclear inspection program. At issue was the marking, or segregation, of certain critical withdrawn uranium fuel rods for eventual sampling to determine how much plutonium had been accumulated. If the IAEA cannot properly monitor, that is, sample, the withdrawn fuel rods, the agency cannot verify whether or not fuel has been diverted for use in nuclear weapons. By measuring the radioactive fuel content of rods, scientists can determine the amount of plutonium that has been accumulated for nuclear weapons. Uranium fuel rods are replaced every few years. North Korea has said that the present rods are the original rods that were placed in 1986 and that they are almost spent, necessitating their replacement. The United States suspects that many of these fuel rods were secretly replaced in 1989 when the reactor was shut down for 100 days and that the removed fuel rods were ultimately reprocessed for use in nuclear weapons.

After failing to conduct complete inspections in March, the two IAEA teams were again sent to North Korea in May to conduct nuclear inspections. Their efforts were again stymied. Complications were introduced when North Korea told the inspectors that they could observe the removal of fuel rods but that they could not test the rods. They were also informed that rods would not be set aside for future measurements and that IAEA inspectors could neither visit two nuclear waste sites nor complete the inspections at the plutonium reprocessing plant at Yŏngbyŏn. In response, the IAEA demanded an immediate stop to the withdrawal of fuel rods. In late May, one IAEA team confirmed that North Korea had withdrawn approximately 4,000 spent fuel rods out of an estimated 8,000 rods in May. The IAEA wanted 300 critical rods that constitute the core fuel element set aside for sampling.

By late May, the United States had warned that it would cancel new high-level talks if North Korea did not comply with IAEA demands and that it would press for international economic sanctions. North Korea has continued to reject the complete inspection program, claiming that it has a "unique status"—attained in March 1993, when it threatened to withdraw from the NPT but then suspended its threats under United States pressure. North Korea has said that it will never allow the IAEA to mark and sample the rods even if threatened with economic sanctions under a UN resolution. On May 30, Britain, China, France, Russia, and the United States issued a statement urging North Korea to set aside fuel rods for future sampling. The following day, the IAEA telexed North Korea to either halt the withdrawal of fuel rods or follow acceptable procedures for storing the rods under international supervision.

Also in late May, Japanese press reports, confirmed by United States officials, noted that North Korea appeared to be preparing for testing a new short-range ballistic missile within the next few weeks. Such a missile would be capable of reaching much of Japan. Department of Defense officials said that on May 31 North Korea tested a cruise missile in the Sea of Japan designed to hit ships at a range of more than 160 kilometers.

In early June, the uncertainty of the situation on the peninsula continued. On June 2, Hans Blix, director general of the IAEA, sent a letter to the secretary general of the UN stating that the IAEA was unable to "select, segregate and secure fuel rods for later measurements in accordance with agency standards" and that it could not determine the amount of plutonium that "has been diverted in the past." He subsequently announced that all but 1,800 of the 8,000 rods—including the 300 critical rods—had been removed and stored in such a way that the IAEA would be unable to determine their location in the reactor. The letter automatically placed the issue of sanctions on the UN Security Council agenda.

As of early June, the United States had not yet decided on the level of sanctions it would seek. It also faced the difficulty of getting the full council membership—particularly China but also Russia—to agree to impose sanctions against North Korea. The United States extension of most-favored-nation status to China in late May has been viewed as a means of appealing to China to either agree to economic sanctions or to use its leverage with North Korea to oblige it to comply with IAEA requests. Moreover, the level of sanctions Japan would be willing to impose also remained questionable. What remains certain is that the United States, China, Japan, Russia, and South Korea publicly want North Korea to comply with the nuclear inspection program, but they differ in their views on the level, the efficacy, and the timing of such sanctions.

Further complicating matters, North Korea again threatened to withdraw from the NPT, stating that sanctions would violate the 1953 armistice agreement and be considered an act of war. Secretary of Defense William Perry has said that the United States will bolster its troops in South Korea and will defend that country if invaded by North Korea.

In mid-June the nuclear inspections issue continued to dominate events on the Korean Peninsula. The United States effort to garner support for the imposition of economic sanctions on North Korea was halted, however, as a result of events following the visit of former United States president Jimmy Carter to North Korea on June 15–18 and his meetings with Kim Il Sung. The United States agreed to resume its high-level talks (suspended for over a year) with North Korea in Geneva on July 8. In exchange, North Korea agreed to "freeze" its nuclear program: to allow IAEA inspectors to remain at Yŏngbyŏn, to halt reprocessing, and to stop reloading the reactor. However, this position is a short-term one. P'yŏngyang's long-term position on the nuclear issue will likely be contingent on the progress of the talks in Geneva.

During President Carter's visit, Kim Il Sung proposed a summit meeting between the leaders of North Korea and South Korea. On June 28, North Korea and South Korea agreed to hold such a meeting—the first since the division of the peninsula—on July 25–27 in P'yŏngyang. The agenda, however, was not discussed; a second, reciprocal meeting—likely to be held in Seoul—will be part of the agenda at the first meeting.

As of late June, the United States was considering a range of economic and diplomatic incentives in exchange for a freeze on North Korea's nuclear weapons program but planning for other contingencies. The United States Navy is sending two minesweepers and an amphibious vessel to Japan as a "purely defensive" measure in order to reinforce the United States military presence on the Korean Peninsula. The ships are scheduled to arrive by the end of July.

The talks in Geneva will likely be a forum for discussing the nuclear issue in a larger context. The dynamics of the situation will change, determined by the direction and progress, or lack thereof, of the talks.

June 29, 1994

* * *

The uncertainty of the situation on the Korean Peninsula continued with the sudden, unexpected death of Kim Il Sung of an alleged heart attack "owing to heavy mental strains." As a result of Kim's death on July 8, which was also the first day of talks in Geneva between the United States and North Korea, it was announced that subsequent talks between the two countries had been suspended, and that the summit talks between North Korea and South Korea scheduled for late July in P'yŏngyang had been postponed indefinitely. P'yŏngyang announced, however, that it would resume discussions on the nuclear weapons issue after Kim's funeral, and on July 20, the United States announced that these talks were expected to resume within a few weeks. On July 16, Kim's funeral was postponed for two days, causing some speculation among Korea watchers as to whether Kim Jong Il's so far seemingly orderly succession was meeting resistance. For the short term, it is expected that Kim Jong Il will be able to assume the positions for which he has been groomed without overt resistance; his long-term success remains open to question. The constitution makes no provisions for succession; as of this writing, Kim has not been formally proclaimed either president of state or general secretary of the party.

July 20, 1994   Andrea Matles Savada

Chapter 1. Historical Setting

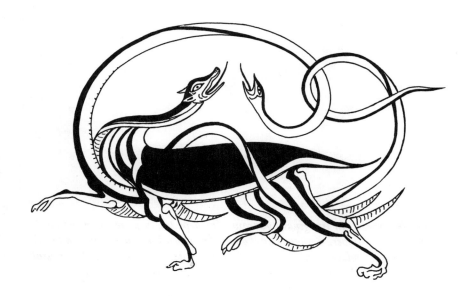

Turtle-serpent, an imaginary guardian, as depicted in a fresco on the north wall, rear chamber, Kangso Big Tomb. The seventh-century tomb, in South P'yŏngan Province, was constructed for the nobles of Koguryŏ. The mural demonstrates the artistic and architectural skills typical of that period.

PRIOR TO THE NATIONAL DIVISION of the Korean Peninsula in 1945, Korea was home to a people with a unitary existence, ethnic and linguistic homogeneity, and a historical bond of exclusionism (see Glossary) toward outsiders—a result of its history of invasion, influence, and fighting over its territory by larger and more powerful neighbors. This legacy continues to influence the contemporary Democratic People's Republic of Korea (DPRK, or North Korea).

There are other parallels between Korea's past and present-day North Korea. The traditions of Confucianism and a bureaucracy administered from the top down and from the center continue to hold sway. Further, just as there was relative stability for more than two millennia on the Korean Peninsula, there has been relative stability in North Korea since Kim Il Sung came to power in 1946. As Confucian doctrine perpetuated the authority of the family system and the importance of education, so too were these elements paramount in Kim Il Sung's North Korea. Politics remain personalistic, and Kim has surrounded himself with a core of revolutionary leaders (now aging), whose loyalty dates back to their days of guerrilla resistance against the Japanese in Manchuria. Kim's *chuch'e* (see Glossary) ideology also has its roots in the self-reliant philosophy of the Hermit Kingdom (as Korea was called by Westerners), and Korea's history of exclusionism also held particular appeal to a people emerging from the period of Japanese colonial domination (1910–45).

North Korea came into being in 1945, in the midst of a prolonged confrontation between the United States and the Soviet Union. North Korea was, and in some ways remains, a classic Cold War state, driven by the demands of the long-standing conflict with the Republic of Korea (ROK, or South Korea) and the United States and its allies. It emerged in the heyday of Stalinism, which influenced North Korea's decision to give priority to heavy industry in its economic program (see Economic Development and Structural Change, ch. 3). North Korea was a state forged in warfare: by a civil struggle fought at the beginning of the regime and by a vicious fratricidal war fought while the system was still in infancy. All these influences combined to produce a hardened leadership that knew how to hold onto power. But North Korea also evolved as a rare synthesis between foreign models and native

3

influences; the political system was deeply rooted in native soil, drawing on Korea's long history of unitary existence on a small peninsula surrounded by greater powers.

The Origins of the Korean Nation

Koreans inhabit a mountainous peninsula protruding southward from the northeastern corner of the Asian continent and surrounded on three sides by water (see fig. 1; The Physical Environment, ch. 2). Although Japan exercised decisive influence by the late sixteenth century, in ancient times the peoples and civilizations on the contiguous Asian continent were far more important. The peninsula is surrounded on three sides by other peoples: Chinese to the west; Japanese to the east; and an assortment of peoples to the north, including "barbarian" tribes, aggressive invaders, and, in the twentieth century, an expanding and deepening Russian presence. Koreans have emerged as a people influenced by the peninsula's internal and surrounding geography.

The northern border between Korea and China formed by the Yalu and Tumen rivers has been recognized for centuries. But these rivers did not always constitute Korea's northern limits; Koreans ranged far beyond this border well into northeastern China and Siberia, and neither Koreans nor the ancient tribes that occupied the plains of Manchuria (northeastern China) considered these riverine borders to be sacrosanct. The harsh winter climate also turned the rivers into frozen pathways for many months, facilitating the back-and-forth migration out of which the Korean people were formed.

Paleolithic excavations show that humans inhabited the Korean Peninsula half a million years ago, but most scholars assume that present-day Koreans are not descended from these early inhabitants. Neolithic-age (from 4000 B.C.) humans also inhabited the area, identified archaeologically by the ground and polished stone tools and pottery they left to posterity. Around 2000 B.C., a new pottery culture spread into Korea from China. These people practiced agriculture in a settled communal life and are widely supposed to have had consanguineous clans as their basic social grouping. Korean historians in modern times sometimes assume that the clan leadership systems characterized by councils of nobles (*hwabaek*) that emerged in the subsequent Silla period can be traced back to these neolithic peoples and that a mythical "child of the *sŏn*," an original Korean, also was born then. There is no hard evidence, however, to support such beginnings for the Korean people.

By the fourth century B.C., a number of walled-town states on the peninsula had survived long enough to come to the attention of China. The most illustrious of these states was Old Chosŏn, which had established itself along the banks of the Liao and the Taedong rivers in southern Manchuria and northwestern Korea. Old Chosŏn prospered as a civilization based on bronze culture and a political federation of many walled towns; the federation, judging from Chinese accounts, was formidable to the point of arrogance. Riding horses and deploying bronze weapons, the Chosŏn people extended their influence to the north, taking most of the Liaodong Basin. But the rising power of the north China state of Yen (1122–255 B.C.) checked Chosŏn's growth and eventually pushed it back to territory south of the Ch'ŏngch'ŏn River, located midway between the Yalu and Taedong rivers. As the Yen gave way in China to the Qin (221–207 B.C.) and the Han (206 B.C.–A.D. 220) dynasties, Chosŏn declined, and refugee populations migrated eastward. Out of this milieu emerged Wiman, a man who assumed the kingship of Chosŏn sometime between 194 and 180 B.C. The Kingdom of Wiman Chosŏn melded Chinese influence, and under the Old Chosŏn federated structure—apparently reinvigorated under Wiman—the state again expanded over hundreds of kilometers of territory. Its ambitions ran up against a Han invasion, however, and Wiman Chosŏn fell in 108 B.C.

These developments coincided with the beginnings of iron culture, enabling the rise of a sophisticated agriculture based on implements such as hoes, plowshares, and sickles. Cultivation of rice and other grains increased markedly. Although the peoples of the peninsula could not yet be called "Korean," there was an unquestioned continuity in agrarian society from this time until the emergence of a unified Korean state many centuries later.

Han Chinese built four commanderies, or local military units, to rule the peninsula as far south as the Han River, with a core area at Lolang (Nangnang in Korean), near present-day P'yŏngyang. It is illustrative of the relentlessly different historiography practiced in North Korea and South Korea, as well as the projection backward of Korean nationalism practiced by both sides, that North Korean historians deny that the Lolang Commandery was centered in Korea. They place it northwest of the peninsula, possibly near Beijing, in order to deemphasize China's influence on ancient Korean history. They perhaps do so because Lolang was clearly a Chinese city, as attested to by the many burial objects showing the affluent lives of Chinese overlords and merchants.

The Period of the Three Kingdoms

From approximately 108 B.C. until A.D. 313, Lolang was a great center of Chinese statecraft, art, industry (including the mining of iron ore), and commerce. Lolang's influence was widespread; it attracted immigrants from China and exacted tribute from several states south of the Han River that patterned their civilization and government after Lolang. In the first three centuries A.D., a large number of walled-town states in southern Korea grouped into three federations known as Chinhan, Mahan, and Pyŏnhan; during this period, rice agriculture had developed in the rich alluvial valleys and plains to such an extent that reservoirs had been built for irrigation.

Chinhan was situated in the middle part of the southern peninsula, Mahan in the southwest, and Pyŏnhan in the southeast. The state of Paekche, which soon came to exercise great influence on Korean history, emerged first in the Mahan area; it is not certain when this happened but Paekche certainly existed by A.D. 246 because Lolang mounted a large attack on it in that year. Paekche, a centralized, aristocratic state that melded Chinese and indigenous influence, was a growing power: within a hundred years, Paekche had demolished Mahan and continued to expand northward into the area of present-day South Korea around Seoul. Contemporary historians believe that the common Korean custom of patrilineal royal succession began with King Kŭn Ch'ogo (r. 346–75) of Paekche. His grandson, Ch'imnyu, inaugurated another long tradition by adopting Buddhism as the state religion in 384 (see The Role of Religion, ch. 2).

Meanwhile, in the first century A.D. two powerful states emerged north of the peninsula: Puyŏ in the Sungari River Basin in Manchuria and Koguryŏ, Puyŏ's frequent enemy to its south, near the Yalu River. Koguryŏ, which like Paekche also exercised a lasting influence on Korean history, developed in confrontation with the Chinese. Puyŏ was weaker and sought alliances with China to counter Koguryŏ but eventually succumbed to it around 312. Koguryŏ expanded in all directions, in particular toward the Liao River in the west and toward the Taedong River in the south. In 313 Koguryŏ occupied the territory of the Lolang Commandery and came into conflict with Paekche.

Peninsular geography shaped the political space of Paekche, Koguryŏ, and a third kingdom, Silla. In the central part of Korea, the main mountain range, the T'aebaek, runs north to south along the edge of the Sea of Japan. Approximately three-fourths of the way down the peninsula, however, roughly at the thirty-seventh parallel, the mountain range veers to the southwest, dividing the peninsula almost in the middle. This southwest extension, the So-baek Range, shielded peoples to the east of it from the Chinese-occupied portion of the peninsula but placed no serious barrier in the way of expansion into or out of the southwestern portion of the peninsula—Paekche's historical territory.

Koguryŏ ranged over a wild region of northeastern Korea and eastern Manchuria that was subjected to extremes of temperature and structured by towering mountain ranges, broad plains, and life-giving rivers; the highest peak, known as Paektu-san (White Head Mountain), is on the contemporary Sino-Korean border and has a beautiful, crystal-pure lake at its summit. Kim Il Sung and his guerrilla band utilized associations with this mountain as part of the founding myth of North Korea, and Kim Jong Il was said to have been born on the slopes of the mountain in 1942. Not surprisingly, North Korea claimed the Koguryŏ legacy as the main element in Korean history.

According to South Korean historiography, however, it was the glories of a third kingdom that were the most important elements. Silla eventually became the repository of a rich and cultured ruling elite, with its capital at Kyŏngju in the southeast, north of the port of Pusan. In fact, the men who ruled South Korea beginning in 1961 all came from this region. It has been the southwestern Paekche legacy that suffered in divided Korea, as Koreans of other regions and historians in both North Korea and South Korea have discriminated against the people of the present-day Chŏlla provinces. But taken together, all three kingdoms continue to influence Korean history and political culture. Koreans often assume that regional traits that they like or dislike go back to the Three Kingdoms period.

Silla evolved from a walled town called Saro. Silla historians are said to have traced its origins to 57 B.C., but contemporary historians regard King Naemul (r. 356–402) as the ruler who first consolidated a large confederated kingdom and established a hereditary kingship. His domain was east of the Naktong River in present-day North Kyŏngsang Province, South Korea. A small number of states located along the south central tip of the peninsula facing the Korea Strait did not join either Silla or Paekche but instead formed the Kaya League, which maintained close ties with states in Japan. Kaya's possible linkage to Japan remains an issue of debate among historians in Korea, Japan, and elsewhere. There is no convincing evidence to definitively resolve the debate, and circumstantial historical archaeological evidence is inconclusive. The debate is significant because its outcome could influence views on the origin of the Japanese imperial family. The Kaya states eventually were absorbed by their neighbors in spite of an attack against Silla in 399 by Wa forces from Japan, who had come to the aid of Kaya. Silla repelled the Wa with help from Koguryŏ.

Centralized government probably emerged in Silla in the last half of the fifth century, when the capital became both an administrative and a marketing center. In the early sixth century, Silla's leaders introduced plowing by oxen and built extensive irrigation facilities. Increased agricultural output presumably ensued, allowing further political and cultural development that included an administrative code in 520, a class system of hereditary ''bone-ranks'' for choosing elites, and the adoption of Buddhism as the state religion around 535.

Militarily weaker than Koguryŏ, Silla sought to fend the former off through an alliance with Paekche. By the beginning of the fifth century, however, Koguryŏ had achieved undisputed control of all of Manchuria east of the Liao River as well as the northern and central regions of the Korean Peninsula. At this time, Koguryŏ had a famous leader appropriately named King Kwanggaet'o (r. 391–412), a name that translates as ''broad expander of territory.'' Reigning from the age of eighteen, he conquered sixty-five walled towns and 1,400 villages, in addition to assisting Silla when the Wa forces attacked. As Koguryŏ's domain increased, it confronted China's Sui Dynasty (581–617) in the west and Silla and Paekche to the south.

Silla attacked Koguryŏ in 551 in concert with King Sŏng (r. 523–54) of Paekche. After conquering the upper reaches of the Han River, Silla turned on the Paekche forces and drove them out of the lower Han area. While a tattered Paekche kingdom nursed its wounds in the southwest, Silla allied with Chinese forces of the Sui and the successor Tang Dynasty (618–907) in combined attacks against Koguryŏ. The Sui emperor, Yang Di, launched an invasion of Koguryŏ in 612, marshaling more than 1 million soldiers, only to be lured by the revered Koguryŏ commander Ŭlchi Mundŏk into a trap, where Sui forces virtually were destroyed. Perhaps as few as 3,000 Sui soldiers survived; the massacre contributed to the fall of the dynasty in 617. Newly risen Tang emperor Tai Zong launched another huge invasion in 645, but Koguryŏ forces won another striking victory in the siege of the An Si Fortress in western Koguryŏ, forcing Tai Zong's forces to withdraw.

Koreans have always viewed these victories as sterling examples of resistance to foreign aggression. Had Koguryŏ not beaten back the invaders, all the states of the peninsula might have fallen under extended Chinese domination. Thus commanders like Ŭlchi

Tourists lining up to see Kim Il Sung's birthplace at Man'gyŏngdae District, P'yŏngyang
Courtesy Tracy Woodward

Mundŏk later became models for emulation, especially during the Korean War (1950–53) (see The Korean War, this ch.).

Paekche could not hold out under combined Silla and Tang attack, however. The latter landed an invasion fleet in 660, and Paekche quickly fell under their assaults. Tang pressure also had weakened Koguryŏ, and after eight years of battle it gave way because of pressure from both external attack and internal strife exacerbated by several famines. Koguryŏ forces retreated to the north, enabling Silla forces to advance and consolidate their control up to the Taedong River, which flows through P'yŏngyang.

Silla emerged victorious in 668. It is from this date that South Korean historians speak of a unified Korea. The period of the Three Kingdoms thus ended, but not before the kingdoms had come under the long-term sway of Chinese civilization and had been introduced to Chinese statecraft, Buddhist and Confucian philosophy, Confucian practices of educating the young, and the Chinese written language. (Koreans adapted Chinese characters to their own language through a system known as *idu.*) The Three Kingdoms also introduced Buddhism, the various rulers seeing a valuable political device for unity in the doctrine of a unified body of believers devoted to Buddha but serving one king. Artists from Koguryŏ

9

and Paekche also perfected a mural art found in the walls of tombs and took it to Japan, where it deeply influenced Japan's temple and burial art. Indeed, many Korean historians believe that wall murals in Japanese royal tombs suggest that the imperial house lineage may have Korean origins.

Korea under Silla

Silla and Paekche had sought to use Chinese power against Koguryŏ, inaugurating another tradition of involving foreign powers in internal Korean disputes. But Silla's reliance on Tang forces to consolidate its control had its price. Because Silla had to resist encroaching Tang forces, its sway was limited to the area south of the Taedong River. Nevertheless, Silla's military power, bolstered by an ideal of the youthful warrior (*hwarang*), was formidable. It seized Tang-occupied Paekche territories by 671, pushed Koguryŏ still farther northward, and drove the Tang commanderies off the peninsula by 676, thereby guaranteeing that the Korean people would develop independently, without outside influences.

The broad territories of Koguryŏ, however, were not conquered, and in 698 a Koguryŏ general named Tae Cho-yŏng established a successor state called Parhae above and below the Yalu and Tumen boundaries. Parhae forced Silla to build a northern wall in 721 and kept Silla forces below a line running from present-day P'yŏngyang to Wŏnsan. By the eighth century, Parhae controlled the northern part of Korea, all of northeastern Manchuria, and the Liaodong Peninsula. Both Silla and Parhae continued to be heavily influenced by Tang Chinese civilization.

Silla and Tang China had a great deal of contact inasmuch as large numbers of students, officials, and monks traveled to China for study and observation. In 682 Silla set up a national Confucian academy to train high officials and later instituted a civil-service examination system modeled on that of the Tang. Parhae modeled its central government even more directly on Tang systems than did Silla and sent many students to Tang schools. Parhae's culture melded indigenous and Tang influences, and its level of civilization was high enough to merit the Chinese designation "flourishing land in the East."

Silla in particular, however, developed a flourishing indigenous civilization that was among the most advanced in the world. Its capital at Kyŏngju in present-day South Korea was renowned as the "city of gold," where the aristocracy pursued a high culture and extravagant pleasures. Tang dynasty historians wrote that elite officials possessed thousands of slaves, with like numbers of horses, cattle, and pigs. Officials' wives wore gold tiaras and earrings of delicate and intricate filigree. Scholars studied the Confucian and Buddhist classics, built up state administration, and developed advanced methods for astronomy and calendrical science. The Dharani sutra, recovered in Kyŏngju, dates as far back as 751 and is the oldest example of woodblock printing yet found in the world. Pure Land Buddhism (Buddhism for the Masses) united the common people, who could become adherents through the repetition of simple chants. The crowning glories of this ''city of gold'' continue to be the Pulguksa temple in the city and the nearby Sŏkkuram Grotto, both built around 750. Both are home to some of the finest Buddhist sculpture in the world. The grotto, atop a coastal bluff near Kyŏngju, houses the historic great stone Sakyamuni Buddha in its inner sanctum; the figure is situated so that the rising sun over the Sea of Japan strikes it in the middle of the forehead.

Ethnic differences between Koguryŏ and the Malgal people native to Manchuria weakened Parhae by the early tenth century, just as Silla's power had begun to dissipate a century earlier when regional castle lords splintered central power and rebellions shook Silla's foundations. Parhae, coming under severe pressure from the Kitan warriors who ruled parts of northern China, Manchuria, and Mongolia, eventually fell in 926. Silla's decline encouraged a restorationist named Kyŏnhwŏn to found Later Paekche at Chŏnju in 892 and another restorationist, named Kungye, to found Later Koguryŏ at Kaesŏng in central Korea. Wang Kŏn, the son of Kungye who succeeded to the throne in 918, shortened the dynastic name to Koryŏ and became the founder of a new dynasty by that name, from which came the modern term *Korea*.

Unification by Koryŏ

Wang Kŏn's army fought ceaselessly with Later Paekche for the next decade, with Silla in retreat. After a crushing victory in 930 over Paekche forces at present-day Andong, South Korea, Koryŏ obtained a formal surrender from Silla and proceeded to conquer Later Paekche by 935—amazingly, with troops led by former Paekche king Kyŏnhwŏn, whose son had treacherously cast him aside. After this accomplishment, Wang Kŏn became a magnanimous unifier. Regarding himself as the proper successor to Koguryŏ, he embraced survivors of the Koguryŏ lineage who were fleeing the dying Parhae state, which had been conquered by Kitan warriors in 926. He then took a Silla princess as his wife and treated the Silla aristocracy with great generosity. Wang Kŏn established a regime embodying the remnants of the Later Three Kingdoms— what was left after the almost fifty years of struggle between the forces of Kyŏnhwŏn and Kungye—and accomplished a true unification of the peninsula.

Placing the regime's capital at Kaesŏng, the composite elite of the Koryŏ Dynasty (918–1392) forged a tradition of aristocratic continuity that lasted to the modern era. The elite fused aristocratic privilege and political power through marriage alliances and control of land and central political office, and they made class position hereditary. This practice established a pattern for Korea in which landed gentry mingled with a Confucian- or Buddhist-educated stratum of scholar-officials; often scholars and landlords were one and the same person. In any case, landed wealth and bureaucratic position were powerfully fused. This fusion occurred at the center, where a strong bureaucracy influenced by Confucian statecraft emerged. Thereafter, this bureaucracy sought to dominate local power and thus militated against the Japanese or European feudal pattern of parcelized sovereignty, castle domains, and military tradition. By the thirteenth century, two dominant government groupings had emerged: the civil officials and the military officials, known thereafter as *yangban* (see Glossary).

The Koryŏ elite admired the Chinese civilization that emerged during the Song Dynasty (960–1279). Official delegations and ordinary merchants brought Koryŏ gold, silver, and ginseng to China in exchange for Song silk, porcelain, and woodblock books. The treasured Song porcelain stimulated Koryŏ artisans to produce an even finer type of inlaid celadon porcelain. Praised for the pristine clarity of its blue-green glaze—celadon glazes also were yellow green—and the delicate art of its inlaid portraits (usually of flowers or animals), Koryŏ celadon displayed the refined taste of aristocrats and later had great influence on Japanese potters.

Buddhism coexisted with Confucianism throughout the Koryŏ period; it deeply affected daily life and perhaps bequeathed to modern Korea its eclecticism of religious beliefs. Koryŏ Buddhist priests systematized religious practice by rendering the Chinese version of the Buddhist canon into mammoth woodblock print editions, known as the Tripitaka. The first edition was completed in 1087 but subsequently was lost; another, completed in 1251 and still extant, is located at the Haeinsa temple near Taegu, South Korea. Its accuracy, combined with its exquisite calligraphic carvings, makes it the finest of some twenty Tripitaka in East Asia. By 1234, if not earlier, Koryŏ had also invented moveable iron type, two centuries before its use in Europe.

This high point of Koryŏ culture coincided with internal disorder and the rise of the Mongols, whose power swept most of Eurasia during the thirteenth century. Koryŏ was not spared; Khubilai

Khan's forces invaded and demolished Koryŏ's army in 1231, forcing the Koryŏ government to retreat to Kanghwa Island (off modern-day Inch'ŏn). But after a more devastating invasion in 1254, in which countless people died and some 200,000 people were captured, Koryŏ succumbed to Mongol domination and its kings intermarried with Mongol princesses. The Mongols then enlisted thousands of Koreans in ill-fated invasions of Japan in 1274 and 1281, using Korean-made ships. Both invasions were repelled with aid, as legend has it, from opportune typhoons known as "divine wind," or kamikaze. The last period of Mongol influence was marked by the appearance of a strong bureaucratic stratum of scholar-officials, or literati (*sadaebu* in Korean). Many of them lived in exile outside the capital, and they used their superior knowledge of the Confucian classics to condemn the excesses of the ruling families, who were backed by Mongol power.

The overthrow of the Mongols by the founders of the Ming Dynasty (1368–1644) in China gave a rising group of military men, steeled in battle against coastal pirates from Japan, the opportunity to contest for power. When the Ming claimed suzerainty over former Mongol domains in Korea, the Koryŏ court was divided between pro-Mongol and pro-Ming forces. Two generals marshaled their forces for an assault on Ming armies on the Liaodong Peninsula. One of the generals, Yi Sŏng-gye, was pro-Ming. When he reached the Yalu River, he abruptly turned back and marched on the Koryŏ capital, which he subdued quickly. He thus became the founder of Korea's longest dynasty, the Yi, or Chosŏn (1392–1910). The new state, Chosŏn, harked back to the old Chosŏn kingdom fifteen centuries earlier; its capital was built at Seoul.

The Chosŏn Dynasty: Florescence

One of General Yi's first acts was to carry out a sweeping land reform long advocated by Confucian literati reformers. After a national cadastral survey, all extant land registers were destroyed. Except for land doled out to loyalists called merit subjects, Yi Sŏng-gye declared everything to be owned by the state, thus undercutting Buddhist temples, which held vast farm lands, and locally powerful clans. Both groups had exacted high rents from peasants, leading to social distress in the late Koryŏ period. These reforms also greatly enhanced the taxation power of the central government.

Buddhist influence in and complicity with the old system made it easier for the Confucian literati to urge an extirpation of Buddhist economic and political influence and of exile in the mountains

13

for monks and their disciples. Indeed, the literati accomplished a deep Confucianization of Chosŏn society, which particularly affected the position of women. Often prominent in Koryŏ society, women were now relegated to domestic chores of child-rearing and housekeeping, as so-called inside people.

As neo-Confucian doctrines swept the old order away, Korea effectively developed a secular society. Common people, however, retained attachments to folk religions, shamanism, geomancy, and fortune-telling, influences condemned by both Confucianism and the world at that time. This Korean mass culture created remarkably lively and diverse art forms: uniquely colorful and unpretentiously naturalistic folk paintings of animals, popular novels in Korean vernacular, and characters like the *mudang,* shamans who summoned spirits and performed exorcisms in *kŭt,* or shamanistic, rituals.

For more than a century after its founding, Chosŏn flourished as an exemplary agrarian bureaucracy deeply influenced by a cadre of learned scholar-officials who were steeped in the doctrines of neo-Confucianism. Like Koryŏ, the Chosŏn Dynasty lacked the typical features of a feudal society. It was instead a classic agrarian bureaucracy.

Chosŏn possessed an elaborate procedure for entry to the civil service, a highly articulated civil service, and a practice of administering the country from the top down and from the center. The system rested on an agrarian base, making it different from modern bureaucratic systems; the particular character of agrarian-bureaucratic interaction also provided one of Korea's departures from the typical Chinese experience.

James B. Palais, a widely respected historian of the Chosŏn Dynasty, has shown that conflict between bureaucrats seeking revenues for government coffers and landowners hoping to control tenants and harvests was a constant during the Chosŏn Dynasty and that in this conflict over resources the landowners often won out. Controlling land theoretically owned by the state, private landed interests soon came to be stronger and more persistent in Korea than in China. Although Korea had a centralized administration, the ostensibly strong center was more often a façade concealing the reality of aristocratic power.

One interpretation suggests that Korea's agrarian bureaucracy was superficially strong but actually rather weak at the center. A more conventional interpretation is that the Chosŏn Dynasty was ruled by a highly centralized monarchy served by a hereditary aristocracy that competed via civil and military service examinations

*The United Front Tower, a
13.5-meter-high monument
rebuilt in 1990 to commemorate
the North-South Joint Conference
on national salvation
and reunification held in
P'yŏngyang on April 19, 1948*
Courtesy Democratic People's
Republic of Korea,
No. 417, 1991

for access to bureaucratic office. The state ostensibly dominated the society, but in fact landed aristocratic families kept the state at bay and perpetuated local power for centuries. This pattern persisted until the late 1940s, when landed dominance was obliterated in a northern revolution and attenuated in southern land reform; since then the balance has shifted toward strong central power and top-down administration of the whole country in both Koreas. The disruptions caused by the Korean War magnified the sociopolitical consequences of these developments.

The scientific Korean written alphabet *han'gŭl* (see Glossary) was systematized in the fifteenth century under the greatest of Korean kings, Sejong (r. 1418–50), who also greatly increased the use of metal moveable type for book publications of all sorts (see The Korean Language, ch. 2). Korean is thought to be part of the Altaic group of languages, which includes Turkic, Mongol, Hungarian, Finnish, Tungusic (Manchu), and possibly Japanese. In spite of the long influence of written Chinese, Korean remains very different in lexicon, phonology, and grammar. The new *han'gŭl* alphabet did not come into general use until the twentieth century, however. Since 1948 North Koreans have used the Korean alphabet exclusively while South Koreans have retained usage of a mixed Sino-Korean script.

Confucianism is based on the family and an ideal model of relations between family members. It generalizes this family model to the state and to an international system—the Chinese world order. The principle is hierarchy within a reciprocal web of duties and obligations: the son obeys the father by following the dictates of filial piety; the father provides for and educates the son. Daughters obey mothers and mothers-in-law; younger siblings follow older siblings; wives are subordinate to husbands. The superior prestige and privileges of older adults make longevity a prime virtue. In the past, transgressors of these rules were regarded as uncultured beings unfit to be members of society. When generalized to politics, the principle meant that a village followed the leadership of venerated elders and that citizens revered a king or emperor, who was thought of as the father of the state. Generalized to international affairs, the Chinese emperor was the big brother of the Korean king.

The glue holding the traditional nobility together was education, meaning socialization into Confucian norms and virtues that began in early childhood with the reading of the Confucian classics. The model figure was the so-called true gentleman, the virtuous and learned scholar-official who was equally adept at poetry and statecraft. In Korea education started very early because Korean students had to master the extraordinarily difficult classical Chinese language—tens of thousands of written ideographs and their many meanings typically learned through rote memorization. Throughout the Chosŏn Dynasty, all official records and formal education and most written discourse were in classical Chinese. With Chinese language and philosophy came a profound cultural penetration of Korea, such that most Chosŏn arts and literature came to use Chinese models.

Confucianism is often thought to be a conservative philosophy, stressing tradition, veneration of a past golden age, careful attention to the performance of ritual, disdain for material goods, commerce, and the remaking of nature, combined with obedience to superiors and a preference for relatively frozen social hierarchies. Much commentary on contemporary Korea focuses on this legacy and, in particular, on its allegedly authoritarian, antidemocratic character. Emphasis on the legacy of Confucianism, however, does not explain the extraordinary commercial bustle of South Korea, the materialism and conspicuous consumption of new elites, or the determined struggles for democratization by Korean workers and students. At the same time, one cannot assume that communist North Korea broke completely with the past. The legacy of Confucianism includes the country's family-based politics, the succession to rule of the leader's son, and the extraordinary veneration of Kim Il Sung.

The Chosŏn Dynasty had a traditional class structure that departed from the Chinese Confucian example, providing an important legacy for the modern period. The governing elite continued to be known as *yangban,* but the term no longer simply connoted two official orders. In the Chosŏn Dynasty, the *yangban* had a virtual monopoly on education, official position, and possession of land. Entry to *yangban* status required a hereditary lineage. Unlike in China, commoners could not sit for state-run examinations leading to official position. One had to prove membership in a *yangban* family, which in practice meant having a forebear who had sat for exams within the past four generations. In Korea as in China, the majority of peasant families could not spare a son to study for the exams, so upward social mobility was sharply limited. But because in Korea the limit also was specifically hereditary, people had even less mobility than in China and held attitudes toward class distinction that often seemed indistinguishable from the attitudes underlying the caste system.

Silla society's "bone-rank" system also underlined that one's status in society was determined by birth and lineage. For this reason, each family and clan maintained an extensive genealogical record, or *chokpo* (see Glossary), with meticulous care. Because only male offspring prolonged the family and clan lines and were the only names registered in the genealogical tables, the birth of a son was greeted with great felicitation.

The elite were most conscious of family pedigree. A major study of all those who passed examinations in the Chosŏn Dynasty (some 14,000) showed that the elite families were heavily represented; other studies have documented the persistence of this pattern into the early twentieth century. Even in 1945, this aristocracy was substantially intact, although it died out soon thereafter.

Korea's traditional class system also included a peasant majority and minorities of petty clerks, merchants, and so-called base classes (*ch'ommin*), that is, castelike hereditary groups (*paekchŏng*) such as butchers, leather tanners, and beggars. Although merchants ranked higher than members of low-born classes, Confucian elites frowned on commercial activity and up until the twentieth century squelched it as much as possible. Peasants or farmers ranked higher than merchants because they worked the land, but the life of the peasantry was almost always difficult during the dynasty and became more so later on. Most peasants were tenants, were required to give up at least half their crop to landlords as tax, and were subject to various additional exactions. Those in the low-born classes were probably worse off, however, given very high rates of slavery for much of the Chosŏn period. One source reported more than 200,000 government slaves in Seoul alone in 1462, and recent scholarship has suggested that at one time as much as 60 percent of Seoul's population may have been slaves. In spite of slavery being hereditary, however, rates of escape from slavery and manumission also were unusually high. Class and status hierarchies also were built into the Korean language and have persisted into the contemporary period. Superiors and inferiors were addressed quite differently, and elaborate honorifics were used to address elders. Even verb endings and conjugations differed according to station.

Chosŏn Dynasty Confucian doctrines also included a foreign policy known as "serving the great" (*sadae*), in this case, China. Chosŏn lived within the Chinese world order, which radiated outward from China to associated states, of which Korea was the most important. Korea was China's little brother, a model tributary state, and in many ways the most important of China's allies. Koreans revered things Chinese, and China responded for the most part by being a good neighbor, giving more than it took away. China assumed that enlightened Koreans would follow it without being forced. Absolutely convinced of its own superiority, China indulged in a policy that might be called benign neglect, thereby allowing Korea substantive autonomy as a nation.

This sophisticated world order was broken up by Western and Japanese influence in the late nineteenth century. Important legacies for the twentieth century remained, however. As a small power, Korea had to learn to be shrewd in foreign policy. Since at least the seventh century, Koreans have cultivated the sophisticated art of "low determines high" diplomacy, a practice whereby a small country maneuvers between two larger countries and seeks to use foreign power for its own ends. Although both North Korea and South Korea have often struck foreign observers as rather dependent on big-power support, both have not only claimed but also have strongly asserted their absolute autonomy and independence as nation-states, and both have been adept at manipulating their big-power clients. Until the mid-1980s, North Korea was masterful not only in getting big powers to fight its battles but also in maneuvering between the Soviet Union and China to obtain something from each and to prevent either from domination. And just as in the traditional period, P'yŏngyang's heart was with Beijing.

Nonetheless, the main characteristic of Korea's traditional diplomacy was isolationism, even what scholar Kim Key-hyuk has called exclusionism. After the Japanese invasions of the 1590s, Korea isolated itself from Japan, although the Edo Shogunate and the Chosŏn Dynasty established diplomatic relations early in the seventeenth century and trade was conducted between the two countries. Korea dealt harshly with errant Westerners who came to the country and kept the Chinese at arm's length. Westerners called Korea the Hermit Kingdom, a term suggesting the pronounced hostility toward foreign power and the deep desire for independence that marked traditional Korea.

Dynastic Decline

A combination of literati purges in the early sixteenth century, Japanese invasions at the end of the century, and Manchu invasions in the middle of the seventeenth century severely debilitated the Chosŏn state, and it never regained the heights of the fifteenth century. This period also saw the Manchus sweep away the Ming Dynasty in China, ending a remarkable period when Korean society seemed to develop apace with China, while making many independent innovations.

The doctrinaire version of Confucianism that was dominant during the Chosŏn Dynasty made squabbles between elites particularly vicious. The literati based themselves in neo-Confucian metaphysics, which reached a level of abstraction virtually unmatched elsewhere in East Asia in the writings of Yi Hwang, also known as Yi T'oe-gye, who was regarded as Korea's Zhu Xi after the Chinese founder of the neo-Confucian school. For many other scholar-officials, however, the doctrine rewarded arid scholasticism and obstinate orthodoxy. First, one had to commit his mind to one or another side of abstruse philosophical debate, and only then could the practical affairs of state be put in order. This situation quickly led to so-called literati purges, a series of upheavals beginning in the mid-fifteenth century and lasting more than 100 years. The losers found their persons, their property, their families, and even their graves at risk from victors determined to extirpate their influence—always in the name of a higher morality. Later in the dynasty, the concern with ideological correctness exacerbated more mundane factional conflicts that debilitated central power. The emphasis on ideology also expressed the pronounced Korean concern with the power of ideas; this emphasis is still visible in Kim Il Sung's *chuch'e* doctrine, which assumes that rectification of one's thinking precedes correct action, even to the point of Marxist heresy in which ideas determine material reality. By the end of the sixteenth century,

19

the ruling elite had so homogenized its ideology that there were few noncomformists left: all were presumably united in one idea.

At the end of the sixteenth century, Korea suffered devastating foreign invasions. The first came shortly after Toyotomi Hideyoshi ended Japan's internal disorder and unified the territory; he launched an invasion that put huge numbers of Japanese soldiers in Pusan in 1592. His eventual goal, however, was to control China. The Chosŏn court responded to the invasion by fleeing to the Yalu River, an action that infuriated ordinary Koreans and led slaves to revolt and burn the registries. Japanese forces marched through the peninsula at will until they were routed by General Yi Sun-sin and his fleet of armor-clad ships, the first of their kind. These warships, the so-called turtle ships, were encased in thick plating with cannons sticking out at every point on their oval shape. The Japanese fleets were destroyed wherever they were found, and Japan's supply routes were cut. Facing Ming forces and so-called righteous armies that rose up to fight a guerrilla war (even Buddhist monks participated), the Japanese were forced to retreat to a narrow redoubt near Pusan.

After desultory negotiations and delay, Hideyoshi launched a second invasion in 1597. The Korean and Ming armies were ready this time. General Yi returned with a mere dozen warships and demolished the Japanese forces in Yellow Sea battles near the port of Mokp'o. Back in Japan, Hideyoshi died of illness, and his forces withdrew to their home islands, where they nursed an isolationist policy for the next 250 years. In spite of the victory, the peninsula had been devastated. Refugees wandered its length, famine and disease were rampant, and even basic land relationships had been overturned by widespread destruction of registers.

Korea had barely recovered when the Manchus invaded from the north, fighting on all fronts to oust the Ming Dynasty. Invasions in 1627 and 1636 established tributary relations between Korea and the Manchu's Qing Dynasty (1644–1911). The invasions, however, were less destructive than the Japanese invasions, except in the northwest where Manchu forces wreaked havoc. Thereafter, the dynasty had a period of revival that, had it continued, might have left Korea much better prepared for its encounter with the West.

The Confucian literati were particularly reinvigorated by an intellectual movement advocating that philosophy be geared to solving real problems of the society. Known as the Sirhak (Practical Learning) Movement, it spawned people like Yu Hyŏng-wŏn (1622–73), from a small farming village, who poured over the classics seeking reform solutions to social problems. He developed a thorough,

Revolutionary art in the Taean Heavy Machinery Works, Taean, Namp'o,
urges workers to march forward toward new victory
under the leadership of the party.
Courtesy Tracy Woodward

detailed critique of nearly all the institutional aspects of Chosŏn politics and society, and a set of concrete reforms to invigorate it. Chŏng Yag-yong (1762–1836) was thought to be the greatest of the Sirhak scholars, producing several books that offered his views on administration, justice, and the structure of politics. Still others like Yi Su-kwang (1563–1628) traveled to China and returned with the new Western learning then spreading in Beijing, while Yi Ik (1681–1763) wrote a treatise entitled *Record of Concern for the Under-privileged.*

A new vernacular fiction also developed in the seventeenth and eighteenth centuries, much of it taking the form of social criticism. The best known is *The Tale of Ch'unhyang,* which argues for the common human qualities of lowborn, commoners, and *yangban* alike. Often rendered as a play, it has been a favorite in both North Korea and South Korea. An older poetic form called *sijo,* which consists of short stanzas, became another vehicle for free expression of distaste for the castelike inequities of Korean society. Meanwhile, Pak Chi-wŏn journeyed to Beijing in 1780 and authored *Jehol Diary,* which compared Korean social conditions unfavorably with his observations of China.

21

The economy diversified as the transplanting of rice seedlings boosted harvests and some peasants became enterprising small landlords. Commercial crops such as tobacco, ginseng, and cotton developed, and merchants proliferated at big markets like those in Seoul at East Gate and South Gate, at the gate to China at Ŭiju, and at the gate to Japan at Tongnae, near Pusan. The use of coins for commerce and for paying wages increased, and handicraft production increased outside government control. The old Koryŏ capital at Kaesŏng became a strong center of merchant commerce and conspicuous wealth. Finally, throughout the seventeenth century, Western learning filtered into Korea, often through the auspices of a spreading Roman Catholic movement, which especially attracted commoners by its creed of equality.

Korea in the Nineteenth-Century World Order

The early nineteenth century witnessed a period of sharp decline in which most of these new developments were extinguished. Harsh persecution of Roman Catholics began in 1801, and agricultural production declined, forcing many peasants to pursue slash-and-burn agriculture in the mountains. Popular uprisings began in 1811 and continued sporadically throughout the rest of the century, culminating in the Tonghak (Eastern Learning) Movement (see Glossary) of the 1860s, which spawned a major peasant rebellion in the 1890s.

Korean leaders were aware that China's position had been transformed by the arrival of powerful Western gunboats and traders, but they reacted to the Opium War (1839–42) between China and Britain by shutting Korea's doors even tighter. In 1853 United States Navy commodore Matthew C. Perry and his "black ships" entered Edo Bay, beginning the process of opening Japan to foreign trade. Korea, however, continued its isolationist policy. Japan's drastic reform of its institutions—the Meiji Restoration of 1868—and subsequent industrialization were attributed by Korean literati to Japan's alleged inferior grasp of Confucian doctrine. Through its successful rebuff of French and American attempts to ''open'' Korea, the regime was encouraged to think it could hold out indefinitely against external pressure. (The U.S.S. *General Sherman* steamed up the Taedong River in 1866 almost to P'yŏngyang, whereupon the natives burned the ship and killed all its crew; Kim Il Sung claimed that his great-grandfather was involved in this incident.)

Reforms from 1864 to 1873 under a powerful leader named the Taewŏn'gun, or Grand Prince (Yi Ha-ung, 1821–98), offered further evidence of Korean resilience; Yi Ha-ung was able to reform the bureaucracy, bring in new talent, extract new taxes from both the *yangban* and commoners, and keep the imperialists at bay. Korea's descent into the maelstrom of imperial rivalry was quick after this, however, as Japan succeeded in imposing a Western-style unequal treaty in February 1876, giving its nationals extra-territorial rights and opening three Korean ports to Japanese commerce. China sought to reassert its traditional position in Korea by playing the imperial powers off against each other, with the result that Korea entered into unequal treaties with the United States, Britain, Russia, Italy, and other countries. These events split the Korean court into pro-Chinese, pro-Japanese, pro-United States, and pro-Russian factions, each of which influenced policy until the final annexation of Korea by Japan in 1910. Meanwhile, various Korean reform movements sought to get under way, influenced by either Japanese or American progressives.

A small group of politically frustrated Korean aristocrats in the early 1880s came under the influence of a Japanese educator and student of Western knowledge, Fukuzawa Yukichi. This group of Koreans saw themselves as the vanguard of Korea's "enlighten-ment," a term that referred to their nation's release from its tradi-tional subordination to China and its intellectual views and political institutions. The group, led by Kim Ok-kyun, included Kim Hong-jip, Yun Ch'i-ho, and Yu Kil-chun. Yun became an influential modernizer in the twentieth century, and Yu became the first Korean to study in the United States—at the Governor Drummer Academy in Byfield, Massachusetts. Kim Ok-kyun, impressed by the Meiji Restoration, sought to stage a coup d'état in 1884 with a handful of progressives, including Philip Jaisohn (Sŏ Chae-p'il, 1866–1948), and about 200 Japanese legation soldiers. Resident Chinese troops quickly suppressed it, however, and Kim fled to Japan. Philip Jaisohn, a Korean who had studied in the United States, was the first Korean to become a United States citizen. He had returned to Korea in 1896 to publish one of its first newspapers.

For a decade thereafter, China reasserted a rare direct influence when Yuan Shikai momentarily made China first among the for-eign powers resident in Korea. He represented the scholar-general and governor of Tianjin, Li Hongzhang, as director-general resi-dent in Korea of diplomatic and commercial relations in Seoul in 1885. A reformer in China, Yuan had no use for Korean reform-ers and instead blocked the slightest sign of Korean nationalism.

Japan put a definitive end to Chinese influence during the Sino-Japanese War of 1894–95, seizing on the reinvigorated Tonghak Movement, which spawned a large rebellion in 1894. Uniting peasants against Western pressure, growing Japanese economic penetration and their own corrupt and ineffectual government, the rebellion spread from the southwest into the center of the peninsula, thus threatening Seoul. The hapless court invited China to send troops to put the rebellion down, whereupon Japan had the pretext it needed to send troops to Korea. After defeating Chinese forces, Japan declared Korea independent, thus breaking its long tributary relationship with China. Thereafter, Japan pushed through epochal reforms that ended the old civil service examination system, abolished traditional class distinctions, ended slavery, and established modern fiscal and judicial mechanisms.

Korean reformers influenced by the West, such as Philip Jaisohn, launched an Independence Club (Tongnip Hyŏphoe) in 1896 to promote Westernization. They used the vernacular *han'gŭl* in their newspaper, the *Tongnip simmun* (The Independent), publishing alternate pages in English. The club included many Koreans who had studied Western learning in Protestant missionary schools, and for a while it influenced not only young reformers but also elements of the Korean court; one of the reformers was Yi Sŭng-man, otherwise known as Syngman Rhee (1875–1965), who later served as the first president of South Korea. The club was repressed, and it collapsed after two years.

The Korean people gradually became more hostile toward Japan. In 1897 King Kojong (r. 1864–1907), fleeing Japanese plots, ended up in the Russian legation; he conducted the nation's business from there for a year and shortly thereafter declared Korea to be the "Great Han [Korean] Empire," from which comes the name *Taehan Min'guk,* or Republic of Korea. It was a futile last gasp for the Chosŏn; the only question was which imperial power would colonize Korea.

By 1900 the Korean Peninsula was the focus of an intense rivalry between the powers then seeking to carve out spheres of influence in East Asia. Russia was expanding into Manchuria and Korea and briefly enjoyed ascendancy on the peninsula when King Kojong sought its help in 1897. In alliance with France and Germany, Russia had forced Japan to return the Liaodong Peninsula, which it had acquired from China as a result of its victory in the First Sino-Japanese War (1894–95). Japan promptly leased the region from China and continued to develop it; shortly thereafter, in 1900, Japanese forces intervened with the other imperial powers to put down the Boxer Uprising, a xenophobic conflict in China against Christians and foreigners. Russia continued to develop the railroad system in Manchuria and to exploit forests and gold mines in the northern part of Korea. The United States, fearing complete exclusion from the region—especially from China—had declared its open door policy in 1900 but lacked the means to assert its will. During this period, however, Americans also were given concessions for rail and trolley lines, waterworks, Seoul's new telephone network, and mines. Japan briefly pulled back from the peninsula, but its 1902 alliance with Britain emboldened Japan to reassert itself there.

Russia and Japan initially sought to divide their interests in Korea, suggesting at one point that the thirty-eighth parallel be the dividing line between their spheres of influence. The rivalry devolved into the Russo-Japanese War (1904–05) when Japan launched a successful surprise attack on the Russian fleet at Port Arthur (Dalian; or Japanese, Dairen). Japan electrified all of Asia by becoming the first nonwhite country to subdue one of the "great powers."

Under the peace treaty brokered by Theodore Roosevelt in a conference at Portsmouth, New Hampshire, and signed in 1905, Russia recognized Japan's paramount rights in Korea. Japan would not question the rights of the United States in its colony, the Philippines, and the United States would not challenge Japan's new protectorate, established in 1905 to control Korea's foreign policy. Japan installed a resident-general and, two years later, deposed King Kojong. Significant Korean resistance followed this deposition, spreading through several provinces as local *yangban* organized militias for guerrilla warfare against Japan. In 1909 An Chung-gŭn, a Korean assassin, shot Itō Hirobumi, the former Japanese resident-general who had concluded the protectorate agreement; two expatriate Koreans in San Francisco also gunned down Durham Stevens, a foreign affairs adviser to the Japanese who had lauded their efforts in Korea. It was too little and too late. In 1910 Japan turned Korea into its colony, thus extinguishing Korea's hard-fought independence, which had first emerged with Silla and Koguryŏ resistance to Chinese pressures.

Under Japanese imperial pressure that began in earnest with Korea's opening in 1876, the Chosŏn Dynasty faltered and then collapsed in a few decades. The dynasty had had an extraordinary five-century longevity, but although the traditional system could adapt to the changes necessary to forestall or accommodate domestic or internal conflict and change, it could not withstand the onslaught of technically advanced imperial powers with strong armies. The old agrarian bureaucracy had managed the interplay of different and competing interests by having a system of checks and balances that tended over time to equilibrate the interests of different parties. The king and the bureaucracy kept watch over each other, the royal clans watched both, scholars criticized or remonstrated from the moral position of Confucian doctrine, secret inspectors and censors went around the country to watch for rebellion and ensure accurate reporting, landed aristocrats sent sons into the bureaucracy to protect family interests, and local potentates influenced the county magistrates sent down from the central administration. The Chosŏn Dynasty was not a system that modern Koreans would wish to restore, but it was a sophisticated political system, adaptable enough and persistent enough to have given unified rule to Korea for half a millennium.

The Legacy of Japanese Colonialism

Korea did not escape the Japanese grip until 1945, when Japan lay prostrate under the Allied victory that brought World War II to a close. The colonial experience that shaped postwar Korea was intense and bitter. It brought development and underdevelopment, agrarian growth and deepened tenancy, industrialization and extraordinary dislocation, and political mobilization and deactivation. It also spawned a new role for the central state, new sets of Korean political leaders, communism and nationalism, and armed resistance and treacherous collaboration. Above all, it left deep fissures and conflicts that have gnawed at the Korean national identity ever since.

Colonialism was often thought to have created new countries where none existed before, drawn national boundaries, brought diverse tribes and peoples together, tutored the natives in self-government, and prepared for the day when the colonialist power decided to grant independence. But all this had existed in Korea for centuries before 1910. Furthermore, by virtue of their relative proximity to China, Koreans had always felt superior to Japan and blamed Japan's devastating sixteenth-century invasions for hindering Korean wealth and power in subsequent centuries.

Thus the Japanese engaged not in creation but in substitution after 1910: substituting a Japanese ruling elite for the Korean *yangban* scholar-officials, colonial imperative coordination for the old central state administration, Japanese modern education for Confucian classics, Japanese capital and expertise for the budding Korean versions, Japanese talent for Korean talent, and eventually the Japanese language for Korean. Koreans never thanked the Japanese for these substitutions, did not credit Japan with creations, and instead saw Japan as snatching away the ancient regime, Korea's sovereignty and independence, its indigenous if incipient modernization, and above all its national dignity. Koreans never saw Japanese rule as anything but illegitimate and humiliating. Furthermore, the very closeness of the two nations—in geography, in common Chinese cultural influences, and in levels of development until the nineteenth century—made Japanese dominance all the more galling to Koreans and gave a peculiar intensity to their love/hate relationship.

Japan built bureaucracies in Korea, all of them centralized and all of them big by colonial standards. Unlike the relatively small British colonial cadre in India, there were 700,000 Japanese in Korea by the 1940s, and the majority of colonizers worked in government service. For the first time in history, Korea had a national police, responsive to the center and possessing its own communications and transportation facilities. The huge Japanese Oriental Development Company organized and funded industrial and agricultural projects and came to own more than 20 percent of Korea's arable land; it employed an army of officials who fanned out through the countryside to supervise agricultural production. The official Bank of Korea performed central banking functions such as regulating interest rates and provisioned credit to firms and entrepreneurs, almost all of them Japanese. Central judicial bodies wrote new laws establishing an extensive, "legalized" system of racial discrimination against Koreans, making them second-class citizens in their own country. Bureaucratic departments proliferated at the Seoul headquarters of Japan's Government-General of Korea, turning it into the nerve center of the country. Semiofficial companies and conglomerates, including the big *zaibatsu* (commercial conglomerates) such as Mitsubishi and Mitsui, laid railroads, built ports, installed modern factories, and ultimately remade the face of old Korea.

Japan held Korea tightly, watched it closely, and pursued an organized, architectonic colonialism in which the planner and administrator were the model, not the swashbuckling conqueror. The strong, highly centralized colonial state mimicked the role that the Japanese state had come to play in Japan—intervening in the economy, creating markets, spawning new industries, and suppressing dissent. Politically, Koreans could barely breathe, but economically there was significant, if unevenly distributed, growth. Agricultural output rose substantially in the 1920s, and a hothouse industrialization occupied the 1930s. Growth rates in the Korean economy often outstripped those in Japan itself; one estimate suggested an annual growth rate for Korea of 3.57 percent in the 1911–38 period and a rate of 3.36 percent for Japan itself.

Koreans have always thought that the benefits of this growth went entirely to Japan and that Korea would have developed rapidly without Japanese help. Nonetheless, the strong colonial state, the multiplicity of bureaucracies, the policy of administrative guidance

27

of the economy, the use of the state to found new industries, and the repression of labor unions and dissidents provided a surreptitious model for both Koreas in the postwar period. Japan showed them an early version of the ''bureaucratic-authoritarian'' path to industrialization, and it was a lesson that seemed well learned by the 1970s.

The Rise of Korean Nationalism and Communism

The colonial period brought forth an entirely new set of Korean political leaders, spawned by both the resistance to and the opportunities of Japanese colonialism. In 1919 mass movements swept many colonial and semicolonial countries, including Korea. Drawing on Woodrow Wilson's promises of self-determination, on March 1, 1919, a group of thirty-three intellectuals petitioned for independence from Japan and touched off nationwide mass protests that continued for months. These protests were put down fiercely by the Japanese, causing many younger Koreans to become militant opponents of colonial rule. The year was a watershed for imperialism in Korea: the leaders of the movement, predominantly Christian and Western in outlook, were moderate intellectuals and students who sought independence through nonviolent means and support from progressive elements in the West. Their courageous witness and the nationwide demonstrations that they provoked remained a touchstone of Korean nationalism. The movement succeeded in provoking reforms in Japanese administration, but its failure to realize independence also stimulated radical forms of anticolonial resistance. In the 1930s, new groups of armed resisters, bureaucrats, and—for the first time—military leaders emerged. Both North Korea and South Korea were profoundly influenced by the political elites and the political conflicts generated during colonial rule.

The emergence of nationalist and communist groups dates back to the 1920s; it was in this period that the left-right splits of postwar Korea began. The transformation of the *yangban* aristocracy also began during the 1920s. Although the higher scholar-officials were pensioned off and replaced by Japanese, landlords were allowed to retain their holdings and encouraged to continue disciplining peasants and extracting rice. The traditional landholding system was put on a new basis through new legal measures and a full cadastral survey shortly after Japan took over, but tenancy continued and was systematically deepened throughout the colonial period. By 1945 Korea had an agricultural tenancy system with few parallels in the world. More traditional landlords were content to sit back and let Japanese officials increase output; by 1945 such people were widely viewed as treacherous collaborators with the Japanese, and strong demands emerged that they share out land to their tenants. During the 1920s, however, another trend began: landlords became entrepreneurs.

Some Korean militants went into exile in China and the Soviet Union and founded early communist and nationalist resistance groups. The Korean Communist Party (KCP) was founded in Seoul in 1925; one of the organizers was Pak Hŏn-yŏng, who became the leader of Korean communism in southern Korea after 1945. Various nationalist groups also emerged during this period, including the exiled Korean Provisional Government (KPG) in Shanghai, which included Syngman Rhee and another famous nationalist, Kim Ku, among its members.

Police repression and internal factionalism made it impossible for radical groups to exist for any length of time. Many nationalist and communist leaders were jailed in the early 1930s (they reappeared in 1945). When Japan invaded and then annexed Manchuria in 1931, however, a strong guerrilla resistance embracing both Chinese and Koreans emerged (see fig. 2). There were well over 200,000 guerrillas—all loosely connected and including bandits and secret societies—fighting the Japanese in the early 1930s; after murderous but effective counterinsurgency campaigns, the numbers declined to a few thousand by the mid-1930s. It was from this milieu that Kim Il Sung (originally named Kim Sŏng-ju, born in 1912) emerged. By the mid-1930s, he had become a significant guerrilla leader whom the Japanese considered one of the most effective and dangerous of guerrillas. They formed a special counterinsurgent unit to track Kim down, and they put Koreans in it as part of their divide-and-rule tactics.

Both Koreas have spawned myths about the guerrilla resistance: North Korea claims that Kim single-handedly defeated the Japanese, and South Korea claims that the present-day ruler of North Korea is an imposter who stole the name of a revered patriot. Nonetheless, the resistance is important for understanding postwar Korea. Resistance to Japan became the main legitimating doctrine of North Korea: North Koreans trace the origin of their army, leadership, and ideology back to this resistance. For the next five decades, the top North Korean leadership was dominated by a core group that had fought the Japanese in Manchuria. (Kim Il Sung's tenure in a Russian reconnaissance brigade also had an influence.)

Japan declared war on China in 1937 and on the United States in 1941. As this war took on global dimensions, Koreans for the first time had military careers opened to them. Although most

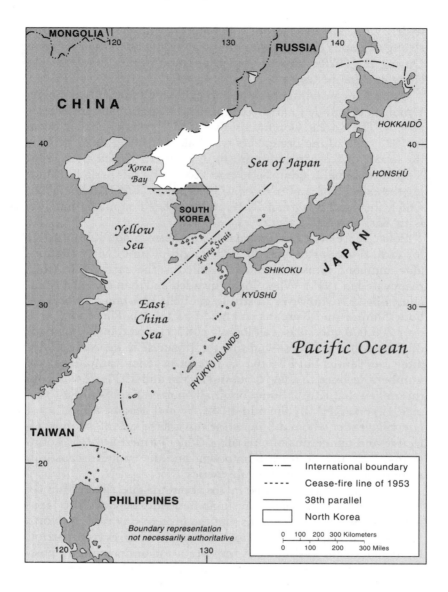

Figure 2. North Korea in Its Asian Setting, 1993

Koreans were conscripted foot soldiers, a small number achieved officer status and a few attained high rank. The officer corps of the South Korean army during the Rhee period was dominated by Koreans with experience in the Japanese army. At least in part, the Korean War became a matter of Japanese-trained military officers fighting Japanese-spawned resistance leaders.

Japan's far-flung war effort also caused a labor shortage throughout the empire. In Korea this situation meant that bureaucratic positions were more available to Koreans than at any previous time; thus a substantial cadre of Koreans received administrative experience in government, local administration, police and judicial work, economic planning agencies, banks, and the like. That this occurred in the last decade of colonialism created a divisive legacy, however, for this period also was the harshest period of Japanese rule, the time Koreans remember with the greatest bitterness. Korean culture was quashed, and Koreans were required to speak Japanese and take Japanese names. The majority suffered badly at the precise time that a minority was doing well. This minority was tainted by collaboration, and that stigma was never lost. Korea from 1937 to 1945 was much like Vichy France in the early 1940s: bitter experiences and memories continued to divide people, even within the same family. Because it was too painful to confront directly, the experience became buried history and continued to play on the national identity.

In the mid-1930s, Japan's colonial policy entered a phase of heavy industrialization that embraced all of Northeast Asia. Unlike most colonial powers, Japan located heavy industry in its colonies and brought the means of production to the labor and raw materials. Manchuria and northern Korea got steel mills, automotive plants, petrochemical complexes, and enormous hydroelectric facilities. The region was held exclusively by Japan and tied together with the home market to the point that national boundaries had became less important than the new transnational, integrated production. To facilitate this production, Japan also built railroads, highways, cities, ports, and other modern transportation and communication facilities. By 1945 Korea proportionally had more kilometers of railroads than any other Asian country save Japan, leaving only remote parts of the central east coast and the wild northeastern Sino-Korean border region untouched by modern means of conveyance. These changes were externally induced and served Japanese, not Korean, interests. Thus they represented a kind of overdevelopment.

The same exogenous changes fostered underdevelopment in Korean society as a whole. The Korean upper and managerial classes did not develop; instead, their development was retarded or swelled suddenly at Japanese behest. Among the majority peasant class, change was advanced. Koreans became the mobile human capital used to work the new factories in northern Korea and Manchuria, mines and other enterprises in Japan, and urban factories in southern Korea. From 1935 to 1945, Korea began its industrial revolution with many of the usual characteristics: uprooting of peasants from the land, emergence of a working class, urbanization, and population mobility. In Korea the process was telescoped, giving rise to comparatively remarkable population movements. By 1945 about 11 percent of the entire Korean population was abroad (mostly in Japan and Manchuria), and 20 percent of all Koreans were either abroad or in a province other than that in which they were born, with most of the interprovincial movement being southern peasants moving into northern industry. This was, by and large, a forced or mobilized movement; by 1942 it often meant drafted, conscripted labor. Peasants lost land or rights to work land, only to end up working in unfamiliar factory settings, doing the dirty work for a pittance.

Perhaps the most important characteristic of Korea's colonial experience was the manner in which it ended: the last decade of a four-decade imperium was a pressure cooker. The colonial situation built to a crescendo, abruptly collapsed, and left the Korean people and two opposing great powers to deal with the results.

When the colonial system was abruptly terminated in 1945, millions of Koreans sought to return to their native villages from these far-flung mobilization details. But they were no longer the same people: they had grievances against those who had remained secure at home, they had suffered material and status losses, they had often come into contact with new ideologies, and they had all seen a broader world beyond the villages. It was these circumstances that loosed upon postwar Korea a mass of changed and disgruntled people who deeply disordered the early postwar period and the plans of the United States and the Soviet Union.

The National Division and the Origins of the Democratic People's Republic of Korea

The crux of the period of national division and opposing states in Korea was the decade from 1943 to 1953, and the politics of contemporary Korea cannot be understood without comprehending this decade. It was the breeding ground of the two Koreas, of war, and of a reordering of international politics in Northeast Asia.

From the time of the tsars, Korea had been a concern of Russian security. The Russo-Japanese War of 1904–05 was fought in part over the disposition of the Korean Peninsula. It was often surmised that the Russians saw Korea as a gateway to the Pacific, especially to warm-water ports. However, the Russians did not get a warm-water port out of their involvement in Korea.

There was greater complexity than this in Soviet policy. Korea had one of Asia's oldest communist movements. Although it would appear that postwar Korea was of great concern to the Soviet Union, many have thought that its policy was a simple matter of Sovietizing northern Korea, setting up a puppet state, and then, in 1950, directing Kim Il Sung to unify Korea by force. However, the Soviet Union did not have an effective relationship with Korean communists; Joseph Stalin purged and even executed many of the Koreans who had functioned in the Communist International, and he did not help Kim Il Sung and other guerrillas in their struggle against Japan.

The United States took the initiative in big-power deliberations on Korea during World War II, suggesting a multilateral trusteeship for postwar Korea to the British in March 1943 and to the Soviet leaders at the end of the same year. President Franklin D. Roosevelt, concerned about the disposition of enemy-held colonial territories and aware of colonial demands for independence, sought a gradualist, tutelary policy of preparing former colonials—such as the Koreans—for self-government and independence. At the Cairo Conference in December 1943, the Allies, under United States urging, declared that after Japan was defeated Korea would become independent "in due course," a phrase consistent with Roosevelt's ideas. At about the same time, planners in the United States Department of State reversed the traditional United States policy of noninvolvement in Korea by defining the security of the peninsula as important to the security of the postwar Pacific, which was, in turn, very important to United States security.

At a midnight meeting in Washington on August 10 and 11, 1945, War Department officials, including John J. McCloy and Dean Rusk, decided to make the thirty-eighth parallel the dividing line between the Soviet and United States zones in Korea. Neither the Soviet forces nor the Koreans were consulted. As a result, when 25,000 American soldiers occupied southern Korea in early September 1945, they found themselves up against a strong Korean impulse for independence and for thorough reform of colonial legacies. By and large, Koreans wished to solve their problems themselves and resented any inference that they were not ready for self-government.

During World War II, Stalin was mostly silent in his discussions with Roosevelt about Korea. From 1941 to 1945, Kim Il Sung and other guerrillas were given sanctuary in Sino-Soviet border towns, trained at a small school, and dispatched as agents into Japanese-held territory. Recent research suggests that Chinese, not Soviet, communists controlled the border camps. Although the United States suspected that as many as 30,000 Koreans were being trained as Soviet guerrilla agents, postwar North Korean documents captured by General Douglas A. MacArthur showed that there could not have been more than a few hundred guerrilla agents. When Soviet troops occupied Korea north of the thirty-eighth parallel in August 1945, they brought these Koreans, now in the Soviet army, with them. They were often termed Soviet-Koreans, even though most of them were not Soviet citizens. Although this group was not large, several of them became prominent in the regime, for example, Hŏ Ka-i, an experienced party organizer, who was Soviet-born, and Nam Il, who became well known during the Korean War when he led the North Korean delegation in peace talks. The Soviet side quietly acquiesced to the thirty-eighth parallel decision and then accepted the United States plan for a multilateral trusteeship at a foreign ministers' meeting in December 1945. Over the next two years, the two powers held so-called joint commission meetings, trying to resolve their differences and establish a provisional government for Korea.

The United States military command, along with emissaries dispatched from Washington, tended to interpret resistance to United States desires in the south as radical and pro-Soviet. When Korean resistance leaders set up an interim ''people's republic'' and people's committees throughout southern Korea in September 1945, the United States saw this fundamentally indigenous movement as part of a Soviet master plan to dominate all of Korea. Radical activity, such as the ousting of landlords and attacks on Koreans in the former colonial police force, usually was a matter of settling scores left over from the colonial period, or of demands by Koreans to run their own affairs. But it immediately became wrapped up with United States-Soviet rivalry, such that the Cold War arrived early in Korea—in the last months of 1945.

Once the United States occupation force chose to bolster the status quo and resist radical reform of colonial legacies, it immediately ran into monumental opposition to its policies from the majority of South Koreans. The United States Army Military Government in Korea (1945–48) spent most of its first year suppressing the many people's committees that had emerged in the provinces. This action provoked a massive rebellion in the fall of 1946; after the rebellion was suppressed, radical activists developed a significant guerrilla movement in 1948 and 1949. Activists also touched off a major rebellion at the port of Yŏsu in South Korea in October 1948. Much of this disorder resulted from unresolved land problems caused by conservative landed factions who used their bureaucratic power to block redistribution of land to peasant tenants. North Koreans sought to take advantage of this discontent, but the best

*P'yŏngyang's Arch of Triumph, unveiled in April 1982, on
the site of Kim Il Sung's 1945 speech celebrating national liberation
Courtesy Democratic People's Republic of Korea
Mission to the United Nations*

evidence shows that most of the dissidents and guerrillas were
southerners upset about southern policies. Indeed, the strength of
the left wing was in those provinces most removed from the thirty-
eighth parallel—in the southwest, which had historically been re-
bellious (the Tonghaks came from there), and in the southeast,
which had felt the greatest impact from Japanese colonialism.

By 1947 Washington was willing to acknowledge formally that
the Cold War had begun in Korea and abandoned attempts to
negotiate with the Soviet government to form a unified, multilateral
administration. Soviet leaders had also determined that the postwar world would be divided into two blocs, and they deepened their
controls over North Korea. When President Harry S. Truman announced the Truman Doctrine and the containment policy in the
spring of 1947, Korea was very nearly included along with Greece
and Turkey as a key containment country; Department of State
planners foresaw an enormous US$600 million package of economic
and military aid for southern Korea, and backed away only when
the United States Congress and the War Department balked at such
a huge sum. Instead, the decision was made to seek United Nations (UN) backing for United States policy in Korea and to

35

hold a UN-supervised plebiscite in all of Korea if the Soviet Union would go along, in southern Korea alone if it did not. North Korea refused to cooperate with the UN. The plebiscite was held in May 1948 and resulted in the establishment of the Republic of Korea in August of the same year.

From August 1945 until January 1946, Soviet forces worked with a coalition of communists and nationalists led by a Christian educator named Cho Man-sik. Kim Il Sung did not appear in North Korea until October 1945; what he did in the two months after the Japanese surrender is not known. When he reappeared, Soviet leaders presented Kim to the Korean people as a guerrilla hero. The Soviet leaders did not set up a central administration, nor did they establish an army. In retrospect, their policy was more tentative and reactive than American policy in South Korea, which moved forward with plans for a separate administration and army. In general, Soviet power in the Asia-Pacific region was flexible and resulted in the withdrawal of Soviet troops from Manchuria in early 1946.

Whether in response to United States initiatives or because most Koreans despised the trusteeship agreement that had been negotiated at the end of 1945, separate institutions began to emerge in North Korea in early 1946. In February 1946, an Interim People's Committee led by Kim Il Sung became the first central government. The next month, a revolutionary land reform took place, dispossessing landlords without compensation. In August 1946, a powerful political party, the North Korean Workers' Party, dominated politics as a result of a merger with the Korean Communist Party; in the fall the rudiments of a northern army appeared. Central agencies nationalized major industries that previously had been mostly owned by the Japanese and began a two-year economic program based on the Soviet model of central planning and priority for heavy industry. Nationalists and Christian leaders were ousted from all but pro forma participation in politics, and Cho Man-sik was placed under house arrest. Kim Il Sung and his allies dominated all the political parties, ousting resisters.

Within a year of the liberation from Japanese rule, North Korea had a powerful political party, a growing economy, and a single powerful leader, Kim Il Sung. Kim's emergence and that of the Kim system dated from mid-1946, by which time he had placed close, loyal allies at the heart of power (see Party Leadership and Elite Recruitment, ch. 4). His prime assets were his background, his skills at organization, and his ideology. Only thirty-four years old when he came to power, Kim was fortunate to emerge in the last decade of a forty-year resistance that had killed off many leaders of the older generation. North Korea claimed that Kim was the leader of all Korean resisters, when, in fact, there were many other leaders. But Kim won the support and firm loyalty of several hundred people like him: young, tough, nationalistic guerrillas who had fought in Manchuria. Because the prime test of legitimacy in postwar Korea was one's record under the hated Japanese regime, Kim and his core allies possessed nationalist credentials superior to those of the South Korean leadership. Furthermore, Kim's backers had military force at their disposal and used it to their advantage against rivals with no military experience.

Kim's organizational skills probably came from experience gained in the Chinese Communist Party in the 1930s. He was also a dynamic leader. Unlike traditional Korean leaders and intellectual or theoretical communists such as Pak Hŏn-yŏng, he pursued a style of mass leadership that involved using his considerable charisma and getting close to the people. He often visited a factory or a farm for so-called "on-the-spot guidance" and encouraged his allies to do the same. Led by Kim, the North Koreans went against Soviet orthodoxy by including masses of poor peasants in the party; indeed, they termed the party a "mass" rather than a "vanguard" party.

Since the 1940s, from 12 to 14 percent of the population has been enrolled in the communist party, compared with 1 to 3 percent for communist parties in most countries. The Korean Workers' Party (KWP) was formed by a merger of the communist parties in North Korea and South Korea in 1949. The vast majority of KWP members were poor peasants with no previous political experience. Membership in the party gave them status, privileges, and a rudimentary form of political participation (see The Korean Workers' Party, ch. 4).

Kim's ideology in the 1940s tended to be revolutionary-nationalist rather than communist. The *chuch'e* ideology had its beginnings in the late 1940s, although the term *chuch'e* was not used until a 1955 speech in which Kim castigated some of his comrades for being too pro-Soviet. The concept of *chuch'e,* which means placing all foreigners at arm's length, has resonated deeply with Korea's Hermit Kingdom past. *Chuch'e* doctrine stresses self-reliance and independence but also draws on neo-Confucian emphasis on rectification of one's thinking before action in the real world. Soon after Kim took power, virtually all North Koreans were required to participate in study groups and re-education meetings, where regime ideology was inculcated.

In the 1940s, Kim faced factional power struggles among his group. Factions included communists who had remained in Korea during the colonial period, called the domestic faction; Koreans associated with Chinese communism, the Yan'an faction; Kim's Manchurian partisans, the Kapsan faction and Soviet Union loyalists, the Soviet faction. In the aftermath of the Korean War, amid much false scapegoating for the disasters of the war, Kim purged the domestic faction, many of whose leaders were from southern Korea; Pak Hŏn-yŏng and twelve of his associates were pilloried in show trials under ridiculous charges that they were American spies, and ten of them subsequently were executed. In the mid-1950s, Kim eliminated key leaders of the Soviet faction, including Hŏ Ka-i, and overcame an apparent coup attempt by members of the Yan'an faction, after which he purged many of them. Some, such as the guerrilla hero Mu Chŏng, a Yan'an faction member, reportedly escaped to China. These power struggles took place only during the first decade of the regime. Later, there were conflicts within the leadership, but they were relatively minor and did not successfully challenge Kim's power.

In the period 1946 to 1948, there was much evidence that the Soviet Union hoped to dominate North Korea. In particular, it sought to involve North Korea in a quasi-colonial relationship in which Korean raw materials, such as tungsten and gold, were exchanged for Soviet manufactured goods. The Soviet Union also sought to keep Chinese communist influence out of Korea; in the late 1940s, Maoist doctrine had to be infiltrated into North Korean newspapers and books (see The Media, ch. 4). Soviet influence was especially strong in the media, where major organs were staffed by Koreans from the Soviet Union, and in the security bureaus. Nonetheless, the Korean guerrillas who fought in Manchuria were not easily molded and dominated. They were tough, highly nationalistic, and determined to have Korea for themselves. This was especially so for the Korean People's Army (KPA), which was an important base for Kim Il Sung and which was led by Ch'oe Yŏng-gŏn, another Korean guerrilla who had fought in Manchuria. At the army's founding ceremony on February 8, 1948, Kim urged his soldiers to carry forward the tradition of the Koreans who had fought against the Japanese in Manchuria.

The Democratic People's Republic of Korea (DPRK, or North Korea) was established on September 9, 1948, three weeks after the Republic of Korea had been formed in Seoul. Kim Il Sung was named premier, a title he retained until 1972, when, under a new constitution, he was named president (see Constitutional Framework, ch. 4). At the end of 1948, Soviet occupation forces were withdrawn from North Korea. This decision contrasted strongly with Soviet policies in Eastern Europe. Tens of thousands of Korean soldiers who fought in the Chinese civil war from 1945 to

1949 also filtered back to Korea. All through 1949, tough crack troops with Chinese, not Soviet, experience returned to be integrated with the KPA; the return of these Korean troops inevitably moved North Korea toward China. It enhanced Kim's bargaining power and enabled him to maneuver between the two communist giants. Soviet advisers remained in the Korean government and military, although far fewer than the thousands claimed by South Korean sources. There probably were 300 to 400 advisers posted to North Korea, but many of those were experienced military and security people. Both countries continued to trade, and the Soviet Union sold World War II-vintage weaponry to North Korea.

In 1949 Kim Il Sung had himself named *suryŏng* (see Glossary), an old Koguryŏ term for "leader" that the Koreans always modified by the adjective "great"—as in "great leader" (Widaehan Chidoja). The KPA was built up through recruiting campaigns for soldiers and bond drives to purchase Soviet tanks. The tradition of the Manchurian guerrillas was burnished in the party newspaper, *Nodong simmun* (Workers' Daily), perhaps to offset the influence of powerful Korean officers, who like Mu Chŏng and Pang Ho-san, had fought with the Chinese communists.

The Korean War

In early 1949, North Korea seemed to be on a war footing. Kim's New Year's speech was bellicose and excoriated South Korea as a puppet state. The army expanded rapidly, soldiers drilled in war maneuvers, and bond drives began to amass the necessary funds to purchase Soviet weaponry. The thirty-eighth parallel was fortified, and border incidents began breaking out. Neither Seoul nor P'yŏngyang recognized the parallel as a permanent legitimate boundary.

Although many aspects of the Korean War remain murky, it seems that the beginning of conventional war in June 1950 was mainly Kim's decision and that the key enabling factor was the existence of as many as 100,000 troops with battle experience in China. When the Rhee regime, with help from United States military advisers, severely reduced the guerrilla threat in the winter of 1949–50, the civil war moved into a conventional phase. Kim sought Stalin's backing for his assault, but documents from Soviet and Chinese sources suggest that he got more support from China.

Beginning on June 25, 1950, North Korean forces fought their way south through Seoul. South Korean resistance collapsed as the roads south of Seoul became blocked with refugees, who were fleeing

North Korean columns spearheaded with tanks supplied by the Soviet Union. Task Force Smith, the first United States troops to enter the war, made a futile stand at Suwŏn, a town some fifty kilometers south of Seoul. Within a month of the start of the invasion, North Korean forces had seized all but a small corner of southeastern Korea anchored by the port city of Pusan. Repeated North Korean efforts, blunted by heavy United States Air Force bombing and stubborn resistance by the combined United States and South Korean forces on the Pusan perimeter, denied Kim Il Sung forceful reunification of the peninsula. The fortunes of war reversed abruptly in early September when General MacArthur boldly landed his forces at Inch'ŏn, the port city for Seoul in west-central Korea. This action severed the lines of communication and supply between the North Korean army and its base in the north. The army quickly collapsed, and combined United States and South Korean forces drove Kim Il Sung's units northward and into complete defeat.

The United States thrust in the fall of 1950, however, motivated China to bring its forces—the Chinese People's Volunteer Army—in on the northern side; these ''volunteers'' and the North Korean army pushed United States and South Korean forces out of North Korea within a month. Although the war lasted another two years, until the summer of 1953, the outcome of early 1951 was definitive: both a stalemate and a United States commitment to containment that accepted the de facto reality of two Koreas.

By the time the armistice was signed in 1953, North Korea had been devastated by three years of bombing attacks that had left almost no modern buildings standing. Both Koreas had watched as their country was ravaged and the expectations of 1945 were turned into a nightmare. Furthermore, when Kim's regime was nearly extinguished in the fall of 1950, the Soviet Union did very little to save it. China picked up the pieces.

The Postwar Economy and Patterns of Industrialization

North Korea has a socialist command economy. Beginning with the Three-Year Plan (1954–56) at the end of the Korean War and the shortened Five-Year Plan (1957–60) that succeeded it, reconstruction and the priority development of heavy industry has been stressed, with consumer goods a low priority. This strategy of industrialization, biased toward heavy industry, pushed the economy forward at record growth rates in the 1950s and 1960s. The First Seven-Year Plan (1961–70—extended for three years because of Soviet aid stoppages in the early 1960s caused by North Korea's support for China in the Sino-Soviet dispute)—also projected a higher than average growth rate (see Economic Development and Structural Change, ch. 3).

By the early 1970s, North Korea had clearly exhausted extensive development of its industries based on its own, prewar Japanese, or new Soviet technologies and therefore turned to the West and Japan to purchase turnkey plants. These purchases ultimately caused North Korea's problems with servicing its external debt—estimated at between US$2 billion and US$3 billion for the years 1972–79 (see Foreign Trade, ch. 3). Later seven- and ten-year plans failed to reach projected growth rates; still, a study published by the United States Central Intelligence Agency in 1978 estimated that North Korea's per capita gross national product (GNP—see Glossary) equaled South Korea's as late as 1976. Since that time, however, it has fallen behind South Korea's, and transportation bottlenecks and fuel resource problems have plagued the economy (see Industry, ch. 3).

Agriculture was collectivized after the Korean War, in stages that went from mutual-aid teams to second-stage cooperatives, but stopped short of building the huge state farms found in the Soviet Union or the communes of China (see Organization and Management, ch. 3). Relying mostly on cooperative farms corresponding to the old natural villages and using material incentives (there was apparently little ideological bias against using such incentives), North Korea pushed agricultural production ahead, and its general agricultural success was acknowledged. The United States government estimated in 1978 that grain production had grown more rapidly in North Korea than in South Korea and that living standards in North Korea's rural areas had probably improved more quickly than those in South Korea. Nevertheless, production has fallen behind, and North Korea has failed to reach projected targets, for example, the production of 10 million tons of grain by 1986.

Corporatism and the *Chuch'e* Idea

Marxism did not present a political model for achieving socialism, only an opaque set of prescriptions. This political vacuum opened the way for the development of an indigenous political culture (see Political Ideology: The Role of *Chuch'e,* ch. 4). The strongest foreign influence on North Korea's leadership has been the Chinese communist model. Like Mao Zedong, Kim Il Sung has been very much a mass line leader, making frequent visits to factories and the countryside, sending cadres down to local levels to help policy implementation and to solicit local opinion, requiring small-group political study and so-called criticism and self-criticism, using periodic campaigns to mobilize people for production or education, and encouraging soldiers to engage in production in good "people's army" fashion.

The North Korean political system also differs in many respects from China and the former Soviet Union. The symbol of the KWP is a hammer and sickle with a superimposed writing brush, symbolizing the "three-class alliance" of workers, peasants, and intellectuals. Unlike Mao's China, the Kim regime has never excoriated intellectuals as a potential "new class" of exploiters; instead, it has followed an inclusive policy toward them, perhaps because postwar Korea was short of intellectuals and experts and because so many had left North Korea for South Korea in the 1945–50 period. For P'yŏngyang, the term *intellectual* refers to experts and technocrats, of which there are exceedingly few in North Korea. North Korea's political system is thus a mix of Marxism-Leninism, Korean nationalism, and indigenous political culture. The term that perhaps best captures this system is corporatism (see Glossary). Socialist corporatist doctrine has always preferred an organic politic to the liberal, pluralist conception: a corporeal body politic rather than a set of diverse groups and interests.

North Korea's goal of tight unity at home has produced a remarkable organicism, unprecedented in any existing communist regime. Kim Il Sung is not just the "iron-willed, ever-victorious commander," the "respected and beloved Great Leader"; he also is the "head and heart" of the body politic (even "the supreme brain of the nation"!). The flavor of this politics can be demonstrated through quotations taken from KWP newspapers in the spring of 1981:

> Kim Il Sung . . . is the great father of our people . . . Long is the history of the word *father* being used as a word representing love and reverence . . . expressing the unbreakable blood ties between the people and the leader. *Father.* This familiar word represents our people's single heart of boundless respect and loyalty . . . The love shown by the Great Leader for our people is the love of kinship. Our respected and beloved Leader is the tender-hearted father of all the people . . . Love of paternity . . . is the noblest ideological sentiment possessed only by our people.
>
> His heart is a traction power attracting the hearts of all people and a centripetal force uniting them as one . . . Kim Il Sung is the great sun and great man . . . thanks to this great heart, national independence is firmly guaranteed.

*Preparations in Kim Il Sung Square, P'yŏngyang, for the eighteenth birthday celebration of Kim Il Sung, April 1992
Courtesy Tracy Woodward*

This type of language was especially strong when the succession of Kim Jong Il was publicly announced at the Sixth Party Congress in 1980. The KWP often is referred to as the "Mother" party, the mass line is said to provide "blood ties," the leader always is "fatherly," and the country is one big "family." Kim Il Sung is said to be paternal, devoted, and benevolent, and the people presumably respond with loyalty, obedience, and mutual love.

North Korean ideology buries Marxism-Leninism under the ubiquitous, always-trumpeted *chuch'e* idea. By the 1970s, *chuch'e* had fundamentally triumphed over Marxism-Leninism as the basic ideology of the regime, but the emphases were there from the beginning. *Chuch'e* is the opaque core of North Korean national solipsism (see Glossary).

National solipsism expresses an omnipotent theme found in North Korean written materials: an assumption that Korea is the center of the world, radiating outward the rays of *chuch'e,* especially to Third World countries that are thought by the North Koreans to be ready for *chuch'e.* The world tends toward Korea, with all eyes on Kim Il Sung. The presence of such an attitude is perhaps the most bizarre aspect of North Korea, but also one of the most noticeable. The model of ever-widening concentric circles—at the center of which is Kim Il Sung, next his family, next the guerrillas who fought with him, and then the KWP elite—is profoundly Korean and has characterized North Korea since 1946. This core circle controls everything at the top levels of the regime. The core moves outward and downward concentrically to encompass other elements of the population and provides the glue holding the system together. As the penumbra of workers and peasants is reached, trust gives way to control on a bureaucratic basis and to a mixture of normative and remunerative incentives. Nonetheless, the family remains the model for societal organization. An outer circle distinguishes the Korean from the foreign, a reflection of the extraordinary ethnic and linguistic unity of Koreans and Korea's history of exclusionism. Yet the circle keeps on expanding, as if to encompass foreigners under the mantle of Kim and his *chuch'e* idea.

International Relations

Since the end of the Korean War, the two Koreas have faced each other across the Demilitarized Zone (DMZ—see Glossary), engaged most of the time in unremitting, withering, unregenerate hostility, punctuated by occasional, brief thaws and increasing exchanges between P'yŏngyang and Seoul. Huge armies still are poised to fight at a moment's notice (see Military Heritage, ch. 5). The emergence of the Sino-Soviet conflict in 1969, the United States opening to China in 1971–72, and the end of the Second Indochina War in 1975, however, were some of the watershed changes in world politics that both seemed to empty the Cold War logic of its previous meaning and changed the great power configuration.

The strategic logic of the 1970s had an immediate and beneficial impact on Korea. The Nixon administration withdrew a division of United States soldiers from South Korea. North Korea responded by virtually halting attempts at infiltration (compared with 1968, when more than 100 soldiers died along the DMZ and the United States spy ship *Pueblo* was seized) and by significantly reducing the defense budget in 1971. In what seemed to be a miraculous development, the Koreas held talks at a high level. These talks between the director of the Korean Central Intelligence Agency and Kim Yŏng-ju, Kim Il Sung's younger brother, in early 1972, culminated in a July 4, 1972, announcement that both sides would seek reunification peacefully, independently of outside forces, and with common efforts toward creating a "great national unity" that would transcend the many differences between the two systems. Within a year, however, this initiative had effectively failed (see Foreign Policy, ch. 4).

United States policy again shifted, if less dramatically, when the administration of Jimmy Carter announced plans for a gradual but complete withdrawal of United States ground forces from South Korea (air and naval units would remain deployed in or near Korea). At that time, a prolonged period of North Korean courting of the United States began. In 1978, however, the first of the large-scale military exercises called Team Spirit, involving more than 200,000 United States and South Korean troops, was held. And, in 1979, the Carter administration dropped its program of troop withdrawal in reaction to North Korea's rapid and extensive upgrading of its army and the discovery of North Korean-built tunnels under the DMZ; the administration committed itself to a modest but significant buildup of force and equipment levels in South Korea.

In the late 1970s, P'yŏngyang's policy toward Moscow and Beijing was somewhat of a balancing act. Nonetheless, North Korea began using a term of opprobrium for Soviet imperialism, *dominationism (chibaejuŭi)*, a term akin to the Chinese term, *hegemonism*. By and large, P'yŏngyang adhered to the Chinese foreign policy line during the Carter years, while taking care not to antagonize the Soviet Union needlessly. When Vietnam invaded Cambodia in 1978, North Korea forcefully and publicly condemned the invasion while maintaining a studied silence when China responded by invading Vietnam.

By the early 1980s, changing United States-China relations also had repercussions in the two Koreas. China said publicly that it wished to play a role in reducing tension on the Korean Peninsula. In January 1984, for the first time, a major North Korean initiative called for three-way talks among the United States, South Korea, and North Korea. Through most of the 1980s, China sought to sponsor talks between Washington and P'yŏngyang—talks that occasionally took place in Beijing at the minister-counselor level—and encouraged Kim Il Sung to take the path of diplomacy.

The reemergence of détente between the United States and the Soviet Union in the mid-1980s has provided a major opportunity to resolve the Korean confrontation. Seoul, more than P'yŏngyang, has been effective in exploiting these new opportunities. As Seoul's prestige has grown, it has clearly put P'yŏngyang on the defensive, perhaps more than at any time since the Korean War. The sharp changes in world politics in the late 1980s placed the fate of the Kim regime in the balance. If North Korea survives amid the failure of most other communist systems, it will be because of the historical, nationalistic, and indigenous roots that its leaders have sought to foster since the 1940s. Drawing on a tradition of resistance to foreign pressure going back to the states of Koguryŏ and Parhae, the North Koreans demonstrated their tenacity and their resilience during the time of the Korean War. They will probably find the 1990s equally challenging.

*   *   *

For additional reading on pre-twentieth century history, see Carter J. Eckert, Ki-baik Lee, Young Ick Lew, Michael Robinson, and Edward W. Wagner's *Korea Old and New;* Han Woo-keun's *The History of Korea;* and James B. Palais's *Politics and Policy in Traditional Korea.* For the colonial period, consult Carter J. Eckert's *Offspring of Empire;* Sang Chul Suh's *Growth and Structural Changes in the Korean Economy, 1910–1945;* and Michael Robinson's *Cultural Nationalism in Korea, 1920–25.* On the origins of Korean nationalism and communism, see Chong-Sik Lee's *The Politics of Korean Nationalism;* Robert A. Scalapino and Chong-Sik Lee's *Communism in Korea* (2 vols.); and Dae-sook Suh's *The Korean Communist Movement, 1918–48* and *Kim Il Sung.*

The Korean War and its origins are covered in Bruce Cumings's *The Origins of the Korean War* (2 vols.); Rosemary Foote's *The Wrong War;* and Peter Lowe's *The Origins of the Korean War.* On North Korea, see the volumes by Robert A. Scalapino and Chong-Sik Lee, and Ellen Brun and Jacques Hersh's *Socialist Korea.* A good study of North Korea's agrarian socialism is provided in Mun Woong Lee's *Rural North Korea under Communism.* A recent survey of North Korea's international relations and United States policy toward North Korea can be found in Selig S. Harrison's *Dialogue with North Korea.* (For further information and complete citations, see Bibliography.)

Chapter 2. The Society and Its Environment

Young woman with a changgo, *the most popular Korean instrument. The* changgo, *which is played with the palm of the hand and a thick stick, is an hourglass-shaped drum covered by skins of different thicknesses. It is used in orchestral and ensemble music and as an accompaniment for vocal and instrumental musical solos. The instrument is sometimes also carried by dancers.*

THE KOREAN PENINSULA, located at the juncture of the northeast Asian continent and the Japanese archipelago, has been home to a culturally and linguistically distinct people for more than two millennia. The ancestors of modern Koreans are believed to have come from northeast and Inner Asia. Like their Japanese neighbors, they have been deeply influenced by Chinese civilization. The elite culture and social structure of traditional Korea, especially during the Chosŏn Dynasty (1392–1910) founded by General Yi Sŏng-gye, reflected neo-Confucian norms (see The Origins of the Korean Nation, ch. 1). Despite centuries of Chinese cultural influence, an episode of Japanese colonialism (1910–45), division into United States and Soviet spheres after World War II (1939–45), and the Korean War (1950–53, known in North Korea as the Fatherland Liberation War), the Korean people have retained their ethnic and cultural distinctiveness. Indeed, cultural distinctiveness, autonomy, and creativity have become central themes in the North Korean regime's *chuch'e* (see Glossary) ideology.

The Democratic People's Republic of Korea (DPRK, or North Korea) is a socialist society with a Soviet-style authoritarian political system in which the leadership emphasizes the formulation of a distinctively Korean style of socialism termed *chuch'e*. Its antithesis is "flunkeyism" (see Glossary), or *sadaejuui,* which traditionally referred to subordination to Chinese culture but has come to mean subservience to a foreign power. North Korean leaders label as "flunkeyism" anything that they wish to criticize as excessively dependent on foreign influence.

The North Korean regime has attempted to break with its China-dependent Confucian past, but the more authoritarian strains in Confucian thought are reinforced by the authoritarianism of Marxism-Leninism and Stalinism and by contemporary social values. Like the ideal Confucian ruler, North Korean leaders Kim Il Sung and Kim Jong Il are depicted as morally perfect leaders whose boundless benevolence earns them the gratitude and loyalty of the masses.

Kim Il Sung's domination of the political system after 1948 and his formulation of *chuch'e* ideology have made him the focus of an intense personality cult comparable to, and perhaps even more extreme than, that of Joseph Stalin. Through means of the state-controlled media and the education system, which includes an elaborate network of "social education" institutions aimed at creating a proper environment for the rearing of North Korean youth, Kim Il Sung and Kim Jong Il are the focus of nationwide veneration.

North Korea's rigidly hierarchical social structure resembles that of pre-modern Korea: an unequal society, in terms of both status and economic rewards. The rulers are at the apex, next come a small elite of Korean Workers' Party (KWP) officers, then a larger group of KWP cadres (see Glossary), and, finally, the majority of the population. At the bottom of the social-political pyramid are the politically suspect, including those whose relatives fled to the Republic of Korea (ROK, or South Korea) after 1945. The treatment of people is largely determined by political criteria. For example, talented people with "tainted" political backgrounds usually find it impossible to attend a college or university.

Insight into this cloistered society has benefited since the late 1980s from North Korea's release of statistics about its population, health conditions, educational enrollment, and other data previously kept secret. This information suggests that as of July 1991, the approximately 21.8 million North Koreans have life expectancies, health conditions, and mortality rates roughly equivalent to those of South Korea, which at that time had about twice the population. In the early 1990s, however, relatively limited information was available on living standards, especially for those living outside the capital city of P'yŏngyang.

The Physical Environment

The Korean Peninsula extends for about 1,000 kilometers southward from the northeast Asian continental landmass. The main Japanese islands of Honshū and Kyūshū are located some 200 kilometers to the southeast across the Tsushima Strait, the southeast part of the Korea Strait; China's Shandong Peninsula lies 190 kilometers to the west (see fig. 2). Japan's Tsushima Island lies between the peninsula's southeast coast and Kyūshū. The Korean Peninsula's west coast is bordered by the Yellow Sea (or Korea Bay as it is called in North Korea). The east coast is bordered by the Sea of Japan (known in Korea as the East Sea; North Korean sources sometimes refer to the Yellow and Japan seas as the West and East seas of Korea, respectively). The 8,460-kilometer coastline of Korea is highly irregular, with North Korea's half of the peninsula having 2,495 kilometers of coastline. Some 3,579 islands lie adjacent to the Korean Peninsula, mostly along the south and west coasts.

Korea's northern land border is formed by the Yalu (or Amnok) and Tumen rivers, which have their sources in the region around Paektu-san (Mount Paektu or White Head Mountain), an extinct volcano and Korea's highest mountain (2,744 meters). The Yalu River flows into the Yellow Sea, and the Tumen River flows east into the Sea of Japan. The northern border extends for 1,433 kilometers; 1,416 kilometers are shared with the Chinese provinces of Jilin and Liaoning, and the remaining seventeen kilometers are shared with Russia. Part of the border with China near Paektu-san has yet to be clearly demarcated.

At the end of World War II, the Korean Peninsula was divided along the thirty-eighth parallel into Soviet and United States occupation zones. With the signing of an armistice marking the end of the Korean War in 1953, the border between North Korea and South Korea became the Demarcation Line (see Glossary), which runs through the middle of the Demilitarized Zone (DMZ—see Glossary). This heavily guarded, 4,000-meter-wide strip of land runs east and west along the line of cease-fire for a distance of 241 kilometers (238 kilometers of that line form the land boundary with South Korea). The North Korean government claims territorial waters extending twelve nautical miles from shore. It also claims an exclusive economic zone 200 nautical miles from shore. In addition, a maritime military boundary that lies fifty nautical miles offshore in the Sea of Japan and 200 nautical miles offshore in the Yellow Sea demarcates the waters and airspace into which foreign ships and airplanes are prohibited from entering without permission.

The total land area of the Korean Peninsula, including islands, is 220,847 square kilometers, of which 55 percent, or 120,410 square kilometers, constitute the territory of North Korea. The combined territories of North Korea and South Korea are about the same size as the United Kingdom or the state of Minnesota. North Korea alone is about the size of the state of New York or Louisiana.

Topography and Drainage

Early European visitors to Korea remarked that the country resembled ''a sea in a heavy gale'' because of the many successive mountain ranges that crisscross the peninsula (see fig. 3). Some 80 percent of North Korea's land area is composed of mountains and uplands, with all of the peninsula's mountains with elevations of 2,000 meters or more located in North Korea. The great majority of the population lives in the plains and lowlands.

The land around Paektu-san near the China border is volcanic in origin and includes a basalt lava plateau with elevations of between 1,400 and 2,000 meters above sea level. The Hamgyŏng Range, located in the extreme northeastern part of the peninsula, has many high peaks, including Kwanmo-san at approximately

1,756 meters. Other major ranges include the Nangnim Range, which is located in the north-central part of North Korea and runs in a north-south direction, making communication between the eastern and western parts of the country rather difficult, and the Kangnam Range, which runs along the North Korea-China border. Kŭmgang-san, or Diamond Mountain (approximately 1,638 meters) in the T'aebaek Range, which extends into South Korea, is famous for its scenic beauty.

For the most part, the plains are small. The most extensive are the P'yŏngyang and Chaeryŏng plains, each covering about 500 square kilometers. Because the mountains on the east coast drop abruptly to the sea, the plains are even smaller there than on the west coast.

The mountain ranges in the northern and eastern parts of North Korea form the watershed for most of its rivers, which run in a westerly direction and empty into the Yellow Sea (Korea Bay). The longest is the Yalu River, which is navigable for 678 of its 790 kilometers. The Tumen River, one of the few major rivers to flow into the Sea of Japan, is the second longest at 521 kilometers but is navigable for only eighty-five kilometers because of the mountainous topography. The third longest river, the Taedong River, flows through P'yŏngyang and is navigable for 245 of its 397 kilometers. Lakes tend to be small because of the lack of glacial activity and the stability of the earth's crust in the region. Unlike neighboring Japan or northern China, North Korea experiences few severe earthquakes. The country is well endowed with spas and hot springs, which number 124 according to one North Korean source.

Climate

Located between 38° and 43° north latitude, North Korea has a continental climate with four distinct seasons. Long winters bring bitterly cold and clear weather interspersed with snowstorms as a result of northern and northwestern winds that blow from Siberia. The daily average high and low temperatures for P'yŏngyang in January are − 3°C and − 13°C. Average snowfall is thirty-seven days during the winter. The weather is likely to be particularly harsh in the northern, mountainous regions. Summer tends to be short, hot, humid, and rainy because of the southern and southeastern monsoon winds that bring moist air from the Pacific Ocean. The daily average high and low temperatures for P'yŏngyang in August are 29°C and 20°C. On average, approximately 60 percent of all precipitation occurs from June to September. Typhoons affect the peninsula on an average of at least once every summer.

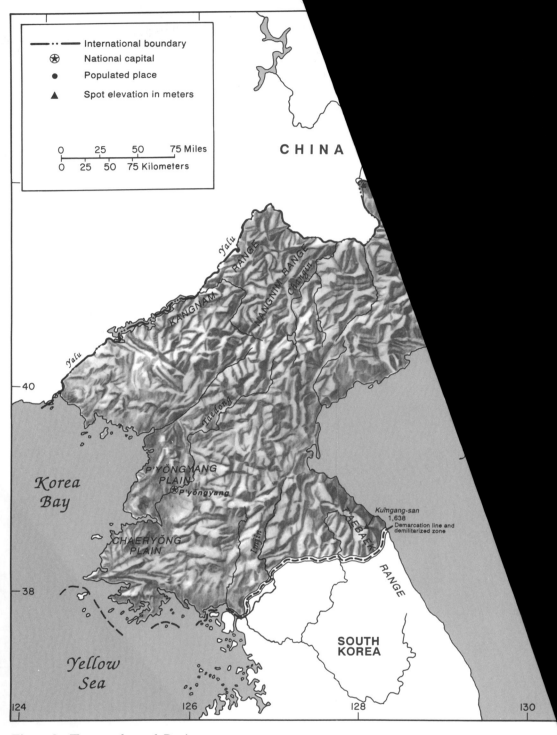

Figure 3. Topography and Drainage

54

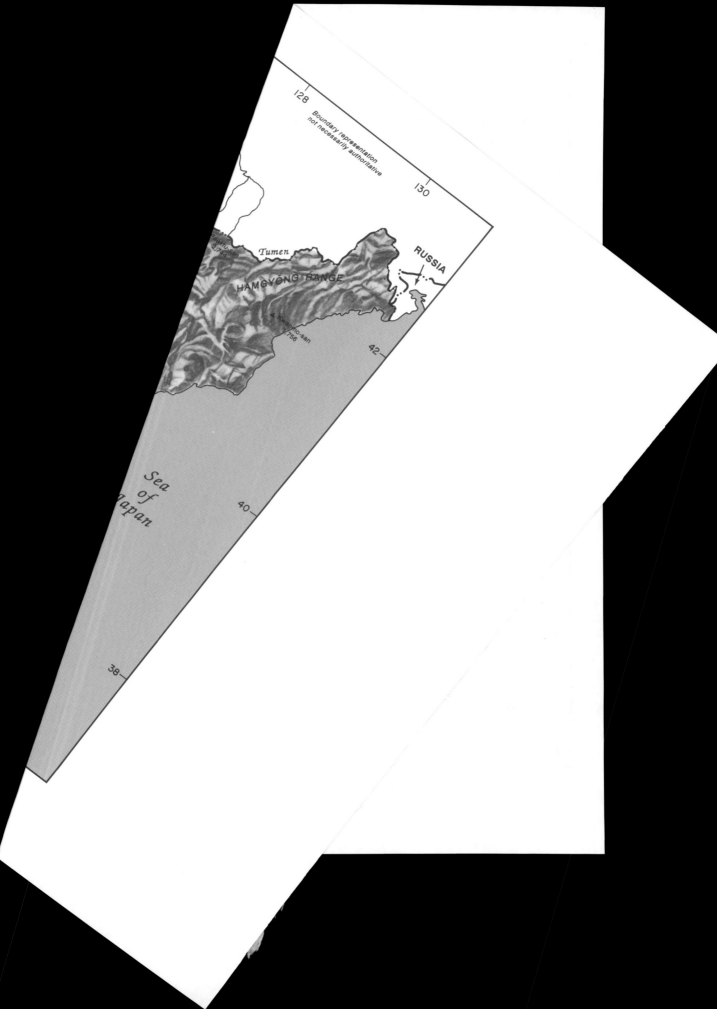

128

130

RUSSIA

Tumen

HAMGYÖNG RANGE

▲ Kwanmo-san
/756

42

40

38

*Sea
of
Japan*

Spring and autumn are transitional seasons marked by mild temperatures and variable winds and bring the most pleasant weather.

Environmental Protection

Lack of information makes it difficult to assess the extent to which industrialization and urbanization have damaged North Korea's natural environment. Using generally obsolete technology transferred from the former Soviet Union and China, the country embarked on a program of ambitious industrialization after the Korean War. Poland, Czechoslovakia, and Romania, which had similar industrial policies, had some of the world's worst air, water, and soil pollution in the early 1990s.

The April 1986 passage of an environmental protection law by the Supreme People's Assembly, the country's national legislature, suggested that North Korea might also have serious pollution problems. Speaking about the bill, Vice President Yi Chong-ok claimed that "big successes" had been accomplished in this field in the past and that "visitors to the DPRK can easily confirm that pollution has not reached the levels experienced in other countries." Although Yi described the law as a preventive rather than a curative measure, a German publication noted that the attendance of representatives from the cities of Namp'o, Hamhŭng, and Ch'ŏngjin at preliminary discussions of the bill suggested that these localities might have more serious pollution problems than other North Korean cities.

Air pollution is moderated by the extensive reliance on electricity rather than on fossil fuels, both for industry and for the heating of urban residences. Air pollution is further limited by the absence of private automobiles and restrictions on using gasoline-powered vehicles because of the critical shortage of oil. The extent of water pollution is unknown, but it did not seem to be a serious problem in the P'yŏngyang area as of early 1993.

Population

Estimating the size, growth rate, sex ratio, and age structure of North Korea's population has been extremely difficult. Until release of official data in 1989, the 1963 edition of the *North Korea Central Yearbook* was the last official publication to disclose population figures. After 1963 demographers used varying methods to estimate the population. They either totaled the number of delegates elected to the Supreme People's Assembly (each delegate representing 50,000 people before 1962 and 30,000 people afterward) or relied on official statements that a certain number of persons, or percentage of the population, was engaged in a particular activity. Thus, on the basis of remarks made by President Kim Il Sung in 1977 concerning school attendance, the population that year was calculated at 17.2 million persons. During the 1980s, health statistics, including life expectancy and causes of mortality, were gradually made available to the outside world.

In 1989 the Central Statistics Bureau released demographic data to the United Nations Fund for Population Activities (UNFPA) in order to secure the UNFPA's assistance in holding North Korea's first nationwide census since the establishment of the DPRK in 1948. Although the figures given to the United Nations (UN) might have been purposely distorted, it appears that in line with other attempts to open itself to the outside world, the North Korean regime has also opened somewhat in the demographic realm. Although the country lacks trained demographers, accurate data on household registration, migration, and births and deaths are available to North Korean authorities. According to the United States scholar Nicholas Eberstadt and demographer Judith Banister, vital statistics and personal information on residents are kept by agencies on the *ri,* or *ni* (village, the local administrative unit) level in rural areas and the *dong* (district or block) level in urban areas.

Size and Growth Rate

In their 1992 monograph, *The Population of North Korea,* Eberstadt and Banister use the data given to the UNFPA and also make their own assessments. They place the total population at 21.4 million persons in mid-1990, consisting of 10.6 million males and 10.8 million females. This figure is close to an estimate of 21.9 million persons for mid-1988 cited in the 1990 edition of the *Demographic Yearbook* published by the UN. *Korean Review,* a book by Pan Hwan Ju published by the P'yŏngyang Foreign Languages Press in 1987, gives a figure of 19.1 million persons for 1986.

The figures disclosed by the government reveal an unusually low proportion of males to females: in 1980 and 1987, the male-to-female ratios were 86.2 to 100 and 84.2 to 100, respectively. Low male-to-female ratios are usually the result of a war, but these figures were lower than the sex ratio of 88.3 males per 100 females recorded for 1953, the last year of the Korean War. The male-to-female ratio would be expected to rise to a normal level with the passage of years, as happened between 1953 and 1970, when the figure was 95.1 males per 100 females. After 1970, however, the ratio declined. Eberstadt and Banister suggest that before 1970 male and female population figures included the whole population, yielding ratios in the ninetieth percentile, but that after that time the male military population was excluded from population figures. Based on the figures provided by the Central Statistics Bureau, Eberstadt and Banister estimate that the actual size of the "hidden" male North Korean military had reached 1.2 million by 1986 and that the actual male-to-female ratio was 97.1 males to 100 females in 1990. If their estimates are correct, 6.1 percent of North Korea's total population was in the military, numerically the world's fifth largest military force, in the late 1980s (see The Armed Forces, ch. 5).

The annual population growth rate in 1960 was 2.7 percent, rising to a high of 3.6 percent in 1970 but falling to 1.9 percent in 1975. This fall reflected a dramatic decline in the fertility rate: the average number of children born to women decreased from 6.5 in 1966 to 2.5 in 1988. Assuming the data are reliable, reasons for falling growth rates and fertility rates probably include late marriage, urbanization, limited housing space, and the expectation that women would participate equally in terms of work hours in the labor force. The experience of other socialist countries suggests that widespread labor force participation by women often goes hand-in-hand with more traditional role expectations; in other words, they are still responsible for housework and childrearing. The high percentage of males aged seventeen to twenty-six may also have contributed to the low fertility rate. According to Eberstadt and Banister's data, the annual population growth rate in 1991 was 1.9 percent.

The North Korean government seems to perceive its population as too small in relation to that of South Korea. In its public pronouncements, P'yŏngyang has called for accelerated population growth and encouraged large families. According to one Korean-American scholar who visited North Korea in the early 1980s, the country has no birth control policies; parents are encouraged to have as many as six children. The state provides *t'agaso* (nurseries) in order to lessen the burden of childrearing for parents and offers a seventy-seven-day paid leave after childbirth (see Family Life; The Role of Women, this ch.). Eberstadt and Banister suggest, however, that authorities at the local level make contraception information readily available to parents and that intrauterine devices are the most commonly adopted birth control method. An interview with a former North Korean resident in the early 1990s revealed that such devices are distributed free at clinics.

Population Structure and Projections

Demographers determine the age structure of a given population by dividing it into five-year age-groups and arranging them chronologically in a pyramidlike structure that "bulges" or recedes

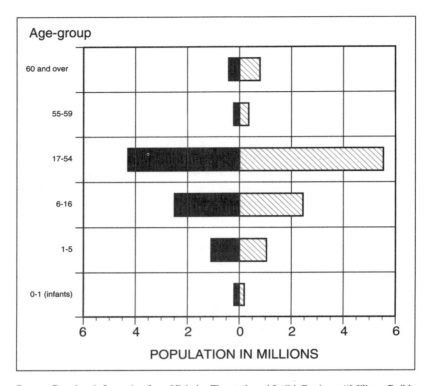

Age-group

POPULATION IN MILLIONS

Source: Based on information from Nicholas Eberstadt and Judith Banister, "Military Build-up in the DPRK: Some New Indications from North Korean Data," *Asian Survey*, 31, No. 11, November 1991, 1101.

Figure 4. Civilian Population Distribution by Age and Sex, 1986

in relation to the number of persons in a given age cohort. Many poor, developing countries have a broad base and steadily tapering higher levels, which reflects a large number of births and young children but much smaller age cohorts in later years as a result of relatively short life expectancies. North Korea does not entirely fit this pattern; data reveal a "bulge" in the lower ranges of adulthood (see fig. 4). In 1991 life expectancy at birth was approximately sixty-six years for males and almost seventy-three years for females.

It is likely that annual population growth rates will increase in the future, as well as difficulties in employing the many young men and women entering the labor force in a socialist economy already suffering from stagnant growth. Eberstadt and Banister estimate that the population will increase to 25.5 million by the end of the century and to 28.5 million in 2010. They project that the population will stabilize (that is, cease to grow) at 34 million persons in 2045 and will then experience a gradual decline. By comparison, South Korea's population is expected to stabilize at 52.6 million people in 2023.

Settlement Patterns and Urbanization

North Korea's population is concentrated in the plains and lowlands. The least populated regions are the mountainous Chagang and Yanggang provinces adjacent to the Chinese border; the largest concentrations of population are in North P'yŏngan and South P'yŏngan provinces, in the municipal district of P'yŏngyang, and in South Hamgyŏng Province, which includes the Hamhŭng-Hŭngnam urban area (see fig. 1). Eberstadt and Banister calculate the average population density at 167 persons per square kilometer, ranging from 1,178 persons per square kilometer in P'yŏngyang municipality to forty-four persons per square kilometer in Yanggang Province. By contrast, South Korea had an average population density of 425 persons per square kilometer in 1989.

Like South Korea, North Korea has experienced significant urban migration since the end of the Korean War. Official statistics reveal that 59.6 percent of the total population was classified as urban in 1987. This figure compares with only 17.7 percent in 1953. It is not entirely clear, however, what standards are used to define urban populations. Eberstadt and Banister suggest that although South Korean statisticians do not classify settlements of under 50,000 as urban, their North Korean counterparts include settlements as small as 20,000 in this category. And, in North Korea, people who engage in agricultural pursuits inside municipalities sometimes are not counted as urban.

Urbanization in North Korea seems to have proceeded most rapidly between 1953 and 1960, when the urban population grew between 12 and 20 percent annually. Subsequently, the increase slowed to about 6 percent annually in the 1960s and between 1 and 3 percent from 1970 to 1987.

In 1987 North Korea's largest cities were P'yŏngyang, with approximately 2.3 million inhabitants; Hamhŭng, 701,000; Ch'ŏngjin, 520,000; Namp'o, 370,000; Sunch'ŏn, 356,000; and Sinŭiju, 289,000. In 1987 the total national population living in P'yŏngyang was 11.5 percent. The government also restricts and monitors migration to cities and ensures a relatively balanced distribution of population in provincial centers in relation to P'yŏngyang.

Koreans Living Overseas

Large-scale emigration from Korea began around 1904 and

continued until the end of World War II. During the Japanese colonial occupation (1910–45), many Koreans emigrated to Manchuria (China's three northeastern provinces of Heilongjiang, Jilin, and Liaoning), other parts of China, the Soviet Union, Hawaii, and the continental United States. People from Korea's northern provinces went mainly to Manchuria, China, and Siberia; many from the southern provinces went to Japan. Most émigrés left for economic reasons because employment opportunities were scarce; many Korean farmers had lost their land after the Japanese colonial government introduced a system of private land tenure, imposed higher land taxes, and promoted the growth of an absentee landlord class charging exorbitant rents.

In the 1980s, more than 4 million ethnic Koreans lived outside the peninsula. The largest group, about 1.7 million people, lived in China; most had assumed Chinese citizenship. Approximately 1 million Koreans, almost exclusively from South Korea, lived in North America. About 389,000 ethnic Koreans resided in the former Soviet Union. One observer noted that Koreans have been so successful in running collective farms in Soviet Central Asia that being Korean is often associated by other citizens there with being rich, and as a result there is growing antagonism toward Koreans. Smaller groups of Koreans are found in Central America and South America (85,000), the Middle East (62,000), Europe (40,000), Asia (27,000), and Africa (25,000).

Many of Japan's approximately 680,000 Koreans have below-average standards of living. This situation is partly because of discrimination by the Japanese. Many resident Koreans, loyal to North Korea, remain separate from, and often hostile to, the Japanese social mainstream. The pro-North Korean Choch'ongryŏn (General Association of Korean Residents in Japan, known as Chōsen sōren or Chōsōren in Japanese) (see Glossary) initially was more successful than the pro-South Korean Mindan (Association for Korean Residents in Japan) in attracting adherents among residents in Japan.

Between 1959 and 1982, Choch'ongryŏn encouraged the repatriation of Korean residents in Japan to North Korea. More than 93,000 Koreans left Japan, the majority (80,000 persons) in 1960 and 1961. Thereafter, the number of repatriates declined, apparently because of reports of hardships suffered by their compatriots. Approximately 6,637 Japanese wives accompanied their husbands to North Korea, of whom about 1,828 retained Japanese citizenship in the early 1990s. P'yŏngyang had originally promised that the wives could return home every two or three years to visit their relatives. In fact, however, they are not allowed to do so, and few have had contact with their families in Japan. In normalization talks between North Korean and Japanese officials in the early 1990s, the latter urged unsuccessfully that the wives be allowed to make home visits.

Social Structure and Values

Confucian and Neo-Confucian Values

Neo-Confucianism, the dominant value system of the Chosŏn Dynasty (1392–1910), combines the social ethics of the classical Chinese philosophers Confucius (Kong Zi, 551–479 B.C.) and Mencius (Meng Zi, 372–289 B.C.) with Buddhist and Daoist metaphysics. One of neo-Confucianism's basic ideas is that the institutions and practices of a properly ordered human community express the immutable principles or laws that govern the cosmos. Through correct social practice, as defined by Confucian sages and their commentators, individuals can achieve self-cultivation and a kind of spiritual unity with heaven (although this was rarely described in mystic or ecstatic terms). Neo-Confucianism defines formal social relations on all levels of society. Social relations are not conceived in terms of the happiness or satisfaction of the individuals involved, but in terms of the harmonious integration of individuals into a collective whole, which, like the properly cultivated individual, mirrors the harmony of the natural order.

During the Chosŏn Dynasty, Korean kings made the neo-Confucian doctrine of the Chinese philosopher Zhu Xi (1130–1200) their state ideology. Although it was a foreign philosophy, Korean neo-Confucian scholars, of whom the most important was Yi Hwang, also known as Yi T'oe-gye (1501–70), played a role in adapting Zhu Xi's teachings to Korean conditions. This was done without denying the cultural superiority of China as the homeland of civilized thought and forms of life.

Neo-Confucianism in Korea became quite rigid and conservative by the mid-sixteenth century. In practice, the doctrine emphasized hierarchy in human relations and self-control for the individual. The Five Relationships (*o ryun* in Korean; *wu lun* in Chinese), formulated by classical Chinese thinkers such as Mencius and subsequently sanctified by Zhu Xi and other neo-Confucianist metaphysicians, governed proper human relations: that "between father and son there should be affection; between ruler and minister there should be righteousness; between husband and wife there should be attention to their separate functions; between old and young there should be proper order; and between friends there should be faithfulness." Only the last was a

61

relationship between equals; the others were based on authority and subordination.

Throughout traditional Korean society, from the royal palace and central government offices in the capital to the humblest household in the countryside, the themes of hierarchy and inequality were pervasive. There was no concept of the rights of the individual. In the context of the wider society, a well-defined elite of scholar-officials versed in neo-Confucian orthodoxy was legitimized in terms of the traditional ethical distinction between the educated ''superior man'' or ''gentleman,'' who seeks righteousness, and the ''small man,'' who seeks only profit. This theme was central in the writings of both Confucius and Mencius. Confucianism and neo-Confucianism as political philosophies proposed a benevolent paternalism: the masses had no role in government, but the scholar-officials were supposed to look after them as fathers look after their children. In the Chosŏn Dynasty, status and power inequalities, defined precisely within a vertical hierarchy, were generally considered both natural and good. The hierarchy extended from the household relationships of fathers and children through the intermediary relationships of ruler and ruled within the kingdom, to Korea's subordinate status as a tributary of China.

There is a danger, however, in overstressing the idea of Korea as a homogeneously Confucian society, even during the Chosŏn Dynasty. Foreign observers have been impressed with the diversity of the Korean character as expressed in day-to-day human relations. There is, on the one hand, the image of Koreans as self-controlled, deferential, and meticulous in the fulfillment of their social obligations; on the other hand, there is the Korean reputation for volatility and emotionalism. The ecstasy and euphoria of shamanistic religious practices, one of Korea's most characteristic cultural expressions, contrast sharply with the austere self-control idealized by Confucianists. Although relatively minor themes in the history of Korean ethics and social thought, the concepts of equality and respect for individuals are not entirely lacking. The doctrines of Ch'ŏndogyo (see Glossary), an indigenous religion that arose in the nineteenth century and combined elements of Buddhism, Daoism, shamanism, Confucianism, and Catholicism, taught that every human being ''bears divinity'' and that one must ''treat man as god.''

Chosŏn Dynasty Social Structure

In the Chosŏn Dynasty, four distinct social strata developed: the scholar-officials (or nobility), collectively referred to as the *yangban* (see Glossary); the *chungin* (literally, ''middle people''), technicians and administrators subordinate to the *yangban;* the commoners or *sangmin,* a large group composed of farmers, craftsmen, and merchants; and the *ch'ŏmmin* (despised, or base people, often slaves) at the bottom of society. To arrest social mobility and ensure stability, the government devised a system of personal tallies in order to identify people according to their status, and elites kept detailed genealogies, or *chokpo* (see Glossary; The Origins of the Korean Nation, ch. 1).

In the strictest sense of the term, *yangban* referred to government officials or officeholders who had passed the civil service examinations, which tested knowledge of the Confucian classics and their neo-Confucian interpretations. They were the Korean counterparts of the scholar-officials, or mandarins, of imperial China. The term *yangban,* first used during the Koryŏ Dynasty (918–1392), literally means two groups, that is, civil and military officials. Over the centuries, however, its usage became rather vague, so the term can be said to have several overlapping meanings. A broader use of the term included within the *yangban* two other groups that could be considered associated with, but outside, the ruling elite. The first included those scholars who had passed the preliminary civil service examination and sometimes the higher examinations but failed to secure government appointment. In the late Chosŏn Dynasty, there were many more successful examination candidates than there were positions. The second included the relatives and descendants of government officials because formal *yangban* rank was hereditary. Even if these people were poor and did not themselves serve in the government, they were considered members of a "*yangban* family" and thus shared the aura of the elite so long as they retained Confucian culture and rituals.

In principle, however, the *yangban* were a meritocratic elite. They gained their positions through educational achievement. Although certain groups of persons (including artisans, merchants, shamans [*mudang*], slaves, and Buddhist monks) were prohibited from taking the higher civil service examinations, they formed only a small portion of the population. In theory, the examinations were open to the majority of people, who were farmers. In the early years of the Chosŏn Dynasty, some commoners may have been able to attain high positions by passing the examinations and advancing on sheer talent. Later, talent was a necessary but not a sufficient prerequisite for getting into the core elite because of the surplus of successful examinees. Influential family connections were virtually indispensable for obtaining high official positions. Moreover, special posts called "protection appointments" were inherited by descendants of the Chosŏn royal family and certain high officials.

Despite the emphasis on educational merit, the *yangban* became in a very real sense a hereditary elite. Thus, when progressive officials enacted the 1984 Kabo Reforms, a program of social reforms, they found it necessary to abolish the social distinctions between *yangban* and commoners.

Below the *yangban,* yet superior to the commoners, were the *chungin,* a small group of technical and administrative officials. This group included astronomers, physicians, interpreters, and career military officers. Local functionaries, who were members of an inferior hereditary class, were an important and frequently oppressive link between the *yangban* and the common people and were often the de facto rulers of a local region.

The *sangmin,* or commoners, comprised about 75 percent of the total population. These farmers, craftsmen, and merchants bore the burden of taxation and were subject to military conscription. Farmers had higher prestige than merchants, but lived a hard life. Below the commoners, the *ch'ŏmmin* performed what was considered vile or low-prestige work. They included servants and slaves in government offices and resthouses, jailkeepers and convicts, shamans, actors, female entertainers (*kisaeng*), professional mourners, shoemakers, executioners, and, for a time, Buddhist monks and nuns. Also included in the category were the *paekchŏng* who dealt with meat and the hides of animals; they were considered ''unclean'' and lived in segregated communities. Slaves were treated as chattel but could own property and even other slaves. Although slaves were numerous at the beginning of the Chosŏn Dynasty, their numbers had dwindled by the time slavery was officially abolished with the Kabo Reforms.

The Traditional Family and Kinship

Filial piety (*hyo* in Korean; *xiao* in Chinese), the first of the Five Relationships defined by Mencius, had traditionally been the normative foundation of Korean family life. Historically, the Korean family was patrilineal. The most important concern of the family group was to produce a male heir to carry on the family line and to perform ancestor rituals in the household and at the family gravesite. The first son customarily assumed leadership of the family after his father's death and inherited his father's house and a greater portion of land than his younger brothers. His birthright enabled him to carry out the ritually prescribed obligations to the family ancestors.

The special reverence shown to ancestors was both a social ethic and a religion. Koreans were taught that deceased family members did not pass into oblivion, to a remote afterlife, or, as Buddhists believed, to rebirth as humans or animals in some remote place; rather, they remained, in spiritual form, securely within the family circle. Even in the early 1990s, the presence of the deceased was intensely real and personal for traditionally minded Koreans. Fear of death is blunted by the consoling thought that even in the grave one will be cared for by one's own people. Succeeding generations are obligated to remember the deceased in a yearly cycle of rituals and ceremonies.

The purpose of marriage was to produce a male heir, not to provide mutual companionship and support for husband and wife, even though this sometimes happened. Marriages were arranged. A go-between or matchmaker, usually a middle-aged woman, carried on the negotiations between the two families involved; because of a very strict law on exogamy, these two families sometimes did not know each other and often lived in different communities. The bride and groom met for the first time at the marriage ceremony, a practice that was gradually abandoned in urban areas before World War II.

The traditional Korean kinship system, defined in terms of different obligations in relation to the reverence shown to ancestors, was complex. Anthropologists generally view it in terms of four separate levels, beginning with the household at the lowest level and reaching to the clan, which included many geographically dispersed members. The household, *chip*, or *jip* (see Glossary), consisted of a husband and wife, their children, and, if the husband was the eldest son, his parents. The eldest son's household, the stem family, was known as the "big house" (*k'ŭnchip*, or *k'ŭnjip*); that of each of the younger sons, a branch family containing husband, wife, and children only, was known as a "little house" (*chagŭnchip*, or *chagŭnjip*). It was through the stem family of the eldest son that the main line of descent was traced from generation to generation.

The second level of kinship was the "mourning group" (*changnye*), which consisted of all those descendants of a common patrilineal forebear up to four generations back. Its role was to organize ceremonies at gravesites. These included the reading of a formal message by the eldest male descendant of the *changnye* progenitor and the offering of elaborate and attractive dishes to the ancestral spirits.

Similar rituals were carried out at the third level of kinship organization, the lineage, *p'a* (see Glossary). A lineage might comprise only a handful of households, or hundreds or even thousands of households. The lineage was responsible for rites to ancestors of the fifth generation or above, performed at a common gravesite. During the Chosŏn Dynasty, the lineage commonly possessed land, gravesites, and buildings. Croplands were allocated to support the ancestral ceremonies. The *p'a* also performed other functions—aiding poor or distressed lineage members, educating children at schools maintained by the *p'a,* and supervising the behavior of younger lineage members. Because most people living in a single village were members of a common lineage during the Chosŏn Dynasty, the *p'a* performed many social services at the local level that, in the 1990s, were provided by state-run schools, public security organs, and the state system of clinics and hospitals.

The fourth and most inclusive kinship organization was the clan or, more accurately, the surname origin group (*tongsŏng*). Members of the same *munjung* (extended family) shared both a surname and origins in the generally remote past. For example, the Chŏnju Yi, who originated in Chŏnju in North Chŏlla Province (in contemporary South Korea), claimed, and continue to claim, as their progenitor the founder of the Chosŏn Dynasty, Yi Sŏng-gye. Unlike members of smaller kinship groups, however, they often lacked strong feelings of solidarity. In many if not most cases, the real function of the surname origin group was to define groups of permissible marriage partners. The strict rule of exogamy prohibited marriage between people from the same *tongsŏng* and *tongbon* (ancestral origin) even if their closest common ancestors had lived centuries earlier. Confucianists regarded this prohibition, which originated during the Chosŏn Dynasty, as a sign of Korea's civilized status; they believed that only barbarians married within their own clan or kin group.

The Colonial Transformation of Korean Society

The social strata of the Chosŏn Dynasty and the family system were sustained by a highly stable environment composed, for the most part, of rural communities. The Hermit Kingdom, as it was called by Westerners, had very little contact with the outside world even in the late nineteenth century. Rapid changes, however, occurred during the Japanese colonial period, which disrupted the centuries-old ways of life and caused considerable personal hardship.

These changes were particularly disruptive in rural areas. Traditionally, all land belonged to the king and was granted by him to his subjects. Although specific tracts of land tended to remain within the same family from generation to generation (including communal land owned by clans and lineages), land occupancy, use, and ownership patterns were often ambiguous and varied from one part of the country to another. Land was not privately held.

Between 1910 and 1920, the Japanese carried out a comprehensive land survey in order to place land ownership on a modern legal footing. Farmers who had tilled the same land for generations but could not prove ownership had their land confiscated. Such land ended up in the hands of the colonial government, to be sold to Japanese enterprises, such as the Oriental Development Company, or to Japanese immigrants.

These policies forced many Koreans to emigrate overseas or to become tenant farmers. Still other Koreans fled to the hills to become "fire-field," or slash-and-burn, farmers, living under extremely harsh and primitive conditions. By 1936 there were more than 1.5 million slash-and-burn farmers. Other former farmers moved to urban areas to work in factories.

The fortunes of the *yangban* elite were mixed. Some prospered under the Japanese as landlords or even entrepreneurs. Those *yangban* who remained aloof from their country's new overlords, however, often fell into poverty. A few Koreans educated in modern Japanese or foreign missionary schools formed the nucleus of a modern middle class.

The Japanese built railroads and highways—a logistic system—and schools and hospitals. A modern system of administration was established to link the colonial economy more effectively with that of Japan. These changes also fostered employment for Koreans as mid- and lower-level civil servants and technicians. During the 1930s and early 1940s, industrial development projects, especially in the border area between Korea and China, employed thousands of Koreans as workers and lower-level industrial managers. All the top posts were held by Japanese; prewar and wartime industrialization nevertheless created new classes of workers and managers.

At the end of World War II, Korea's traditional social fabric, based on rural communities and stable social hierarchies, was tattered but not entirely destroyed. In South Korea, the traditional social system survived, although drastically altered by urbanization and economic development. In North Korea, an occupation by Soviet troops, the communist revolution, and the rule of Kim Il Sung transformed the society.

Tradition and Modernity in North Korea

The extent to which the Confucian values of the Chosŏn Dynasty continue to exert an influence on North Korean society in the 1990s is an intriguing question that cannot be adequately answered until outside observers can gain greater access to the country. The regime practices a very strict regimen of "revolutionary tourism" for those few people allowed to visit the country, so observing everyday life and gleaning opinions and attitudes are impossible. The average tourist views countless monuments to Kim

Il Sung, revolutionary theatrical performances, model farms and factories, large, new apartment complexes, and scenic splendor, but hears little of what the people really think or feel. Confucianism clearly does not serve as a formal ideology or social ethic (being condemned because of its history of class exploitation, its cultural subservience to a foreign state, and as a contradiction of the *chuch'e* ideology). Yet its more authoritarian and hierarchical themes seem to have made the population receptive to the personality cult of Kim Il Sung.

This authoritarian strain of Confucianism has apparently survived, transformed by socialist and *chuch'e* ideology. It appears that P'yŏngyang has chosen to co-opt some of the traditional values rather than to eradicate them. For example, the education system and the media strongly emphasize social harmony. But the nature of education beginning at the preschool level and the limited amount of time parents are able to spend with children because of work schedules subordinate parental authority to that of the state and its representatives. Some aspects of filial piety remain salient in contemporary North Korea; for example, children are taught by the state-controlled media to respect their parents. However, filial piety plays a secondary role in relation to loyalty to the state and Kim Il Sung.

Kim Il Sung is not only a fatherly figure but was described, in childhood, as a model son. A 1980 article entitled "Kim Il Sung Termed Model for Revering Elders" tells of how he warmed his mother's cold hands with his own breath after she returned from work each day in the winter and gave up the pleasure of playing on a swing because it tore his pants, which his mother then had to mend. "When his parents or elders called him, he arose from his spot at once no matter how much fun he had been having, answered 'yes' and then ran to them, bowed his head and waited, all ears, for what they were going to say." According to Kim, "Communists love their own parents, wives, children, and their fellow comrades, respect the elderly, live frugal lives and always maintain a humble mien." The "dear leader," or Kim Jong Il, is also described as a filial son; when he was five years old, a propagandist wrote, he insisted on personally guarding his father from evil imperialists with a little wooden rifle.

The personality cult of Kim Il Sung resembles those of Stalin in the Soviet Union in the 1930s and 1940s and Nicolae Ceauşescu in Romania until his overthrow in 1989. But in North Korea, special attention is paid to the theme of Kim's benevolence and the idea that North Koreans must repay that benevolence with unquestioning loyalty and devotion, recalling old Confucian values of repaying debts of gratitude. Kim's birthday, April 15, is a national holiday. His eightieth birthday, celebrated in 1992, was the occasion for massive national celebrations. The state-run media similarly depicts Kim Jong Il in a benevolent light.

One enthusiastic Japanese writer related in a 1984 book how the younger Kim, learning of the poor living standards of lighthouse keepers and their families on a remote island, personally arranged for various life-style improvements, including water storage tanks, television sets, special scholarships for the children, and "colorful clothes, coats and caps of the kind that were worn by children in P'yŏngyang." In the writer's words, "the lighthousemen and their families shed tears of gratitude to the Secretary [Kim Jong Il] for his warm-hearted care for them." The writer also described the "bridge of love," built on Kim's order in a remote area in order to allow thirteen children to cross a river on the way to school. He emphasized that the bridge had absolutely "no economic merit."

Chuch'e and Contemporary Social Values

Chuch'e is a significant break with the Confucian past. Developed during the period of revolutionary struggle against Japanese imperialism, *chuch'e* is the product of Kim Il Sung's thinking. *Chuch'e* emphasizes the importance of developing the nation's potential, using its own resources and reserves of human creativity (see Political Ideology: The Role of *Chuch'e*, ch. 4). *Chuch'e* legitimizes cultural, economic, and political isolationism by stressing the error of imitating foreign countries or of becoming excessively "international." During the 1970s, Kim Jong Il suggested that *chuch'e* ideology be renamed Kim Il Sung Chuui (Kim Il Sungism). Kim Il Sungism, epitomizing *chuch'e*, is described as superior to all other systems of human thought, including (apparently) Marxism.

Chuch'e thought is not, at least in principle, xenophobic. P'yŏngyang has devoted considerable resources to organizing *chuch'e* study societies around the world and bringing foreign visitors to North Korea for national celebrations—for example, 4,000 persons were invited to attend Kim Il Sung's eightieth birthday celebrations.

The government opposes "flunkeyism." Kim Jong Il, depicted as an avid student of Korean history in his youth, was said to have made the revolutionary proposal that Kim Yushin, the great general of the Silla Dynasty (668–935), was a "flunkeyist" rather than a national hero because he enlisted the aid of Tang Dynasty (618–907) China in order to defeat Silla's rivals, Koguryŏ and Paekche, and unify the country. *Chuch'e*'s opposition to flunkeyism, moreover, is probably also a reaction to the experience of Japanese colonialism (see The Legacy of Japanese Colonialism, ch. 1).

Apart from the North Korean people's almost complete isolation from foreign influences, probably the most significant impact of *chuch'e* thought and Kim Il Sungism with regard to daily life is the relentless emphasis on self-sacrifice and hard work. The population is told that everything can be accomplished through dedication and the proper revolutionary spirit. This view is evident in the perennial "speed battles" initiated by the leadership to dramatically increase productivity; another example is the bizarre phenomenon called the "drink no soup movement," apparently designed to keep workers on the factory floor rather than going to the lavatory (see Budget and Finance, ch. 3). Moreover, *chuch'e* provides a "proper" standpoint from which to create or judge art, literature, drama, and music, as well as a philosophical underpinning for the country's educational system.

Classes and Social Strata

Although socialism promises a society of equals in which class oppression is eliminated, most evidence shows that great social and political inequality continued to exist in North Korea in the early 1990s. The state is the sole allocator of resources, and inequalities are justified in terms of the state's political and economic imperatives. Kim Il Sung and Kim Jong Il are described by unsympathetic foreign observers as living like kings. (The South Korean film director Sin Sangok and his actress wife, Ch'oe Unhui, who were apparently kidnapped and taken to North Korea on Kim Jong Il's orders, described him as a fanatic film buff with a library of 15,000 films; they claimed that he alone could view these films, which were collected for his benefit by North Korean diplomats abroad.) Equally important from the standpoint of social stratification, however, is a small and clearly defined elite within the ruling KWP, who, like the privileged communists listed in the former Soviet Union's *nomenklatura*, a listing of positions and personnel, have emerged as a "new class" with a relatively high standard of living and access to consumer goods not available to ordinary people.

According to North Korean sources cited by Eberstadt and Banister, total membership in the KWP in 1987 was "over 3 million," or almost 15 percent of the estimated population of 20.3 million that year. Membership in the party requires a politically "clean" background. Given the KWP's status as a revolutionary "vanguard party," these individuals clearly constitute an elite; it is unclear, however, how the standards of living of lower echelon party members differ from those of nonparty members (see Party Leadership and Elite Recruitment, ch. 4). Nonetheless, party membership is clearly the smoothest path for upward social mobility. It opens opportunities such as university attendance to members and their children. The state-controlled media repeatedly exhort party members to eschew "bureaucratism" and arrogance in dealing with nonparty people. But it is unclear how successful the regime is in uprooting the centuries-old tradition of *kwanjon minbi* (honor officials, despise the people), which often makes the traditional aristocratic *yangban* elite insufferably arrogant.

Although Japan had promoted some industrialization in the northern part of its Korean colony during the occupation, most of the Korean Peninsula's population before 1945 were farmers. North Korea's industrialization after the Korean War, however, transformed the nature of work and occupational categories. In the late 1980s, the government divided the labor force into four categories: "workers," who were employed at state-owned enterprises; "farmers," who worked on agricultural collectives; "officials," who performed nonmanual labor and probably included teachers, technicians, and health care workers as well as civil servants and KWP cadres; and workers employed in "cooperative industrial units," which Eberstadt and Banister suggest constitute a minuscule private sector. North Korean government statistics showed that the state "worker" category constituted the largest category in 1987, or 57 percent of the labor force. Farmers constituted the second largest category at 25.3 percent; and officials and industrial cooperative workers, 16.8 percent and 0.9 percent, respectively. Within the "worker" category, skilled workers in the fisheries and in the heavy, mining, and defense industries tend to be favored in terms of economic incentives over their counterparts in light and consumer industries; the labor force in urban areas tends to be favored over farmers (see Agriculture, Forestry, and Fisheries, ch. 3). Despite the small size of the "cooperative industrial sector," that is, the industrial counterpart of the cooperative (collective) farms enterprise, a black market apparently exists, with prices as much as ten times higher than those in the official distribution system. Farmers' markets also exist. The black market is not likely to be large enough to foster the emergence of a sizable, shadowy class of smugglers and entrepreneurs.

Food and other necessities of life are strictly rationed, and different occupational groups are reported to receive different qualities and kinds of goods. Sin Sangok and Ch'oe Unhui wrote in the South Korean media in the late 1980s that consumption of beef and pork is largely restricted to "middle-class" and "upper-class people"; "ordinary people" can obtain no meat except dog meat, which is not rationed. An exception is made for the New Year's holidays, Kim Il Sung's birthday, and other holidays, when pork is made

71

available to all. They also report that the regime is actively encouraging sons to assume the occupations of their fathers and that "job succession is regarded as a cardinal virtue in North Korea."

Housing is another area of social inequality. According to a South Korean source, North Korea has five types of standardized housing allotted according to rank; the highest ranks—the party and state elite—live in one- or two-story detached houses. Sixty percent of the population, consisting of ordinary workers and farmers, live in multi-unit dwellings of no more than one or two rooms, including the kitchen.

Family background, in terms of political and ideological criteria, is extremely relevant to one's social status and standard of living. Sons and daughters of revolutionaries and those who died in the Korean War are favored for educational opportunities and advancement. For these children, a special elite school, the Mangyŏng-dae Revolutionary Institute, was established near P'yŏngyang at the birthplace of Kim Il Sung. South Korean scholar Lee Mun Woong wrote that illegitimate children are also favored because they are raised entirely in state-run nurseries and schools and are not subject to the corruption of traditionally minded parents.

Conversely, the children and descendants of "exploiting-class" parents—those who collaborated with the Japanese during the colonial era, opposed agricultural collectivization in the 1950s, or were associated with those who had fled to South Korea—are discriminated against. They are considered "contaminated" by the bad influences of their parents and have to work harder to acquire reputable positions. Relatives of those who had fled to South Korea are especially looked down on and considered "bad elements." Persons with unfavorable political backgrounds are often denied admission to institutions of higher education, despite their intellectual qualifications.

With the exception of disabled Korean War veterans, physically handicapped people appear to be subject to special discrimination, according to international human rights organizations. For example, they are not allowed to enter P'yŏngyang, and those who manage to live in the capital are periodically sought out by the police and expelled. These sources also allege that persons of below-normal height (dwarfs) have been forced to live in a special settlement in a remote rural area. South Korean sources also cite examples of single women over forty years of age who are considered social misfits and are thus harassed.

Urban Life

According to reports by defectors from North Korea and

information gleaned from the limits imposed by "revolutionary tourism," urban life in P'yŏngyang probably resembles that in other East Asian cities, such as Seoul or Tokyo, in that living space is extremely limited. Little remains of traditional architecture, however; with its modern-style, high-rise buildings, P'yŏngyang appears to lack lively neighborhoods, as well as the local festivals and bustling market life of other Asian cities. Spacious highways span the metropolis but seem devoid of traffic except for military vehicles. Unlike the residents of Tokyo and Seoul, however, residents of P'yŏngyang have access to expansive parks and green spaces (see Architecture and City Planning, this ch.).

Beginning in the 1980s, several high-rise apartment complexes were built in P'yŏngyang, some of them reaching forty stories. The Kwangbok New Town, opened in 1989 as housing for representatives to the Thirteenth World Festival of Youth and Students, has been described as accommodating 25,000 families of the KWP elite. A sympathetic Japanese visitor reports that units are 110 square meters in area, with a kitchen-dining room and three or four additional rooms. Maintenance fees (not rent) for the housing of manual workers and office workers constitute 0.3 percent of their monthly income; utilities, including heating, cost about 3 percent of monthly income. Heating in rural areas during the frigid winters seems to be supplied primarily by charcoal briquettes.

Although urban standards of living—at least in P'yŏngyang—appear to be better than rural standards of living, observers note that city shops have limited supplies of necessities. Visitors to the capital during the celebration of Kim Il Sung's eightieth birthday (as well as at other times), however, have toured department stores full of goods. One widely repeated rumor suggests that crowds of local residents are paid by the day to throng department stores but that virtually the only goods actually on sale for them are soap and special consignments of notebooks. Otherwise, access to most department stores in P'yŏngyang is limited to KWP members and foreigners.

Village Life

A land reform law enacted in 1946 confiscated the holdings of big landowners and distributed them to poor farmers and tenants. The consequences of this compulsory redistribution were as much social as economic. Many rich farmers fled to the United States-occupied half of the peninsula south of the thirty-eighth parallel.

Rural collectivization, carried out in three stages between 1945 and 1958, had profound implications for a society consisting mainly of farmers living in small hamlets scattered throughout the

74

Kwangbok Street, Man'gyŏngdae District, P'yŏngyang. The high-rise buildings lining the street contain 25,000 family units. Courtesy Democratic People's Republic of Korea Mission to the United Nations

countryside. The new class of individual landholders—whose holdings could not exceed five *chŏngbo* (see Glossary) in lowland areas, or twenty *chŏngbo* in mountainous ones—had little time to enjoy their status as independent proprietors because the state quickly initiated a process of collectivization. In the initial stage, "permanent mutual aid teams" were formed in which landholders managed their own land as private property but pooled labor, draft animals, and agricultural tools. This stage was followed by the stage of "semi-socialist cooperatives," in which land, still privately held, was pooled. The cooperative purchased animals and tools out of a common fund, and the distribution of the harvest depended on the amount of land and labor contributed. The third and final stage involved the establishment of "complete socialist cooperatives" in which all land was turned over to collective ownership and management. Cooperative members were paid solely on the basis of labor contributed.

The 1959 edition of the *North Korea Central Yearbook* reported that approximately 80 percent of all farmers had joined socialist cooperatives by December 1956 and that by August 1958 all had joined. A land law passed in 1977 stipulated that all land held by cooperatives would be transferred gradually to state ownership or "ownership by the entire people."

The state encouraged the merging of cooperatives so that they would coincide with the *ri,* or *ni* (village). The number of cooperatives with between 101 and 200 households increased from 222 cooperatives in 1954 to 1,074 cooperatives in 1958. The number of cooperatives with between 201 and 300 households increased from twenty cooperatives in 1955 to 984 cooperatives in 1958.

The merging process had important implications for kinship and family life: it broke down the isolation of the single hamlet by making the socialist cooperative the basic local unit and thus diluted *p'a* ties. The traditional kinship system and its strict rules of exogamy worked best in the isolation of hamlets. With the passing of the hamlets, the traditional kinship system and its strict rules of exogamy were seriously undermined.

Family Life

The family is regarded by North Korean authorities as a "cell," or basic unit of society, but not an economic entity. A person participates in production in a cooperative, factory, or office and individually earns "work points." Although on a socialist cooperative payment for work points earned by family members goes to the family unit as a whole, the family head—the father or the

Traditional-style houses in Kaesŏng
Courtesy Tracy Woodward

grandfather—no longer manages and organizes the family's economic life.

Both in urban areas and in socialist cooperatives, family size tends to be small—between four and five people and usually no more than two generations, as opposed to the three generations or more found in the traditional "big house." Parents often live with their youngest, rather than oldest, son and his wife. Observers discovered, however, that sons are still more desired than daughters for economic reasons and for continuing the family name. The eldest son's wedding is a lavish affair compared with those of his brothers. But the traditionally oppressive relationship between mother-in-law and daughter-in-law common to East Asian countries seems to have been fundamentally transformed. A South Korean source reported that an overly demanding mother-in-law might be criticized by a local branch of women's organizations such as the Korean Democratic Women's Union.

A Korean-American scholar learned in discussions with North Korean officials in the early 1980s that a wife's inability to bear a son still gives a husband grounds for divorce. If a man desires a divorce, he has to obtain his wife's permission. A woman, however, is able to divorce without her husband's consent. A South Korean source reported the opposite—that it is easier for a husband to obtain a divorce than it is for a wife. Divorce from those branded "reactionaries," or "bad elements," is granted rather easily in the case of either gender and in fact often is strongly encouraged by the authorities. In general, the authorities seem to discourage divorce with the exceptions noted above. Eberstadt and Banister, using statistics provided by the Central Statistics Bureau, indicate that the number of divorces granted annually between 1949 and 1987 ranged between 3,000 and 5,000 (a low of 3,021 in 1965 and a high of 4,763 in 1949).

The legal age for males to marry is eighteen years; for females, seventeen years. Marrying in one's late twenties or early thirties is common because of work and military service obligations; late marriage also affects fertility rates. Most marriages seem to be between people in the same rural cooperative or urban enterprise. Traditional arranged marriages have by and large disappeared, in favor of "love matches"; nevertheless, children still seem to seek their parents' permission before getting married. The taking of secondary wives, a common practice in traditional times, is prohibited.

Wedding ceremonies are much simpler and less costly than in traditional times. However, they still contain such practices as meetings between families of the bride and groom, gift exchanges, formal letters of proposal, and wedding feasts. Among farming families, weddings usually take place after the fall harvest and before the spring plowing; this is when families have the most resources to invest and the bride can bring her yearly income from work points to her new household.

In 1946 the North Korean regime confiscated the remaining lineage land, and the elaborate ceremonies of the past lost their economic base. Since that time, the traditional ceremonies surrounding death and veneration of the ancestors have been simplified. The remains are no longer carried in a special carriage, but, in rural areas, in a cart or tractor. One Korean source reported that at the funeral of his grandmother in North Korea incense was offered in front of a photograph of the deceased; the source also said that the ceremony generally retains the outlines of the traditional rites. Relatives and neighbors apparently still donate some money to the family of the deceased. Some "revolutionary" content has been added to funeral practices. One traditional chant has been rewritten to include the phrase "though this body is deceased, the spirit of the revolution still lives." Widowers frequently remarry, but widows rarely do.

Gravesites are still preserved and remain a common feature of the North Korean landscape. According to one observer, if construction projects necessitate disturbing graves, relatives are notified beforehand, and graves are carefully relocated. If no relative claims the graves, they are still relocated elsewhere. The custom of visiting graves at certain times of the year apparently continues, even though large kinship groups cannot meet—not because the state has prohibited it but because the groups are scattered across the country and travel restrictions make it difficult for them to get together.

In households in which both parents work and no grandparents live nearby, infants over three months usually are placed in a *t'agaso* (nursery). They remain in these nurseries until they are four years old. Although *t'agaso* are not part of the compulsory education system, most families find them indispensable. In the early 1970s, North Korean statistics counted 8,600 *t'agaso*. The nurseries not only free women from child care but also provide infants and small children with the foundations of a thorough ideological and political education. A South Korean source reported that when meals are given to the infants, they are expected to give thanks to a portrait of "Father Kim Il Sung."

The Role of Women

In the Chosŏn Dynasty, women were expected to give birth to and rear male heirs to ensure the continuation of the family line. Women had few opportunities to participate in the social, economic, or political life of society. There were a few exceptions to limitations imposed on women's roles. For example, female shamans were called on to cure illnesses by driving away evil spirits, to pray for rain during droughts, or to perform divination and fortune-telling.

Few women received any formal education in traditional Korean society. After the opening of Korea to foreign contact in the late nineteenth century, however, Christian missionaries established girls' schools, thus allowing young Korean females to obtain a modern education.

The social status and roles of women were radically changed after 1945. On July 30, 1946, authorities north of the thirty-eighth parallel passed the Sex Equality Law. The 1972 constitution asserted that "women hold equal social status and rights with men." The 1990 constitution stipulates that the state creates various conditions for the advancement of women in society. In principle, North Korea strongly supports sexual equality.

In contemporary North Korea, women are expected to fully participate in the labor force outside the home. Apart from its ideological commitment to the equality of the sexes, the government views women's employment as essential because of the country's labor shortage. No able-bodied person is spared from the struggle to increase production and compete with the more populous southern half of the peninsula. According to one South Korean source, women in North Korea are supposed to devote eight hours a day to work, eight hours to study (presumably, the study of *chuch'e* and Kim Il Sungism), and eight hours to rest and sleep. Women who have three or more children apparently are permitted to work only six hours a day and still receive a full, eight-hour-a-day salary.

The media showcase role models. The official newspaper *P'yŏng-yang Times,* in an August 1991 article, described the career of Kim Hwa Suk, a woman who had graduated from compulsory education (senior middle school), decided to work in the fields as a regular farmer in a cooperative located in the P'yŏngyang suburbs, and gradually rose to positions of responsibility as her talents and dedication became known. After serving as leader of a youth workteam, she attended a university. After graduating, she became chairperson of her cooperative's management board. Kim was also chosen as a deputy to the Supreme People's Assembly.

Despite such examples, however, it appears that women are not fully emancipated. Sons are still preferred over daughters. Women do most if not all of the housework, including preparing a morning and evening meal, in addition to working outside the home; much of the responsibility of childrearing is in the hands of *t'agaso* and the school system. The majority of women work in light industry, where they are paid less than their male counterparts in heavy industry. In office situations, they are likely to be engaged in secretarial and other low-echelon jobs.

Different sex roles, moreover, are probably confirmed by the practice of separating boys and girls at both the elementary and the higher middle-school levels (see Education, this ch.). Some aspects of school curricula for boys and girls also are apparently different, with greater emphasis on physical education for boys and on home economics for girls. In the four-year university system, however, women majoring in medicine, biology, and foreign languages and literature seem especially numerous.

The Role of Religion

Koreans are traditionally pragmatic and eclectic in their religious commitments. Their religious outlook is not conditioned by a single, exclusive faith but by a combination of indigenous beliefs and creeds, such as Confucianism, Daoism, and Buddhism. Belief in a world inhabited by spirits is probably the oldest Korean religion. Daoism and Buddhism were introduced from China around the fourth century A.D., the latter becoming predominant during the

Students in P'yŏngyang rehearse for Kim Il Sung's eightieth birthday celebration, April 1992.
Courtesy Tracy Woodward

Silla Dynasty (668–935), but reaching its height during the Koryŏ Dynasty (918–1392). Buddhism suffered a decline, however, and Buddhists were persecuted to some extent during the Chosŏn Dynasty. For the average Korean in late traditional and early modern times, the elaborate rituals of ancestor veneration connected to Confucianism were generally the most important form of religious life. Korean neo-Confucian philosophers, moreover, developed concepts of the cosmos and humanity's place in it that were, in a basic sense, religious rather than philosophical.

In 1785 the first Christian missionary, a Roman Catholic, entered Korea. The government prohibited the propagation of Christianity, and by 1863 there were only some 23,000 Roman Catholics in the country. Subsequently, the government ordered harsh persecution of Korean Christians, a policy that continued until the country was opened to Western countries in 1881. Protestant missionaries began entering Korea during the 1880s. They established schools, universities, hospitals, and orphanages and played a significant role in the modernization of the country. Before 1948 P'yŏngyang was an important Christian center; one-sixth of its population of about 300,000 residents were converts.

Another important religious tradition is Ch'ŏndogyo. A new

religion that developed out of the Tonghak (Eastern Learning) Movement (see Glossary) of the mid- and late nineteenth century, Ch'ŏndogyo emphasizes the divine nature of all people (see Korea in the Nineteenth-Century World Order, ch. 1). A syncretic religion, Ch'ŏndogyo contains elements of shamanism, Buddhism, Daoism, Confucianism, and Roman Catholicism.

Between 1945, when Soviet forces first occupied the northern half of the Korean Peninsula, and the end of the Korean War in 1953, many Christians, considered "bad elements" by North Korean authorities, fled to South Korea to escape the socialist regime's antireligious policies. The state co-opted Buddhism, which had weakened over the centuries. P'yŏngyang has made a concerted effort to uproot indigenous animist beliefs. In the early 1990s, the practices of shamanism and fortune-telling seemed to have largely disappeared.

Different official attitudes toward organized religion are reflected in various constitutions. Article 14 of the 1948 constitution noted that "citizens of the Democratic People's Republic of Korea shall have the freedom of religious belief and of conducting religious services." Article 54 of the 1972 constitution, however, stated that "citizens have religious liberty and the freedom to oppose religion" (also translated as "the freedom of antireligious propaganda"). Some observers argued that the change occurred because in 1972 the political authorities no longer needed the support of the much-weakened organized religions. In the 1992 constitution, Article 68 grants freedom of religious belief and guarantees the right to construct buildings for religious use and religious ceremonies. The article also states, however, that "No one may use religion as a means by which to drag in foreign powers or to destroy the state or social order." This provision may be linked to North Korea's representation at international religious conferences by state-sponsored religious organizations, such as the Korean Buddhists' Federation, the Christian Federation, and the Ch'ŏndogyo Youth Party.

Many churches and temples have been taken over by the state and converted to secular use. Buddhist temples, such as those located at Kŭmgang-san and Myohyang-san, are considered "national treasures," however, and have been preserved and restored. This action is in accord with the *chuch'e* principle that the creative energies of the Korean people in the past must be appreciated.

In the late 1980s, it became apparent that North Korea was beginning to use the small number of Christians remaining in the country to establish contacts with Christians in South Korea and the West. Such contacts are considered useful for promoting the regime's political aims, including reunifying the peninsula. In 1988 two new churches, the Protestant Pongsu Church and the Catholic Changchung Cathedral, were opened in P'yŏngyang. Other signs of the regime's changing attitude toward Christianity include holding the International Seminar of Christians of the North and South for the Peace and Reunification of Korea in Switzerland in November 1988, allowing papal representatives to attend the opening of the Changchung Cathedral in October-November of the same year, and sending two North Korean novice priests to study in Rome. Moreover, a new association of Roman Catholics was established in June 1988. A North Korean Protestant pastor reported at a 1989 meeting of the National Council of Churches in Washington, D.C., that his country has 10,000 Protestants and 1,000 Catholics who worship in 500 home churches. In March-April 1992, American evangelist Billy Graham visited North Korea to preach and to speak at Kim Il Sung University.

A limited revival of Buddhism is apparently taking place. This includes the establishment of an academy for Buddhist studies and the publication of a twenty-five-volume translation of the Korean Tripitaka, or Buddhist scriptures, which had been carved on 80,000 wooden blocks and kept at the temple at Myohyang-san in central North Korea. A few Buddhist temples conduct religious services.

Many if not most observers of North Korea would agree that the country's official religion is the cult of Kim Il Sung. North Korean Christians attending overseas conferences claim that there is no contradiction between Christian beliefs and the veneration of the "great leader" or his secular *chuch'e* philosophy. This position does not differ much from that of the far more numerous Japanese Christian communities before and during World War II, which were pressured into acknowledging the divine status of the emperor.

Ethnicity, Culture, and Language in Contemporary Society

In terms of ethnicity, the population of the Korean Peninsula is one of the world's most homogeneous. Descended from migratory groups who entered the Korean Peninsula from Siberia, Manchuria, and Inner Asia several thousands of years ago, the Korean people are distinguished from the neighboring populations of mainland Asia and Japan in terms of ethnicity, culture, and language, even though they share many cultural elements with these peoples.

Since the establishment of the Han Chinese colonies in the northern Korean Peninsula 2,000 years ago, Koreans have been under the cultural influence of China. During the period of Japanese domination (1910–45), the colonial regime attempted to force Koreans to adopt the Japanese language and culture. Neither the long and pervasive Chinese influence nor the more coercive and short-lived Japanese attempts to make Koreans loyal subjects of the Japanese emperor, however, succeeded in eradicating their ethnic, cultural, and linguistic distinctiveness. The desire of the North Korean regime to preserve its version of Korean culture, including many traditional aspects such as food, dress, art, architecture, and folkways, is motivated in part by the historical experience of cultural domination by both the Chinese and the Japanese.

Chuch'e ideology asserts Korea's cultural distinctiveness and creativity as well as the productive powers of the working masses. The ways in which *chuch'e* rhetoric is used show a razor-thin distinction between revolutionary themes of self-sufficient socialist construction and a virulent ethnocentrism. In the eyes of North Korea's leaders, the ''occupation'' of the southern half of the peninsula by ''foreign imperialists'' lends special urgency to the issue of cultural-ethnic identity. Not only must the people of South Korea be liberated from foreign imperialism, but also they must be given the opportunity to participate in the creation of a new, but still distinctively Korean, culture.

Contemporary Cultural Expression

The role of literature and art in North Korea is primarily didactic; cultural expression serves as an instrument for inculcating *chuch'e* ideology and the need to continue the struggle for revolution and reunification of the Korean Peninsula. There is little subtlety in most contemporary cultural expression. Foreign imperialists, especially the Japanese and the Americans, are depicted as heartless monsters; revolutionary heroes and heroines are seen as saintly figures who act from the purest of motives. The three most consistent themes are martyrdom during the revolutionary struggle (depicted in literature such as *The Sea of Blood*), the happiness of the present society, and the genius of the ''great leader.''

Kim Il Sung himself was described as a writer of ''classical masterpieces'' during the anti-Japanese struggle. Novels created ''under his direction'' include *The Flower Girl, The Sea of Blood, The Fate of a Self-Defense Corps Man,* and *The Song of Korea;* these are considered ''prototypes and models of *chuch'e* literature and art.'' A 1992 newspaper report describes Kim in semiretirement as writing his memoirs—''a heroic epic dedicated to the freedom and happiness of the people.''

The state and the KWP control the production of literature and art. In the early 1990s, there was no evidence of any underground literary or cultural movements such as those that existed in the Soviet Union or in China. The party exercises control over culture through its Propaganda and Agitation Department and the Culture and Arts Department of the KWP's Central Committee. The KWP's General Federation of Korean Literature and Arts Unions, the parent body for all literary and artistic organizations, also controls cultural activity.

The population has little or no exposure to foreign cultural influences apart from performances by song-and-dance groups and other entertainers brought in periodically for limited audiences. These performances, such as the Spring Friendship Art Festival held annually in April, are designed to show that the peoples of the world, like the North Koreans themselves, love and respect the "great leader." During the 1980s and the early 1990s, the North Korean media gave Kim Jong Il credit for working ceaselessly to make the country a "kingdom of art" where a cultural renaissance unmatched in other countries was taking place. Indeed, the younger Kim is personally responsible for cultural policy.

A central theme of cultural expression is to take the best from the past and discard "reactionary" elements. Popular, vernacular styles and themes in literature, art, music, and dance are esteemed as expressing the truly unique spirit of the Korean nation. Ethnographers devote much energy to restoring and reintroducing cultural forms that have the proper "proletarian" or "folk" spirit and that encourage the development of a collective consciousness. Lively, optimistic musical and choreographic expression are stressed. Group folk dances and choral singing are traditionally practiced in some but not all parts of Korea and were being promoted throughout North Korea in the early 1990s among school and university students. Farmers' musical bands have also been revived. Kim Il Sung condemns such cultural expressions as plaintive *p'ansori* (see Glossary) ballads. Kim also condemns the sad "crooning tunes" composed during the Japanese colonial occupation, although he apparently has made an exception for songs that indirectly criticize the injustices of the colonial society.

P'yŏngyang and other large cities offer the broadest of a necessarily narrow selection of cultural expression. "Art propaganda squads" travel to production sites in the provinces to perform poetry readings, one-act plays, and songs in order to "congratulate workers on their successes" and "inspire them to greater successes through their artistic agitation." Such squads are prominent in the countryside during the harvest season and whenever "speed battles" to increase productivity are held.

Literature, Music, and Film

Literature and music are other venues for politics. A series of historical novels—*Pulmyouui yoksa* (Immortal History)—depict the heroism and tragedy of the preliberation era. The Korean War is the theme of *Korea Fights* and *The Burning Island*. Since the late 1970s, five "great revolutionary plays" have been promoted as prototypes of *chuch'e* literature: *The Shrine for a Tutelary Deity;* a theatrical rendition of *The Flower Girl; Three Men, One Party; A Letter from a Daughter;* and *Hyolbun mangukhoe* (Resentment at the World Conference).

"Revolutionary operas," derived from traditional Korean operas, known as *ch'angguk,* often utilize variations on Korean folk songs. Old fairy tales have also been transformed to include revolutionary themes. As part of the *chuch'e* policy of preserving the best from Korea's past, moreover, premodern vernacular works such as the *Sasong kibong* (Encounter of Four Persons) and the *Ssangch'on kibong* (Encounter at the Two Rivers) have been reprinted.

Musical compositions include the "Song of General Kim Il Sung," "Long Life and Good Health to the Leader," and "We Sing of His Benevolent Love"—hymns that praise the "great leader." According to a North Korean writer, "Our musicians have pursued the party's policy of composing orchestral music based on famous songs and folk songs popular among our people and produced numerous instrumental pieces of a new type." This music includes a symphony based on the theme of *The Sea of Blood,* which has also been made into a revolutionary opera.

Motion pictures are recognized as "the most powerful medium for educating the masses" and play a central role in "social education." According to a North Korean source, "films for children contribute to the formation of the rising generation, with a view to creating a new kind of man, harmoniously evolved and equipped with well-founded knowledge and a sound mind in a sound body." One of the most influential films, "An Chung-gŭn Shoots Itō Hirobumi," tells of the assassin who killed the Japanese resident-general in Korea in 1909. An is depicted as a courageous patriot, but one whose efforts to liberate Korea were frustrated because, in the words of one reviewer, the masses had not been united under "an outstanding leader who enunciates a correct guiding thought and scientific strategy and tactics." Folk tales such as "The Tale of Chun Hyang," about a nobleman who marries a servant girl, and "The Tale of Ondal" have also been made into films.

Architecture and City Planning

Arguably the most distinct and impressive forms of contemporary

*Students playing traditional Korean instruments
in a music class at the Man'gyŏngdae Schoolchildren's Palace,
P'yŏngyang, opened in May 1989
Courtesy Tracy Woodward*

cultural expression in North Korea are architecture and city planning. P'yŏngyang, almost completely destroyed during the Korean War, has been rebuilt on a grand scale. Many new buildings have been constructed during the 1980s and 1990s in order to enhance P'yŏngyang's status as a capital.

Major structures are divided architecturally into three categories: monuments, buildings that combine traditional Korean architectural motifs and modern construction, and high-rise buildings of a totally modern design. Examples of the first include the Ch'ŏllima (see Glossary) Statue; a twenty-meter-high bronze statue of Kim Il Sung in front of the Museum of the Korean Revolution (itself, at 240,000 square meters, one of the largest structures in the world); the Arch of Triumph (similar to its Parisian counterpart, although a full ten meters higher); and the Tower of the Chuch'e Idea, 170 meters high, built on the occasion of Kim's seventieth birthday in 1982. According to a North Korean publication, the tower is covered with 25,550 pieces of granite, each representing a day in the life of the "great leader."

The second architectural category makes special use of traditional tiled roof designs and includes the People's Culture Palace and the

People's Great Study Hall, both in P'yŏngyang, and the International Friendship Exhibition Hall at Myohyang-san. The latter building displays gifts given to Kim Il Sung by foreign dignitaries. In light of Korea's tributary relationship to China during the Chosŏn Dynasty, it is significant that the section of the hall devoted to gifts from China is the largest.

The third architectural category includes high-rise apartment complexes and hotels in the capital. The most striking of these buildings is the Ryugong Hotel, still unfinished in the early 1990s and noted by some observers to be clearly leaning and perhaps not able to be completed. Described as the world's tallest hotel at 105 stories, its triangular shape looms over north-central P'yŏngyang. The Koryŏ Hotel is an ultramodern, twin-towered structure forty-five stories high.

A flurry of construction occurred before celebrations of Kim Il Sung's eightieth birthday, including the building of apartment complexes and the Reunification Expressway, a four-lane road connecting the capital and the Demilitarized Zone. According to a journalist writing in the *Far Eastern Economic Review,* the highway is "an impressive piece of engineering" that "cuts a straight path through mountainous terrain with 21 tunnels and 23 bridges on the 168 kilometers route to P'anmunjŏm." As in many other construction projects, the military provided the labor (see Transportation and Communications, ch. 3; Role in National Life, ch. 5).

The Korean Language

There is a consensus among linguists that Korean is a member of the Altaic family of languages, which originated in northern Asia and includes the Mongol, Turkic, Finnish, Hungarian, and Tungusic (Manchu) languages. Although a historical relationship between Korean and Japanese has not been established, the two languages have strikingly similar grammatical structures. Both, for example, employ particles after nouns to indicate case (the particle used to indicate "of," as in "the wife of Mr. Li," is *no* in Japanese and *ui* in Korean).

Both Korean and Japanese possess what is sometimes called "polite" or "honorific" language, the use of different levels of speech in addressing persons of superior, inferior, or equal rank. These distinctions depend both on the use of different vocabulary and on basic structural differences in the words employed. For example, in Korean, the imperative "go" can be rendered *kara* for speaking to an inferior or a child, *kage* to an adult inferior, *kao* or *kaseyo* to a superior, and *kasipsio* to a person of still higher rank. The proper use of polite language, or of the levels of polite language, is extremely complex and subtle. Like Japanese, Korean is extremely sensitive to the nuances of hierarchical human relationships. Two people who meet for the first time are expected to use the more distant or formal terms, but they will shift to more informal or "equal" terms if they become friends. Younger people invariably use formal language in addressing elders; the latter use "inferior" terms in "talking down" to those who are younger.

The Korean language may be written using a mixture of Chinese characters (*hancha*) and a native Korean alphabet known as *han'gŭl* (see Glossary), or in *han'gŭl* alone. *Han'gŭl* was invented by scholars at the court of King Sejong (r.1418–50), not solely to promote literacy among the common people as was sometimes claimed but also, as Professor Gari K. Ledyard has noted, to assist in studies of Chinese historical phonology. According to a statement by the king, an intelligent man could learn *han'gŭl* in a morning's time, and even a fool could master it in ten days. As a result, it was scorned and relegated to women and merchants. Scholars of linguistics consider the script one of the most scientific ever devised; it reflects quite consistently the phonemes of the spoken Korean language.

Although the Chinese and Korean languages are not related in terms of grammatical structure, a large percentage of the Korean vocabulary has been derived from Chinese loanwords, a reflection of China's long cultural dominance. In many cases, there are two words—a Chinese loanword and an indigenous Korean word—that mean the same thing. The Chinese-based word in Korean often has a bookish or formal nuance. Koreans select one or the other variant to achieve the proper register in speech or in writing and to make subtle distinctions in accordance with established usage.

There is considerable divergence in the Korean spoken north and south of the DMZ. It is unclear to what extent the honorific language and its grammatical forms have been retained in the north. However, according to a South Korean scholar, Kim Il Sung "requested people to use a special, very honorific deference system toward himself and his family and, in a 1976 publication, *Our Party's Language Policy,* rules formulated on the basis of Kim Il Sung's style of speech and writing were advocated as the norm."

During the colonial period, large numbers of Chinese character compounds coined in Japan to translate modern Western scientific, technical, social science, and philosophical concepts came into use in Korea. The North Korean regime has attempted to eliminate as many of these loanwords as possible, as well as older terms of Chinese origin; Western loanwords are also being dropped.

P'yŏngyang regards *hancha,* or Chinese characters, as symbols of "flunkeyism" and has systematically eliminated them from all publications. *Kŭlloja* (The Worker), the monthly KWP journal of the Central Committee, has been printed exclusively in *han'gŭl* since 1949. An attempt has also been made to create new words of exclusively Korean origin. Parents are encouraged to give their children Korean rather than Chinese-type names. Nonetheless, approximately 300 Chinese characters are still taught in North Korean schools.

North Koreans refer to their language as "Cultured Language" (*munhwa*), which uses the regional dialect of P'yŏngyang as its standard. The "Standard Language" (*p'yojuno*) of South Korea is based on the Seoul dialect. North Korean sources vilify Standard Language as "coquettish" and "decadent," corrupted by English and Japanese loanwords and full of nasal twangs. Two documents, or "instructions," by Kim Il Sung, "Some Problems Related to the Development of the Korean Language," promulgated in 1964, and "On the Development of the National Language: Conversations with Linguists," published in 1966, define basic policy concerning Cultured Language.

Education

Formal education has played a central role in the social and cultural development of both traditional Korea and contemporary North Korea. During the Chosŏn Dynasty, the royal court established a system of schools that taught Confucian subjects in the provinces as well as in four central secondary schools in the capital. There was no state-supported system of primary education. During the fifteenth century, state-supported schools declined in quality and were supplanted in importance by private academies, the *sŏwŏn,* centers of a neo-Confucian revival in the sixteenth century. Higher education was provided by the Sŏnggyungwan, the Confucian national university, in Seoul. Its enrollment was limited to 200 students who had passed the lower civil service examinations and were preparing for the highest examinations.

The late nineteenth and early twentieth centuries witnessed major educational changes. The *sŏwŏn* were abolished by the central government. Christian missionaries established modern schools that taught Western curricula. Among them was the first school for women, Ehwa Woman's University, established by American Methodist missionaries as a primary school in Seoul in 1886. During the last years of the dynasty, as many as 3,000 private schools that taught modern subjects to both sexes were founded by missionaries and others. Most of these schools were concentrated in the

An English class at P'yŏngyang Senior Middle School No. 9
Courtesy Tracy Woodward

northern part of the country. After Japan annexed Korea in 1910, the colonial regime established an educational system with two goals: to give Koreans a minimal education designed to train them for subordinate roles in a modern economy and make them loyal subjects of the emperor; and to provide a higher quality education for Japanese expatriates who had settled in large numbers on the Korean Peninsula. The Japanese invested more resources in the latter, and opportunities for Koreans were severely limited. In 1930 only 12.2 percent of Korean children aged seven to fourteen attended school. A state university modeled on Tokyo Imperial University was established in Seoul in 1923, but the number of Koreans allowed to study there never exceeded 40 percent of its enrollment; the rest of its students were Japanese. Private universities, including those established by missionaries such as Sungsil College in P'yŏngyang and Chosun Christian College in Seoul, provided other opportunities for Koreans desiring higher education.

After the establishment of North Korea, an education system modeled largely on that of the Soviet Union was established. The system faces serious obstacles. According to North Korean sources, at the time of North Korea's establishment, two-thirds of school-age children did not attend primary school, and most adults, numbering 2.3 million, were illiterate. In 1950 primary education became compulsory. The outbreak of the Korean War, however, delayed attainment of this goal; universal primary education was not achieved until 1956. By 1958 North Korean sources claimed that seven-year compulsory primary and secondary education had been implemented. In 1959 "state-financed universal education" was introduced in all schools; not only instruction and educational facilities but also textbooks, uniforms, and room and board are provided to students without charge. By 1967 nine years of education became compulsory. In 1975 the compulsory eleven-year education system, which includes one year of preschool education and ten years of primary and secondary education, was implemented; that system remained in effect as of 1993. According to a 1983 speech given by Kim Il Sung to education ministers of nonaligned countries in P'yŏngyang, universal, compulsory higher education was to be introduced "in the near future." At that time, students had no school expenses; the state paid for the education of almost half of North Korea's population of 18.9 million.

Educational Themes and Methods

As in other communist countries, politics come first in the education system. In his 1977 "Theses on Socialist Education," Kim Il Sung wrote that "political and ideological education is the most important part of socialist education. Only through a proper political and ideological education is it possible to rear students as revolutionaries, equipped with a revolutionary world outlook and the ideological and moral qualities of a communist. And only on the basis of sound political and ideological education will the people's scientific and technological education and physical culture be successful." Education is a "total experience" encompassing not only formal school education but also extracurricular "social education" and work-study adult education. According to the "Theses on Socialist Education," the socialist state should not only organize and conduct comprehensive educational programs, eliminating the need for private educational institutions, but also should "run education on the principle of educating all members of society continuously—the continued education of all members of society is indispensable for building socialism and communism."

Chuch'e is a central theme in educational policy. According to Kim Il Sung, "in order to establish *chuch'e* in education, the main emphasis should be laid on things of one's own country in instruction and people should be taught to know their own things well." In his 1983 speech to education ministers of nonaligned countries, Kim also emphasized that *chuch'e* in education was relevant to all Third World countries. Kim asserted that although "flunkeyism" should be avoided, it might be necessary to adopt some techniques from developed countries.

Closely tied to the central theme of *chuch'e* in education is the "method of heuristic teaching"—a means of developing the independence and creativity of students and a reaction against the traditional Confucian emphasis on rote memorization. "Heuristics give students an understanding of the content of what they are taught through their own positive thinking, and so greatly help to build up independence and creativeness." Coercion and "cramming" should be avoided in favor of "persuasion and explanation," particularly in ideological education.

Primary and Secondary Education

In the early 1990s, the compulsory primary and secondary education system was divided into one year of kindergarten, four years of primary school (people's school) for ages six to nine, and six years of senior middle school (secondary school) for ages ten to fifteen) (see fig. 5). There are two years of kindergarten, for children aged four to six; only the second year (upper-level kindergarten) is compulsory.

In the mid-1980s, there were 9,530 primary and secondary schools. After graduating from people's school, students enter either a regular secondary school or a special secondary school that concentrates on music, art, or foreign languages. These schools teach both their specialties and general subjects. The Man'gyŏngdae Revolutionary Institute is an important special school.

In the early 1990s, graduation from the compulsory education system occurred at age sixteen. Eberstadt and Banister report that according to North Korean statistics released in the late 1980s, primary schools enrolled 1.49 million children in 1987; senior middle schools enrolled 2.66 million that same year. A comparison with the total number of children and youths in these age brackets shows that 96 percent of the age cohort is enrolled in the primary and secondary educational system.

School curricula in the early 1990s were balanced between academic and political subject matter. According to South Korean scholar Park Youngsoon, subjects such as Korean language, mathematics, physical education, drawing, and music constitute the bulk of instruction in people's schools; more than 8 percent of instruction is devoted to the "Great Kim Il Sung" and "Communist Morality." In senior middle schools, politically oriented subjects, including the "Great Kim Il Sung" and "Communist Morality," as well as "Communist Party Policy," comprise only 5.8 percent of instruction. However, such statistics understate the

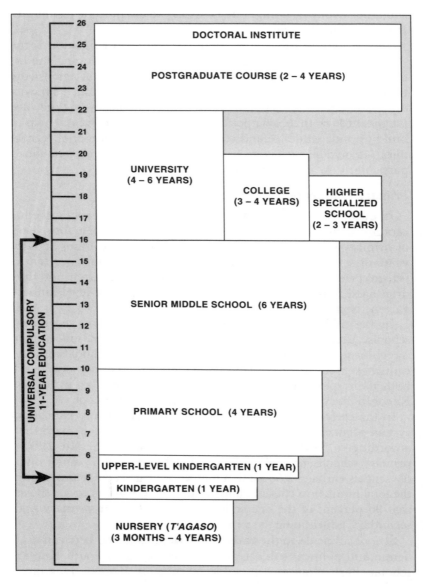

Source: Based on information from Kŭktong Munje Yon'guso, *Pukhan Chŏnsŏ, 1945–1980* (A Complete North Korean Handbook), Seoul, 1980, 595; "Public Education System of the DPRK," in *Do You Know about Korea?*, P'yŏngyang, 1989, 50; and Park Youngsoon, "Language Policy and Language Education in North Korea," *Korea Journal* [Seoul], 31, No. 1, Spring 1991, 33.

Figure 5. Structure of the Education System, 1991

political nature of primary and secondary education. Textbooks in the Korean language, for example, include titles such as *We Pray for "Our Master," Following Mrs. Kim, Our Father, Love of Our Father,* and *Kim Jong Il Looking at Photos.* Kindergarten children receive instruction in "Marshal Kim's Childhood" and "Communist Morality." Park noted that when students read Kim Il Sung's writings in the classroom, they are expected to do so "loudly, and slowly and with a feeling of respect." They also are taught a special way of speaking toward Kim, in terms of pronunciation, speed, and a special deference system and attitude."

Social Education

Outside the formal structure of schools and classrooms is the extremely important "social education." This education includes not only extracurricular activities but also family life and the broadest range of human relationships within society. There is great sensitivity to the influence of the social environment on the growing child and its role in the development of his or her character. The ideal of social education is to provide a carefully controlled environment in which children are insulated from bad or unplanned influences. According to a North Korean official interviewed in 1990, "School education is not enough to turn the rising generation into men of knowledge, virtue, and physical fitness. After school, our children have many spare hours. So it's important to efficiently organize their afterschool education."

In his 1977 "Theses on Socialist Education," Kim Il Sung described the components of social education. In the Pioneer Corps and the Socialist Working Youth League (SWYL), young people learn the nature of collective and organizational life; some prepare for membership in the KWP. In students' and schoolchildren's halls and palaces, managed by the SWYL Central Committee, young people participate in many extracurricular activities after school. There also are cultural facilities such as libraries and museums, monuments and historical sites of the Korean revolution, and the mass media dedicated to serving the goals of social education. Huge, lavishly appointed "schoolchildren's palaces" with gymnasiums and theaters have been built in P'yŏngyang, Man'gyŏngdae, and other sites. These palaces provide political lectures and seminars, debating contests, poetry recitals, and scientific forums. The Students' and Children's Palace in P'yŏngyang attracted some 10,000 children daily in the early 1990s.

Although North Korean children would not seem to have much time to spend at home, the family's status as the "basic unit" of society also makes it a focus of social education. According to a

North Korean publication, when "homes are made revolutionary," parents are "frugal . . . courteous, exemplary in social and political life," and children have proper role models.

Higher Education

Institutions of higher education in the early 1990s included colleges and universities; teachers' training colleges with a four-year course for preparing kindergarten, primary, and secondary instructors; colleges of advanced technology with two- or three-year courses; medical schools with six-year courses; special colleges for science and engineering, art, music, and foreign languages; and military colleges and academies. Kim Il Sung's report to the Sixth Party Congress of the KWP in October 1980 revealed that there were 170 "higher learning institutions" and 480 "higher specialized schools" that year. In 1987 there were 220,000 students attending two- or three-year higher specialized schools and 301,000 students attending four- to six-year colleges and university courses. According to Eberstadt and Banister, 13.7 percent of the population sixteen years of age or older was attending, or had graduated from, institutions of higher education in 1987-88. In 1988 the regime surpassed its target of producing "an army of 1.3 million intellectuals," graduates of higher education, a major step in the direction of achieving the often-stated goal of "intellectualization of the whole society."

Kim Il Sung University, founded in October 1946, is the country's only comprehensive institution of higher education offering bachelor's, master's, and doctoral degrees. It is an elite institution whose enrollment of 16,000 full- and part-time students in the early 1990s occupies, in the words of one observer, the "pinnacle of the North Korean educational and social system." Competition for admission to its faculties is intense. According to a Korean-American scholar who visited the university in the early 1980s, only one student is admitted out of every five or six applicants. An important criterion for admission is senior middle-school grades, although political criteria are also major factors in selection. A person wishing to gain acceptance to any institution of higher education has to be nominated by the local "college recommendation committee" before approval by county- and provincial-level committees.

Kim Il Sung University's colleges and faculties include economics, history, philosophy, law, foreign languages and literature, geography, physics, mathematics, chemistry, atomic energy, biology, and computer science. There are about 3,000 faculty members, including teaching and research staff. All facilities are located on a modern, high-rise campus in the northern part of P'yŏngyang.

Students at the Grand People's Study House, P'yŏngyang
Courtesy Cho Yung Soon

Adult Education

Because of the emphasis on the continued education of all members of society, adult or work-study education is actively supported. Practically everyone in the country participates in some educational activity, usually in the form of "small study groups." In the 1980s, the adult literacy rate was estimated at 99 percent.

In the early 1990s, people in rural areas were organized into "five-family teams." These teams have educational and surveillance functions; the teams are the responsibility of a schoolteacher or other intellectual, each one being in charge of several such teams. Office and factory workers have two-hour "study sessions" after work each day on both political and technical subjects.

Adult education institutions in the early 1990s include "factory colleges," which teach workers new skills and techniques without forcing them to quit their jobs. Students work part-time, study in the evening, or take short intensive courses, leaving their workplaces for only a month or so. There also are "farm colleges," where rural workers can study to become engineers and assistant engineers, and a system of correspondence courses. For workers and peasants who are unable to receive regular school education, there are "laborers' schools" and "laborers' senior middle schools," although in the early 1990s these had become less important with the introduction of compulsory eleven-year education.

Public Health

North Korea claimed a dramatic improvement in the health and longevity of its population with the creation of a state-funded and state-managed public health system based on the Soviet model. According to North Korean statistics, the average life expectancy at birth for both sexes was a little over thirty-eight years in the 1936–40 period. By 1986 North Korean statistics claimed life expectancy had risen to 70.9 years for males and 77.3 years for females. According to UN statistics, life expectancy in 1990 was about sixty-six years for males and almost seventy-three years for females. North Korean sources reported that crude death rates fell from 20.8 per 1,000 people in 1944 to 5 per 1,000 in 1986; infant mortality, from 204 per 1,000 live births to 9.8 per 1,000 in the same period. Eberstadt and Banister report that these mortality figures were probably understated (they estimate infant mortality at around 31 per 1,000 live births in 1990); they conclude, however, that the statistics "suggest that the mortality transition in North Korea over the past three decades has not only improved overall

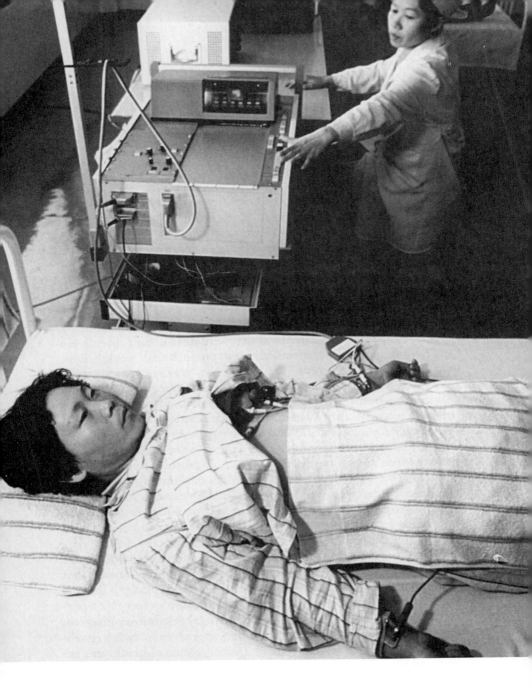

Patient being given a cardiographic sonogram at the San Won "Mother's Palace" Maternity Hospital, P'yŏngyang
Courtesy Tracy Woodward

survival chances but reduced previous differences in mortality between urban and rural areas.''

North Korean statistics reveal a substantial increase in the number of hospitals and clinics, hospital beds, physicians, and other health care personnel since the 1950s. Between 1955 and 1986, the number of hospitals grew from 285 to 2,401; clinics increased from 1,020 to 5,644; hospital beds per 10,000 population, from 19.1 to 135.9; physicians per 10,000 population, from 1.5 to 27; and nurses and paramedics per 10,000 population, from 8.7 to 43.2. There are hospitals at the provincial, county, *ri*, and *dong* levels. Hospitals are also attached to factories and mines. Specialized hospitals, including those devoted to treating tuberculosis, hepatitis, and mental illness, are generally found in large cities.

Preventive medicine is the foundation for health policies. According to the Public Health Law enacted on April 5, 1980, ''The State regards it as a main duty in its activity to take measures to prevent the people from being afflicted by disease and directs efforts first and foremost to prophylaxis in public health work.'' Disease prevention is accomplished through ''hygiene propaganda work,'' educating the people on sanitation and healthy life-styles, and the ''section-doctor system.'' This system, also known as the ''doctor responsibility system,'' assigns a single physician to be responsible for an area containing several hundred individuals. In general, medical examinations are required twice a year, and complete records are kept at local hospitals. According to one source, persons are required to follow the orders of their assigned physician and cannot refuse treatment. In the countryside, medical examination teams (*kŏmjindae*) composed of personnel from the provincial central hospital make rounds to investigate health conditions; local doctors also make frequent rounds.

North Korean statistics reveal that the major causes of death are similar to those in developed countries; 1986 figures showed that 45.3 percent of reported deaths were caused by circulatory ailments such as heart disease and stroke, 13.9 percent by cancer, 10.4 percent by digestive diseases, and 9.4 percent by respiratory diseases. Infectious diseases and parasitism, major causes of death in earlier decades, were a relatively insignificant cause of death and accounted for only 3.9 percent of reported deaths in 1986. As of 1990, the latest year for which data were available, no cases of acquired immune deficiency syndrome (AIDS) had been reported.

Although shamanistic medicine has been repudiated as superstition, herbal medicine, known as Eastern Medicine (Tonguihak), is still highly esteemed. Practitioners of Eastern Medicine not only give preparations orally but also practice moxibustion (burning herbs and grasses on the skin) and acupuncture. The high value accorded traditional herbal medicine reflects not only its efficacy but also the *chuch'e* emphasis on using native products and ingenuity. Moreover, in 1979 Kim Il Sung published an essay entitled "On Developing Traditional Korean Medicine." Central Eastern Medicine Hospital in P'yŏngyang, the Research Institute of Eastern Medicine in the Academy of Medical Sciences, and many pharmacies deal in traditional herbal remedies.

Over the centuries, Korean physicians have developed an extensive pharmacopeia of curative herbs. North Korean sources claim that herbal medicines are superior to Western medicines because they have no dangerous side effects. According to a 1991 article in the *P'yŏngyang Times*, "[t]he combination of Korean medicine with Western medicine has reached 70 percent in the primary medical treatment," and "[t]he native system is popular among the people for its effectiveness in internal and surgical treatment, obstetrics and gynecology, pediatrics and other sectors of clinical treatment and health and longevity." Natural products with medical properties distributed by pharmacies include extracts of *insam* (ginseng), deer placenta, and a "metabolism activator" called *tonghae chongsimhwan*, a mixture of herbs and animal and mineral products collected around Kwanmo-san and along the coast of the East Sea.

Physical education is an important part of public health. Children and adults are expected to participate in physical exercise during work breaks or school recesses; they are also encouraged to take part in recreational sports activities such as running, gymnastics, volleyball, ice skating, and traditional Korean games. Group gymnastic exercises are considered an art form as well as a form of discipline and education. Mass gymnastic displays, involving several tens of thousands of uniformed participants, are frequently organized. Some of the largest were held in commemoration of the eightieth birthday of Kim Il Sung and the fiftieth birthday of Kim Jong Il, both celebrated in 1992.

* * *

Traditional Korean society and social values are amply discussed in James B. Palais's *Politics and Policy in Traditional Korea* and Kibaik Lee's *A New History of Korea*. Lee Kwang-kyu provides a detailed description of the Korean family system in his two-volume *Kinship System in Korea*.

Reliable information on North Korean society is scarce, although the gradual opening of the country to the outside world during the early 1990s has improved the situation to some extent. Probably the best single English-language source is Nicholas Eberstadt and Judith Banister's *The Population of North Korea,* published in 1992. Working from newly released North Korean statistics as well as their own computer projections, Eberstadt and Banister provide extensive data on the population, health, urbanization, educational enrollment, and other aspects of the contemporary society as well as their own interpretations of this information.

Chuch'e ideology and its application to social life are discussed extensively in *Kim Il Sung: Selected Works;* for example, his 1977 ''Theses on Socialist Education'' provides the ideological foundation for the nation's schools. The North Korean government publishes several periodicals that describe the country's social, cultural, and artistic life. These include the magazines *Democratic People's Republic of Korea* and *Korea Today,* as well as the newspaper *P'yŏngyang Times.* South Korean sources publish occasional articles on North Korea in *Korea Journal,* and more extensive coverage is found in *North Korea News* published by the Naewoe Press in Seoul. *North Korea Quarterly,* published by the Institute of Asian Affairs in Hamburg, Germany, is one of the best Western sources on the country.

Because of historical connections, geographical proximity, and concerns about stability on the Korean Peninsula, Japanese sources on North Korea are relatively plentiful. A highly sympathetic account of North Korea is provided by Inoue Shūhachi in *Modern Korea and Kim Jong Il,* which has been translated into English. Interesting accounts of daily life are provided in a Japanese translation of reports by the South Korean Yonhap News Agency entitled *Kita Chōsen wa dō natte iru ka?* (What will become of North Korea?). (For further information and complete citations, see Bibliography.)

Chapter 3. The Economy

Flying horse, symbol of the Ch'ŏllima production drives of the late 1950s; the slogans proclaim self-reliance and three revolutions.

THE DEMOCRATIC PEOPLE'S REPUBLIC OF KOREA
(DPRK, or North Korea) possesses extensive economic resources
with which to build a modern economy. These include sizable
deposits of coal, other minerals, and nonferrous metals. The river
systems of the Yalu, Tumen, Taedong, and lesser rivers supplement North Korea's coal reserves and form an abundant source
of power. Although the mountainous terrain prohibits paddy rice
cultivation except in the coastal lowlands, corn, wheat, and soybeans grow well on dry field plateaus. The country's hilly areas
also provide for timber forests, livestock grazing, and orchards.

North Korea inherited the basic infrastructure of a modern economy at the end of the Japanese colonial era (1910–45) and achieved
considerable success because of the ability of the communist regime to marshall unutilized resources and idle labor and to impose a low rate of consumption. Around the beginning of the 1960s,
however, the economy had reached a stage where delays and bottlenecks began to emerge. Once growth could be achieved only by
raising productivity through increased efficiency, an expanded resource base, and technological advances, slowdowns and setbacks
occurred. Slow economic growth continued into the 1970s and
1980s. Based on *chuch'e* (see Glossary), the self-reliant economic
policy emphasizes heavy industry. This policy, coupled with economic difficulties, has resulted in a poor record of exports, chronic
trade deficits, and a sizable foreign debt, as well as foreign trade
primarily oriented toward other communist countries. At the outset of the 1990s, North Korea's economy was in a deep slump and
in great disarray, and was hopelessly behind its rival, the Republic of Korea (ROK, or South Korea), which has become a world-
class economic powerhouse.

North Korea's economy remains one of the world's last centrally planned systems. The role of market allocation is sharply
limited—mainly in the rural sector where peasants sell produce from
small private plots. There are almost no small businesses. Although
there have been scattered and limited attempts at decentralization,
as of mid-1993, P'yŏngyang's basic adherence to a rigid command
economy continues, as does its reliance on fundamentally non-
pecuniary incentives. A North Korean decision to create Chinese-
style special economic zones represents a major breakthrough in
decentralizing the economy.

As the country faces the 1990s, great challenges lie ahead. The collapse of communist regimes, particularly North Korea's principal benefactor, the Soviet Union, have forced the already depressed North Korean economy to fundamentally realign its foreign economic relations. Economic exchanges with South Korea have even begun in earnest.

Economic Setting

Korea under the Japanese Occupation

North Korea inherited the basic infrastructure of a modern economy because of Japan's substantial investment in development during the Japanese occupation. The Japanese had developed considerable heavy industry, particularly in the metal and chemical industries, hydroelectric power, and mining in the northern half of Korea, where they introduced modern mining methods. The southern half of the country produced most of the rice and a majority of textiles. The hydroelectric power and chemical plants were said to be second to none in Asia at that time in terms of both their scale and technology. The same applied to the railroad and communication networks.

There were, however, serious defects in the industrial structures and their location. The Korean economy, geared primarily to benefit the Japanese homeland, was made dependent on Japan for final processing of products; heavy industry was limited to the production of mainly raw materials, semifinished goods, and war supplies, which were then shipped to Japan proper for final processing and consumption. Japan did not allow Korea to develop a machine tool industry. Most industrial centers were strategically located on the eastern or western coasts near ports so as to connect them efficiently with Japan. Railroad networks ran mainly along the north-south axis, facilitating Japan's access to the Asian mainland. Because the Japanese occupied almost all the key government positions and owned and controlled the industrial and financial enterprises, few Koreans benefited from acquiring basic skills essential for modernization. Moreover, the Japanese left behind an agrarian structure—land tenure system, size of landholdings and farm operation, pattern of land use and farm income—that needed much reform. Farms were fragmented and small, and landownership was extremely unequal. Toward the end of the Japanese occupation, about 50 percent of all farm households in Korea were headed by tenant farmers.

The sudden withdrawal of the Japanese and the subsequent partition of the country created economic chaos. Severance of the complementary "agricultural" south from the "industrial" north and from Japan meant that North Korea's traditional markets for raw materials and semifinished goods—as well as its sources of food and manufactured goods—were cut off. Furthermore, the withdrawal of the entrepreneurial and engineering skills supplied mainly by Japanese personnel affected the economic base. Thus the task facing the communist regime in North Korea was to develop a viable economy, which it reoriented mainly toward other communist countries, while at the same time to rectify the "malformation" in the colonial industrial structure. Subsequently, the problem was compounded further by the devastation of industrial plants during the Korean War (1950–53) (see The Legacy of Japanese Colonialism, ch. 1). North Korea's economic development therefore did not tread a new path until after the Korean War.

Developmental Strategy

As of mid-1993, North Korea's economy remained one of the world's most highly centralized and planned, even by pre-1990 communist standards. Complete "socialization" of the economy was accomplished by 1958, when private ownership of the means of production, land, and commercial enterprises was replaced by state or cooperative (collective) ownership and control. As a result, industrial firms were either state-owned or cooperatives, the former contributing more than 90 percent of total industrial output in the 1960s.

Unlike in industry, collectives are the predominant form of ownership and production in agriculture; the remaining rural enterprises are organized as state farms. The sole negligible exception to state and collective ownership in agriculture is the ownership of small garden plots and fruit trees, as well as the raising of poultry, pigs, bees, and the like, which are permitted both for personal consumption and sale at the peasant market. Private plots can be no more than roughly 160 square meters in area. State and cooperative ownership and control extends to foreign trade, as well as to all other sectors of the economy, including banking, transportation, and communications.

In commerce nearly all goods are distributed through either state-operated or cooperative stores. Less than 1 percent of retail transactions are carried out at peasant markets, where surplus farm products are sold at free-market prices.

As in other Soviet-type or "command" economies, all economic decisions concerning the selection of output, output targets, allocation of inputs, prices, distribution of national income, investment, and economic development are implemented through the economic plan devised at the center and are "blueprinted" by the State Planning Committee (see Planning, this ch.; Organization of the Government, ch. 4). In the face of the worldwide political and economic collapse of communist regimes in the early 1990s, North Korea defiantly continues to sing the praises of a command economy. Attempts to increase production through rigid central control and exhortations and other non-pecuniary incentives have not ceased, as exemplified by the campaign entitled "Speed of the 1990s." On-site industrial visits by President Kim Il Sung and his son and heir-apparent, Kim Jong Il, continue.

However, there have been some minor efforts toward relaxing central control of the economy that involve industrial enterprises. Encouraged by Kim Jong Il's call to strengthen the implementation of the independent accounting system (*tongnip ch'aesangje*) of enterprises in March 1984, interest in enterprise management and the independent accounting system has increased, as evidenced by increasing coverage of the topic in various North Korean journals (see The Media, ch. 4). Under the system, factory managers still are assigned output targets but are given more discretion in making decisions about labor, equipment, materials, and funds.

In addition to fixed capital, each enterprise is allocated a minimum of working capital from the state through the Central Bank and is required to meet various operating expenses with the proceeds from sales of its output. Up to 50 percent of the "profit" is taxed, the remaining half being kept by the enterprise for purchase of equipment, introduction of new technology, welfare benefits, and bonuses. As such, the system provides some built-in incentives and some degree of micro-level autonomy, unlike the budget allocation system, under which any surplus is turned over to the government in its entirety.

Another innovation, the August Third People's Consumer Goods Production Movement, is centered on consumer goods production. This measure was so named after Kim Jong Il made an inspection tour of an exhibition of light industrial products held in P'yŏngyang on August 3, 1984. The movement charges workers to use locally available resources and production facilities to produce needed consumer goods. On the surface, the movement does not appear to differ much from the local industry programs in existence since the 1960s, although some degree of local autonomy is allowed. However, a major departure places output, pricing, and purchases outside central planning. In addition, direct sales stores have been established to distribute goods produced under the movement directly to consumers. The movement is characterized as a third sector in the production of consumer goods, alongside centrally controlled light industry and locally controlled traditional light industry. Moreover, there were some reports in the mid-1980s of increasing encouragement of small-scale private handicrafts and farm markets. As of 1992, however, no move was reported to expand the size of private garden plots.

All these measures appear to be minor stop-gap measures to alleviate severe shortages of consumer goods by infusing some degree of incentives. In mid-1993 no significant moves signaling a fundamental deviation from the existing system had occurred. The reluctance to initiate reform appears to be largely political. It is, perhaps, the linkage between economic reform and political liberalization that worries the leadership. This concern is based on the belief that economic reform will produce new interests that will demand political expression, and that demands for the institutionalization of such pluralism eventually will lead to political liberalization. There clearly exists a catch-22 situation for Kim Il Sung and, particularly, for Kim Jong Il. In order to legitimize his power base, the younger Kim needs an economic base. However, his economic reforms challenge his position as the advancer of *chuch'e* and may eventually undo the regime.

In the mid-1980s, the speculation that North Korea would emulate China in establishing Chinese-style special economic zones was flatly denied by then deputy chairman of the Economic Policy Commission Yun Ki-pok (Yun became chairman as of June 1989). China's special economic zones typically are coastal areas established to promote economic development and the introduction of advanced technology through foreign investment. Investors are offered preferential tax terms and facilities. The zones, which allow greater reliance on market forces, have more decision-making power in economic activities than do provincial-level units. Over the years, China has tried to convince the North Korean leadership of the advantages of these zones by giving tours of the various zones and explaining their values to visiting high-level officials.

In December 1991, North Korea established a "zone of free economy and trade" to include the northeastern port cities of Unggi, Ch'ŏngjin, and Najin. The establishment of this zone also had ramifications on the questions of how far North Korea would go in opening its economy to the West and to South Korea, the future of the development scheme for the Tumen River area, and, more important, how much North Korea would reform its economic system.

Economic Development and Structural Change

North Korea's reliance on a command economy has led to an

inward-looking development strategy, demonstrated in policies on domestic industrial development, foreign trade, foreign capital, imported technology, and other forms of international economic cooperation. Priority is assigned to establishing a self-sufficient industrial base. Consumer goods are produced primarily to satisfy domestic demand, and private consumption is held to low levels. This approach is in sharp contrast to South Korea's outward-oriented strategy begun in the mid-1960s, which started with light industry in order to meet the demands of growing domestic and foreign markets and export expansion.

As a consequence of the government's policy of establishing economic self-sufficiency, the North Korean economy has become increasingly isolated from that of the rest of the world, and its industrial development and structure do not reflect its international competitiveness. Domestic firms are shielded from international as well as domestic competition; the result is chronic inefficiency, poor quality, limited product diversity, and underutilization of plants. This protectionism also limits the size of the market for North Korean producers, which, in turn, prevents them from taking advantage of economies of scale.

Beginning in the mid-1980s, and particularly around the end of the decade, North Korea began slowly to modify its rigid self-reliant policy. The changes, popularly identified as the open-door policy, included an increasing emphasis on foreign trade, a readiness to accept direct foreign investment by enacting a joint venture law, the decision to open the country to international tourism, and economic cooperation with South Korea.

Record of Economic Performance

A lack of reliable data inhibits an accurate quantitative assessment of North Korea's economic performance. In mid-1993 North Korea remains one of the most secretive nations in the world, limiting the release of its economic data to the outside world and, for that matter, to its own population. Until about 1960, North Korea released economic data relatively more freely. Beginning in the 1960s, the publication of economic data began to dwindle dramatically; the withholding of information coincided with the beginning of the economy's slowdown.

The small amount of data that is published suffers from ambiguities and gaps and—more often than not—is in the form of percentages that do not provide base figures or explain the precise meaning of aggregated data. Moreover, North Korean macroeconomic aggregates such as national income, which is based on Marxist definitions, have to be modified in order to be comparable to customary

Male workers at the Taean Heavy Machinery Complex, Taean, Namp'o Courtesy Tracy Woodward

Western standards. In the 1980s and early 1990s, only limited quantitative or qualitative information about the North Korean economy was available. Quantitative information on foreign trade is a welcome exception because the statistical returns from North Korea's trade partners are gathered by such international organizations as the United Nations (UN) and the International Monetary Fund (IMF—see Glossary), and South Korean organizations such as the National Unification Board.

Estimating gross national product (GNP—see Glossary) is a difficult task because of the dearth of economic data, the national income accounting procedures based on the Marxist definition of production, and the problem of choosing an appropriate rate of exchange for the *wŏn* (see Glossary)—the nonconvertible North Korean currency. The South Korean government's estimate placed North Korea's GNP in 1991 at US$22.9 billion, or US$1,038 per capita. This estimate of economic accomplishment pales next to South Korea's GNP of US$237.9 billion with a per capita income of US$5,569 that same year. North Korea's GNP in 1991 showed a 5.2 percent decline over 1989, and preliminary indications were that the decline would continue. In contrast, South Korea's GNP grew by 9.3 percent and 8.4 percent, respectively, in 1990 and 1991.

Postwar Economic Planning

During what North Korea called the ''peaceful construction'' period before the Korean War, the fundamental task of the economy was to overtake the level of output and efficiency attained toward the end of the Japanese occupation; to restructure and develop a viable economy reoriented toward the communist-bloc countries; and to begin the process of socializing the economy. Nationalization of key industrial enterprises and land reform, both of which were carried out in 1946, laid the groundwork for two successive one-year plans in 1947 and 1948, respectively, and the Two-Year Plan of 1949–50. It was during this period that the piece-rate wage system and the independent accounting system began to be applied and that the commercial network increasingly came under state and cooperative ownership.

The basic goal of the Three-Year Plan, officially named the Three-Year Post-war Reconstruction Plan of 1954–56, was to reconstruct an economy torn by the Korean War. The plan stressed more than merely regaining the prewar output levels. The Soviet Union, China, and East European countries provided reconstruction assistance. The highest priority was developing heavy industry, but an earnest effort to collectivize farming also was begun. At the end of 1957, output of most industrial commodities had returned to

1949 levels, except for a few items such as chemical fertilizers, carbides, and sulfuric acid, whose recovery took longer.

Having basically completed the task of reconstruction, the state planned to lay a solid foundation for industrialization while completing the socialization process and solving the basic problems of food and shelter during the Five-Year Plan of 1957–60. The socialization process was completed by 1958 in all sectors of the economy, and the Ch'ŏllima Movement (see Glossary) was introduced. Although growth rates reportedly were high, there were serious imbalances among the different economic sectors. Because rewards were given to individuals and enterprises that met production quotas, frantic efforts to fulfill plan targets in competition with other enterprises and industries caused disproportionate growth among various enterprises, between industry and agriculture and between light and heavy industries. Because resources were limited and the transportation system suffered bottlenecks, resources were diverted to politically well-connected enterprises or those whose managers complained the loudest. An enterprise or industry that performed better than others often did so at the expense of others. Such disruptions intensified as the target year of the plan approached.

Until the 1960s, North Korea's economy grew much faster than South Korea's. Although P'yŏngyang was behind in total national output, it was ahead of Seoul in per capita national output, because of its smaller population relative to South Korea. For example, in 1960 North Korea's population was slightly over 10 million persons, while South Korea's population was almost 25 million persons. Phenomenal annual economic growth rates of 30 percent and 21 percent during the Three-Year Plan of 1954–56 and the Five-Year Plan of 1957–60, respectively, were reported. After claiming early fulfillment of the Five-Year Plan in 1959, North Korea officially designated 1960 a ''buffer year''—a year of adjustment to restore balances among sectors before the next plan became effective in 1961. Not surprisingly, the same phenomenon recurred in subsequent plans. Because the Five-Year Plan was fulfilled early, it became a de facto four-year plan. Beginning in the early 1960s, however, P'yŏngyang's economic growth slowed until it was stagnant at the beginning of the 1990s.

Various factors explain the very high rate of economic development of the country in the 1950s and the general slowdown since the 1960s. During the reconstruction period after the Korean War, there were opportunities for extensive economic growth—attainable through the communist regime's ability to marshall idle resources and labor and to impose a low rate of consumption. This general pattern of initially high growth resulting in a high rate of capital

113

formation was mirrored in other Soviet-type economies. Toward the end of the 1950s, as reconstruction work was completed and idle capacity began to diminish, the economy had to shift from the extensive to the intensive stage, where the simple communist discipline of marshalling underutilized resources became less effective. In the new stage, inefficiency arising from emerging bottlenecks led to diminishing returns. Further growth would only be attained by increasing efficiency and technological progress.

Beginning in the early 1960s, a series of serious bottlenecks began to impede development. Bottlenecks were pervasive and generally were created by the lack of arable land, skilled labor, energy, and transportation, and deficiencies in the extractive industries. Moreover, both land and marine transportation lacked modern equipment and modes of transportation. The inability of the energy and extractive industries as well as of the transportation network to supply power and raw materials as rapidly as the manufacturing plants could absorb them began to slow industrial growth.

The First Seven-Year Plan (initially 1961–67) built on the groundwork of the earlier plans but changed the focus of industrialization. Heavy industry, with the machine tool industry as its linchpin, was given continuing priority. During the plan, however, the economy experienced widespread slowdowns and reverses for the first time, in sharp contrast to the rapid and uninterrupted growth during previous plans. Disappointing performance forced the planners to extend the plan three more years, until 1970. During the last part of the de facto ten-year plan, emphasis shifted to pursuing parallel development of the economy and of defense capabilities. This shift was prompted by concern over the military takeover in South Korea by General Park Chung Hee (1961–79), escalation of the United States involvement in Vietnam, and the widening Sino-Soviet split. It was thought that stimulating a technological revolution in the munitions industry was one means to achieve these parallel goals. In the end, the necessity to divert resources to defense became the official explanation for the plan's failure.

The Six-Year Plan of 1971–76 followed immediately in 1971. In the aftermath of the poor performance of the preceding plan, growth targets of the Six-Year Plan were scaled down substantially. Because some of the proposed targets in the First Seven-Year Plan had not been attained even by 1970, the Six-Year Plan did not deviate much from its predecessor in basic goals. The Six-Year Plan placed more emphasis on technological advance, self-sufficiency in industrial raw materials, improving product quality, correcting imbalances among different sectors, and developing the power and extractive industries; the last of these had been deemed largely responsible for slowdowns during the First Seven-Year Plan. The plan called for attaining a self-sufficiency rate of 60 to 70 percent in all industrial sectors by substituting domestic raw materials wherever possible and by organizing and renovating technical processes to make the substitution feasible. Improving transport capacity was seen as one of the urgent tasks in accelerating economic development—understandable since it was one of the major bottlenecks of the Six-Year Plan (see Transportation and Communications, this ch.).

North Korea claimed to have fulfilled the Six-Year Plan by the end of August 1975, a full year and four months ahead of schedule. Under the circumstances, it was expected that the next plan would start without delay in 1976, a year early, as was the case when the First Seven-Year Plan was instituted in 1961. Even if the Six-Year Plan had been completed on schedule, the next plan should have started in 1977. However, it was not until nearly two years and four months later that the long-awaited plan was unveiled—1977 had become a "buffer year."

The inability of the planners to continuously formulate and institute economic plans reveals as much about the inefficacy of planning itself as the extent of the economic difficulties and administrative disruptions facing the country. For example, targets for successive plans have to be based on the accomplishments of preceding plans. If these targets are underfulfilled, all targets of the next plan—initially based on satisfaction of the plan—have to be reformulated and adjusted. Aside from underfulfillment of the targets, widespread disruptions and imbalances among various sectors of the economy further complicate plan formulation.

The basic thrust of the Second Seven-Year Plan (1978–84) was to achieve the three-pronged goals of self-reliance, modernization, and "scientification." Although the emphasis on self-reliance was not new, it had not previously been the explicit focus of an economic plan. This new emphasis might have been a reaction to mounting foreign debt originating from large-scale imports of Western machinery and equipment in the mid-1970s. Through modernization North Korea hoped to increase mechanization and automation in all sectors of the economy. "Scientification" is a buzzword for the adoption of up-to-date production and management techniques. The specific objectives of the economic plan were to strengthen the fuel, energy, and resource bases of industry through priority development of the energy and extractive industries; to modernize industry; to substitute domestic resources for certain imported raw materials; to expand freight-carrying capacity in railroad, road, and marine transportation systems; to centralize and containerize the transportation system; and to accelerate a technical revolution in agriculture.

In order to meet the manpower and technology requirements of an expanding economy, the education sector also was targeted for improvements. The quality of the comprehensive eleven-year compulsory education system was to be enhanced to train more technicians and specialists, and to expand the training of specialists, particularly in the fields of fuel, mechanical, electronic, and automation engineering (see Education, ch. 2).

Successful fulfillment of the so-called nature-remaking projects also was part of the Second Seven-Year Plan. These projects referred to the five-point program for nature transformation unveiled by Kim Il Sung in 1976: completing the irrigation of non-paddy fields; reclaiming 100,000 hectares of new land; building 150,000 hectares to 200,000 hectares of terraced fields; carrying out afforestation and water conservation work; and reclaiming tidal land.

From all indications, the Second Seven-Year Plan was not successful. North Korea generally downplayed the accomplishments of the plan, and no other plan received less official fanfare. It was officially claimed that the economy had grown at an annual rate of 8.8 percent during the plan, somewhat below the planned rate of 9.6 percent. The reliability of this aggregate measure, however, is questionable. During the plan, the target annual output of 10 million tons of grains (cereals and pulses) was attained. However, by official admission, the targets of only five other commodities were fulfilled. Judging from the growth rates announced for some twelve industrial products, it is highly unlikely that the total industrial output increased at an average rate of 12.2 percent as claimed. After the plan concluded, there was no new economic plan for two years, indications of both the plan's failure and the severity of the economic and planning problems confronting the economy in the mid-1980s.

The main targets of the Third Seven-Year Plan of 1987–93 are to achieve the so-called "Ten Long-Range Major Goals of the 1980s for the Construction of the Socialist Economy" (see table 2, Appendix). These goals, conceived in 1980, are to be fulfilled by the end of the decade. The fact that these targets are rolled over to the end of the Third Seven-Year Plan is another indication of the disappointing economic performance during the Second Seven-Year Plan. The three policy goals of self-reliance, modernization, and "scientification" were repeated. Economic growth was set at 7.9 percent annually, lower than the previous plan. Although achieving the ten major goals of the 1980s is the main thrust of the Third

Women workers at the Taean Heavy Machinery Complex
Courtesy Tracy Woodward

Seven-Year Plan, some substantial changes have been made in specific quantitative targets. For example, the target for the annual output of steel has been drastically reduced from 15 million tons to 10 millon tons. This reduction will have serious negative secondary effects on heavy industry. The output targets of cement and non-ferrous metals—two major export items—have been increased significantly. The June 1989 introduction of the Three-Year Plan for Light Industry as part of the Third Seven-Year Plan is intended to boost the standard of living by addressing consumer needs.

The Third Seven-Year Plan gives a great deal of attention to developing foreign trade and joint ventures, the first time a plan has addressed these issues. By the end of 1991, however, two years before the termination of the plan, no quantitative plan targets had been made public, an indication that the plan has not fared well. The diversion of resources to build highways, theaters, hotels, airports, and other facilities in order to host the Thirteenth World Festival of Youth and Students in July 1989, must have had a negative impact on industrial and agricultural development, although the expansion and improvement of social infrastructure have resulted in some long-term economic benefits.

The shortage of foreign exchange because of a chronic trade deficit, a large foreign debt, and dwindling foreign aid has constrained economic development. In addition, North Korea has been diverting scarce resources from developmental projects to defense; it spent more than 20 percent of GNP on defense toward the end of the 1980s, a proportion among the highest in the world (see The Armed Forces, ch. 5). These negative factors, compounded by the declining efficiency of the central planning system and the failure to modernize the economy, have slowed the pace of growth since the 1960s. The demise of the communist regimes in the Soviet Union and East European countries—North Korea's traditional trade partners and benefactors—has compounded the economic difficulties in the early 1990s.

Concomitant with the socialization of the economy and the growth in the total magnitude of national output has been a dramatic and revealing change in the relative share of output, indicating that the economy has been transformed from being primarily agricultural to primarily industrial. Whereas in 1946 industrial and agricultural outputs were 16.8 percent and 63.5 percent, respectively, of total national output, the relative position has reversed fundamentally since then so that the respective shares in 1970 were 57.3 percent and 21.5 percent. Judging from the agricultural share of 24 percent in 1981, there were slight reverses in the relative composition in the 1970s.

Growth and changes in the structure and ownership pattern of the economy also have changed the labor force. By 1958 individual private farmers, who once constituted more than 70 percent of the labor force, had been transformed into or replaced by state or collective farmers. Private artisans, merchants, and entrepreneurs had joined state or cooperative enterprises. In the industrial sector in 1963, the last year for which such data are available, there were 2,295 state enterprises and 642 cooperative enterprises. The size and importance of the state enterprises can be surmised by the fact that state enterprises, which constituted 78.1 percent of the total number of industrial enterprises, contributed 91.2 percent of total industrial output.

Budget and Finance

The Ministry of Finance controls all aspects of the government's budget and finance, including banks. The Central Bank issues currency, regulates the money supply, sets official foreign exchange rates, deals with the purchase and sale of gold and foreign exchange, and handles foreign loans. The Foreign Trade Bank, under the supervision of the Central Bank, handles transactions and letters of credit related to foreign trade, and controls the foreign exchange payments of foreign trade organizations and other enterprises.

The Kŭmgang Bank is a specialized bank that handles transactions of foreign trade organizations dealing with exports and imports of machinery, metals, mineral products, and chemical products. The Daesŏng Bank handles transactions of the Daesŏng Trading Company and other trading organizations. There are also three joint venture banks.

The state budget is a major government instrument in carrying out the country's economic goals. Expenditures represented about three-quarters of GNP in the mid-1980s—the allocation of which reflected the priorities assigned to different economic sectors. Taxes were abolished in 1974 as "remnants of an antiquated society." This action, however, was not expected to have any significant effect on state revenue because the overwhelming proportion of government funds—an average of 98.1 percent during 1961–70—was from turnover (sales) taxes, deductions from profits paid by state enterprises, and various user fees on machinery and equipment, irrigation facilities, television sets, and water.

In order to provide a certain degree of local autonomy as well as to lessen the financial burden of the central government, a "local budget system" was introduced in 1973. Under this system, provincial authorities are responsible for the operating costs of institutions and enterprises not under direct central government control, such as schools, hospitals, shops, and local consumer goods production. In return, they are expected to organize as many profitable ventures as possible and to turn over profits to the central government.

Around November of every year, the state budget for the following calendar year is drafted, subject to revision around March. Typically, total revenue exceeds expenditure by a small margin, with the surplus carried over to the following year. The largest share of state expenditures goes to the "people's economy," which averaged 67.3 percent of total expenditures between 1987 and 1990, followed in magnitude by "sociocultural," "defense," and "administration."

Defense spending, as a share of total expenditures, has increased significantly since the 1960s: from 3.7 percent in 1959 to 19 percent in 1960, and, after averaging 19.8 percent between 1961 and 1966, to 30.4 percent in 1967. After remaining around 30 percent until 1971, the defense share decreased abruptly to 17 percent in 1972, and continued to decline throughout the 1980s. Officially, in both 1989 and 1990 the defense share remained at 12 percent, and for 1991 it was 12.3 percent with 11.6 percent planned for 1992 (see table 3, Appendix; Role in National Life, ch. 5). The declining trend is consistent with the government's announced intentions to stimulate economic development and increase the social benefits. However, Western experts estimate that actual military expenditures are higher than budget figures indicate.

Organization and Management of the Economy

Since the government is the dominant force in the development and management of the economy, bureaus and departments have proliferated at all administrative levels. There are fifteen committees—such as the agricultural and state planning committees—one bureau, and twenty departments under the supervision of the State Administration Council; of these, twelve committees, one bureau, and sixteen departments are involved in economic management. In the early 1990s, several vice premiers of the State Administration Council supervised economic affairs. Organizations undergo frequent reorganization. Many of these agencies have their own separate branches at lower levels of government while others maintain control over subordinate sections in provincial and county administrative agencies.

Planning

Although general economic policy objectives are decided by the Central People's Committee (CPC), it is the task of the State Planning Committee to translate the broad goals into specific annual and long-term development plans and quantitative targets for the economy as a whole, as well as for each industrial sector and enterprise. Under the basic tenets of the 1964 reforms, the planning process is guided by the principles of "unified planning" (*ilwŏnhwa*) and of "detailed planning" (*saebunhwa*).

Under "unified planning," regional committees are established in each province, city, and county to systematically coordinate planning work. These committees do not belong to any regional organization and are directly supervised by the State Planning Committee. As a result of a reorganization in 1969, they are separated into provincial planning committees, city/county committees, and enterprise committees (for large-scale enterprises).

The various planning committees, under the auspices of the State Planning Committee, coordinate their planning work with the existing planning offices of the various economy-related government organizations in each of the corresponding regional and local areas. The system attempts to enable the regional planning staffs to better coordinate with economic establishments in their areas, which are directly responsible to them with regard to planning, as well as to communicate directly with staff at the CPC. "Detailed planning" seeks to construct plans with precise accuracy and scientific methods based on concrete assessment of the available resources, labor, funds, plant capacities, and all other necessary information.

There are four stages in drafting the final national economic plan. The first stage is collecting and compiling preliminary statistical data. These figures, which are used as the basic planning data on the productive capacities of various economic sectors, originally are prepared by lower level economic units and aggregated on a national level by respective departments and committees. Simultaneously, the regional, local, and enterprise planning committees prepare their own data and forward them to the CPC. Through this two-channel system of simultaneous but separate and independent preparation of statistical data by economic units and planning committees, the government seeks to ensure an accurate, objective, and realistic data base unfettered by local and bureaucratic bias. The second stage is preparing the control figures by the CPC based on the preliminary data in accordance with the basic plan goals presented by the Central People's Committee. In the third stage, a draft plan is prepared.

The draft plan, prepared by the CPC, is the result of coordinating all draft figures submitted by the lower level economic units, which, in turn, base their drafts on the control figures handed down from the committee. In the fourth stage, the CPC submits a unified national draft plan to the Central People's Committee and the State Administration Council for confirmation. After approval by the Supreme People's Assembly, the draft becomes final and is distributed to all economic units as well as to regional and local planning committees. The plan then becomes legal and compulsory. Frequent directives from the central government contain changes in the plan targets or incentives for meeting the plan objectives.

Although the central government is most clearly involved in the formulation and evaluation of the yearly and long-term plans, it also reviews summaries of quarterly or monthly progress. Individual enterprises divide the production period into daily, weekly, ten-day, monthly, quarterly, and annual periods. In general, the monthly plan is the basic factory planning period.

The success of an economic plan depends on the quality and detail of information received, the establishment of realistic targets, coordination among different sectors, and correct implementation. High initial growth during the Three-Year Plan and, to a lesser extent, during the Five-Year Plan contributed to a false sense of confidence among the planners. Statistical overreporting—an inherent tendency in an economy where rewards lie in fulfilling the quantitative targets, particularly when the plan target year approaches—leads to overestimation of economic potential, poor product quality, and eventually to plan errors. Inefficient utilization of plants, equipment, and raw materials also adds to planning errors. Lack of coordination in planning and production competition among sectors and regions cause imbalances and disrupt input-output relationships. The planning reforms in 1964 were supposed to solve these problems, but the need for correct and detailed planning and strict implementation of plans was so great that their importance was emphasized in the report unveiling the Second Seven-Year Plan, indicating that planning problems persisted in the 1980s.

The Ch'ŏngsan-ni Method

The Ch'ŏngsan-ni Method, or Chŏngsan-ri Method (see Glossary), of management was born out of Kim Il Sung's February 1960 visit to the Ch'ŏngsan-ni Cooperative Farm in South P'yŏngan Province. Kim and other members of the KWP Central Committee offered "on-the-spot guidance" and spent fifteen days instructing and interacting with the workers. The avowed objective of this new method is to combat "bureaucratism" and "formalism" in the farm management system.

The leadership claimed that farm workers were unhappy and produced low output because low-ranking party functionaries, who expounded abstract Marxist theories and slogans, were using incorrect tactics that failed to motivate. To correct this, the leadership recommended that the workers receive specific guidance in solving production problems and be promised readily available material incentives. The Ch'ŏngsan-ni Method called for high-ranking party officials, party cadres (see Glossary), and administrative officials to emulate Kim Il Sung by making field inspections. The system also provided opportunities for farmers to present their grievances and ideas to leading cadres and managers.

Perhaps more important than involving administrative personnel in on-site inspections was the increased use of material incentives, such as paid vacations, special bonuses, honorific titles, and monetary rewards. In fact, the Ch'ŏngsan-ni Method appeared to accommodate almost any expedient to spur production. The method, however, subsequently was undercut by heavy-handed efforts to increase farm production and amalgamate farms into ever-larger units. Actual improvement in the agricultural sector began with the adoption of the subteam contract system as a means of increasing peasant productivity by adjusting individual incentives to those of the immediate, small working group. Thus the increasing scale of collective farms was somewhat offset by the reduction in the size of the working unit. "On-the-spot guidance" by high government functionaries, however, continues in the early 1990s,

Construction workers on Tongil Street, P'yŏngyang
Courtesy Tracy Woodward

as exemplified by Kim Il Sung's visits to such places as the Wang-jaesan Cooperative Farm in Sŏsŏng County and the Kyŏngsŏn Branch Experimental Farm of the Academy of Agricultural Sciences between August 20 and 30, 1991.

The Taean Work System

The industrial management system developed in three distinct stages. The first stage was a period of enterprise autonomy that lasted until December 1946. The second stage was a transitional system based on local autonomy, with each enterprise managed by the enterprise management committee under the direction of the local people's committee. This system was replaced by the "one-man management system," with management patterned along Soviet lines as large enterprises were nationalized and came under central control. The third stage, the Taean Work System (see Glossary), was introduced in December 1961 as an application and refinement of agricultural management techniques to industry. The Taean industrial management system grew out of the Ch'ŏngsan-ni Method.

The highest managerial authority under the Taean system is the party committee. Each committee consists of approximately twenty-five to thirty-five members elected from the ranks of managers, workers, engineers, and the leadership of "working people's organizations" at the factory. A smaller "executive committee," about one-fourth the size of the regular committee, has practical responsibility for day-to-day plant operations and major factory decisions. The most important staff members, including the party committee secretary, factory manager, and chief engineer, make up its membership. The system focuses on cooperation among workers, technicians, and party functionaries at the factory level.

Each factory has two major lines of administration, one headed by the manager, the other by the party committee secretary. A chief engineer and his or her assistants direct a general staff in charge of all aspects of production, planning, and technical guidance. Depending on the size of the factory, varying numbers of deputies oversee factory logistics, marketing, and workers' services. The supply of materials includes securing, storing, and distributing all materials for factory use, as well as storing finished products and shipping them from the factory.

Deputies are in charge of assigning workers to their units and handling factory accounts and payroll. Providing workers' services requires directing any farming done on factory lands, stocking factory retail shops, and taking care of all staff amenities. Deputies in charge of workers' services are encouraged to meet as many of the factory's needs as possible using nearby agricultural cooperatives and local industries.

The secretary of the party committee organizes all political activities in each of the factory party cells and attempts to ensure loyalty to the party's production targets and management goals. According to official claims, all management decisions are arrived at by consensus among the members of the party committee. Given the overwhelming importance of the party in the country's affairs, it seems likely that the party secretary has the last say in any major factory disputes.

The Taean system heralded a more rational approach to industrial management than that practiced previously. Although party functionaries and workers became more important to management under the new system, engineers and technical staff also received more responsibility in areas where their expertise could contribute the most. The system recognizes the importance of material as well as "politico-moral" incentives for managing the factory workers. The "internal accounting system," a spin-off of the "independent accounting system," grants bonuses to work teams and workshops that use raw materials and equipment most efficiently. These financial rewards come out of enterprise profits.

A measure of the success of the Taean Work System is its longevity and its continued endorsement by the leadership. In his 1991 New Year's address marking the thirtieth anniversary of the creation of the system, Kim Il Sung said that the "Taean work system is the best system of economic management. It enables the producer masses to fulfill their responsibility and role as masters and to manage the economy in a scientific and rational manner by implementing the mass line in economic management, and by combining party leadership organically with administrative, economic, and technical guidance."

Mass Production Campaigns

Parallel to management techniques such as the Ch'ŏngsan-ni Method and the Taean Work System, which were designed to increase output in the course of more normalized and regularized operations of farms and enterprises, the leadership continuously resorts to exhortations and mass campaigns to motivate the workers to meet output targets. The earliest and the most pervasive mass production campaign was the Ch'ŏllima Movement. Introduced in 1958, and fashioned after China's Great Leap Forward (1958–60), the Ch'ŏllima Movement organized the labor force into work teams and brigades to compete at increasing production. The campaign was aimed not only at industrial and agricultural workers but also at organizations in education, science, sanitation and health, and culture. In addition to work teams, units eligible for Ch'ŏllima citations included entire factories, factory workshops, and such self-contained units as a ship or a railroad station. The "socialist competition" among the industrial sectors, enterprises, farms, and work teams under the Ch'ŏllima Movement frantically sought to complete the Five-Year Plan (1957–60), but instead created chaotic disruptions in the economy. The disruptions made it necessary to set aside 1959 as a "buffer year" to restore balance in the economy.

Although the Ch'ŏllima Movement was replaced in the early 1960s by the Ch'ŏngsan-ni Method and the Taean Work System, the regime's reliance on some form of mass campaign continued into the early 1990s. Campaigns conducted after the Ch'ŏllima Movement have been narrower in scope and have concentrated on specific time frames for a particular industry or economic sector. Often, the mass production movement takes the form of a "speed battle"—the "100-day speed battle" being most common. The fact that the leadership has to resort to these campaigns points to the weakness or improper functioning of the regular day-to-day management system, as well as to a lack of incentives for workers

125

to achieve the desired economic results. The leadership frequently resorts to speed battles toward the end of a certain period (such as a month, a year, or a particular economic plan) to reach production targets. The "Speed of the 1990s" is designed to carry out the economic goals of the decade.

Industry

North Korea's self-reliant development strategy assigned top priority to developing heavy industry, with parallel development in agriculture and light industry. This policy was achieved mainly by giving heavy industry preferential allocation of state investment funds. More than 50 percent of state investment went to the industrial sector during the 1954–76 period (47.6 percent, 51.3 percent, 57.0 percent, and 49.0 percent, respectively, during the Three-Year Plan, Five-Year Plan, First Seven-Year Plan, and Six-Year Plan). As a result, gross industrial output grew rapidly.

As was the case with the growth in national output, the pace of growth has slowed markedly since the 1960s. The rate declined from 41.7 percent and 36.6 percent a year during the Three-Year Plan and Five-Year Plan, respectively, to 12.8 percent, 16.3 percent, and 12.2 percent, respectively, during the First Seven-Year Plan, Six-Year Plan, and Second Seven-Year Plan. As a result of faster growth in industry, that sector's share in total national output increased from 16.8 percent in 1946 to 57.3 percent in 1970. Since the 1970s, industry's share in national output has remained relatively stable. From all indications, the pace of industrialization during the Third Seven-Year Plan up to 1991 is far below the planned rate of 9.6 percent. In 1990 it was estimated that the industrial sector's share of national output was 56 percent.

Industry's share of the combined total of gross agricultural and industrial output climbed from 28 percent in 1946 to well over 90 percent in 1980 (see Agriculture, Forestry, and Fisheries, this ch.). Heavy industry received more than 80 percent of the total state investment in industry between 1954 and 1976 (81.1 percent, 82.6 percent, 80 percent, and 83 percent, respectively, during the Three-Year Plan, Five-Year Plan, First Seven-Year Plan, and Six-Year Plan), and was overwhelmingly favored over light industry.

North Korea claims to have fulfilled the Second Seven-Year Plan (1978–84) target of raising the industrial output in 1984 to 120 percent of the 1977 target, equivalent to an average annual growth rate of 12.2 percent. Judging from the production of major commodities that form the greater part of industrial output, however, it is unlikely that this happened. For example, the increase during the 1978–84 plan period for electric power, coal, steel, metal-cutting machines, tractors, passenger cars, chemical fertilizers, chemical fibers, cement, and textiles, respectively, was 78 percent, 50 percent, 85 percent, 67 percent, 50 percent, 20 percent, 56 percent, 80 percent, 78 percent, and 45 percent.

Development in Major Sectors

Growth in total industrial output was accompanied by changes in the composition of industry, but large gaps and inconsistencies in official statistics made it impossible to assess specific changes accurately. In 1965, the last year for which data were available for several sectors, the machine building and metal processing sector—the "engineering sector"—accounted for the largest share of total industrial production—29 percent. This figure was a dramatic change from 1946, when the share of this sector was only 5.1 percent. Machine building was regarded as the key to industrialization. The next largest shares in total industrial production in 1965 were 17.2 percent for textiles and 9.1 percent for the food processing and luxury goods industries (see table 4, Appendix). The share of the machinery manufacturing industry increased further to 33.7 percent of gross industrial output in 1980. Although the production of consumer goods was given more emphasis in the 1970s and 1980s, most economic resources continue to be devoted to the production of minerals, metals, and heavy machinery. In fact, most industry is located around the major mining and machinery manufacturing centers that form the focal points of the transportation and communications networks. At the start of the 1990s, the country had a variety of relatively well developed industries, and in per capita production of some industrial items was comparable to those of many middle-income countries.

Mining and Metal Processing

The economy depends to a considerable degree on the extraction of its many mineral resources for fuels, industrial raw materials, and metal processing as well as for exports. Anthracite coal, with estimated reserves of 1.8 billion tons, is the most abundant of the country's mineral resources. It is produced in large quantity for both domestic consumption and export. Coal mines, largely concentrated in South P'yŏngan Province, produced 68 million tons and 22 million tons, respectively, of anthracite and the less abundant lignite coal in 1990. Despite a fairly steady increase in the 1980s, coal production has not been able to catch up with rising demand. This situation has created a persistent energy shortage because the country relies on coal as its main energy source and lacks any reserves of oil or gas.

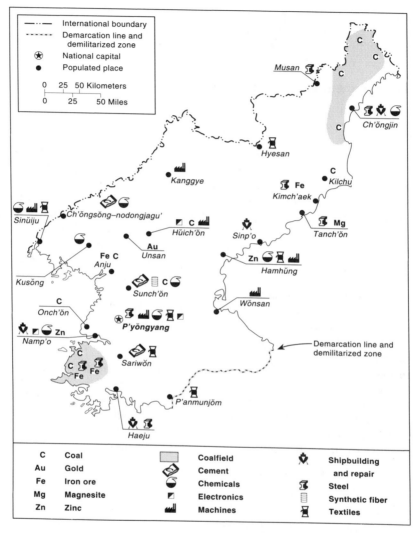

Source: Based on information from *Korea* (Länderkarte.), Gotha, Germany, 1990; Australia, Ministry of Defence, Joint Intelligence Organisation, *North and South Korea Economic Activities*, Canberra, 1975; and K.P. Wang et al., *Mineral Industries of the Far
East and South Asia*, Washington, 1988, 70–72.

Figure 6. Selected Industrial and Mining Activity, 1990

The lagging coal industry remains a major bottleneck. The aging of existing mining equipment and facilities, the inefficiency that
arises from the increasing need to mine deeper seams, and a lack

of modern, efficient equipment are the primary reasons for the production lag in extractive industries. The persistence of these problems prompted Kim Il Sung to stress the importance of developing the mining and power industries and rail transport even in his 1992 New Year's address—the same theme he had repeated annually in his New Year's address for at least the previous fifteen years.

Because of the lack of domestic reserves, the country continues to rely on foreign sources for bituminous coal. Toward the end of the 1980s, China was the chief source of coking coal, followed by the Soviet Union.

The Anju District coal mining complex is the leading coal producer (see fig. 6). A large-scale open-pit mine was being developed in the Anju District in 1990. High-quality anthracite deposits are located in the Paegam District of Yanggang Province, and have estimated reserves of at least 1 million tons. Coal deposits amounting to 10 million tons also exist in Chunbi, T'ŏ-gol, and Kangdong in Kangdong District.

With estimated reserves of 400 million tons, iron ore continues to be important for domestic industry and is a major source of foreign exchange. According to Western estimates, annual iron ore output increased from 8 million tons in 1985 to 10 million tons in 1990. In the 1980s, new mines were added at Tŏksŏng and Sŏhaeri; they supplemented older mines at Musan, Ŭnryul, Tŏkch'ŏn, Chaeryŏng, and Hasŏng, all of which received considerable state investment. The expansion projects started in early 1988 to increase the production capacity of the Musan Mining Complex to 10 millions tons per year were completed in 1989. The long-term annual output target, however, is 15 million tons. The Chŏngp'yŏng Mine in South Hamgyŏng Province was commissioned to produce ores in February 1991.

North Korea possesses the largest and some of the best quality magnesite deposits in the world—an estimated 490 million tons. The mining of magnesite is important for the domestic industrial ceramics industry and for exports. Magnesite mines are concentrated in the Tanch'ŏn District in South Hamgyŏng Province; annual output of magnesite in 1990 was estimated at 1.5 million tons. With the completion of expansion projects of the Tanch'ŏn Magnesia Plant and the construction of the Unsŏng Crushing and Screening Plant in 1987, the production capacity of magnesia increased to 2 million tons annually. The government also began efforts to expand output capacity of magnesia in the Taehŭng District toward the end of the 1980s.

Other important minerals are lead, zinc, tungsten, mercury, copper, phosphates, gold, silver, and sulfur; manganese, graphite, apatite, fluorite, barite, limestone, and talc also are found in great supply. Zinc and lead ingots, among the leading exports, are produced at domestic smelting plants in Tanch'ŏn, Namp'o, Haeju, and Munpyŏng. With a capacity of 15 million tons, the Kŭmdŏk Mining Complex in South Hamgyŏng Province is one of the leading producers. An estimated 200,000 tons of high-grade electrolytic zinc and an estimated 80,000 tons of lead were produced in 1990.

A joint venture project to redevelop the Unsan Gold Mine was unveiled in March 1987. The successful reexploitation of the mine, originally opened by a United States firm in 1896, with deposits estimated at more than 1,000 tons, could make it one of the world's major gold mines.

Building materials, such as the cement used in almost every construction project, are manufactured in large as well as small-scale local industrial plants. Annual cement output was estimated at 11.77 million tons and 12.02 millon tons, respectively, in 1989 and 1990.

Manufacturing

The machine building industry grew rapidly beginning in the mid-1950s and had become the most important industrial sector by 1960. It supplies machinery needed for domestic industry and agriculture, such as tractors and other farm machinery, as well as an extensive range of military equipment (see Military Industry, ch. 5). Production levels since the early 1960s, however, have been disappointing. The output of metal cutting machines reached 30,000 units in 1975, but was far below the planned target of 50,000 units in 1984. Output in 1990 was estimated at 35,000 units. Similarly, the output of tractors in 1984 was estimated to be less than 40,000 units, below the Second Seven-Year Plan target of 45,000 units per year. Annual automobile production in 1990 was estimated at 33,000 units.

The quality of machinery generally is considered below international standards. Some of the largest machinery plants are the Yongsŏng Machinery Works and the Rakwŏn Machinery Works. The Taean Heavy Machinery Works, built during the Second Seven-Year Plan (1978–84) with Soviet assistance, is the country's largest machinery plant.

During the Third Seven-Year Plan (1987–93), the government plans to modernize the machinery industry by introducing high-technology and high-speed precision machines and equipment. For example, it was reported in 1990 that the Huich'ŏn Machine Tool

General Works had completed a flexible manufacturing process by introducing robots into the plant's numerically controlled machine tools and that the Ch'ŏngjin Machine Tool Plant and others were hastening to do the same. The Third Seven-Year Plan calls for an increase of 150 percent in machinery output, slightly higher than the claimed increase of 130 percent during the previous plan.

Utilizing the country's relatively abundant iron ore, the steel industry is a major industrial sector. The Kimch'aek Integrated Iron and Steel Works has surpassed the Hwanghae Iron Works to become the largest steel and iron center. The planned annual production targets for the Second Seven-Year Plan of 6.4 million tons to 7 million tons of pig-iron and granulated iron, 7.4 million tons to 9 million tons of crude steel, and 5.6 million tons to 6 million tons of rolled and structural steel were not met. Estimated output of crude and rolled steel in 1990 was 5.9 million tons and 4 million tons, respectively. Outdated technology, a lack of coking coal, and the low purity of domestic iron ore created serious problems for the iron and steel industry. These difficulties forced the government to scale down the crude steel target by the end of the Third Seven-Year Plan compared with the earlier target of 15 million tons by the end of the 1980s. Completion of the second-stage expansion of Kimch'aek in 1988 reportedly increased the output capacity of the complex to 5 million tons or more per year. New expansion projects completed in 1989 added a 100-ton converter, an oxygen plant, and other production and auxiliary systems.

Capacity expansion projects have been under way at the Ch'ŏngjin and Ch'ŏllima steel complexes. In October 1989, the Large Size Stamp-Forging Plant of the Ch'ŏllima Steel Complex, with a capacity of 2 million tons a year and equipped with a 100,000-ton press, began operation. An expansion project completed in 1989 at the Sŭngri General Motor Works quadrupled the production capacity of the heavy-duty trucks and plant manufactures.

The French-built Ch'ŏngnyŏn Integrated Chemical Works in the Anju District north of P'yŏngyang is the first petrochemical complex designed to produce ethylene, polyethylene, acrylonitrite, and urea. The nearby refinery at Unggi supplies the necessary crude petroleum. The Eight February Synthetic Fiber Integrated Plant, a large-scale complex, produces chemical fibers and has an annual capacity of 50,000 tons. A synthetic fiber complex in Sunch'ŏn, the country's largest, began operation in 1989 after completing its first stage of construction. When all stages are completed, production capacity is expected to reach 100,000 tons of synthetic fiber, 1 million tons of calcium carbide, 750,000 tons of methanol, 900,000 tons of nitrogen fertilizers, 250,000 tons of caustic soda, 250,000 tons of vinyl chloride, and 400,000 tons of soda ash per year.

Light manufacturing has not kept pace with heavy industry. Since the 1970s, the leadership has begun to admit openly the backwardness of consumer goods in terms of quality and variety. The government's stress on providing adequate consumer goods continues into the early 1990s, but is not backed by any real efforts to divert state investment funds from heavy industrial projects. In his 1992 New Year's address, Kim Il Sung stressed achieving the people's long cherished desire that "all people might equally eat rice and meat soup regularly, wear silk clothes, and live in a house with a tiled roof." However, this was preceded by his exhortation that the most important and urgent tasks for 1992 were increasing the production of electricity and coal, and developing rail transport.

The textile industry, the most important light industrial sector, utilizes primarily locally produced synthetics and petrochemically based fibers, as well as cotton and silk. P'yŏngyang, the site of the P'yŏngyang Integrated Textile Mill, is the country's textile capital, but Sinŭiju and Sariwŏn have been gaining in importance. During the Second Seven-Year Plan (1978–84), output of textile fabrics increased by 78 percent registered an annual growth rate of 8.6 percent, and, according to official claims, achieved the 1984 target of 800 million meters. However, foreign estimates placed textile output in 1990 at only 670 million meters. During the Second Seven-Year Plan, knitted goods, particularly those using domestically produced acrylic fibers, were emphasized. Efforts to expand the production capacity of knitwear continue in the Third Seven-Year Plan (1987–93). By modernizing existing equipment and installing new spinning and weaving machines, the government plans to increase the annual output of textiles to 1.5 billion meters by 1993. Judging from the 1990 level of output, it is unlikely that this target will be fulfilled.

The Third Seven-Year Plan emphasizes synthetic fiber production based on indigenous technology using coal and limestone, and on the production of chemical fibers based on petrochemistry. The government has called for accelerating the expansion projects at both the Sinŭiju and Ch'ŏngjin chemical fiber complexes. The planned annual output target for chemical fibers in the Third Seven-Year Plan is 225,000 tons while the output for synthetic resin and plasticizer is targeted at 500,000 tons. Foreign estimates place the output of chemical fibers in 1990 at 177,000 tons. North Korea also has a chemical weapons capability (see Special Weapons, ch. 5).

Since the early 1960s, local industry has been the major supplier of consumer goods and foodstuffs. With the introduction of the

Women waiting at a bus stop in P'yŏngyang
Courtesy Tracy Woodward

August Third People's Consumer Goods Production Movement, in effect since 1984, the government's policy of developing small- and medium-scale local industrial plants simultaneously with large-scale, centrally controlled light industrial plants continues into the 1990s.

Services and Marketing

As in other sectors, the service industries are either under direct state control or cooperatives. The sole, minor exception is the peasant market. One foreign estimate suggests that service industries accounted for 17.2 percent of GNP in 1990. In order to meet the increasing demand for services and distribution channels, the Third Seven-Year Plan calls for expanding retail trade by 110 percent, with particular emphasis on increasing the supply of consumer goods to rural areas. This expansion will be accomplished by extending the network of general and food stores, restaurants, and service centers.

Most retail shops are regulated and operated by the People's Services Committee, which was established in 1972. There are four types of stores. State-run stores include all department stores, vegetable and meat markets, and district shops. Several department stores are located in the national capital, and each provincial capital is supposed to have at least one department store. In the cities, the government planned to have one all-purpose store in each neighborhood, usually located on the ground floor of an apartment building. The second type of store is owned and operated by cooperatives, but since the mid-1960s most have been brought under the control of the People's Services Committee. A third type of store is the factory outlet, usually attached to light industrial factories. Shoppers can buy goods directly from the factory; the price, however, is the same as that of the other retail outlets. Fourth, there are separate stores for military personnel and for railroad workers as well as reports of special luxury shops for high-level cadres. There also are some hard-currency-only stores.

After the August Third People's Consumer Goods Production Movement was introduced, local governments were permitted to establish direct-sale stores within their districts. In January 1990, the number of workers active in the movement nationwide reached several hundred thousand, and the total value of sales under the movement was 9.5 percent of the total retail sales of the traditional distribution network of state and cooperative stores. In the early 1990s, there were 130,000 shops, service establishments, and "food processing and storage bases." Prices for all retail and wholesale goods are fixed by state ministries and do not vary from shop to shop.

The only exception to controlled marketing is the peasant market, where surplus farm products—mostly nongrain daily necessities such as eggs, vegetables, milk, fish, poultry, rabbits, beef, mutton, seasonings, and so on—are sold at free-market prices based on supply and demand. Although North Korea is doctrinally opposed to peasant markets and considers them remnants of capitalism, these markets had gained considerable headway by 1964. The markets are used as stop-gap devices to provide consumers with daily necessities and as a way to reduce black-market activities. One or two of these free markets are located in each county and are opened two or three times a month in central locations. Local officials watch these markets carefully, even though prices are not regulated, to make sure that goods are not being diverted from the state stores.

Agriculture, Forestry, and Fisheries

The task of increasing agricultural production beyond simple recovery from the Korean War was not easy. The country's sparse agricultural resources limit agricultural growth. Climate, terrain, and soil conditions are not particularly favorable for farming (see The Physical Environment, ch. 2). Only about 18 percent of the total landmass, or approximately 2.2 million hectares, is arable; the major portion of the country is rugged mountain terrain. The weather varies markedly according to elevation, and lack of precipitation, along with infertile soil, makes land at elevations higher than 400 meters unsuitable for purposes other than grazing. Precipitation is geographically and seasonally irregular, and in most parts of the country as much as half the annual rainfall occurs in the three summer months. This pattern favors the cultivation of paddy rice in warmer regions that are outfitted with irrigation and flood control networks. Where these conditions are lacking, however, farmers have to substitute other grains for the traditional favorite.

Farming is concentrated in the flatlands of the four west coast provinces, where a longer growing season, level land, adequate rainfall, and good, irrigated soil permit the most intensive cultivation of crops. A narrow strip of similarly fertile land runs through the eastern seaboard Hamgyŏng provinces and Kangwŏn Province, but the interior provinces of Chagang and Yanggang are too mountainous, cold, and dry to allow much farming. The mountains, however, contain the bulk of North Korea's forest reserves while the foothills within and between the major agricultural regions provide lands for livestock grazing and fruit tree cultivation.

Since self-sufficiency remains an important pillar of North Korean ideology, self-sufficiency in food production is deemed a worthy goal. Another aim of government policies—to reduce the "gap" between urban and rural living standards—requires continued investment in the agricultural sector. Finally, as in most countries, changes in the supply or prices of foodstuffs probably are the most conspicuous and sensitive economic concerns for the average citizen. The stability of the country depends on steady, if not rapid, increases in the availability of food items at reasonable prices. In the early 1990s, there also were reports of severe food shortages.

The most far-reaching statement on agricultural policy is embodied in Kim Il Sung's 1964 "Theses on the Socialist Agrarian Question in Our Country," which underscores the government's concern for agricultural development. Kim emphasized technological and educational progress in the countryside as well as collective forms of ownership and management. As industrialization progressed, the share of agriculture, forestry, and fisheries in the total national output declined from 63.5 percent and 31.4 percent, respectively, in 1945 and 1946, to a low of 26.8 percent in 1990. Their share in the labor force also declined from 57.6 percent in 1960 to 34.4 percent in 1989.

135

Resource Development

Resource development in agriculture is a crucial means for increasing agricultural production, recognizing the unfavorable natural endowments—topography, climate, and soil. This development consists of what North Koreans call "nature-remaking" projects. These projects generally increase the quantity of arable land, and rural investment projects, which, in turn, increase the yield of the available land through increased capital and improved technology. "Nature-remaking" projects include irrigation, flood control, and land reclamation. Rural investment projects consist of mechanization, electrification, and "chemicalization"—that is, the increased use of chemical fertilizers and pesticides.

Despite priority allocation of state funds for heavy industry, North Korea has achieved considerable success in irrigation since the Korean War. Irrigation projects began with paddy fields and then continued to non-paddy fields. Irrigated land increased from 227,000 hectares in 1954 to 1.2 million hectares in 1988. North Korea claimed that paddy field irrigation was completed by 1970. In 1990 there were more than 1,700 reservoirs throughout the country, watering 1.4 million hectares of fields with a ramified irrigation network of 40,000 kilometers, which irrigated about 70 percent of the country's arable land. Water-jetting irrigation of non-paddy fields was introduced in the 1980s. In 1989 construction began on a 400-kilometer canal by diverting the flow of the Taedong River along its west coast.

Rural electrification has progressed rapidly. The proportion of villages supplied with electricity increased from 47 percent in 1953 to 92 percent of all villages by the end of 1961. The process of extending electrical lines to the rural areas reportedly was completed in 1970. The annual supply of electricity to the rural areas reached 2.5 billion kilowatt-hours toward the end of the 1980s.

Mechanization is another agricultural target. By 1984 mechanization had reached the level of seven tractors per 100 hectares in the plains and six tractors per 100 hectares in the intermediate and mountainous areas. The fact that the same tractor ratios are quoted in official pronouncements of the early 1990s probably indicates that there is no further improvement in these ratios, and that the planned target of ten tractors per 100 hectares by the end of the Second Seven-Year Plan in 1984 still has not been met. Given the disappointing output record of tractors in recent years, it is doubtful that the target of ten to twelve tractors per 100 hectares will be fulfilled by the end of the Third Seven-Year Plan in 1993. Nonetheless, North Korea claimed that 95 percent of rice planting was mechanized and that there were 5.5 rice transplanting machines per 100 hectares of paddy fields in 1990.

Chemical fertilizers receive much government attention and investment because of their importance for agriculture. Most fertilizers are produced by the enormous fertilizer plant in Hŭngnam, which has an annual capacity of 1 million tons. According to official claims, the output of 4.7 million tons in 1984, compared with 3 million tons in 1976, had fulfilled the 1978–84 plan target. Judging from a foreign estimate of 3.5 million tons in 1990, however, production of chemical fertilizers has been deteriorating. The Sariwŏn Potassium Fertilizer Complex, which has an annual capacity of 3 million tons of potassium feldspar, began construction in 1988 and when completed is expected to raise the country's potassium fertilizer capacity to 500,000 tons, aluminum capacity to 420,000 tons, and cement capacity to 10 million tons per year. In his 1991 New Year's address, Kim Il Sung noted that the complex still was under construction.

By 1977 the "chemicalization" process had increased the average fertilizer application to 1.3 tons per hectare and 1.2 tons per hectare, respectively, for paddy and non-paddy fields, and the 1984 target of two tons per hectare was claimed to have been achieved. The target of the Third Seven-Year Plan is to increase the rate to 2.5 tons. In a 1991 "advisory note" addressing the North Korean economy for the years 1992–96, the United Nations Development Programme (UNDP), the only international agency resident in P'yŏngyang, warned that the practice of intensive chemicalization has led to land degradation—that is, declining soil fertility, falling organic matter content, erosion and soil acidification, and water pollution, with resulting environmental damage.

The objectives of the "nature-remaking program" launched in 1976 are to complete the irrigation of non-paddy lands, to reclaim 100,000 hectares of new land, to build 150,000 hectares to 200,000 hectares of terraced fields, to reclaim tidal land, and to conduct afforestation and water conservation projects. The reclamation of 6,200 hectares of tideland at Taedong Bay was underway as part of the 1987-93 plan to reclaim a total of 300,000 hectares of tidal land. The largest land reclamation scheme, the West Sea Barrage, involves an eight-kilometer-long sea wall across the Taedong River, and was completed in June 1986. The multipurpose project, five years in construction at a reported cost of US$4 billion, consists of a main dam, three locks, and thirty-six sluices, and reportedly was the longest dam in the world as of 1992.

Production and Distribution of Crops and Livestock

The total cropland of about 2.2 million hectares is overwhelmingly planted with grains, of which rice accounted for 30.1 percent in 1989–90. Official data on cropland distribution and agricultural production are scanty, and there are discrepancies in the methods of calculating the weight of rice (husked or unhusked). North Korea claims to have produced 10 million tons of grains in 1984. The grain output in 1989 was estimated at 12.04 million tons by the Food and Agriculture Organization (FAO) of the UN. In 1989 the output of the two most important crops, rice and corn, was estimated at 6.4 million tons and 3 million tons, respectively. The output of potatoes was 2.05 million tons in 1989. Other important crops are wheat, barley, millet, sorghum, oats, and rye. Corn grows in most areas, except for parts of Yanggang and North Hamgyŏng provinces. Barley and wheat are cultivated mostly in both Hwanghae provinces and in South P'yŏngan Province. Rice is exported, but other grains, such as wheat, are imported. P'yŏngyang's goal is to increase the grain output to 15 million tons by 1993.

Major rice production centers are located in the provinces of North and South Hwanghae and in the provinces of North and South P'yŏngan. North Korea's climate precludes double-cropping of rice in most areas, and different methods had to be devised to increase productivity. One method is to use cold-bed seeding, a process that enables farmers to begin rice growing before the regular season by planting seedlings in protected, dry beds.

Fruits, vegetables, and livestock also are important, particularly around cities and in upland areas unsuited to grain cultivation. Fruit orchards are concentrated in both Hamgyŏng provinces, South P'yŏngan Province, and South Hwanghae Province. Soybeans, whose output was around 450,000 tons toward the end of the 1980s, are raised in many parts of the country, but primarily in South P'yŏngan Province.

The post-Korean War trend of increasing the share of livestock in the total value of agricultural output continued during the 1980s, judging from the steady growth, which outpaced grain production. Cattle are raised in the mountainous parts of the two P'yŏngan provinces, and sheep and goats are kept in the rugged areas of the two Hamgyŏng provinces and in Yanggang and Kangwŏn provinces. Pigs and poultry, probably the most important types of livestock, are raised near P'yŏngyang and in North P'yŏngan and South Hwanghae provinces. The government is particularly proud of its large chicken farms.

According to a 1988 agreement with the UNDP, North Korea was to receive livestock aid from the UNDP, along with assistance in modernizing vegetable farms, fruit production and storage, rice cultivation, and construction of a fish farm and soil and plant experimental stations. A rice nursery and a vegetable research institute began operation in March 1991. The Third Seven-Year Plan called for attaining an annual output of 1.7 million tons of meat, 7 billion eggs, and 2 million tons of fruit by 1993.

In the early 1990s, there were persistent reports of severe food shortages as a result of several years of consecutive crop failures, coupled with distribution problems that had serious consequences for food rationing. An indirect admission of food shortages came in Kim Il Sung's 1992 New Year's address, in which he defined 1992 as the "year of put-greater-efforts-into-agriculture" in order to provide the population with sufficient food.

Organization and Management

Efforts to increase agricultural production include a variety of experiments with land tenure, farm organization, and managerial techniques. Following a typical communist pattern, land initially was redistributed to tillers in a sweeping land reform in 1946 soon after the communists took over the country. By 1958 private farming, which ironically was given a boost by land reform, was completely collectivized.

The Land Reform Act of March 1946 had, in the remarkably short period of one month, abolished tenancy and confiscated and redistributed more than 1 million hectares of land. The government reallocated most of the land formerly owned by the Japanese colonists and all properties exceeding five hectares to individual farming households. The number of peasant holdings increased dramatically, but the average size of individual holdings dropped from 2.4 hectares to 1.4 hectares. It was difficult to determine the effect of such massive land distribution on production because the Korean War interrupted farming in the early 1950s. The reform, however, was quickly replaced by a drive for collectivization.

During the 1954–58 transition period, farm holdings went through three progressively collective phases: "permanent mutual-aid teams," "semisocialist cooperatives," and "complete socialist cooperatives." In the final stage, all land and farm implements are owned collectively by the members of each cooperative. The pace of collectivization quickened during 1956, and by the end of that year about 80 percent of all farmland was cooperatively owned. By the time this process was completed in August 1958, more than 13,300 cooperatives with an average of eighty households and 130 hectares of land dotted the countryside. Only two months later, however, the government increased the size of the average cooperative to 300 households managing 500 hectares of land through consolidation of all farms in each *ri,* or *ni* (village, the lowest administrative unit) into one. As a result, the number of cooperatives decreased but their average size increased. Judging from the timing of the consolidation of farms, this sudden decision to increase the size of the cooperatives appears to have been influenced by the introduction of communes in China. Newly consolidated farms established and operated such nonagricultural institutions as clinics, rest homes, day nurseries, schools, and community dining halls.

Each cooperative farm elects a management committee to oversee all aspects of farm activity, including retail services and marketing, and the local party committee closely supervises its management. The party committee chairman usually is the vice chairman of the management committee. Within the management committee, an auditing unit wields the most power and controls the management of farm accounts, work points, cooperative shops, and credit facilities. Auditors report to the plenary session of the management committee as well as to county authorities.

The basic unit of production and accounting on the cooperative farm is the work team, which is further divided into subteams. Most cooperatives have several agricultural work teams and at least one animal husbandry work team. In some cooperatives, work teams or subteams specialize in vegetable farming, sericulture, fruit cultivation, aquaculture, or other activities. Work is allocated to teams and subteams according to physical ability. Most able-bodied men and women are assigned to rice growing units, which require the most effort. Wages are distributed in both cash and kind.

State farms are considered the more ideologically "advanced" agricultural organizations. Both the means of production and output are state owned, and farmers receive standardized wages on the basis of an eight-hour workday rather than shares of production. Managers of state farms, appointed by the state farm bureau of the national-level Agricultural Committee, run the farms as if they were industrial enterprises. State farms often are coterminous with a county and are model farms that experiment with new cropping methods or specialize in livestock or fruit production. Their larger scale allows for greater mechanization, and their output per worker is undoubtedly higher because their operations are more efficient than those of the rural cooperative farms. State farms attempt to integrate all county agricultural and industrial activities into one complementary and integrated management system. Utilizing

The Yonggwang Station of the P'yŏngyang Metro
Courtesy Korea Pictorial

about 10 percent of the country's total cropland, they contribute about 20 percent of total agricultural output. Kim Il Sung often stresses the need for transforming agriculture from cooperative ownership to "all-people's" or state ownership, but as of 1993 no action had been taken to change cooperative farms to state farms.

Dissatisfied with low levels of agricultural production, the government developed a new administrative structure to perform for the rural cooperatives what the management of state farms is supposed to have accomplished. The county Cooperative Farm Management Committee, established in 1962, took over all the economic functions of the county people's committees. The new committee was to bring agricultural management closer to the ideal "industrial method," by "the strengthening of technical guidance of production and the planification and systematization of all management activities of the enterprise."

The composition of the management committee varies from county to county, but the staff usually consists of agronomists, technicians, directors of county agricultural agencies, and, where appropriate, forestry and fishery agents. The function of the committee is to set production targets for the cooperatives within its jurisdiction, allocate resources and materials necessary to achieve these goals, and monitor the payment of wage shares and the collection of receipts. County managers report to their counterparts at the provincial-level Rural Management Committee, who in turn direct all their reports to the General Bureau for Cooperative Farm Guidance at the national-level Agricultural Committee.

In spite of lagging agricultural output, there have been no significant changes in the agricultural organization and management system in place since the early 1960s. Furthermore, as exemplified by Kim Il Sung's exhortation to strengthen the application of the Ch'ŏngsan-ni Method of farming, no fundamental changes in the agricultural incentive system have been introduced. The strategy for achieving greater agricultural production continues to emphasize "industrialization" of agriculture through increased irrigation, fertilizer use, and mechanization while maintaining the existing administrative, management, and incentive systems.

Forestry

North Korea's forests have a variety of trees and other plant life. Predominant trees include larch, poplar, oak, alder, pine, spruce, and fir. In the early 1990s, approximately 80 percent of the total area of the country, or 9.4 million hectares, was made up of forests and woodlands; over 70 percent of these reserves were in the mountainous Hamgyŏng provinces, and in Yanggang and Chagang provinces. Much of this area was severely damaged by overcutting during the last years of Japanese colonial rule and by the effects of the Korean War. The government has promoted afforestation projects to make up for these losses, and during the First Seven-Year Plan an estimated 914,000 hectares were planted, with an average of 2,900 trees per hectare. In the early 1970s, however, the rate of afforestation dropped to about 10,000 hectares per year.

Timber production was estimated at 600,000 cubic meters in 1977, basically unchanged since the late 1960s. In 1987, however, timber production was estimated at 3 million cubic meters. The amount of fuelwood available for rural households increased by 11 percent from 1970 to 1977, when approximately 4.6 million cubic meters were used for heating.

The Ministry of Forestry was established in 1980 to oversee the development of the forestry industry. The ministry sent agents to the county level to manage the rotation of harvest and replanting. Since the 1980s, almost no official quantitative information on forestry has been forthcoming. The government failed to mention the performance of the forestry sector in its report on the fulfillment of the Second Seven-Year Plan, and the Third Seven-Year Plan does not even contain any reference to forestry.

Fisheries

North Korea's coastline of about 2,495 kilometers, mixture of warm and cold ocean currents, and many rivers, lakes, and streams make its potential for fishery development better than for most other countries. Not until the early 1960s, however, did the domestic fishing industry begin to expand rapidly, receiving increased investment in vessels, equipment, and port facilities. Total marine products increased from 465,000 tons in 1960 to 1.14 million tons in 1970, registering an annual growth rate of 9.4 percent compared with the planned rate of 14.5 percent. The Six-Year Plan target of 1.6 million tons was met in 1976, as was the target of 3.5 million tons for the Second Seven-Year Plan in 1984. The output target for the Third Seven-Year Plan was 11 million tons by 1993, including a catch of 3 million tons of fish. With an estimated total output of 1.5 million tons in 1990, down from 1.6 million tons in 1989, it is highly unlikely that the 1993 target for marine products will be met.

The major fishing grounds are in the coastal areas of the Sea of Japan, or East Sea, to the east and the Yellow Sea to the west. Deep-sea fishing began in earnest in the 1970s. The principal catch from the Sea of Japan is pollack, a favorite fish of most Koreans;

sardine and squid catches also are significant. From the west coast, yellow covina and hairtail are the most common varieties of fish. Deep-sea catches include herring, mackerel, pike, and yellowtail. The main fishery ports are Sinp'o, Kimch'aek, and the nearby deep-sea fishery bases of Yanghwa and Hongwŏn. Most large-scale storage and canning facilities also are located on the east coast. Besides the fishery stations, smaller fishery cooperatives are located along both coasts in traditional fishing centers. Aquaculture and freshwater fishing take place on regular cooperative farms.

In order to expand marine products, the Third Seven-Year Plan calls for modernizing the fishery industry. Specifically, the plan urges increasing the numbers of 14,000-ton class processing ships, 3,750-ton class stern-trawlers, and 1,000-ton and 480-ton class fishing vessels, as well as generally increasing the size of vessels. The government also called for widespread introduction of modern fishing implements and rationalizing the fishery labor system. Improvements also are slated for expanding and modernizing the cold-storage and processing facilities in order to facilitate speedy processing of catches. The slow progress in state investment, combined with the shortages of oil, are the main factors in the disappointing record of marine output in the late 1980s and early 1990s.

Infrastructure

An inadequate and outmoded infrastructure, particularly the transportation network, has severely impeded industrial growth, especially since the end of the disappointing Six-Year Plan. The magnitude of the problem was such that in 1977 Kim Il Sung identified the "transportation front" as the sector requiring the greatest effort that year. During the Second Seven-Year Plan, priority was assigned to modernizing and expanding the freight-carrying capacity in rail, road, and marine transport, as well as to centralizing and containerizing transport. The expansion and renovation of port facilities also received much investment in order to alleviate congestion and delay in the handling of cargo at ports. The same theme was basically repeated in the Third Seven-Year Plan.

Transportation and Communications
Railroads

Railroads, the main means of transportation, had a total route length of 5,045 kilometers in 1990. In 1990 railroads hauled 90 percent of all freight, with 7 percent carried on roads and 3 percent of transport hauled by water. The comparative figures for passenger traffic were 62 percent, 37 percent, and 1 percent, respectively.

By 1990 approximately 63 percent of the rail network was electrified, an important factor in improving traction capacity in mountainous terrain. Two major lines run north-south, one each along the east and west coasts. Two east-west lines connect P'yŏngyang and Wŏnsan by a central and a southerly route, and a part of a third link line constructed in the 1980s connects provinces in the mountainous far north near the Chinese border (see fig. 7). The railroad system is linked with those of China and Russia, although gauge inconsistencies necessitated some dual gauging with Russia. The Third Seven-Year Plan targeted an increase of 60 percent for railroad traffic through continued efforts in electrification, development of centralized and containerized transport, and modernization of transport management.

Maritime Transportation

Water transport on the major rivers and along the coasts plays only a minor, but probably growing, role in freight and passenger traffic. Except for the Yalu and Taedong rivers, most of the inland waterways, totaling 2,253 kilometers, are navigable only by small craft. Coastal traffic is heaviest on the eastern seaboard, whose deeper waters can accommodate larger vessels. The major ports are Namp'o on the west coast and Najin, Ch'ŏngjin, Wŏnsan, and Hamhŭng on the east coast. The country's harbor loading capacity in the 1990s was estimated at almost 35 million tons a year. In the early 1990s, North Korea possessed an oceangoing merchant fleet, largely domestically produced, of sixty-eight ships (of at least 1,000 gross-registered tons), totaling 465,801 gross-registered tons (709,442 deadweight tons), which includes fifty-eight cargo ships and two tankers. There is a continuing investment in upgrading and expanding port facilities, developing transportation—particularly on the Taedong River—and increasing the share of international cargo by domestic vessels.

Civil Aviation

North Korea's international air connections are limited. There are regularly scheduled flights (about once or twice a week) from the international airport at Sunan—twenty-four kilometers north of P'yŏngyang—to Moscow, Khabarovsk, and Beijing, and irregular flights from Sunan to Tokyo as well as to East European countries, the Middle East, and Africa. Information on the frequency of the latter flights is not available. An agreement to initiate a service between P'yŏngyang and Tokyo was signed in 1990. Internal flights are limited to routes between P'yŏngyang, Hamhŭng, Wŏnsan, and Ch'ŏngjin. All civil aircraft, an estimated eighteen planes in

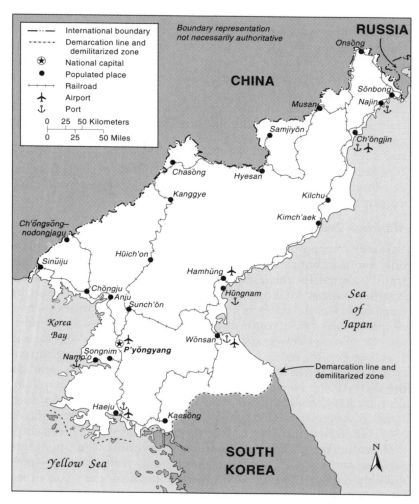

Source: Based on information from *Korea* (Länderkarte.), Gotha, Germany, 1990.

Figure 7. Primary Railroads, Ports, and Airports, 1990

1991, were purchased from the Soviet Union. From 1976 to 1978, three Tu-154 jets were added to the small fleet of propeller-driven An-24s.

Roads

Fuel constraints and the near absence of private automobiles have relegated road transportation to a secondary role. The road network was estimated between 23,000 and 30,000 kilometers in 1990, of which only 1,717 kilometers—7.5 percent—are paved; the rest are of dirt, crushed stone, or gravel, and are poorly maintained (see fig. 8). There are three major multilane highways: a 200-kilometer expressway connecting P'yŏngyang and Wŏnsan on the east coast, a forty-three-kilometer expressway connecting P'yŏngyang and its port, Namp'o, and a four-lane 100-kilometer highway linking P'yŏngyang and Kaesŏng. The overwhelming majority of the estimated 264,000 vehicles in use in 1990 were for the military. Rural bus service connects all villages, and cities have bus and tram services. In 1973 an extravagantly outfitted, two-line 30.5-kilometer subway system was completed in P'yŏngyang.

Telecommunications

Based on the limited information available in the early 1990s about the country's telecommunications network, telephone services—an estimated 30,000 telephones in 1985—mainly were available at government offices, factories, cooperatives, and other workplaces. By 1970 automatic switching facilities were in use in P'yŏngyang, Sinŭiju, Hamhŭng, and Hyesan. A few public telephone booths were beginning to appear in P'yŏngyang around 1990. Ordinary citizens do not have private telephone lines. There are international connections via Moscow and Beijing, and in late 1989 international direct dialing service was introduced from Hong Kong. A satellite ground station near P'yŏngyang provides direct international communications using the International Telecommunications Satellite Corporation (Intelsat) Indian Ocean satellite. A satellite communications center was installed in P'yŏngyang in 1986 with French technical support. An agreement to share in Japan's telecommunications satellites was reached in 1990. North Korea joined the Universal Postal Union in 1974 but has direct postal arrangements with only a select group of countries.

The Korean Central Television Station is located in P'yŏngyang, and there also are stations in major cities, including Ch'ŏngjin, Kaesŏng, Hamhŭng, Haeju, and Sinŭiju. There are three channels in P'yŏngyang but only one channel in other cities. Imported Japanese-made color televisions have a North Korean brand name superimposed, but nineteen-inch black-and-white sets have been produced locally since 1980. One estimate places the total number of television sets in use in the early 1990s at 250,000 sets.

North Korea has two amplitude modulation (AM) radio broadcasting networks, P'yŏngyang Broadcasting Station (Radio P'yŏngyang) and Korean Central Broadcasting Station, and one frequency modulation (FM) network, P'yŏngyang FM Broadcasting Station.

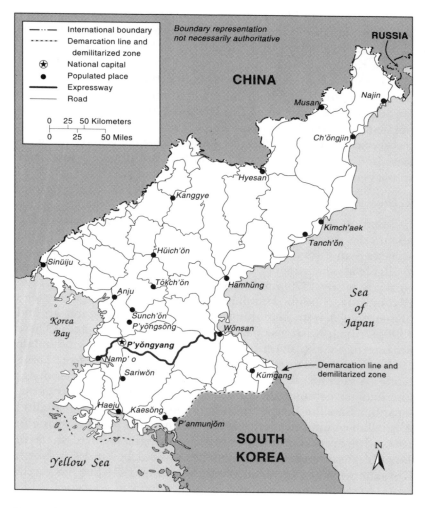

Source: Based on information from *Atlas of North Korea*, Seoul, 1992; and *Korea (Länder-karte.)*, Gotha, Germany, 1990.

Figure 8. Primary Roads, 1992

All three networks have stations in major cities that offer local programming. There also is a powerful shortwave transmitter for overseas broadcasts in several languages. In the early 1990s, North Korea had an estimated 3.75 million radio sets; radio dials, however, are fixed to receive only designated frequencies, preventing reception of foreign broadcasts.

Energy and Power

An abundance of coal and water resources has allowed North Korea to build a well-developed electric power network. North Korea's preeminence as an energy producer began during the Japanese occupation with the Sup'ung Hydroelectric Plant, located in the northwest; at the time the plant was the largest of its kind in Asia. North Korea supplied more than 90 percent of the electricity in the Korean Peninsula before partition.

Since the 1970s, the country has increasingly turned to coal as an energy source. Compared with hydroelectrical plants, coal-based thermal plants can be built at locations near industrial and population centers at lower initial costs, require shorter construction time, and are not subject to instability arising from periods of drought.

Thermal plants tend to be less efficient and have higher operating costs. North Korea's installed generating capacity was estimated at 7.14 million kilowatts in 1990, with 60 percent—4.29 million kilowatts—from hydropower and the remainder from thermal sources. With output estimated at 50 billion kilowatt-hours (Kwh) and 55 billion Kwh, in 1984 and 1988, respectively, the Second Seven-Year Plan target of 56 billion Kwh to 60 billion Kwh had not yet been fulfilled five years after the plan had ended. It is therefore unlikely that the 1993 target of 100 billion Kwh will be realized.

The only oil-fired thermal plant is at Unggi, near the Russian border. The 200-megawatt plant receives its fuel oil from the nearby Unggi refinery, which uses crude petroleum imported from Russia.

In the early 1990s, many power plants were under construction, including the T'aech'ŏn power station, in the northwest, reportedly the largest hydroelectric plant in North Korea when completed. Other large-scale projects include the Kŭmgang-san, Hŏch'ŏn, Nam-gang, Kŭmyagang, and Ŏrang-ch'on plants. In addition, thermal power plants such as the East P'yŏngyang Power Plant and the Hamhŭng Power Plant were under construction in the early 1990s. Four large hydroelectric plants—some built with Chinese aid—are situated along the Yalu River; they supply power jointly to both countries.

In 1986 the Soviet Union announced that it was building a 1,760-megawatt nuclear power plant in North Korea. According to South Korean sources, the construction of the plant began in 1990 in the Sinp'o District. Completion of the plant, originally targeted for 1992, is in doubt because of pressure exerted by the International Atomic Energy Agency (IAEA—see Glossary) and termination of assistance from the former Soviet Union, which is burdened with its own economic difficulties. Wood-burning is still significant for domestic heating and related purposes.

There are no domestic oil reserves. The capacity of North Korea's two oil refineries totals 4.5 million tons a year. Oil is imported from China and the Soviet Union by pipeline, and from Iran by sea. Because both Russia and China have insisted on hard currency payments at international prices for oil since 1991, Iran is becoming the major oil source under a 1989 agreement to supply 40,000 barrels of oil per day.

Foreign Economic Relations

Foreign economic relations have been shaped largely by *chuch'e* ideology and the development strategy of building a virtually autarkic economy. These factors have led to an inward-looking and import-substituting trade policy, which has resulted in a small scale of foreign trade and a chronic trade deficit. North Korea's main trade partners have been communist countries, principally the Soviet Union and China, and Japan has been a major trading partner since the 1960s.

Although still adhering to the basic principle of self-reliance, P'yŏngyang is flexible in its application whenever the economic need arises. After the Korean War, North Korea received a substantial amount of economic aid from communist countries for reconstructing its war-torn economy. In the early 1970s, the country accepted a massive infusion of advanced machinery and equipment from Western Europe and Japan in an effort to modernize its economy and to catch up with South Korea. By the late 1980s, P'yŏngyang had moved toward making exporting a priority in order to garner foreign exchange so as to be able to import advanced technologies needed for industrial growth and to pay for oil imports.

The most recent and important manifestation of a flexible and practical application of self-reliance—prompted by severe economic difficulties—is the gradual move toward an open-door policy. This policy shift, which involves North Korea's attitudes toward foreign trade, tourism, direct foreign investment, joint ventures, and economic cooperation with South Korea, has the potential to significantly change the country's foreign economic relations.

The importance of trading with Western developed countries was expounded by Kim Il Sung as early as 1975. The origin of the open-door policy, however, was Kim Il Sung's 1979 New Year's address, in which he mentioned the need to expand foreign trade rapidly in order to meet the requirements of an expanding economy. Kim publicly alluded to some serious problems impeding North Korean exports, exhorting the population to adhere to a reliability-first principle: improving product quality, strictly meeting delivery dates, and expanding harbor facilities and the number of cargo vessels. In his 1980 New Year's address, Kim repeated this theme and announced that foreign trade had increased 30 percent in 1979 over 1978. This speech marked the first time in a decade that trade statistics had been made public—even in this limited and relative form. Unexpectedly and uncharacteristically, North Korea joined the UNDP in 1979 and accepted US$8.85 million in technical assistance. This action was further evidence of a small opening to outside economic involvement.

The year 1984 was the benchmark in officially launching the open-door policy. The Supreme People's Assembly's policy statement, entitled "For Strengthening South-South Cooperation and External Economic Work and Further Developing Foreign Trade," stressed the need to expand economic relations with the developing world as well as to promote economic and technical cooperation with advanced industrial countries. The document also repeated the export bottlenecks listed by Kim in his 1979 and 1980 New Year's addresses. North Korea indicated its readiness to accept direct foreign investment by enacting a joint venture law in 1984. And, since 1986, the country has begun to encourage tourism by accepting some tour groups from the West.

The most far-reaching change in foreign economic relations occurred in 1988 when North Korea began to trade with South Korea (see Inter-Korean Affairs, ch. 4). Inter-Korean trade has grown rapidly, and by 1993 the two Koreas expanded into joint ventures and other forms of economic cooperation. North Korea's readiness to open its economy to the West and to South Korea is, no doubt, prompted by its need to import sophisticated Western industrial equipment, plants, and up-to-date technologies in order to modernize and jump-start the economy, and to catch up with South Korea. Given its sizable foreign debt, sagging exports, and the dissolution of the Soviet Union, its largest trade partner, North Korea does not have much choice and recognizes the need to revise its trade laws so as to encourage foreign investment.

Economic Assistance

Economic assistance from communist countries plays an important role in securing resources for economic development. Estimates vary, but it is likely that the equivalent of US$4.75 billion of aid was accepted between 1946 and 1984. Almost 46 percent of the assistance came from the Soviet Union, followed by China with about 18 percent, and the rest from East European communist countries (see table 5, Appendix). Most of the assistance—about two-thirds—was in the form of loans; the rest were outright grants. Understandably, grants dominated in the years immediately after the Korean War, but subsequently loans became the predominant form of aid. Whereas in 1954 aid receipts made up one-third of national revenues, by 1960 foreign assistance had dropped to less than 3 percent of total revenues. Officially, declining foreign aid in the 1960s was blamed for being partly responsible for poor economic performance during the First Seven-Year Plan. In the 1970s, loans (for importing Western machinery and plants) from Japan and Western Europe were larger than those from communist countries. Grants, terminated since the 1960s, were restored when China gave approximately US$300 million between 1978 and 1984. In November 1990, China reportedly promised North Korea economic aid amounting to US$150 million over five years, largely made up of deliveries of grain and oil. North Korea receives no multilateral economic assistance other than from the UNDP.

Between 1949 and 1990, the Soviet Union helped North Korea build or rehabilitate 170 large plants in sectors such as power, mining, ferrous and non-ferrous metals, chemicals, construction materials, oil-refining, machinery, textiles, food, transportation, and communications. During the same period, these plants reportedly produced about 60 percent of all electric power, 40 percent of steel and rolled steel, 50 percent of oil products, 10 percent of coke, 13 percent of fertilizers, 19 percent of fabrics, and 40 percent of iron ore. Soviet assistance also was important in the construction of expanded port facilities at Najin. In addition, a total of 6,000 Soviet engineers and experts were sent to North Korea to train 20,000 Korean workers, and 2,000 North Koreans received technical training in the Soviet Union.

Beginning in the late 1970s, Soviet assistance began to take the form of output-sharing ventures. Enterprises under these ventures include an enamel wire plant, a small electric motor plant, a car battery plant, a cold rolled steel shop, and a hot rolled steel shop at the Kimch'aek Integrated Iron and Steel Works. Under a buyback arrangement, Soviet assistance for constructing industrial projects was paid for with commodities produced at the plants.

There were reports in 1978 that approximately 10,000 Chinese laborers were working on construction projects. Chinese workers had assisted in the construction of the Sup'ung and Unbong hydroelectric power stations, from which China also drew electricity.

In spite of its domestic economic difficulties, North Korea also is an aid donor on a fairly modest scale. Between 1980 and 1989, North Korea provided a total of approximately US$26.4 million in aid to Third World countries, of which almost 74 percent went to African countries in the form of technical agricultural assistance.

Foreign Trade

North Korea's foreign trade is characterized by its relatively low value, chronic trade deficits, and small number of trading partners. In 1990 almost 83 percent of total trade was conducted with the Soviet Union, China, and Japan. Although modest in scale, accompanied by wide and frequent swings from year to year, and even negative growth in some years, trade levels have grown over the years. Based on estimates from the returns of trading partners, exports and imports grew from US$307.7 million and US$434.1 million, respectively, in 1970, to US$1.86 billion and US$2.92 billion, respectively, in 1990 (see tables 6 and 7, Appendix). North Korea's total exports were comparable to only 2.9 percent of South Korea's exports of US$65.02 billion in 1990. North Korea's trade value also is small in relative terms when compared with that of South Korea and other newly industrializing economies. The trade ratio (total trade value relative to GNP) in 1990 was 20.7 percent, with export and import ratios of 8.1 percent and 12.6 percent, respectively. The comparative ratio for South Korea was 56.7 percent—with 27.3 percent and 29.4 percent, respectively, for exports and imports.

Except for a few years since 1946, the trade balance has been characteristically unfavorable. North Korea attracted worldwide notoriety in 1976 when it defaulted on its payment of foreign debt to Western countries. The debt had resulted from massive purchases of capital goods from West European countries and Japan in the early 1970s, which had drastically increased the trade deficit. Imports are supposed to be paid for by increased export earnings and short-term credits, neither of which has occurred. The oil shock of late 1973 and the onset of the recession and worldwide stagflation also took their toll. Prices of North Korea's minerals declined sharply because of a worldwide recession that lowered demand. Foreign exchange reserves dwindled, leading to the debt crisis. After suspending payments, North Korea tried to reschedule the payments, but its payment record is erratic; the debts continue in the early 1990s, and unpaid interest continues to mount. At the end of 1989, the total foreign debt was estimated at US$6.78 billion: 45.9 percent, or US$3.13 billion, was owed to the Soviet Union; US$900 million to China; and US$530 million to Japan. According to South Korean sources, the total debt had increased to US$7.86 billion at the end of 1990.

Despite North Korea's flirtation with Western developed countries, the Soviet Union, China, and Japan remain its principal trading partners. In the late 1940s and 1950s, more than 90 percent of trade was conducted with communist countries. In the 1960s, this dependency began to gradually decrease, and in the mid-1970s, with P'yŏngyang's sudden turn to the West for imports of machinery and equipment, the slide accelerated. This dependency fell to its lowest point in 1974—only 51.5 percent of total trade; it began to rise again when North Korea, having defaulted on payment of its debt, found it difficult to obtain credit to finance imports from the West. The ratio of trade with communist countries was 72.7 percent and 71.4 percent, respectively, in 1989 and 1990.

The Soviet Union has consistently been North Korea's largest trading partner, accounting for about half of total two-way trade in the late 1980s and 55.9 percent and 56.8 percent in 1989 and 1990, respectively. It is followed by China, with 12.5 percent and 11.4 percent in 1989 and 1990, respectively. Since the early 1960s, Japan has emerged as the third largest trading partner—10.7 percent and 19.7 percent in 1989 and 1990, respectively. Japan remains a major continuing link with the advanced market economies. For some years in the mid-1980s, imports from Japan exceeded those of China. Most of the trade deficits originate in communist countries; an exception was in 1974–75 when an import surplus from Western countries exceeded that from communist countries.

The Soviet Union also is the largest source of import surpluses. In 1989 and 1990, trade deficits with the Soviet Union constituted 63.5 percent and 57.7 percent, respectively, of the total deficit. The corresponding ratio for China was 20.3 percent and 28.6 percent, respectively. North Korea had depended predominantly on the Soviet Union and China for its trade credits in the late 1980s, but in 1990 P'yŏngyang began to lean more toward Beijing. From 1987 to 1990, North Korea consistently accumulated a trade surplus with Japan.

A major factor in North Korea's renewed reliance on the Soviet Union in the 1980s—both as supplier of imports as well as the chief destination for exports—was the difficulty of marketing its products elsewhere; a second important factor was the West's reluctance to extend additional credits. In a trade agreement signed in November 1990, North Korea was required, for the first time, to use hard currency in its commercial transactions with the Soviet Union beginning in 1991. China also notified North Korea to use hard currency in their mutual trade beginning in 1992. This requirement will have a serious adverse effect on the trade value, the balance

*The West Sea Barrage, an eight-kilometer-long sea wall, helps
to irrigate the west coast.
Painting at the West Sea Barrage depicting Kim Il Sung
and Kim Jong Il at the construction site
Courtesy Tracy Woodward*

of payments, and the domestic energy situation. There are signs that the initial attempts to enforce the hard currency rule caused Soviet-North Korean trade to plummet in early 1991. For example, petroleum deliveries from the Soviet Union plunged from 410,000 tons in 1990 to 45,000 tons in the first half of 1991. In order to prevent a further decline, the Soviets conceded some unidentifiable amount of transition time before fully enforcing hard currency payments. Because of the decline in oil imports, the Soviet-aided Sŭngri oil refinery in Ch'ŏngjin was at least temporarily closed. Consequently, North Korea has increasingly turned to China and Iran for petroleum.

North Korea's principal exports are non-ferrous metals—mostly zinc, lead, barites, gold, iron, and steel, and textile yarn and fabrics, magnesium, metal-working machine tools, military equipment, cement, vegetables, and fishery products. Its main imports are advanced machinery, transport equipment, high-grade iron and steel products, crude petroleum, wheat, and chemicals. Of almost US$1.7 million of imports from the Soviet Union in 1990, machinery and transport equipment constituted by far the largest category of imports—22.4 percent; garments constituted 53.6 percent of exports, amounting to approximately US$1 million that same year. Petroleum and petroleum products imported from the Soviet Union declined sharply from 21.5 percent in 1987, to 10.9 percent in 1988, and to 6.7 percent in 1990.

North Korea's main imports from China are energy-related products--coal, briquettes, petroleum, and petroleum products; they constituted 38.4 percent and 38.5 percent of imports, respectively, for 1989 and 1990. Other imports include cereals and cereal preparations, oil seeds, rubber products, textile fibers, fruits and vegetables, foodstuffs, and machinery and equipment. Metallurgical exports, including magnesium, steel, and nonferrous metals, are the largest category of exports to China, comprising 37.2 percent of total exports in 1990. Other exports to China include anthracite coal, cement, fish, and seafood.

Machinery is the largest import from Japan, making up 23 percent of the total, followed by textile fibers and products, base metal and products, chemicals, plastic and rubber products, and electric and transport equipment. Making up about 40 percent of the total in 1989–90, the main exports to Japan are minerals, in particular iron and steel, zinc, magnesium, aluminum, and lead. Other export items to Japan are vegetables, marine products, textile fibers, anthracite coal, apparel and clothing accessories, and precious metals.

Foreign Investment and Joint Ventures

Direct foreign investment in North Korea had been virtually absent until 1984, when North Korea made a surprising turnabout by proclaiming the Joint Venture Law. The twenty-six-article law on joint ventures appears to have been fashioned after China's law on the same subject. Joint ventures are allowed in "industries necessary for the people's economy," specifically electronics, automation equipment, metals, machine building, chemicals, food processing, clothing-processing industries, consumer goods, construction, transportation, and tourism. Overseas Koreans, particularly those in Japan, are singled out as parties who might wish to participate in joint ventures. Foreign participants are allowed to repatriate profits. There are no stated limits on foreign equity shares. A Ministry of Joint Venture Industry was created in 1988 but in 1990 was scaled down to a bureau, presumably under the Ministry of External Economic Affairs, which handles foreign market development, foreign investment, and joint ventures.

Attempts to accelerate the transfer of hoped-for and much-needed advanced technology and the infusion of capital through joint ventures have had limited success. Until the early 1990s, North Korea was unable to attract major investment by West European or mainstream Japanese firms. Many factors influence the slow pace and low level of participation in joint ventures by firms other than those owned by Choch'ongryŏn (General Association of Korean Residents in Japan) (see Glossary)—an organization of North Korea-supporting Korean residents of Japan. In fact, the majority of joint venture deals have been concluded with Choch'ongryŏn firms. Of a total of 100 joint ventures reported toward the end of 1991, with a total capitalization of 13 billion yen (approximately US$96.5 million), over 70 percent involve Choch'ongryŏn firms.

Because the foreign debt problem still is unresolved, North Korea has not improved its shaky credit rating. As a result, Western firms consider any venture with North Korea highly risky. Although the joint venture law is liberal with regard to the repatriation of profits, the dearth of hard currency holdings makes profit repatriation questionable, thus discouraging potential investors. Another inhibiting factor is the relatively small size of the domestic market, particularly in terms of per capita income. Moreover, the market's restrictive nature—with prices and distribution channels controlled by the state—makes the prospect of successful penetration both dim and problematic.

Approximately ten joint ventures have Chinese participation; other partner countries include the Soviet Union and Bulgaria.

The largest joint venture project is the Hamhŭng Rare Earth Separator Plant, which has both Chinese and Choch'ongryŏn participation and an investment of approximately US$10.25 million. There also are thirty overseas joint ventures; they are mostly in the former Soviet Union with a few in China. The majority of the firms are engaged in light manufacturing. The first joint venture with China, begun in 1989, was a marine fishery products firm located in Ch'ŏngjin that had an initial capitalization of US$1 million. The Hŭich'ŏn-Gorky joint venture company run by the Hŭich'ŏn Machine Tool General Works of North Korea and the Gorky Machine Production Complex of the Soviet Union was commissioned in October 1989. Other projects under way include a joint shipping company, a luxury hotel, a store selling soft drinks, a department store, an apparel plant, a restaurant, a silk fabric plant, and a gold mine. Both Kim Il Sung and Kim Jong Il attended an exhibition of goods produced by a joint venture with Choch'ongryŏn firms from Japan in P'yŏngyang on April 13, 1991; the first such event ever held in North Korea.

Inter-Korean Economic Cooperation

The first inter-Korean exchange of goods occurred in 1988. This development had the potential to significantly alter both North Korea's future economic development and its foreign economic relations. Trade began modestly with the November 21, 1988, arrival of forty kilograms of North Korean clams at the South Korean port of Pusan. A second transaction, in January 1989, involved South Korean imports of North Korean art, such as paintings, pottery, woodwork, and industrial artworks. In July 1990, North Korea swallowed its pride and accepted delivery of some 800 tons of South Korean rice collected by Christians through a "Rice of Love" campaign for the poor.

In December 1990, the first contract between a South Korean company and a North Korean company was signed. Doosung Company, a small, little-known trading company in Seoul, signed a direct barter trade contract with Kŭmgang-san International Trade and Development Company. The contract called for exchanging US$1.3 million worth of goods by the end of February 1992. Doosung was to ship 500 refrigerators and 240 color television sets and to receive North Korean cement, artifacts, and paintings of equal value. A total of 11,243 North Korean works of art worth US$650,000 arrived in Pusan on February 15, 1991, followed shortly thereafter by a shipment of electronic products to North Korea. Before this deal, some 200 North-South transactions—involving no fewer than 150 South Korean firms and nine North Korean firms—had taken place, but all these transactions had been indirect and had been conducted through brokers in Hong Kong or Japan.

On March 29, 1991, Cheongji Trading Company became the second South Korean trading company to sign a formal barter agreement with Kŭmgang-san International Trade and Development Company. The two companies agreed to exchange 100,000 tons of rice for 11,000 tons of cement and 30,000 tons of coal. The initial rice shipment of 5,000 tons left Mokp'o in July 1991. Seoul was ready to compensate fully any losses to Cheongji through an inter-Korean cooperation fund established in August 1990. The fund was to provide loans and financial assistance for expenses related to promoting inter-Korean trade and other forms of economic cooperation.

In addition to direct agreements with smaller South Korean firms, North Korea also began to trade with South Korea's conglomerates, or *chaebŏl* (see Glossary). Lucky-Goldstar signed a contract in February 1991 with a Chinese broker to ship 30,000 barrels of high sulfur diesel oil to North Korea for US$1.4 million payable in cash. The diesel oil was to be shipped from Yosu, South Korea, to Namp'o, North Korea. Two *chaebŏl*, Samsung and Lucky-Goldstar, bought almost 135 kilograms of North Korean gold bullion in 1991 from brokers in Hong Kong. This transaction was South Korea's first purchase of gold from North Korea.

Immediately after the two Koreas were admitted to the United Nations in 1991, South Korean traders, including Samsung and Hyundai, began to increase imports of products from North Korea. Samsung signed a contract to import steel sheets, zinc ingots, farm crops, and yarn; the company planned to pay for the steel sheets by exporting color television sets, sugar, and refrigerators. Another South Korean conglomerate, Ssangyong, imported iron ingots in September 1991 and planned to import more. Hyundai planned to import 1,500 tons of iron ingots in October 1991. Based on South Korean figures, the value of the two-way trade increased from US$23.34 million in 1989, to US$25.61 million in 1990, and to US$190 million in 1991.

One indication of North Korea's readiness to trade with South Korea was the early 1992 report that North Korea had ordered US$800 million to US$1 billion of consumer goods from South Korea to be known as "April 15 goods" in honor of Kim Il Sung's eightieth birthday. These goods, ranging from toothbrushes and clothing to refrigerators and washing machines, were to be sold or handed out to North Koreans as gifts during the birthday celebrations. The South Korean firms were asked not to attach brand names to the goods.

At the beginning of inter-Korean trade, North Korea exported hot-rolled coil, iron and zinc ingots, coal, steel sheets, cement, potatoes, electrolyte copper, Alaskan pollack, dried squid, raw silk, and other products. Textiles, sock looms, electrical appliances, and other goods were imported. A turning point was reached in 1991, when inter-Korean economic cooperation moved beyond commodity trade.

South Korean *chaebŏl,* concerned about rising wages in South Korea, are inclined toward joint ventures in labor-intensive manufactures such as petroleum and the assembly of electronic products, and appear to be competing with each other in their march toward North Korea. Hyundai's Chung Ju Yung returned from his first visit to North Korea in 1989 with a promise to develop Kŭmgang-san (Diamond Mountain) as a resort. Although North Korea later reneged on the project, Chung planned to lead a delegation of Hyundai executives to North Korea in 1992. Samsung sent a senior executive in 1991 to discuss opening a branch office in P'yŏngyang and wanted to explore the feasibility of a US$20-million joint venture with Japanese and Hong Kong partners for a textile and garment plant in Ch'ŏngjin. A pilot project by the Kolon textiles group is said to be fully operational—socks are produced on machines imported from Seoul under a South Korean supervisor.

In January 1992, Daewoo chairman Kim Woo Choong visited North Korea as the first officially invited South Korean business leader. While in P'yŏngyang, Kim concluded a joint venture agreement with the North Korean government to establish an industrial park in Namp'o for the exclusive use of Daewoo and other South Korean firms. Daewoo will spend between US$10 million and US$20 million to build the complex; North Korea will provide the labor and land. Consumer goods such as clothes, leather goods, footware, toys, and kitchen utensils will be produced for export to third countries. Daewoo is expected to make a separate agreement involving investment guarantees, shipping arrangements, sales methods, and technology transfer. As the goods are not to be used for internal consumption, it is likely that some kind of compensation trade arrangement was reached whereby Daewoo's payment for its investment will come from selling the finished products in third countries. On February 10, 1992, Seoul announced its approval of Daewoo's joint venture projects in North Korea.

Economic Outlook

It appeared for a time that North Korea could not remain immune indefinitely to the fallout from the political and economic collapse of communist regimes as well as to the rise of South Korea as an economic powerhouse. Eventually, the severe economic difficulties and adverse changes in the international environment will become serious enough to compel the North Korean leadership to introduce some changes in the economic institutions. At the outset of 1993, however, it does not seem that North Korea will fundamentally overhaul its economic system. Only selective reforms—such as the gradual expansion of peasant and handicraft markets, extension of free-market-based retail outlets dealing with local consumer goods, and a much wider application of the independent accounting system in industrial enterprises with more discretion for the disposition of the "profits"—are expected to be implemented.

North Korea's leadership probably drew a lesson from China's experience: in spite of popular demands that political liberalization follow economic liberalization, communist rule can still be prolonged if leaders have sufficient will and power. The decision to adopt both Chinese-style joint ventures and special economic zones shows that North Korean leaders are willing to make that gamble. But they are more likely to open the economy to foreign trade and direct investment than to approve fundamental economic reforms.

Expanding economic ties with South Korea and diplomatic normalization with Japan offers the greatest future economic opportunities. One important component of the on-again-off-again negotiations for normalization that began in 1990 is North Korea's demand that Japan provide reparations as compensation for its colonial rule over Korea. Both reparations and improved political relations with Japan will ease North Korea's economic hardships. Reparations can be used immediately to repay part of North Korea's debt to Japan, alleviating a longstanding source of friction between the two countries and paving the way toward importing much-needed advanced capital goods and technology from Japan.

The possibility of joint ventures with South Korean firms and, to a lesser extent, with mainstream Japanese firms is particularly promising. North Korea's cheap labor force will be a strong magnet for South Korean and Japanese firms, at least initially. In time, North Korean workers will need more technical training, and the communist managers will have to be taught Western management practices, both of which will add to labor costs.

The economic role of formerly communist allies, particularly that of the former Soviet Union, is expected to decline drastically. By the end of the decade, Japan will likely become North Korea's second largest trading partner after Russia and then possibly its largest trading partner—or at least its largest source of imports. Inter-Korean trade, however, has the potential to increase to the point that South Korea may eventually overtake Japan in a decade or so to become North Korea's largest trading partner. If this occurs, China and Russia will probably become North Korea's third and fourth largest trading partners, respectively.

North Korea's admission to the UN in 1991 makes it eligible for various types of economic, scientific, and technical assistance from the UN and its various specialized agencies. UN membership also increases the possibility that North Korea can participate in international organizations such as the World Bank (see Glossary) and the IMF.

Reparations payments and economic aid from Japan, trade credits from South Korea, and participation in various international organizations will substantially help North Korea's modernization. A modernized and expanded infrastructure—with particular attention to transportation and communications—will have to precede the commitment of scarce resources to modernizing a specific industrial sector or plant.

In order to alleviate chronic energy shortages and meet growing industrial needs, rebuilding and restructuring the energy industry will have to take precedence over other industrial projects. Restructuring could eventually alter the practice of relying equally on coal-powered and hydroelectric plants, gradually replacing coal with alternative sources such as nuclear energy. Doing so would make electric-power generation less vulnerable to the faltering coal industry and to the vagaries of rainfall. The extractive industries will also have to receive substantial investment before North Korea can take advantage of its mineral resources. Easily accessed coal may have been depleted; as with iron ores, zinc, and other minerals, deeper seams will have to be mined. It also will be necessary to introduce modern mining equipment and techniques.

Although poor harvests frequently are attributed to bad weather, farming is relatively well developed. Nonetheless, productivity can be greatly increased by introducing modern farm machinery, high-quality seeds, and more and better distribution of fertilizer. The prospects for improving farm output through decollectivization, however, appear to be dim in the near future.

With the Cold War over and the signing of the Agreement on Reconciliation, Nonaggression, Exchanges, and Cooperation between the two Koreas in December 1991, reduced defense expenditures are a real possibility in the near future. Arms control already is on the agenda in the inter-Korean talks. Diverting some or most of North Korea's defense spending to economic development projects would make a substantial contribution toward economic progress.

As of mid-1993, however, it did not appear that the nonaggression pact would soon pave the way to economic integration and reunification of the two Koreas. Significant differences in the unification formulas remain. There is little likelihood of a German-style absorption of North Korea by South Korea, and North Korea has voiced its concern and opposition to the possibility of absorption to the South Korean authorities. If South Korea had ever entertained the idea of a German-style unification, the hindsight of the German experience has forced it to take a more sober and realistic appraisal of the possibility. The huge cost of absorption would economically overwhelm South Korea and have the potential of destabilizing the entire Korean Peninsula. However, inter-Korean economic cooperation through trade and joint ventures has the potential of significantly jump starting and modernizing the North Korean economy by introducing South Korean capital and technological and managerial know-how. Improvements in the North Korean economy will, in turn, facilitate and increase the probability of economic integration and eventual reunification.

* * *

Because of the secretive nature of the North Korean regime, the scarcity of consistent and reliable economic data, particularly since the 1960s, makes studying its economy a challenge. Among the North Korean sources that consistently contain economic topics are *Chosŏn chungyang yŏngam* (Korean Central Yearbook), an annual with sections on the economy and other related topics; *Kŭlloja* (The Worker), a monthly journal of the KWP Central Committee; *Nodong simmun* (Workers' Daily), the KWP's daily newspaper; and *Foreign Trade of the Democratic People's Republic of Korea* and *Korea Today,* monthly English-language periodicals. *Kŭlloja* and other Korean-languages periodicals, as well as those in other languages such as Japanese, are available in English as the Korean Affairs Report series issued by the United States Joint Publications Research Service.

The most useful Japanese source is *Kita Chōsen no keizai to bōeki no tenbō* (North Korean Economic and Trade Prospects), an annual published by the Japan External Trade Organization (JETRO) that contains up-to-date surveys of the economy and statistical data on trade. Another informative Japanese source is the monthly periodical *Kita Chōsen kenkyū* (Studies on North Korea). Two additional useful South Korean sources are issued monthly: *Vantage Point,* an English-language periodical of the Naewoe Press in Seoul devoted to events in North Korea, and *Pukhan* (North Korea). Other South Korean English-language periodicals frequently contain articles on the North Korean economy: *Asian Perspective,* a biannual published by the Institute for Far Eastern Studies of Kyungnam University; *Korea Observer,* a quarterly of the Institute of Korean Studies; and *Korea and World Affairs,* a quarterly by the Research Center for Peace and Unification of Korea.

Other valuable English-languages sources are the weekly *Far Eastern Economic Review* and its annual publication, *Asia Yearbook; Country Report: China, North Korea,* a quarterly report put out by the Economist Intelligence Unit, and its annual survey, *Country Profile: China, North Korea;* January issues of *Asian Survey,* which carry the annual survey on North Korea; *Yearbook of International Trade Statistics* by the United Nations; the *Direction of Trade Statistics* of the International Monetary Fund; and the United States Foreign Broadcast Information Service *Daily Report: East Asia.* (For further information and complete citations, see Bibliography.)

Chapter 4. Government and Politics

Kim Il Sung, the "great leader," as depicted in a statue at the Samjiyŏn Grand Monument, Lake Samji. The monument, unveiled in May 1979, immortalizes the revolutionary exploits of Kim Il Sung during the anti-Japanese revolutionary struggle.

THE DEMOCRATIC PEOPLE'S REPUBLIC OF KOREA (DPRK, or North Korea) was liberated from Japanese colonial rule by the Soviet Union at the end of World War II (1939–45). When Kim Il Sung, born April 15, 1912, returned to North Korea from the Soviet Union where he and his guerrillas had been based from 1941–45, the Soviet occupation forces in the northern part of the country presented him to the North Korean people as a hero. In mid-1993 Kim Il Sung was general secretary of North Korea's ruling party and president of the state.

North Korea is a classic example of the "rule of man." Overall, political management is highly personalized and is based on loyalty to Kim Il Sung and the Korean Workers' Party (KWP). The cult of personality, the nepotism of the Kim family, and the strong influence of former anti-Japanese partisan veterans and military leaders are unique features of North Korean politics.

Kim Il Sung's eldest son Kim Jong Il, born February 16, 1942, is a secretary of the KWP Central Committee Secretariat and chairman of the National Defense Commission. On December 24, 1991, Kim Jong Il succeeded his father as commander of the Korean People's Army.

In addition, as of mid-1993, Kim Il Sung's wife, Kim Song-ae, was a member of the KWP Central Committee, a member of the Standing Committee of the Supreme People's Assembly, a deputy to the assembly, and chairwoman of the Korean Democratic Women's Union Central Committee. Kim Il Sung's daughter, Kim Kyong-hui, was a member of the KWP Central Committee and deputy to the Supreme People's Assembly (SPA), and his son-in-law, Chang Song-taek, was a candidate member of the KWP Central Committee and deputy to the SPA. Kang Song-san, Kim Il Sung's cousin by marriage, was premier and a member of the KWP Central Committee and Political Bureau, deputy to the SPA, and member of the state Central People's Committee (CPC). The late Ho Tam, who died in 1991, was Kim Il Sung's brother-in-law, a member of the KWP Central Committee and Political Bureau, chairman of the SPA Foreign Affairs Committee, deputy to the SPA, and chairman of the Committee for the Peaceful Reunification of the Fatherland.

Although the Korean communist party dates from the 1920s, North Korea claims that the KWP was founded by Kim Il Sung in 1945. Since that time, North Korea has been under the one-party rule of the KWP. The party is by far North Korea's most politically significant entity; its preeminence in all spheres of society places it beyond the reach of dissent or disagreement. Party membership is composed of the "advanced fighters" among North Korea's working people: workers, peasants, and working intellectuals who struggle devotedly for the success of the socialist and communist cause. The KWP claimed a membership of "over three million" people in 1988. The ruling elite considers KWP members the major mobilizing and developmental cadres (see Glossary). In principle, every worker, peasant, soldier, and revolutionary element can join the party. Among KWP members, however, the military has a major political role, and all key military leaders have prestigious positions in top party organs.

The political system originally was patterned after the Soviet model. The party is guided by the concept of *chuch'e* (see Glossary)—"national self-reliance" in all activities. The essence of *chuch'e* is to apply creatively the general principles of Marxism and Leninism in the North Korean way (*woorisik-dero salja*). *Chuch'e* is a response to past political economic dependence. As historian Dae-Sook Suh has noted, *chuch'e* is "not the philosophical exposition of an abstract idea; rather it is firmly rooted in the North Korean people and Kim Il Sung."

In the decades since the departure of Soviet occupation forces in 1948, and as the party leadership gradually has grown more confident in its management of various problems, the system has been somewhat modified in response to specific domestic circumstances. In April 1992, North Korea promulgated an amended constitution that deleted Marxism and Leninism as principal national ideas and emphasized *chuch'e*. The constitutional revisions also granted supreme military power to the chairman of the National Defense Commission, Kim Jong Il.

Another salient feature of the country's political system is glorification of Kim Il Sung's authority and cult of personality. Kim uses the party and the government to consolidate his power. He is addressed by many honorary titles: the "great leader," the son of the nation, national hero, liberator, and the fatherly leader. According to the party, there can be no greater honor or duty than being loyal to him "absolutely and unconditionally." Kim's executive power is not checked by any constitutional provision. The party's principal concern is to ensure strict popular compliance with the policies of Kim Il Sung and the party; such compliance implants an appearance of institutional imprimatur on Kim's highly personalized and absolute rule. Politics as a function of competition for power by aspiring groups and promotion of the interests of special groups is not germane to the North Korean setting.

Personalism centers on Kim Il Sung, but he has been gradually preparing Kim Jong Il as heir apparent since 1971. Between 1971 and 1980, Kim Jong Il was given positions of increasing importance in the KWP hierarchy. Since the Sixth Party Congress in October 1980, Kim Jong Il's succession has been consolidated with his phased assumption of control over the civil administration, followed by his designation as supreme commander of the Korean People's Army in December 1991.

Relationship Between the Government and the Party

As of the early 1990s, the philosophy underlying the relationship between the government and the party had not changed since independence. Government organs are regarded as executors of the general line and policies of the party. They are expected to implement the policies and directives of the party by mobilizing the masses. All government officials or functionaries are exhorted to behave as servants of the people, rather than as overbearing "bureaucrats." The persistence in party literature of admonitory themes against formalism strongly suggests that authoritarian bureaucratic behavior remains a major source of concern to the party leadership. This concern may explain in part the party's intensified efforts since the early 1970s to wage an ideological struggle against the bureaucratic work style of officials. The general trend is toward tightened party control and supervision of all organs of administrative and economic policy implementation.

In January 1990, Kim Jong Il introduced the slogan "to serve the people" and directed party functionaries to mingle with the people and to devotedly work as faithful servants of the people. Kim said that the collapse of socialism in some countries is a stern lesson to North Korea and is related to failures in party building and party activity. He stressed the importance of reinforcing the party's ideological unity and cohesion, and elucidated tasks that would strengthen education in the principle of *chuch'e*, revolutionary traditional education, and socialist and patriotic education.

The party is the formulator of national purpose, priorities, and administrative hierarchy. It is the central coordinator of administrative and economic activities at the national and local levels. Through its own organizational channels, which permeate all government and economic agencies, the party continues to oversee administrative operations and enforce state discipline. Without exception, key government positions are filled by party loyalists, most of whom are trained in the North Korean system, which emphasizes ideology and practical expertise.

The Korean Workers' Party

The Korean Workers' Party (KWP) is North Korea's most politically significant entity. In theory, according to Article 21 of the Rules and Regulations of the Korean Workers' Party as revised in October 1980 (hereafter referred to as the party rules), the national party congress is the supreme party organ. The party congress approves reports of the party organs, adopts basic party policies and tactics, and elects members to the KWP Central Committee and the Central Auditing Committee. The election, however, is perfunctory because the members of these bodies are actually chosen by Kim Il Sung and his few trusted lieutenants. When the party congress is not in session, the Central Committee acts as the official agent of the party, according to Article 14 of the party rules. As of September 1992, the KWP had 160 Central Committee members and 143 Central Committee alternate (candidate) members. The Central Committee meets at least once every six months. Article 24 of the party rules stipulates that the Central Committee elects the general secretary of the party, members of the Political Bureau Presidium (or the Standing Committee), members of the Political Bureau (or Politburo), secretaries, members of the Central Military Commission, and members of the Central Inspection Committee. A party congress is supposed to be convened every five years, but as of 1993, one had not been held since the Sixth Party Congress of October 1980. Party congresses are attended by delegates elected by the members of provincial-level party assemblies at the ratio of one delegate for every 1,000 party members.

The long-delayed Sixth Party Congress, convened from October 10–14, 1980, was attended by 3,220 party delegates (3,062 full members and 158 alternate members) and 177 foreign delegates from 118 countries. Approximately 1,800 delegates attended the Fifth Party Congress in November 1970. The 1980 congress was convened by the KWP Central Committee to review, discuss, and endorse reports by the Central Committee, the Central Auditing Committee, and other central organs covering the activities of these bodies since the last congress.

The Sixth Party Congress reviewed and discussed the report on the work of the party in the ten years since the Fifth Party Congress. It also elected a new Central Committee. In his report to the congress, Kim Il Sung outlined a set of goals and policies for the 1980s. He proposed the establishment of a Democratic Confederal Republic of Koryŏ as a reasonable way to achieve the independent

Kim Il Sung, general secretary of the Korean Workers' Party since October 1966 and president of the Democratic People's Republic of Korea since 1972 Courtesy Democratic People's Republic of Korea Mission to the United Nations

and peaceful reunification of the country. Kim Il Sung also clarified a new ten-point policy for the unified state and stressed that North Korea and South Korea (the Republic of Korea, or ROK) should recognize and tolerate each other's ideas and social systems, that the unified central government should be represented by P'yŏng-yang and Seoul on an equal footing, and that both sides should exercise regional autonomy with equal rights and duties. Specifically, the unified government should respect the social systems and the wishes of administrative organizations and of every party, every group, and every sector of people in the North and the South, and prevent one side from imposing its will on the other.

Kim Il Sung also emphasized the Three Revolutions (see Glossary), which were aimed at hastening the process of political and ideological transformation based on *chuch'e* ideology, improving the material and technical standards of the economy, and developing socialist national culture. According to Kim, these revolutions are the responsibility of the Three Revolution Team Movement (see Glossary)—"a new method of guiding the revolution, which combined political and ideological guidance with scientific and technical guidance. This approach enabled the upper bodies to help the lower levels and rouse masses of the working people to accelerate the Three Revolutions." The teams perform their guidance work by sending their members to factories, enterprises, and cooperative farms. Their members are party cadres, including those from

171

the KWP Central Committee, reliable officials of the government, persons from economic and mass organizations, scientists and technicians, and young intellectuals. Kim Il Sung left no question that the Three Revolution Team Movement had succeeded the Ch'ŏllima Movement (see Glossary) and would remain the principal vehicle through which the party pursued its political and economic objectives in the 1980s.

The linkage between party and economic work also was addressed by Kim Il Sung. In acknowledging the urgent task of economic construction, he stated that party work should be geared toward efficient economic construction and that success in party work should be measured by success in economic construction. Accordingly, party organizations were told to "push forward economic work actively, give prominence to economic officials, and help them well." Party officials were also advised to watch out for signs of independence on the part of technocrats.

The membership and organization of the KWP are specified in the party rules. There are two kinds of party members: regular and probationary. Membership is open to those eighteen years of age and older, but party membership is granted only to those who have demonstrated their qualifications; applications are submitted to a cell along with a proper endorsement from two party members of at least two years in good standing. The application is acted on by the plenary session of a cell; an affirmative decision is subject to ratification by a county-level party committee. A probationary period of one year is mandatory, but may be waived under certain unspecified "special circumstances." Recruitment is under the direction of the Organization and Guidance Department and its local branches. After the application is approved, an applicant must successfully complete a one-year probationary period before becoming a full party member.

Constitutional Framework

The constitutions of North Korea have been patterned after those of other communist states. The constitutional framework delineates a highly centralized governmental system and the relationship between the people and the state. On December 27, 1972, the Fifth Supreme People's Assembly ratified a new constitution to replace the first constitution, promulgated in 1948. Innovations of the 1972 constitution included the establishment of the positions of president and vice presidents and a super-cabinet called the Central People's Committee (CPC). The 1972 constitution was revised in April 1992, and ratified by the Sixth Supreme People's Assembly.

The South Korean press published unofficial translations of the document in late 1992.

The revised constitution has 171 articles and seven chapters (twenty-two more and four less, respectively, than the 1972 constitution). Among the more significant changes are the elevation of *chuch'e* at the expense of Marxism-Leninism, the removal of references to the expulsion of foreign troops, and the addition of articles encouraging joint ventures, guaranteeing the ''legitimate rights and interests of foreigners,'' and establishing a framework for expanded ties with capitalist countries. More important, the new constitution provides a legal framework for the 1991 appointment of Kim Jong Il as supreme commander of the armed forces by removing the military from the command of the president and by placing the military under the control of the National Defense Commission, of which he is chairman.

The eighteen articles of Chapter 1 deal with politics. Article 1 defines North Korea as an independent socialist state representing the interests of all the Korean people. Article 15 states that the DPRK defends the democratic, national rights of overseas Koreans and their legitimate rights under international law. Sovereignty emanates from four expressly mentioned social groups: workers, peasants, soldiers, and working intellectuals. State organs are organized on and operate on the principle of democratic centralism. In a change from the previous constitution, attaining ''the complete victory of socialism in the northern half'' was to be accomplished through the execution of the three revolutions of ideology, technology, and culture, while struggling to realize unification of the fatherland by following the principles of independence, peaceful unification, and grand national unity. Previously socialism was to have been accomplished by driving out foreign forces on a countrywide scale and by reunifying the country peacefully on a democratic basis. Other articles in this chapter refer to the mass line, the Ch'ŏngsan-ni Method (or Ch'ŏngsan-ri—see Glossary) and spirit, and the Three Revolution Team Movement. The constitution states that foreign policy and foreign activities are based on the principles of independence, peace, and friendship. Diplomatic, political, economic, and cultural relations are to be established with all friendly countries based on the principles of complete equality, independence, mutual respect, noninterference in each other's internal affairs, and mutual benefit.

In Chapter 2, economic affairs are codified. The constitution declares that the means of production are owned by state and cooperative organizations. The text reiterates that natural resources, major factories and enterprises, harbors, banks, and transportation and telecommunications establishments are state owned and that land, draft animals, farm implements, fishing boats, buildings, and small- and medium-sized factories and enterprises may be owned by cooperative organizations. Article 24 defines personal property as that for personal use by the working people for the purpose of consumption and derived from the "socialist distribution according to work done and from additional benefits received from the state and society." Benefits derived from supplementary pursuits, such as the small garden plots of collectivized farmers, are considered personal property; such benefits are protected by the state as private property and are guaranteed by law as a right of inheritance. The planned, national economy is directed and managed through the Taean Work System (see Glossary; Planning, ch. 3).

Culture, education, and public health are covered in Chapter 3. Article 45 stipulates that the state develop a mandatory eleven-year education system, including one year of preschool education (see Education, ch. 2). Other articles state that education is provided at no cost and that scholarships are granted to students enrolled in colleges and professional schools. Education in nurseries and kindergartens is also at the state and society's expense. Article 56 notes that medical service is universal and free (see Public Health, ch. 2). Medical care and the right to education are also covered in Chapter 5 articles. Article 57 places environmental protection measures before production; this emphasis is in line with the attention given to preserving the natural environment and creating a "cultural and sanitary" living and working environment by preventing environmental pollution.

Chapter 5 extensively details the fundamental rights and duties of citizens. Citizens over the age of seventeen may exercise the right to vote and be elected to office regardless of gender, race, occupation, length of residency, property status, education, party affiliation, political views, or religion. Citizens in the armed forces may vote or be elected; insane persons and those deprived by court decisions of the right to vote do not have the right to vote and be elected. According to Article 67, citizens have freedom of speech, publication, assembly, demonstration, and association. Citizens also have the right to work, and Article 70 stipulates that they work according to their ability and are remunerated according to the quantity and quality of work performed. Article 71 provides for a system of working hours, holidays, paid leave, sanitoriums, and rest homes funded by the state, as well as for cultural facilities. Article 76 accords women equal social status and rights. Women are also granted maternity leave and shortened working hours when they have large families. Marriage and the family are protected by the state.

Chapter 6, entitled "State Institutions," has eighty articles and eight sections—more sections than any other chapter. The chapter covers the Supreme People's Assembly, the president of the DPRK, the National Defense Commission, the Central People's Committee, the State Administration Council, the local people's assemblies and people's committees, the local administrative and economic committees, and the court and the procurator's office. Chapter 7, which covers the national emblem, the flag, and capital, describes the first two items, designates P'yŏngyang as the capital, and names the national anthem. In a change from the previous constitution, the 1992 revision mandates that "the sacred mountain of the revolution"—Paektu-san—be added to the national emblem. It is to stand above the existing symbols: a hydroelectric power plant, the beaming light of a five-pointed red star, ovally framed ears of rice bound with a red band, and the inscription "Democratic People's Republic of Korea."

Organization of the Government

The Supreme People's Assembly

Although under the constitution the Supreme People's Assembly (SPA) is "the highest organ of state power," it is not influential and does not initiate legislation independently of other party and state organs. Invariably the legislative process is set in motion by executive bodies according to the predetermined policies of the party leadership. The assembly is not known to have ever criticized, modified, or rejected a bill or a measure placed before it, or to have proposed an alternative bill or measure.

The constitution provides for the SPA to be elected every five years by universal suffrage. Article 88 indicates that legislative power is exercised by the SPA and the Standing Committee of the SPA when the assembly is not in session. Elections to the Ninth Supreme People's Assembly were held in April 1990, with 687 deputies, or representatives, elected. The KWP approves a single list of candidates who stand for election without opposition. Deputies usually meet once a year in regular sessions in March or April, but since 1985 they have also met occasionally in extraordinary sessions in November or December. Sessions are convened by the assembly's Standing Committee, whose chairman as of 1992 was Yang Hyong-sop (also a full member of the KWP Central Committee and a vice chairman of the Committee for the Peaceful Reunification of the Fatherland). Assembly members are elected by the deputies, as are the chairman and vice chairmen. The assembly also has five committees: Bills, Budget, Foreign Affairs, Qualifications Screening, and Reunification Policy Deliberation.

Article 91 states that the assembly has the authority to adopt or amend the constitution, laws, and ordinances; formulate the basic principles of domestic and foreign policies; elect or recall the president of the state and other top officials of the government; approve the state economic plan and national budget; and decide whether to ratify or abrogate treaties and questions of war and peace. Matters deliberated are submitted by the president, the Central People's Committee, the assembly's Standing Committee, the State Administration Council (the cabinet), or individual deputies.

Assembly decisions are made by a simple majority and signified by a show of hands. Deputies, each representing a constituency of approximately 30,000 persons, are guaranteed inviolability and immunity from arrest. Between assembly sessions, the Standing Committee does legislative work; this body may also interpret and amend the laws and ordinances in force, conduct the election of deputies to the SPA, organize the election of deputies to local legislative bodies, conduct election of deputies to the SPA, convene sessions of the SPA and people's assessors or lay judges, and elect or recall judges of the Central Court.

The Executive Branch

The President and Vice Presidents

The president is the head of state and the head of government in his capacity as chairman of the Central People's Committee (CPC). The president is elected every four years by the SPA. The title "president" (*chusŏk*) was adopted in the 1972 constitution. Before 1972 an approximate equivalent of the presidency was the chairmanship of the Standing Committee of the SPA. The constitution has no provisions for removing, recalling, or impeaching the president, or for limiting the number of terms of service. On May 24, 1990, the SPA unanimously reelected Kim Il Sung to a fifth presidential term.

Presidential powers are stated only in generalities. The chief executive convenes and guides the State Administration Council as occasion demands. Under the 1972 constitution, he was also the supreme commander of the armed forces and chairman of the National Defense Commission—although Kim Il Sung appointed his son to the former position in December 1991 and to the latter position in April 1993 (see National Command Authority, ch. 5). The president's prior assent is required for all laws, decrees, decisions,

Supreme People's Assembly, P'yŏngyang
Hall inside the Supreme People's Assembly
Courtesy Tracy Woodward

and directives. The president's edicts command the force of law more authoritatively than any other legislation. The president promulgates the laws and ordinances of the SPA; the decisions of the Standing Committee of the SPA; and the laws, ordinances, and decisions of the CPC. The president also grants pardons, ratifies or abrogates treaties, and receives foreign envoys or requests their recall. No one serves in top government posts without the president's recommendation. Even the judiciary and the procurators are accountable to Kim Il Sung.

The constitution states that two vice presidents "assist" the president, but it does not elaborate a mode of succession. As of July 1992, Pak Sŏng-ch'ŏl (elected in 1977) and Yi Chong-ŏk (elected in 1984) were vice presidents of North Korea.

The Central People's Committee

The top executive decision-making body is the Central People's Committee (CPC) created under the 1972 constitution. Seven articles in the 1992 constitution relate to the CPC. The president of the DPRK is the head of the CPC; it is also composed of the vice presidents, the CPC secretary, and unspecified "members." The term is the same as that for the SPA. All CPC members are elected by the SPA and can be recalled by the assembly on presidential recommendation. Inasmuch as CPC members overlap with the top-ranking members of the party's Political Bureau, the CPC provides the highest visible institutional link between the government and the party and serves in effect as a de facto super-cabinet.

The CPC's formal powers are all-inclusive. Among its responsibilities are formulating domestic and foreign policies, directing the work of the State Administration Council and its local organs, directing the judiciary, ensuring the enforcement of the constitution and other laws, appointing or removing the vice premiers and cabinet members, establishing or changing administrative subdivisions or their boundaries, and ratifying or abolishing treaties signed with foreign countries. The CPC also may issue decrees, decisions, and instructions.

The CPC oversees nine commissions: economic policy, foreign policy, internal policy, justice and security, legislative, national defense, parliamentary group, state inspection, and state price fixing. The members of these commissions are appointed by the CPC. The National Defense Commission's vice chairmen (an unspecified number) are elected by the SPA on the recommendation of the president, who also is chairman of the commission.

The State Administration Council

Since 1972 the highest administrative arm of the government has been the State Administration Council. From 1948 to 1972, the cabinet was the highest level of the executive branch. The 1972 constitution changed the name and role of the cabinet. The newly named State Administration Council has a similar function to that of the cabinet, but is directed by the president and the CPC. The State Administration Council is composed of the premier (*chong-ri*), vice premiers (*bochong-ri*), ministers (*boojang*), committee chairmen, and other cabinet-level members of central agencies. Among its duties, the council is responsible for foreign affairs, national defense, public order and safety, economic and industrial affairs, general government operation, concluding treaties with foreign countries and conducting external affairs, and safeguarding the rights of the people. It also has the power to countermand decisions and directives issued by subordinate organs. The formulation of state economic development plans and measures for implementing them, the preparation of the state budget, and the handling of other monetary and fiscal matters also are under the council's jurisdiction.

As of mid-1993, the State Administration Council, headed by Premier Kang Song-san since December 1992, had ten vice premiers. Vice premiers often concurrently are ministers or chairpersons of cabinet-level commissions. Under the premier and vice premiers, there are ministries, commissions, and other bodies of the State Administration Council. Governmental responsibilities that require coordination and a close working relationship among two or more ministries are generally placed under a commission, whose chairman usually holds the title of vice premier.

The Judiciary

In the North Korean judicial process, both adjudicative and prosecuting bodies function as powerful weapons for the proletarian dictatorship. The constitution states that justice is administered by the central court, provincial- or special-city-level courts, the people's courts, or special courts.

The Central Court, the highest court of appeal, stands at the apex of the court system. As of July 1992, it had two associate chief judges, or vice presidents—Choe Yong-song and Hyon Hong-sam. Pang Hak Se, who died in July 1992, had been chief judge, or president, since 1972. In the case of special cities directly under central authority, provincial or municipal courts serve as the courts of first instance for civil and criminal cases at the intermediate level. At

179

the lowest level are the people's courts, established in ordinary cities, counties, and urban districts. Special courts exist for the armed forces and for railroad workers. The military courts have jurisdiction over all crimes committed by members of the armed forces or security organs of the Ministry of Public Security. The railroad courts have jurisdiction over criminal cases involving rail and water transport workers. In addition, the Korean Maritime Arbitration Committee adjudicates maritime legal affairs.

Judges and people's assessors, or lay judges, are elected by the organs of state power at their corresponding levels, those of the Central Court by the SPA's Standing Committee, and those of the lower courts by the provincial- and county-level people's assemblies. Neither legal education nor practical legal experience is required for judgeship. In addition to administering justice based on criminal and civil codes, the courts are in charge of political indoctrination through "reeducation." The issue of punishment is not expressly stated in the constitution or the criminal code.

The collective interests of the workers, peasants, soldiers, and working intellectuals are protected by a parallel hierarchy of organs controlled at the top by the Central Procurator's Office. This office acts as the state's prosecutor and checks on the activities of all public organs and citizens to ensure their compliance with the laws and their "active struggle against all lawbreakers." Its authority extends to the courts, the decisions of which (including those of the Central Court) are subject to routine scrutiny. A judgment of the Central Court may be appealed to the plenary session of the Central Court, of which the state's chief prosecutor is a statutory member.

The chief prosecutor, known as the procurator general, is appointed by and accountable in theory, though not in fact, to the SPA. As of mid-1993, the procurator general was Yi Yong-sŏp. There are three deputy procurators general.

Local Government

There are three levels of local government: province (*do*) (see Glossary) and special province-level municipalities (*chikalsi*, or *jik-halsi*) (see Glossary); ordinary cities (*si*), urban districts (*kuyŏk*), and counties (*gun*, or *kun*); and traditional villages (*ri*, or *ni*). Towns and townships (*myŏn*) no longer functioned as administrative units in North Korea after the Korean War, but still exist in South Korea. At the village level, administrative and economic matters are the responsibility of the chairman of the cooperative farm management committee in each village.

As of mid-1993, there were nine provinces: Changang, North Hamgyŏng and South Hamgyŏng, North Hwanghae and South

Hwanghae, Kangwŏn, North P'yŏngan and South P'yŏngan, and Yanggang; three special provincial-level cities: Kaesŏng, Namp'o, and P'yŏngyang, municipalities under central authority; seventeen ordinary cities under provincial authority; thirty-six urban districts; over 200 counties; and some 4,000 villages (see fig. 9). Among these divisions, the counties serve as the intermediate administrative link between provincial authorities and the grass-roots-level village organizations. Local organs at the county level provide other forms of guidance to such basic units as blocks and workers' districts (*nodongja-ku*).

Three types of local organs elect local officials to carry out centrally planned policies and programs: KWP local committees, local people's assemblies, and local administrative committees (such as local administration, economic guidance, and rural economic committees). These committees are local extensions of the three higher bodies at the national level: the Supreme People's Assembly, the Central People's Committee, and the State Administration Council.

The local people's assemblies, established at all administrative levels, perform the same symbolic functions as the SPA. They provide a façade of popular support and involvement and serve as a vehicle through which loyal and meritorious local inhabitants are given visible recognition as deputies to the assemblies. The assemblies meet once or twice a year for only a few days at each session. Their duties are to approve the plan for local economic development and the local budget; to elect the officers of other local bodies, including the judges and people's assessors of the courts within their jurisdictions; and to review the decisions and directives issued by local organs at their corresponding and lower levels. The local people's assemblies have no standing committees. Between regular sessions, their duties are performed by the local people's committees, whose members are elected by assemblies at corresponding levels and are responsible both to the assemblies and to the local people's committees at higher levels.

The officers and members of the people's committees are influential locally as party functionaries and as senior administrative cadres. These committees can convene the people's assemblies; prepare for the election of deputies to the local assemblies; implement the decisions of the assemblies at the corresponding level and those of the people's committees at higher levels; and control and supervise the work of administrative bodies, enterprises, and social and cooperative organizations in their respective jurisdictions.

The day-to-day affairs of local communities are handled by the local administrative committees. The chairman, vice chairmen,

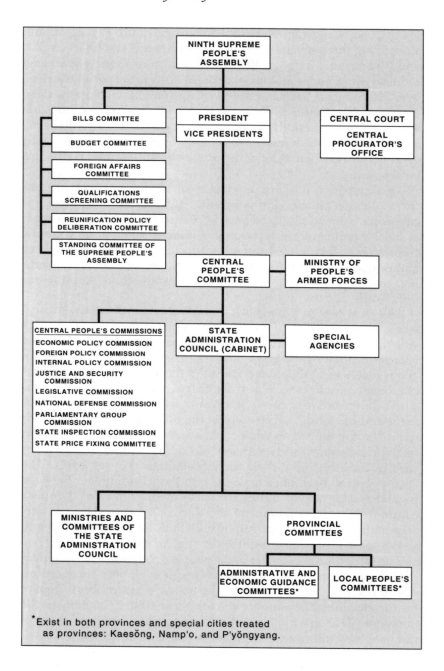

Figure 9. Structure of the Government, 1993

secretary, and members of these bodies are elected by the local people's committees at the corresponding levels.

Political Ideology: The Role of *Chuch'e*

Chuch'e ideology is the basic cornerstone of party construction, party works, and government operations. *Chuch'e* is sanctified as the essence of what has been officially called Kim Il Sung Chuui (Kim Il Sung-ism) since April 1974. *Chuch'e* is also claimed as "the present-day Marxism-Leninism." North Korean leaders advocate *chuch'e* ideology as the only correct guiding ideology in their ongoing revolutionary movement.

Chuch'e also is referred to as "the unitary ideology" or as "the monolithic ideology of the Party." It is inseparable from and, for all intents and purposes, synonymous with Kim Il Sung's leadership and was said to have been "created" or "fathered" by the "great leader" as an original "encyclopedic thought which provides a complete answer to any question that arises in the struggle for national liberation and class emancipation, in the building of socialism and communism." *Chuch'e* is viewed as the embodiment of revealed truth attesting to the wisdom of Kim's leadership as exemplified in countless speeches and "on-the-spot guidance."

Chuch'e was proclaimed in December 1955, when Kim underlined the critical need for a Korea-centered revolution rather than one designed to benefit, in his words, "another country." *Chuch'e* is designed to inspire national pride and identity and mold national consciousness into a potentially powerful focus for internal solidarity centered on Kim and the KWP.

According to Kim, *chuch'e* means "the independent stance of rejecting dependence on others and of using one's own powers, believing in one's own strength and displaying the revolutionary spirit of self-reliance." *Chuch'e* is an ideology geared to address North Korea's contemporary goals—an independent foreign policy, a self-sufficient economy, and a self-reliant defense posture. Kim Il Sung's enunciation of *chuch'e* in 1955 was aimed at developing a monolithic and effective system of authority under his exclusive leadership. The invocation of *chuch'e* was a psychological tool with which to stigmatize the foreign-oriented dissenters and remove them from the center of power. Targeted for elimination were groups of pro-Soviet and pro-Chinese anti-Kim dissenters.

Chuch'e did not become a prominent ideology overnight. During the first ten years of North Korea's existence, Marxism-Leninism was accepted unquestioningly as the only source of doctrinal authority. Nationalism was toned down in deference to the country's connections to the Soviet Union and China. In the mid-1950s, however, *chuch'e* was presented as a "creative" application of Marxism-Leninism. In his attempt to establish an interrelationship between Marxism-Leninism and *chuch'e,* Kim contended that although Marxism-Leninism was valid as the fundamental law of revolution, it needed an authoritative interpreter to define a new set of practical ideological guidelines appropriate to the revolutionary environment in North Korea.

Kim's practical ideology was given a test of relevancy through the mid-1960s. In the late 1950s, Kim was able to mobilize internal support when he purged pro-Soviet and pro-Chinese dissenters from party ranks. During the first half of the 1960s, Kim faced an even more formidable challenge when he had to weather a series of tense situations that had potentially adverse implications for North Korea's economic development and national security. Among these were a sharp decrease in aid from the Soviet Union and China; discord between the Soviet Union and China and its disquieting implications for North Korea's confrontation with the United States and South Korea; P'yŏngyang's disagreements with Moscow and apprehensions about the reliability of the Soviet Union as an ally; and the rise of an authoritarian regime in Seoul under former General Park Chung Hee (1961–79).

These developments emphasized the need for self-reliance—the need to rely on domestic resources, heighten vigilance against possible external challenges, and strengthen domestic political solidarity. Sacrifice, austerity, unity, and patriotism became dominant themes in the party's efforts to instill in the people the importance of *chuch'e* and collective discipline. By the mid-1960s, however, North Korea could afford to relax somewhat; its strained relations with the Soviet Union had eased, as reflected in part by Moscow's decision to rush economic and military assistance to P'yŏngyang.

Beginning in mid-1965, *chuch'e* was presented as the essence of Kim Il Sung's leadership and of party lines and policies for every conceivable revolutionary situation. Kim's past leadership record was put forward as the "guide and compass" for the present and future and as a source of strength sufficient to propel the faithful through any adversity.

Nonetheless, the linkage of *chuch'e* to Marxism-Leninism remains a creed of the party. The April 1972 issue of *Kŭlloja* (The Worker) still referred to the KWP as "a Marxist-Leninist Party"; the journal pointed out that "the only valid policy for Korean Communists is Marxism-Leninism" and called for "its creative application to our realities."

Since 1974 it has become increasingly evident, however, that the emphasis is on the glorification of *chuch'e* as "the only scientific revolutionary thought representing our era of Juche and communist future and the most effective revolutionary theoretical structure that leads to the future of communist society along the surest shortcut.'' This new emphasis was based on the contention that a different historical era, with its unique sociopolitical circumstances, requires an appropriately unique revolutionary ideology. Accordingly, Marxism and Leninism were valid doctrines in their own times, but had outlived their usefulness in the era of *chuch'e,* which prophesies the downfall of imperialism and the worldwide victory of socialism and communism.

As the years have passed, references to Marxism-Leninism in party literature have steadily decreased. By 1980 the terms *Marxism* and *Leninism* had all but disappeared from the pages of *Kŭlloja.* An unsigned article in the March 1980 *Kŭlloja* proclaimed, ''Within the Party none but the leader Kim Il Sung's revolutionary thought, the *chuch'e* ideology, prevails and there is no room for any hodge-podge thought contrary to it.'' The report Kim Il Sung presented to the Sixth Party Congress in October 1980 did not contain a single reference to Marxism-Leninism, in marked contrast to his report to the Fifth Party Congress in November 1970. In the 1980 report, Kim declared: ''The whole party is rallied rock-firm around its Central Committee and knit together in ideology and purpose on the basis of the *chuch'e* idea. The Party has no room for any other idea than the *chuch'e* idea, and no force can ever break its unity and cohesion based on this idea.''

Chuch'e is instrumental in providing a consistent and unifying framework for commitment and action in the North Korean political arena. It offers an underpinning for the party's incessant demand for spartan austerity, sacrifice, discipline, and dedication. Since the mid-1970s, however, it appears that *chuch'e* has become glorified as an end in itself.

In his annual New Year's message on January 1, 1992, Kim Il Sung emphasized the invincibility of *chuch'e* ideology: ''I take great pride in and highly appreciate the fact that our people have overcome the ordeals of history and displayed to the full the heroic mettle of the revolutionary people and the indomitable spirit of *chuch'e* Korea, firmly united behind the party . . . No difficulty is insurmountable nor is any fortress impregnable for us when our party leads the people with the ever-victorious *chuch'e*-oriented strategy and tactics and when all the people turn out as one under the party's leadership.''

Party Leadership and Elite Recruitment

The party congress, the highest KWP organ, meets infrequently.

185

As of mid-1993, the most recently held congress was the Sixth Party Congress of October 1980. The official agent of the party congress is the Central Committee. As of July 1991, the Sixth Party Congress Central Committee had 329 members: 180 full members and 149 alternate members. Nearly 40 percent of these members, 131 members, are first-termers. Among the 329 members, the technocrats—economists, managers, and technicians—are the most numerous.

Influence and prestige within the party power structure are directly associated with the rank order in which the members of the Central Committee are listed. Key posts in party, government, and economic organs are assigned; higher-ranking Central Committee members also are found in the armed forces, educational and cultural institutions, and other social and mass organizations. Many leaders concurrently hold multiple positions within the party, the government, and the military.

The Central Committee holds a plenum, or plenary session, at least once every six months to discuss major issues. The plenum also elects the general secretary, members of the Political Bureau (called the Political Committee until October 1980), and its Standing Committee, or Presidium, which was established in October 1980.

In early 1981, the Political Bureau had thirty-four members: nineteen regular members and fifteen alternate members. This figure was a substantial increase in membership from the Fifth Party Congress, when there were eleven regular members and five alternate members. As of 1992, however, the Political Bureau had only twenty-four members—fourteen regular members and ten alternate members—because a number of the members either had died or had stepped down. The inner circle of powerful leaders within the Political Bureau include the president, premier, vice premiers, and minister of the people's armed forces.

Several central organizations are subordinate to the Political Bureau Presidium. One of the most important executive organs is the Secretariat of the Central Committee, led by General Secretary Kim Il Sung and eleven other secretaries as of mid-1992. Each secretary is in charge of one or more departmental party functions. Other key bodies include the Central Military Commission headed by Kim Il Sung; the Central Auditing Committee, the fiscal watchdog of the party; and the Central Inspection Committee, which enforces party discipline and acts as a trial and appeals board for disciplinary cases.

The various departments of the Secretariat of the Central Committee depend for implementation of party policies and directives on the party committees in the provincial- and county-level

Kim Il Sung statue, P'yŏngyang
Courtesy Tracy Woodward

administrative divisions and in organizations where there are more than 100 party members—for example, major enterprises, factories, government offices, military units, and schools. In the countryside, village party committees are formed with a minimum of fifty party members. The basic party units are cells to which all party members belong and through which they participate in party organizational activities. Attendance at cell meetings and party study sessions, held at least once a week, is mandatory.

Party Members

The KWP claimed a membership of more than 3 million persons as of 1988, a significant increase from the 2 million members announced in 1976. This increase may have been a result of the active mobilization drive for the Three Revolution Team Movement.

The Korean Workers' Party has three constituencies: industrial workers, peasants, and intellectuals, that is, office workers. Since 1948 industrial workers have constituted the largest percentage of party members, followed by peasants and intellectuals. Beginning in the 1970s, when North Korea's population reached the 50 percent urban mark, the composition of the groups belonging to the party changed. More people working in state-owned enterprises became party members and the number of members working in agricultural cooperatives decreased.

Party Cadres

The recruitment and training of party cadres (*kanbu*) has long been the primary concern of party leadership. Party cadres are those officials placed in key positions in party organizations, ranging from the Political Bureau to the village party committees; in government agencies; in economic enterprises; in military and internal security units; in educational institutions; and in mass organizations. The duties of cadres are to educate and lead party and nonparty members of society and to ensure that party policies and directives are carried out faithfully. The party penetrates all aspects of life. Associations and guidance committees exist at all levels of society, with a local party cadre serving as a key member of each committee.

Some cadres are concerned principally with ideological matters, whereas others are expected both to be ideologically prepared and to give guidance to the technical or managerial activities of the state. Regardless of specialization, all party cadres are expected to devote two hours a day to the study of *chuch'e* ideology and Kim Il Sung's policies and instruction.

The party has a number of schools for cadre training. At the national level, the most prestigious school is the Kim Il Sung Higher Party School, directly under the Central Committee. Below the national level are communist colleges established in each province for the education of county-level cadres. Village-level cadres are sent to county training schools.

The rules governing cadre selection have undergone subtle changes in emphasis. Through the early 1970s, "good class origin," individual ability, and ideological posture were given more or less equal consideration in the appointment of cadres. Since the mid-1970s, however, the doctrinally ordained "class principle" has been downgraded on the assumption that the actual social or class status of people should not be judged on the basis of their past family backgrounds but on their "present class preparation and mental attitudes." The party increasingly stresses individual merit and "absolute" loyalty as the criteria for acceptance into the elite status of cadre. Merit and competence have come to mean "a knowledge of the economy and technology." Such knowledge is considered crucial because, as Kim Il Sung stressed in July 1974, "Party organizational work should be intimately linked to economic work and intraparty work should be conducted to ensure success in socialist construction and backup economic work."

An equally important, if not more important criterion for cadre selection is political loyalty inasmuch as not all cadres of correct class origin nor all highly competent cadres are expected to pass the rigorous tests of party life. These tests entail absolute loyalty to Kim Il Sung and the party, thorough familiarity with *chuch'e* ideology, refusal to temporize in the face of adversity, and a readiness to respond to the party's call under any conditions and at all times.

Although information on the composition of cadre membership was limited as of mid-1993, the number of cadres of nonworker and nonpeasant origin has steadily increased. These cadres generally are classified as "working intellectuals" engaged in occupations ranging from party and government activities to educational, technical, and artistic pursuits. Another notable trend is the infusion of younger, better educated cadres into the party ranks. An accent on youth and innovation was very much in evidence after 1973 when Kim Jong Il assumed the leading role in the Three Revolution Team Movement.

The Ruling Elite

Persons with at least one major position in leading party, government, and military organs are considered the ruling elite. This group includes all political leaders who are, at a given time, directly involved in the preparation of major policy decisions and who participate in the inner circle of policy making. The ruling elite include Political Bureau members and secretaries of the KWP, Central People's Committee members, members of the State Administration Council, and members of the Central Military Commission and the National Defense Commission. Because overlapping membership is common in public office, top-ranking office holders number less than 100. In any event, those having the most influential voice in policy formulation are members of the Political Bureau Presidium.

Top leaders share a number of common social characteristics. They belong to the same generation; the average age of the party's top fifty leaders was about sixty-eight years in 1990. By the end of 1989, aging members of the anti-Japanese partisan group accounted for 24 percent of the Political Bureau's full members. There is no clear evidence of regional underrepresentation. Nonetheless, many Hamgyŏng natives are included in the inner circle—for example, O Chin-u, Pak Sŏng-ch'ŏl, Kim Yong-nam, and Kye Ung-t'ae. The latter is a member of the Secretariat of the Central Committee and secretary in charge of economics.

Leadership Succession

Beginning in the fall of 1975, North Koreans used the term *party center* to refer to Kim Jong Il. Kim Jong Il is reported to have concentrated a great deal of effort on the performing arts, and many artists began to use the term when referring to Kim in articles in *Kŭlloja*. However, for a few years after its initial introduction the term was used only infrequently because Kim Il Sung's efforts to promote his son met some resistance. Many of Kim Jong Il's opponents have been purged by Kim Il Sung, however, and neither Kim faces any active opposition.

Kim Il Sung was awarded the rank of generalissimo (*taewŏnsu*) on April 13, 1992. On April 20, 1992, Kim Jong Il, as supreme commander of the armed forces, was given the title marshal (*wŏnsu*) of the DPRK. Kim Il Sung was the president and chairman of the National Defense Commission with command and control of the armed forces until Kim Jong Il assumed the latter position in April 1993. O Chin-u also became a marshal.

There are many scenarios for leadership succession. Some of the prospects are based on a common postulation that Kim Il Sung's succession scheme will take at least a few years because of the decades-long preparation of a succession plan. South Korean scholar Yang Sung Chul labels this "positive skepticism" and calls short-term failure, such as a coup d'état or a revolution, "negative skepticism." "Negative skepticism" is not to be dismissed, however, because of Kim Jong Il's weaknesses—his lack of charisma, poor international recognition, and unknown governing skills—as well as the sagging domestic economy and external factors such as inter-Korean, Japan-DPRK, and United States-DPRK relations (see Foreign Policy, this ch.).

Kim Jong Il's appointment as commander of the Korean People's Army suggests that the succession issue finally has been solved because the military was once considered Kim's weak point; he already has full control of the state and the economic administration. Kim Jong Il also manages political affairs and KWP businesses as a primary authority and handles symbolic roles such as meeting with foreign leaders and appearing at national celebrations.

In addition, Kim Jong Il plays a prominent role in the KWP propaganda machine—mass media, literature, and art. Many literary and art works—including films, operas, and dramas—are produced under the revolutionary tradition of the KWP and Kim's guidance. Kim uses popular culture to broaden his public image and gain popular support.

A flag of Kim Jong Il is displayed on a truck being driven through P'yŏngyang.
Courtesy Tracy Woodward

Kim Jong Il has tried to expedite economic growth and productivity using the Three Revolution Team Movement and the Three Revolution Red Flag Movement. Both movements are designed to inspire the broad masses into actively participating in the Three Revolutions. At the Fifth Party Congress, Kim Il Sung emphasized the necessity of pressing ahead more vigorously with the three revolutions to consolidate the socialist system. In response, Kim Jong Il developed the follow-up slogan, "Let us meet the requirements of the *chuch'e* in ideology, technology and culture." Most units forged ahead with "ideological education" to teach the party members and other workers to become revolutionaries of the *chuch'e* idea. In many spheres of the national economy, productivity also is expected to increase as a result of the technology emphasis of the campaigns. In addition, the "cultural revolution" addresses promoting literacy and cultural identity.

Chuch'e, instrumental in providing a consistent and unifying framework for commitment and action in the political arena, offers a foundation for the party's incessant demand for spartan austerity, sacrifice, discipline, and dedication. It has not yet been determined, however, whether *chuch'e* is an asset or liability for Kim. Nonetheless, Kim is likely to continue to emphasize *chuch'e* as the only satisfactory answer to all challenging questions in North Korea, particularly because he attributes the collapse of communism in the Soviet Union and East European countries to their lack of *chuch'e* ideology.

Graduates of the first class of the Man'gyŏngdae Revolutionary Institute, established in 1947, support Kim Jong Il's power base. Many of these graduates occupy key positions in government and the military. For example, O Guk-nyol and General Paek Haknim—the latter, the minister of public security—are members of the Central Military Commission, KWP Central Committee, and the SPA; Kim Hwan, the former minister of chemical industry and a vice premier as of mid-1993, is a member of both the KWP Central Committee and the SPA; and Kim Yong-sun, a candidate member of the Politburo, is the director of the International Affairs Department, KWP Central Committee.

Mass Organizations

All mass organizations are guided and controlled by the party. A number of political and social organizations appear concerned with the promotion of special interest groups but actually serve as auxiliaries to the party. Many of these organizations were founded in the early years of the KWP to serve as vehicles for the party's efforts to penetrate a broader cross section of the population.

Mass organizations have another important function: to create the impression that there are noncommunist social, political, cultural, and professional groups that can work with their South Korean counterparts toward national reunification. Most of these organizations were established to develop a unified strategy in dealing with the ruling establishment of South Korea and other foreign countries and organizations. As of July 1992, these included the Korean Social Democratic Party headed by Yi Kye-paek; the Chondoist Chongu Party headed by Chong Sin-hyok, the Socialist Working Youth League (SWYL) headed by Ch'oe Yong-hae; the Committee for the Peaceful Reunification of the Fatherland headed by Yun Ki-pok; the Korean Democratic Women's Union headed by Kim Il Sung's wife, Kim Song-ae; the Korean National Peace Committee headed by Chong Chun-ki; the Korean Students Committee headed by Mun Kyong-tok; the General Federation of Trade Unions headed by Han Ki-chang; and many others. In the early 1990s, the Committee for the Peaceful Reunification of the Fatherland was actively involved in the two Koreas' reconciliation talks.

Among auxiliary organizations, one frequently covered in the media is the SWYL. Directly under the party Central Committee, it is the only mass organization expressly mentioned in the charter of the KWP. The league is the party's most important ideological and organizational training ground, with branches and cells wherever there are regular party organizations. Youth league cells exist in the army, factories, cooperative farms, schools, cultural institutions, and government agencies. The organization is hailed as a "militant reserve" of the party; its members are described as heirs to the revolution, reliable reserves, and active assistants of the party. Youths between the ages of fifteen and twenty-six are eligible to join the league regardless of other organizational affiliations, provided they meet requirements similar to those for party membership. The junior version of the youth league is the Young Pioneer Corps, open to children between the ages of nine and fifteen. The Students' and Children's Palace in P'yŏngyang is maintained by the SWYL for the extracurricular activities of Young Pioneer Corps members; these activities include study sessions in *chuch'e* ideology as well as other subjects taught in the primary and secondary schools.

The principal vehicle for P'yŏngyang's united front strategy in dealing with South Korea and foreign counterparts is the Democratic Front for the Reunification of the Fatherland (DFRF), popularly known as the Fatherland Front. The Fatherland Front actually is an umbrella for various other organizations and thus ostensibly is a nonpolitical, nongovernmental organization.

Choch'ongryŏn (General Association of Korean Residents in Japan) (see Glossary), is one of the best known of the foreign auxiliary organizations. Its mission is to enlist the allegiance of the more than 600,000 Korean residents in Japan. At least a third of these residents, who also are assiduously courted by Seoul, are considered supporters of P'yŏngyang. The remaining two-thirds of the members are divided into South Korean loyalists and neutralists. Those who are friendly toward North Korea are regarded by P'yŏngyang as its citizens and are educated at Korean schools in Japan that are financially subsidized by North Korea. These Koreans are expected to work for the North Korean cause either in Japan or as returnees to North Korea.

The activities of these mass organizations are occasionally reported in the news. However, it is difficult to ascertain what these organizations actually do. Organizations such as the Korean Social Democratic Party and the Chondoist Chongu Party publicize only the officially published names of their leaders and do not report anything about their membership or activities.

The Media

Although Article 53 of the constitution states that North Korean citizens have freedom of speech, press, assembly, association, and demonstration, such activities are permitted only in support of government and KWP objectives. Other articles of the constitution require citizens to follow the socialist norms of life; for example, a collective spirit takes precedence over individual political or civil liberties.

Domestic media censorship is strictly enforced, and deviation from the official government line is not tolerated. The regime prohibits listening to foreign media broadcasts, and violators are reportedly subject to severe punishment. Senior party cadres, however, have good access to the foreign media. No external media are allowed free access to North Korea, but an agreement to share in Japan's telecommunications satellites was reached in September 1990.

Newspapers, broadcasting, and other mass media are major vehicles for information dissemination and political propaganda. Although most urban households have radios and some have television sets, neither radios nor televisions can be tuned to anything other than official programming. Only some 10 percent of the radios and 30 percent of the televisions are in private households (see Transportation and Communications, ch. 3). Government control extends to artistic and academic circles, and visitors report that the primary function of plays, movies, books, and the performing arts is to contribute to the cult of personality surrounding Kim Il Sung.

The media are government controlled. As of mid-1993, there were eleven television stations, approximately two dozen AM stations, ten FM stations, eight domestic shortwave stations, and a powerful international shortwave station. The latter broadcast in English, French, Spanish, German, and several Asian languages. Korean Central Broadcasting Station and P'yŏngyang Broadcasting Station (Radio P'yŏngyang) are the central radio stations; there are also several local stations and stations for overseas broadcasts.

A number of newspapers are published. *Nodong simmun* (Workers' Daily), the organ of the party Central Committee, claimed a circulation of approximately 1.5 million as of 1988. *Kŭlloja* (The Worker), the theoretical organ of the party Central Committee, claimed a circulation of about 300,000 readers. *Minju Chosŏn* (Democratic Korea) is the government newspaper, and *Nodong chŏngnyŏn* (Working Youth) is the newspaper of the SWYL. There also are specialized newspapers for teachers, the army, and railway workers.

The Korean Central News Agency (Chosŏn Chungyang Tŏngsinsa—KCNA) is the primary agency for gathering and disseminating news. KCNA publishes the daily paper *Korean Central News* (Chosŏn Chungyang T'ongsin), *Photographic News* (Sajin T'ongsin), and the *Korean Central Yearbook* (Chosŏn Chungyang Yŏnbo). KCNA issues daily press releases in English, Russian, French, and Spanish; newscasts in these languages are beamed overseas. The Foreign Languages Press Group issues the monthly magazine *Korea Today* and the weekly newspaper the *P'yŏngyang Times* published in English, Spanish, and French.

Foreign Policy

North Korea's foreign relations are shaped by a mixture of historical, nationalistic, ideological, and pragmatic considerations. The territorial division of the peninsula looms large in the political thinking of North Korean leaders and is a driving force in their management of internal and external affairs. Over the centuries, unequal relations, foreign depredation, dependence on foreigners for assorted favors, and the emulation of foreign cultures and institutions have been less the exception than the rule in Korea's relationship with the outside world. These patterns have given rise to the widely shared assumption among Koreans that their capacity to control their national destiny is limited by geopolitical constraints.

Inter-Korean Affairs

The reunification of the two Koreas is seen as a difficult goal. Although P'yŏngyang and Seoul agreed in principle in 1972 that unification should be achieved peacefully and without foreign interference, they continued to differ substantially on the practical methods of attaining reunification; this area of disagreement has not narrowed in subsequent years.

North Korea's goal of unification remains constant, but tactics have changed depending on the perception of opportunities and limitations implicit in shifting domestic and external situations. From the beginning, North Korea has insisted that an inter-Korean political formula should be based on parity or coequality, rather than population. Because South Korea has more than twice the population of North Korea, a supreme Korean council set up according to a one-person, one-vote formula will give South Korea a commanding position in that type of relationship. Another constant is P'yŏngyang's insistence that the Korean question be settled as an internal Korean affair without foreign interference.

P'yŏngyang's position that unification should be achieved by peaceful means was belied by circumstances surrounding the outbreak of the Korean War in 1950 and by subsequent infiltrations, the digging of tunnels, and other incidents. North Korea's contention that the conflict was started by South Korea and the United States failed to impress South Korea's population. The war, in effect, reinforced the obvious ideological and systemic incompatibilities that were in place at the time of the division of the peninsula in 1945. At the Geneva Conference in mid-1954, North Korea proposed the formation of an all-Korean commission and a single Korean legislature through elections; the withdrawal of all foreign troops from the Korean Peninsula; and the formal declaration by outside powers of the need for peaceful development and unification in Korea. P'yŏngyang also proposed that the armies of both countries be reduced to 100,000 persons each within a year, that neither side enter into any military alliance, and that measures be taken to facilitate economic and cultural exchanges. Kim Il Sung urged a mutual reduction of armed forces and a sharp cutback in the "heavy burden of military expenditure in South Korea," recognizing that any arms buildup could lead to a renewed arms race on the Korean Peninsula. Kim also called on "South Korean authorities, political parties, social organizations, and individual personages" to have their representatives meet their northern counterparts in P'yŏngyang, Seoul, or P'anmunjŏm to start negotiations on all "burning issues awaiting urgent solution."

In mid-1969 Kim signaled the resumption of peaceful gestures to South Korea. In October 1969, P'yŏngyang announced that the policy of peaceful unification would be renewed, adding that this option had not been stressed "in the last few years" because of alleged war policies being pursued by the United States and South Korea. Beginning in August 1970, Seoul proposed that the two Koreas open "a bona fide competition" to see which side could better satisfy the various needs of the Korean people. This development ended P'yŏngyang's previous monopoly on the rhetoric of neighborly intentions and peaceful unification.

Inter-Korean affairs became more complex in 1970 and 1971, in part because of the United States decision to withdraw some of its troops from South Korea and because of moves by the United States and China to improve their relations. In August 1971, amid signs of a thaw in the Cold War and an uncertain international environment, the Red Cross societies of Seoul and P'yŏngyang agreed to open talks aimed at the eventual reunion of dispersed families. These high-level talks—between Kim Il Sung's brother and the chief of the South Korean Central Intelligence Agency, were held alternately in the two capitals and paralleled behind-the-scenes contacts to initiate political negotiations, reportedly at South

Korea's suggestion. The talks continued to evolve and resulted in a joint communiqué issued on July 4, 1972, in which the two countries agreed to abide by three principles of unification. As such, the two Koreas agreed to work toward reunifying the country independently and without foreign interference; transcending differences in ideology and political systems; and unifying the country peacefully without the use of armed force.

The communiqué also contained an accord designed to ease tensions and foster mutual trust by instructing the two countries to refrain from slandering and defaming each other, expediting the Red Cross talks, installing a hot line between P'yŏngyang and Seoul, and establishing a South-North Coordinating Committee (SNCC) as the machinery for substantive negotiations and for implementing the points of the agreement. The SNCC met three times. The first and third meetings were held in Seoul from November 30 to December 2, 1972, and June 12–14, 1973, respectively; the second meeting was held in P'yŏngyang, March 14–16, 1973. At the second meeting, the committee agreed to set up five subcommittees—political, military, foreign, economic, and cultural affairs—under joint direction. It was stipulated however, that subcommittees would be formed only when progress had been made vis-à-vis SNCC dialogue.

By June 1973, inter-Korean dialogue had become deadlocked. The fourth meeting was scheduled for August 28, 1973, in P'yŏngyang, but North Korea declined to convene it, making it official that it was no longer interested in participating in SNCC meetings. No significant agreement has been reached through the SNCC mechanism.

It quickly became obvious to both sides that they have fundamentally divergent approaches. North Korea's position focuses on three major themes: that the inter-Korean armed confrontation must first be ended; that North Korea's transitional scheme of coexistence called "confederation" be recognized as a practical necessity; and that a one-Korea policy should be pursued under all circumstances. P'yŏngyang seeks to settle military questions first, proposing cessation of the military buildup and the withdrawal of all foreign troops from South Korea. South Korea's position is one of peaceful coexistence based on "peace first, unification later." Seoul seeks recognition of the political systems of the two Koreas, noninterference in each side's internal affairs, and the promotion of mutual economic cooperation. South Korean president Park Chung Hee stressed the importance of preserving peace at all costs, specifying that each side refrain from invading the other or interfering in the other's affairs.

The contrast in positions is especially evident in international relations. South Korea suggested that both Koreas become members of the United Nations (UN) if it were the wish of the majority of UN members and if membership would not impede unification. In reaffirming peace and good-neighborliness as the basis of its foreign policy, Seoul declared its readiness to establish formal relations even with those countries whose ideologies and social institutions were different from South Korea's. In an obvious allusion to communist states, Seoul called on these countries to reciprocate by opening their doors.

North Korea began to urge the United States to refrain from obstructing the dialogue and from giving military aid to South Korea. In March 1974, P'yŏngyang proposed direct negotiations to Washington on the question of replacing the "outdated" Korean armistice agreement with a peace agreement. Relations between North Korea and South Korea had, by 1975, become increasingly complicated because of the ripple effect created by the fall of the government in Saigon. Following Vietnam's reunification in mid-1975, the Nixon administration reduced the United States troop level in South Korea by about one-third. This move, in conjunction with Nixon's opening to China, worried South Korea.

Leaders in both P'yŏngyang and Seoul talked increasingly about the dangers of renewed military conflict on the Korean Peninsula. North Korea called on South Koreans to overthrow President Park's government and reiterated its support for what it called a "massive popular struggle for independence and democracy" in South Korea. In South Korea, the cry of "threat from the North" became more shrill after Vietnam's reunification. In August 1976, against the backdrop of escalating tensions along the Demilitarized Zone (DMZ—see Glossary), the telephone hot line that had linked P'yŏngyang and Seoul ceased operations and remained unused until February 1980.

In the late 1970s, North Korea and South Korea attempted to revive their dialogue. In January 1979, North Korea agreed to South Korea's proposal to resume talks unconditionally, but preliminary talks held in February and March failed to narrow the differences. North Korea maintained that the talks should be within the framework of a "whole-nation congress" composed of political and social groups from both sides. South Korea countered that the talks should be on a government-to-government basis without participation of nongovernmental mass organizations.

In February 1980, preparatory talks got under way at P'anmunjŏm in the DMZ. Through August 1980, the two sides met ten times and agreed on several minor procedural and technical points, even though they were unable to decide on an agenda for the premiers' conference or on an interpretation of such terms as "collaboration," "unity," and "peaceful reunification." Another impediment was disagreement on whether the premiers' talks should be treated as part of broader North-South contacts involving various mass organizations—as North Korea contends—or whether the talks should be on a more manageable government-to-government basis—as South Korea demands. On September 24, 1980, two days before the eleventh scheduled meeting, North Korea suspended the talks, citing "the South Korean military fascist" policy of seeking confrontation and division. On September 25, P'yŏngyang also once again suspended operation of the telephone hot line. In October 1980, at the Sixth Party Congress, Kim Il Sung proposed the establishment of the Democratic Confederal Republic of Koryŏ, a system of unification based on mutual convenience and toleration. According to the proposal, a single unified state would be founded on the principle of coexistence, leaving the two systems intact and federating the two governments. The Democratic Confederal Republic of Koryŏ, so named after a unified state that previously existed in Korea (918–1392), is viewed by North Korea as "the most realistic way of national reunification." A supreme national assembly with an equal number of representatives from north and south and an appropriate number of representatives of overseas Koreans would be formed, with a confederal standing committee to "guide the regional government of the north and the south and to administer all the affairs of the confederal state." The regional governments of the north and south would have independent policies—within limits—consistent with the fundamental interests and demands of the whole nation and strive to narrow their differences in all areas.

The proposal provided that the supreme national confederal assembly and the confederal standing committee—its permanent organ and the de facto central government—would be the unified government of the confederal state and, as such, would be responsible for discussing and deciding domestic and foreign affairs, matters of national defense, and other matters of common concern related to the interests of the whole country and nation. Further, the coordinated development of the country and nation should be promoted. The confederal government would be neutral and nonaligned. South Korea rejected the confederation as another propaganda ploy.

No significant dialogue occurred between the two countries until the middle of 1984, when South Korea suffered a devastating flood. North Korea proposed to send relief goods to flood victims in South Korea; the offer was accepted. This occasion provided the momentum for both sides to resume their suspended dialogue. In 1985 the two countries exchanged performing arts groups, and ninety-two members of separated families met. In January 1986, however, North Korea once again suddenly cut off all talks with South Korea, blaming ''Team Spirit,'' the annual United States-South Korean joint military exercise.

After the inauguration of South Korean president Roh Tae Woo in 1988, a more vigorous dialogue commenced between Seoul and P'yŏngyang. Nordpolitik (see Glossary), South Korea's efforts since 1984 to expand ties with the former communist bloc, and the slowing pace of North Korea's economic development have contributed to a basic change in P'yŏngyang's strategy toward Seoul. Further encouraging this shift were the political upheaval and demise of communism in Eastern Europe and the dissolution of the Soviet Union, one of North Korea's key allies.

Subsequently, North Korea lost its guaranteed access to the market once provided by the Soviet Union and its satellites. At the same time, South Korea established commercial and diplomatic relations with many East European countries. Next, the five permanent members of the UN Security Council approved the simultaneous entry of both Koreas into the UN in September 1991.

Five rounds of meetings were held alternately in Seoul and P'yŏngyang before the Agreement on Reconciliation, Nonaggression, Exchanges, and Cooperation between the South and the North was signed on December 13, 1991 (see table 8, Appendix). The agreement called for reconciliation and nonaggression on the Korean Peninsula. Then North Korean premier Yon Hyong-muk called the agreement ''the most valuable achievement ever made between the South and North Korean authorities.'' It was agreed that further meetings would be held to resolve such issues as creating a nuclear-free Korea, uniting divided families, and discussing economic cooperation.

For the first time, North Korea ''officially recognized'' the existence of South Korea. The accord called for North Korea and South Korea to formally end the Korean War. Among the terms of the accord are agreements to issue a joint declaration of nonaggression, advance warning of troop movements and exercises, and the installation of a hot line between top military commanders. The Agreement on Reconciliation, Nonaggression, Exchanges, and Cooperation has led to the establishment of several joint North-South Korea subcommittees that are to work out the specifics for implementing the general terms of the accord. These subcommittees report to the committees that met in conjunction

Overview of P'yŏngyang, the Taedong River, and the May Day Stadium, upper left. The latter, completed in 1989, was built for the Asian Games and seats 150,000 persons.
Courtesy Tracy Woodward

with the prime ministerial level talks that had begun in September 1990. There are subcommittees on economic cooperation affairs (concerning South Korea's commercial investments in North Korea) and on trade and the opening of lines of travel and communication (including telephonic) between the two Koreas; cultural exchange, concerning the exchange of entertainment and athletic groups and the joint sponsorship of single teams to represent both Koreas in international sports competitions; political affairs, on working to eliminate mutual slander in their respective mass media and to abrogate laws detrimental to improving understanding and cooperation; and military affairs, on devising ways and means to reduce tensions and exchange notice of military exercises. Separate from the prime ministerial dialogue, yet closely associated with it, are talks held between the North and South Korean Red Cross organizations about reunification of families.

The two Koreas also agree that their peninsula should be "free of nuclear weapons." The joint Declaration on the Denuclearization of the Korean Peninsula calls for the establishment of a Joint Nuclear Control Committee (JNCC) to negotiate a credible and effective bilateral nuclear inspection regime as called for in the declaration. Although negotiations in all these areas produced substantive progress toward the drafting of detailed accords for the terms of implementing the Agreement on Reconciliation, Nonaggression, Exchanges and Cooperation, nothing has been implemented as of mid-1993. As for negotiation of a bilateral inspection regime, these talks also had not achieved any significant progress by mid-1993.

China and the Soviet Union

North Korea owes its survival as a separate political entity to China and the Soviet Union. Both countries provided critical military assistance—soldiers and matériel—during the Korean War. From that time and until the early 1990s, China and the Soviet Union both provided North Korea with its most important markets and were its major suppliers of oil and other basic necessities. In turn, China and the Soviet Union were reliable pillars of diplomatic support. The demise of the Soviet Union and the former communist bloc in Eastern Europe, combined with the gradually warming relationship between Beijing and Seoul—which resulted in the establishment of diplomatic relations in August 1992—significantly altered P'yŏngyang's ties with Beijing and Moscow.

More out of economic necessity than ideological compatibility, North Korea sought to maintain good relations with China, despite the latter's increasingly close economic and diplomatic ties with South Korea. In October 1991, Kim Il Sung visited China for ten days, reportedly to ask for economic and military assistance, and to persuade Beijing not to establish diplomatic ties with Seoul. Predictably, North Korea and China reaffirmed their commitment to socialism, but at the time China did not express clear signals for North Korea's other agenda.

Close Sino-North Korean ties continue, but Beijing is striving to maintain a balance in its relationship with the two Koreas, a far cry from its previous four decades of dealing solely with P'yŏngyang. China welcomed the Declaration on the Denuclearization of the Korean Peninsula, making clear its preference for a nonnuclear Korea. Beijing also urged P'yŏngyang to cooperate with the International Atomic Energy Agency (IAEA—see Glossary). Although China remains a crucial trade partner for North Korea, Beijing's former willingness to assist P'yŏngyang economically by extending easy credit is increasingly giving way to no assistance and less and less extension of credit.

The Soviet Union stunned North Korea in September 1990 when it established diplomatic relations with South Korea. Since that time and since the collapse of the Soviet Union in August 1991, North

Korea has worked to build a relationship with Russia's new political leaders. North Korea's efforts to recapture some of the previous closeness and economic benefits of its relationship with the former Soviet Union are seriously hampered, however, by Russia's preoccupation with its own political and economic woes. Trade between the two nations has dropped dramatically since 1990. North Korea cannot compete with the quality of goods South Korea can offer. Whereas the Soviet Union had extended credit without problems to North Korea, Russia has demanded hard currency for whatever North Korea purchases. Russia also has signalled North Korea that it intends to revise the 1961 defense treaty between North Korea and the Soviet Union. The revision will most likely mean Russia will not be obligated to assist North Korea militarily except in the event that North Korea is invaded.

North Korea was diplomatically, politically, and economically far more isolated in mid-1993 than at any time since 1945. Although a member of the UN since 1991, North Korea's relations with its two closest allies—China and the former Soviet Union—have undergone a fundamental shift unlikely to revert to previous patterns. This shift poses a dilemma for North Korea. Will it persist in the pattern of conduct that has made it an international outlaw, or will it set out in a new direction aimed at integrating itself into the international community? In mid-1993 North Korea appears to be on a dual track. On the one hand, P'yŏngyang's signing of the Agreement on Reconciliation, Nonaggression, Exchanges, and Cooperation, and the conclusion of a nuclear safeguards agreement with the IAEA point to its striving for greater acceptance in the international community by measuring up to internationally desired norms. On the other hand, P'yŏngyang continues to act as an international outlaw by selling ballistic missiles abroad, refusing to sign the convention on chemical and biological warfare, and refusing to comply with the terms for nuclear inspections.

Japan

Until the late 1980s, North Korea's post-World War II policy toward Japan was mainly aimed at minimizing cooperation between Japan and South Korea, and at deterring Japan's rearmament while striving for closer diplomatic and commercial ties with Japan. Crucial to this policy was the fostering within Japan of support for North Korea, especially among the Japanese who supported the Japanese communist and socialist parties and the Korean residents of Japan. Over the years, however, North Korea did much to discredit itself in the eyes of many potential supporters in Japan. Japanese who had accompanied their spouses to North Korea had endured severe hardships and were prevented from communicating with relatives and friends in Japan. Japan watched with disdain as North Korea gave safe haven to elements of the Japanese Red Army, a terrorist group. North Korea's inability and refusal to pay its debts to Japanese traders also reinforced popular Japanese disdain for North Korea.

Coincidental with the changing patterns in its relations with China and Russia, North Korea has moved to improve its strained relations with Japan. P'yŏngyang's primary motives appear to be a quest for relief from diplomatic and economic isolation, which has also caused serious shortages of food, energy, and hard currency. Normalization of relations with Japan also raises the possibility of North Korea's gaining monetary compensation for the period of Japan's colonial rule (1910–45), a precedent set when Japan normalized relations with South Korea.

The first round of normalization talks was held January 30–31, 1991, but quickly broke down over the question of compensation. P'yŏngyang has demanded compensation for damages incurred during colonial rule as well as for "sufferings and losses" in the post-World War II period. Japan, however, insists that North Korea first resolve its differences with South Korea over the question of bilateral nuclear inspections. Other points of contention are North Korea's refusal both to provide information about Japanese citizens who had migrated to North Korea with their Korean spouses in the 1960s, and to discuss the case of Yi Un Hee, a Korean resident of Japan whom North Korean agents had allegedly kidnapped to North Korea to teach Japanese in a school for espionage agents. As of mid-1993, several rounds of talks had yet to produce any significant progress toward normalization of relations.

The United States

Since 1945 North Korea's relationship with the United States has been marked by almost continuous confrontation and mistrust. North Korea views the United States as the strongest imperialist force in the world and as the successor to Japanese imperialism. The Korean War only intensified this perception. The United States views North Korea as an international outlaw. The uneasy armistice that halted the intense fighting of the Korean War has occasionally been broken. Perpetuating the mutual distrust was North Korea's 1968 seizure of the United States Navy intelligence-gathering ship *Pueblo,* the downing of a United States reconnaissance plane in 1969, and the 1976 killing of two American soldiers at the P'anmunjŏm "Peace Village" in the middle of the DMZ. North Korea's assassination of several United States-educated South Korean cabinet officials in 1983 and the terrorist bombing of a South Korean airliner in 1987 likewise have reinforced United States perceptions of North Korea as unworthy of having diplomatic or economic ties with the United States.

Following South Korea's lead, the United States in 1988 launched its own modest diplomatic initiative. Washington sought to reduce P'yŏngyang's isolation and to encourage its opening to the outside world. Consequently, the United States government began facilitating cultural, scholarly, journalistic, athletic, and other exchanges with North Korea. After a hesitant start, by the early 1990s almost monthly exchanges were occurring in these areas between the two nations, a halting but significant movement away from total estrangement.

The atmosphere between P'yŏngyang and Washington warmed significantly in 1991 and 1992. The United States supported the simultaneous admission of both Koreas into the UN in September 1991. That same month, President George Bush announced the withdrawal of all tactical nuclear weapons worldwide. In January 1992, after North Korea had publicly committed itself to the signing of a nuclear safeguards agreement with the IAEA and to permitting IAEA inspections of its primary nuclear facility at Yŏngbyŏn, President Bush and South Korean president Roh Tae Woo took the unprecedented step of cancelling their 1992 joint annual military exercise Team Spirit.

In February 1992, United States Department of State Under Secretary for Political Affairs Arnold Kanter met with his North Korean counterpart, Korean Workers' Party Director for International Affairs Kim Yong-sun, in New York. At this meeting, the United States set forth the steps it wanted North Korea to take prior to normalization of relations. North Korea had to facilitate progress in the North-South Korea dialogue; end its export of missile and related technology; renounce terrorism; cooperate with accounting for all Korean War United States military personnel classified as Missing in Action; demonstrate increasing respect for human rights; and conclude a credible and effective North-South nuclear inspection regime designed to complement inspections conducted by the IAEA. Once a credible and effective bilateral North-South Korean inspection regime has been implemented, the United States government will initiate a policy-level dialogue with North Korea to formulate specifics for resolving other outstanding United States concerns.

Prospects

As of mid-1993, North Korea seemed eager to seek reconciliation with South Korea and to open its doors to the outside world. This eagerness is largely the result of demands by the United States, Japan, and other Asian countries that North Korea improve its relations with South Korea as a precondition to improving their own relations with North Korea. At the same time, North Korea also worries that the opening of North Korean society to South Korea and the West will be problematic because it will allow potential ideological contamination.

The IAEA agreement on nuclear facilities poses a challenge to North Korea because both United States and South Korean analysts have indicated that North Korea is working on developing nuclear weapons at a facility in Yŏngbyŏn, approximately 100 kilometers north of P'yŏngyang. On January 30, 1992, P'yŏngyang signed the IAEA Full Scope Safeguards Agreement and agreed to open its nuclear installations for inspection. North Korea also was required to submit to the IAEA an inventory of all of its nuclear materials before inspections.

North Korea is under pressure to embrace opportunities presented by the changing world situation in the 1990s as well as to concentrate on accelerating its economic development. Nonetheless, it is likely that North Korea will continue its present course with respect to internal politics until its economy improves substantially. Economic pressures are forcing P'yŏngyang to hint that it would like to begin to open up to the noncommunist world (see Foreign Economic Relations, ch. 3). In this regard, it has established a special economic zone offering preferential tax rates for foreign investments in the Tumen River area.

From a political perspective, it is unlikely that political liberalization will occur in the near future. Such action would probably lead to subversive tendencies and jeopardize the existing political system. The upheaval in the former Soviet Union and East European countries has aggravated North Korea's economic woes and caused political fear among—and the exercise of caution by—P'yŏngyang's leaders. Because the KWP firmly controls the state and no formally organized dissident movement against the regime exists, the party is likely to continue its political conservatism and to intensify its ''socialist education.''

What changes will occur in terms of political development are uncertain. An accelerated opening of North Korea, fueled by improved relations with South Korea, the United States, and Japan, will erode North Korea's socialism and is hence unlikely to occur. Kim Il Sung's succession plan for handing over power to Kim Jong Il has been reinforced with the younger Kim's assumption of power as the supreme commander of the armed forces. North Korea's sluggish economy, however, is a principal stumbling block for maintenance of the regime and its leadership succession process. Support among top military and political elites for Kim Il Sung's succession plan may depend on the achievement of political stability and economic growth as well as the maintenance of the status quo for those in power. Their support may waver with Kim Il Sung's death.

Overall, North Korea is likely to continue its two-track policy: strengthening ideological indoctrination while increasing economic relations with capitalist countries. Whatever options Kim Jong Il chooses, his references to the need for bolder reforms may be followed immediately both by warnings about moving too fast from hardliners who stress the importance of orthodox ideology over economic reform and by complaints about reforming too slowly from technical experts who stress the urgent need for economic development and technology accumulation. However, given his years of studious apprenticeship, and assuming the absence of major upheavals in the Koreas and the international environment, continuity under Kim Jong Il seems assured, at least for the early 1990s.

*   *   *

Sources on North Korea vary considerably in reliability and balance, so they should be used with care, particularly in the case of information emanating from North Korea. Information from South Korea also has a political bias. Major articles in *Nodong simmun* (Workers' Daily), *Kŭlloja* (The Worker), and other Korean-language publications are translated into English in the Foreign Broadcast Information Service's *Daily Report: East Asia* and the *Korean Affairs Report* issued by the Joint Publications Research Service.

For in-depth coverage of North Korea, one of the most comprehensive sources is *Pukhan Chŏnsŏ* (North Korean Handbook), in Korean, prepared by South Korea's Kuktong Munje Yŏn'guso (Institute for East Asian Studies). *Pukhan* (North Korea), the monthly organ of Pukhan Yŏn'guso, the Research Institute on North Korea in Seoul; and *Kita Chōsen kenkyū* (Studies on North Korea), a Japanese-language monthly of the Kokusai Kankei Kyōdō Kenkyūjo (Joint Research Institute on International Relations) in Tokyo are also useful. *Vantage Point,* an English-language monthly periodical issued by Naewoe Press in Seoul, and *East Asian Review,* an English-language quarterly published by the Institute for East Asian Studies in Seoul, provide in-depth studies of North Korean social, economic, and political developments.

Other sources include the annual survey articles on North Korea in *Asian Survey,* the annual roundup of articles on North Korea in the Far Eastern Economic Review's *Asia Yearbook,* and the now defunct *Yearbook on International Communist Affairs,* published by Hoover Institution Press. (For further information and complete citations, see Bibliography.)

Chapter 5. National Security

Military personnel symbolizing the branches of the Korean People's Army

IN THE EARLY 1990s, the Democratic People's Republic of Korea, (DPRK, or North Korea) was one of the most militarized countries in the world. North Korea's confrontational relationship with the Republic of Korea (ROK, or South Korea) is one of the last legacies of the Cold War; 1992, however, hinted at the beginning of a new era of reconciliation. Nonetheless, the peninsula remains divided, with two large armies tactically deployed forward along the Demilitarized Zone (DMZ—see Glossary) that is demilitarized in name only.

The division of Korea originated as a consequence of a territorial partition imposed at the end of World War II (1939–45). When Japanese forces on the peninsula surrendered, the United States and the Soviet Union agreed to divide the landmass into dual occupation zones at the thirty-eighth parallel, the Soviet Union occupying the north and the United States the south. The arrangement was intended to be temporary, and the country was to be unified after free elections. Instead, diametrically different political systems were set up in the two areas, and all ensuing diplomatic efforts to unify the country have failed.

A communist attempt at reunification by military action in 1950 brought on the Korean War (1950–53), known in North Korea as the Fatherland Liberation War. The fighting was stopped with an armistice in July 1953, but the hostile political and military relationship between the two Koreas remained unsolved, and the North-South military confrontation continues. There is no convincing evidence that P'yŏngyang has ever given up the option of reuniting the peninsula by force of arms. In fact, despite growing economic difficulties, North Korea continues to devote its scarce resources to maintaining a force structure that appears unjustifiable on defensive considerations alone. Some officials in the South Korean government believe that North Korea has designated 1995 as the year for reunification and is accelerating its preparations for war.

In 1992 some observers regarded the possibility of war on the Korean Peninsula as low, a judgment based on the global political changes that have ended the confrontation between East and West. Despite the end in the early 1990s to the Cold War competition that had created South Korea and North Korea, the confrontation on the peninsula has not dissipated. Multiple areas of friction between the two countries, including potential nuclear weapons development by North Korea, continue to suggest the possibility of conflict, either deliberate or as a result of miscalculation.

The North Korean leadership has created a Stalinist state that perhaps even exceeds the model. P'yŏngyang subjects its people to rigid controls: Individual rights are subordinate to those of the state and party. The Ministry of Public Security is charged with maintaining law and order and internal security, and has sweeping powers over the lives of citizens.

The North Korean penal code is draconian and stipulates harsh punishments, particularly for political crimes. Its legal and criminal systems are patterned after Soviet models in force during the occupation after World War II. Little information is available on specific criminal justice procedures and practices.

Although the constitution (adopted in 1948, revised in 1972 and again in 1992) states that courts are independent and that judicial proceedings are carried out in strict accordance with the law—and includes elaborate procedural guarantees to carry out the law— there are strong indications that safeguards are seldom followed in practice. The legal system reflects strong authoritarian impulses and the subordination of the interests of the individual to the state, or to the cause of revolution. Not all details of the law are available to the citizens, and, as of mid-1993, there were indications that liberally defined political crimes were prosecuted with little regard for legal constraints.

Military Heritage

North Korea is heavily militarized, with over a million military personnel. It has been estimated that one out of every five North Korean men between the ages of sixteen and fifty-four was in the military in 1992. The active-duty forces account for at least 6 percent of the population and at least 12 percent of the male population. These capabilities far exceed any conceivable defensive requirement.

This force structure and offensive orientation are relatively new phenomena for the Korean Peninsula. Despite frequent external military challenges, the military has never enjoyed high social status in traditional Korea. The traditional value systems of Buddhism and Confucianism hold the military profession in low esteem. The *yangban* (see Glossary) class initially had two official ranks: civil and military officials. The *yangban* civil official class, which rose to power in the tenth century during the Koryŏ Dynasty (918–1392), feared a powerful military might dominate the government (see The Origins of the Korean Nation, ch. 1; Social Structure and Values, ch. 2). Rivalry for power between the two classes resulted in military dominance over civil officials and contributed to some 100 years of political instability during the Koryŏ Dynasty. Yi Sŏng-gye, a former military general and the founder of the Chosŏn (Yi) Dynasty (1392–1910), sought to break this cycle. Once the dynasty was firmly in place, military officials gradually lost out in the competition for high government positions and civil officials were preferred even in senior military commands. As a result, even through five centuries of Chosŏn Dynasty rule, the ruling elite was seldom compelled to strengthen the military enough to defend the nation. The Chosŏn Dynasty relied upon its tributary status with China for national defense. Despite two major invasions by the Japanese and the Manchus, there is no enduring military tradition in Korea.

In times of emergency, the general population would form a volunteer army (*ŭibyŏng*) to oppose invaders. This practice continued during the Japanese colonial period (1910–45). Several anti-Japanese militias, including Kim Il Sung's group of guerrillas (Kim Il Sung was president of the DPRK and general secretary of the Korean Workers' Party (KWP) in mid-1993), were organized by Koreans and operated independently or as part of the Chinese or Soviet forces.

The origins of military organizations and police forces in what would become North Korea during the Soviet occupation are difficult to understand because of limited and contradictory information, and the confusion of the times. Kim Il Sung originally operated in northern China in forces associated with the Chinese communists. He fled to the Soviet Union and later appeared in Soviet uniform at Wŏnsan in 1945. The North Korean military grew out of the eventual merger of the Chinese communist and Soviet forces (see The National Division and the Origins of the Democratic People's Republic of Korea, ch. 1).

There were factional power struggles among the various Korean troops. The Yan'an faction had its origins in the Korean nationalist movement in China. Mu Chŏng, a veteran of the Chinese Communist Party's Long March (1934–35), established a Korean military unit in Yan'an with Chinese communist backing. Mu was acknowledged by the Chinese communists as the central leader of the Korean communist movement. The Korean Yan'an contingent never was massive, but by mid-1941 most of the Korean anti-Japanese activity had shifted to northern China. Under Chinese communist protection, the Yan'an faction trained a substantial number of military and political cadres and was a political and military force to be reckoned with when it tried to return to Korea in 1945. Mu was commander of the Second Corps during the open phase of the Korean War but reportedly escaped and was purged during the December 1950 plenum because the entry of the Chinese People's Volunteers into the war made him too great a threat to Kim Il Sung's faction.

Kim Il Sung's faction, known as the Kapsan faction, did not operate as an independent anti-Japanese unit in China during World War II. (Kapsan is the name of a place in North Korea near the border with Manchuria—as northeast China was then called—where Kim's forces were headquartered prior to escaping to the Soviet Far Eastern provinces in 1940.) Rather, the faction was part of the Soviet Eighty-Eighth Sniper Brigade—a mixed Chinese, Korean, and Soviet reconnaissance unit stationed in Khabarovsk. Kim Il Sung, commander of one of the battalions, was a captain in the Soviet Army when he reentered Korea in 1945.

Kim Il Sung's Kapsan faction dominated the military leadership even before the Korean War. The role of the Korean People's Army (KPA) in the interfactional struggles of the 1950s, during which Kim Il Sung solidified his control of the KWP and the state, is unclear. With the victory of Kim's faction, all remaining Yan'an (Chinese) faction members were purged.

The first political-military school in North Korea, the P'yŏng-yang Military Academy, headed by Kim Chaek, an ally of Kim Il Sung, was founded in October 1945 under Soviet guidance to train people's guards, or public security units. In 1946 graduates of the school entered regular police and public security/constabulary units. These lightly armed security forces included followers of Kim Il Sung and returned veterans from China. Many veterans from China who had tried to return home immediately after World War II were stopped by Soviet forces at the border. Some were disarmed and allowed to enter North Korea; the rest were returned to Manchuria, where the force was expanded and tempered in the Chinese civil war. While the Chinese-sponsored forces were growing into maturity in Manchuria, Kim Il Sung secured control of the military and security apparatus in North Korea with Soviet sponsorship. His dominant position within the armed forces was crucial to securing control of the state.

Soviet forces withdrew in 1948, leaving an approximately 60,000-man Korean army and a larger paramilitary force that included people's guards, border guards, and railroad security forces. On February 8, 1948, the North Korean Provisional Committee officially announced the formation of the KPA and the establishment of the Ministry of People's Armed Forces, which controlled a central guard battalion, two divisions, and an independent mixed brigade.

The Soviet Union fostered the development of the KPA and supplied weapons and equipment, along with temporarily transferred advisers and personnel who helped to draft the operational plans for the southward invasion in 1950. The core combat units of the KPA, however, traced their origins to the small Korean Volunteer Army (KVA), which had fought with the Chinese communist Eighth Route Army. Aided by a massive influx of Soviet matériel, the KPA grew to between 150,000 and 200,000 men by the time it invaded South Korea in June 1950. As many as 10,000 personnel had received training in the Soviet Union, including ethnic Koreans and Soviet citizens and soldiers. An estimated 40,000 men were battle-hardened veterans of the Chinese civil war who had returned to the north in 1949 and formed the main force units of the KPA.

Information uncovered in 1992 confirmed that both the Soviet Union and China were aware and supportive of North Korea's invasion plans in 1949. Yu Song Cho, deputy chief of staff of the KPA at the time of the invasion, revealed that Soviet military advisers went so far as to rewrite his initial invasion order. Russian statements in 1992 revealed that Soviet air defense and fighter units totalling 26,000 men participated in the Korean War.

The initial stages of the Korean War almost brought victory to the KPA, which had excellent capabilities and successfully applied breakthrough and exploitation techniques. However, the intervention of the United States-led United Nations (UN) forces, the UN Command, denied the KPA victory on the battlefield. Fighting on the Pusan defense perimeter began on August 1 and continued through to the Inch'ŏn landing on September 15. These defeats broke the KPA and virtually destroyed it as a cohesive force.

China, finding the UN Command occupation of North Korea unacceptable and its diplomatic efforts ignored, announced the formation of the Chinese People's Volunteer Army in October 1950. The Chinese People's Liberation Army massed some 850,000 "volunteer troops" north of the Yalu River, launched a major offensive in November 1950, and succeeded in driving the UN Command forces southward. Only the intervention of the Chinese People's Volunteers and the help of massive Soviet material assistance enabled the KPA to reconstitute itself. The front eventually stabilized close to the thirty-eighth parallel.

Hostilities ended inconclusively with an armistice agreement in July 1953, signed by the commanders of the KPA, the UN Command—which included ROK forces—and the Chinese People's Volunteer Army. Technically, the peninsula remained in a state of war restrained by an armistice. The subject of replacing the armistice with a formal peace agreement was mentioned in the 1991 Agreement on Reconciliation, Nonaggression, Exchanges, and Cooperation between North Korea and South Korea, but remained unresolved in mid-1993. KPA losses in the Korean War, called the Fatherland Liberation War by North Korea, totaled more than half a million persons, although North Korea has not released figures. The war also resulted in the virtual destruction of North Korea's economy and infrastructure (see Economic Development and Structural Change, ch. 3). Chinese troops remained in North Korea until October 1958.

After the war, the KPA was reconstituted, but until the early 1960s rebuilding military strength remained less important than economic reconstruction. The signing of treaties of mutual assistance with the Soviet Union and China in 1961 and the promulgation of the Four Military Guidelines in 1962 brought the military back to a position of primacy, which it retained as of mid-1993.

The Armed Forces

National Command Authority

On November 23, 1992, the South Korean government released the text of the revised North Korean state constitution, which had been approved, but not made public, by the Ninth Supreme People's Assembly on April 9, 1992. The document revises the structure of the national command authority.

The KPA is a creation of both the government and the KWP. According to Chapter 7, Article 46 of the KWP constitution, "The Korean People's Army is the revolutionary armed forces of the Korean Workers' Party." The 1992 state constitution groups clauses related to national defense into two sections. Those defining the role and mission of the armed forces are under the subheading entitled National Defense—Chapter 4, Article 58 through Article 62. The text redefining the relationships among the president, Supreme People's Assembly, and National Defense Commission is under the subheading on State Institutions—Chapter 6, Article 111 through Article 114. The duality of the KPA's role is indicated in Article 59, which states, "The mission of the Armed Forces of the Democratic People's Republic of Korea is to defend the interests of the working people, defend the socialist system and the gains of the revolution from external invasion, and protect the freedom, independence and peace of the fatherland." The dual nature of the KPA as the "army of the Party" and of the state is reflected in the national military command structure.

Under the coordinated authority of the party's Military Affairs

Committee and the state National Defense Commission, the Ministry of People's Armed Forces exercises jurisdiction over the KPA (see fig. 10). Eight major organizations constitute the national command authorities: the president; the KWP's Military Affairs Committee; the Civil Defense Department; the Military Affairs Department; the Supreme People's Assembly; the National Defense Commission with special emphasis on its chairman; the Ministry of People's Armed Forces; and the General Political Bureau of the General Staff.

Under previous constitutions, the president was empowered as the supreme commander of the armed forces and as chairman of the National Defense Commission. At the Seventh Supreme People's Assembly on April 5, 1982, the Ministry of People's Armed Forces (along with the Ministry of Public Security and the State Inspection Commission) was separated from the State Administration Council and made responsible to the president alone. On December 24, 1991, however, the constitutional and legal requirements were muddied when it was announced that President Kim's son and heir apparent, Kim Jong Il, had been named supreme commander. The 1992 state constitution, however, deletes clauses in the 1972 constitution that stipulated that the president was supreme commander of the armed forces and chairman of the National Defense Commission, shifting powers instead to the Supreme People's Assembly and the National Defense Commission. Under the revisions, the president retains only the power to recommend the election or recall of the chairman of the National Defense Commission.

The KWP Military Affairs Committee determines broad security policy, including basic military policy, political indoctrination of the armed services, resource allocation, and high-level personnel matters. The committee has under its jurisdiction both the regular and paramilitary forces. The Military Affairs Committee consists of between ten and twenty party officials, typically military officers. In mid-1993 Kim Il Sung, as general secretary of the KWP, headed the committee, and Kim Jong Il was second in command.

Under the 1992 constitution, the Supreme People's Assembly gained the power to elect or to recall the authority of the chairman of the National Defense Commission on the recommendation of the president. On the recommendation of the commission chairman, it has election and recall authority over the first vice chairman, the vice chairman, and members of the commission. According to Article 91.20, it also retains ultimate power to "decide on questions conceding war and peace."

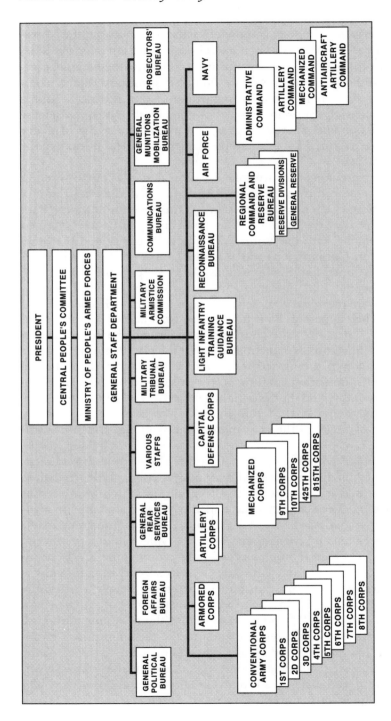

Figure 10. Organization of the Armed Forces, 1993

The 1992 constitution appears to continue a trend of increasing the importance and independence of the National Defense Commission. Links to the Central People's Committee were apparently severed and the commission became directly subordinate to the Supreme People's Assembly. Article 111 states "The National Defense Commission is the supreme military guidance organ of the DPRK sovereign power," and Article 113 declares, "The Chairman of the DPRK National Defense Commission commands and controls all the armed forces." Under Article 114, the commission has the power to declare a state of war and issue mobilization orders in an emergency, guide the armed forces, appoint and dismiss major military cadres, and control general officer promotions. These sweeping changes are apparently aimed at laying the groundwork for readdressing the apparent violation of the constitution when Kim Jong Il was installed as supreme commander of the army in December 1991. Although the commission's position in the state was enhanced, observers believe that, in reality, it adopted and implemented policies based on the KWP's Military Affairs Committee guidelines. The National Defense Commission has a chairman, first vice chairman, one or more additional vice chairmen, and between nine and fifteen members inclusive, usually all military officers. In April 1993, Kim Il Sung turned over the chairmanship to Kim Jong Il.

The Ministry of People's Armed Forces is organizationally subordinate to the state structure but is controlled by the KWP. The ministry is responsible for management and operational control of the armed forces. Prior to 1992, it was under the direct control of the president, with guidance from the National Defense Commission and the KWP Military Affairs Department. The 1992 state constitution shifts its control to the National Defense Commission.

The Ministry of People's Armed Forces has three principal departments. The General Staff Department exercises operational control over the military. The General Political Bureau guides and supervises party organizations and political activities at all levels of the ministry under direction of the party's Military Affairs Committee. The General Rear Services Bureau controls logistics, support, and procurement activities. Other bureaus include the Military Tribunal Bureau and the Prosecutors' Bureau.

Major operational forces include all corps, the Light Infantry Training Guidance Bureau (formerly called the VIII Special Warfare Corps or the Special Forces Corps), the Reconnaissance Bureau, the navy, the air force, the Air Defense Command, and some combat support units. The Artillery Command, the Armor Command, and some twenty-six bureaus, two departments, and two offices are responsible for doctrine, administration, logistics, and training for functional areas, including the field artillery, air defense artillery, armor, mechanized infantry, ordnance, and chemical warfare. Corps-level commands in peacetime are directly commanded by the General Staff Department.

Formulation of National Security Policy

The seemingly complex national security policy-making process was tempered by three factors: interlocking memberships in party and government apparatus, the relative unimportance of the state apparatus in decision making, and the state's relegation to implementing policies decided by the party structure. In general, the party, typically the General Political Bureau and the Military Affairs Committee, has broad policy-making responsibility for military affairs. Within the government, however, the Ministry of the People's Armed Forces controls the military. The General Staff Department and the General Rear Services Bureau of the Ministry of the People's Armed Forces prepare military budgets under the guidance of the Political Bureau and Military Affairs Committee. Proposed budgets are approved by the KWP Military Affairs Committee and passed into law by the essentially rubber stamp legislature, the Supreme People's Assembly (see Organization of the Government, ch. 4).

The Army

Over 90 percent of all KPA personnel in 1992—more than 1 million troops—were in the ground forces, the North Korean army. Ground forces in 1960 may have totalled fewer than 400,000 persons and probably did not rise much above that figure before 1972. The force expanded relentlessly over the next two decades; in 1992, there were approximately 1 million personnel. The size, organization, disposition, and combat capabilities of the army give P'yŏngyang military options both for offensive operations to reunify the peninsula and for credible defensive operations against any perceived threat from South Korea.

The army is largely an infantry force although a decade-long modernization program has significantly improved the mobility and firepower of its active forces. Between 1980 and 1992, North Korea reorganized, reequipped, and forward deployed the majority of its ground forces. The army places great emphasis on special operations and has one of the largest special operations forces in the world—tailored to meet the distinct requirements of Korean terrain.

Organization and Disposition

The army initially was organized along Chinese and Soviet lines. Over time, this organization has adjusted to the unique circumstances of the military problem the KPA faces and to the evolution of North Korean military doctrine and thought.

In the 1980s, the mechanized infantry and armored and artillery forces were reorganized into new mechanized armored and artillery corps to implement the change in strategic thinking. This restructuring suggests that some infantry divisions were used to form the new mechanized forces and then reformed, and that a similar pattern apparently was used to reconstruct the armored corps.

Until 1986 most sources claimed the army had two armored divisions. These divisions disappeared from the order of battle and were replaced by the armored corps and a doubling of the armored brigade count. In the mid-1980s, the heavy caliber self-propelled artillery was consolidated into the first multibrigade artillery corps. At the same time, the restructured mobile exploitation forces were redeployed forward, closer to the DMZ. The forward corps areas of operation were compressed although their internal organization appeared to remain basically the same. The deployment of the newly formed mechanized, armored, and artillery corps directly behind the first-echelon conventional forces provides a potent exploitation force that did not exist prior to 1980.

As of 1992, the army was composed of sixteen corps commands, two separate special operations forces commands, and nine military district commands (or regions) under the control of the Ministry of the People's Armed Forces (see table 9, Appendix). Most sources agree that North Korea's ground forces consist of approximately 145 divisions and brigades, of which approximately 120 are active. There is less agreement, however, on the breakdown of the forces.

In 1992 North Korea was divided among the conventional geographic corps (see fig. 11). The army's armored and mechanized corps, composed of independent combined arms brigades tailored to the restrictive terrain of the peninsula, are positioned along the avenues of approach as exploitation and counterattack forces.

Each province has, independent of the collocated conventional geographic corps, a regional Military District Command dedicated to local defense, which controls predominantly reserve forces organized into divisions and brigades. The Military District Commands apparently were formed during a restructuring of the reserves during the 1980s. Their command structure is unclear, although they apparently control the local reserves, some regular forces, and coastal defense units.

Figure 11. Deployment of Ground and Naval Forces and Air Wings, 1993

Weapons and Equipment

In the 1980s, in order to make the army more mobile and mechanized, there was a steady influx of new tanks, self-propelled artillery, armored personnel carriers (APCs), and trucks. The ground forces seldom retire old models of weapons and tend to maintain a large equipment stock, keeping old models along with upgraded ones in the active force or in reserve.

Beginning in the late 1970s, North Korea began to produce a

modified version of the 115mm gunned T–62 tank, which was the Soviet army's main battle tank in the 1960s. Based on general trends and photography of armed forces parades, it is clear that North Korea has made considerable modifications to the basic Soviet and Chinese designs in its own production.

Although the majority of units remain "straight-leg" infantry forces, that is, lacking significant motorized or mechanized transport, the army contains a significant number of well-equipped mechanized units, with about 2,500 APCs. These mobile forces are equipped with a mix of older Soviet-made APCs, some Chinese-made APCs, and some indigenously produced APCs, such as the M–1985.

Probably because of its initial Soviet tutelage and the limited ground-attack capability of the air force, great emphasis is placed on using massive artillery firepower. North Korean ordnance factories produce a variety of self-propelled guns, howitzers, and gun-howitzers. In the 1980s, North Korea produced a significant amount of self-propelled artillery, mating towed artillery tubes with chassis already in the inventory. North Korean strategic thought also seems to be based on the primacy of developing an offensive capability, reflecting an appreciation for firepower probably dating to the Korean War. Further, P'yŏngyang is willing to invest the time and effort necessary for effective defense of its ground forces from air attack and artillery fire.

With the exception of the 170mm M–1978 Koksan gun first noted in a parade in 1985, a new turreted self-propelled gun observed in a 1992 parade, and perhaps a few other systems, most artillery was developed from older Soviet and Chinese designs. All incorporate proven technologies or components.

North Korea continues to produce a range of Soviet antitank guns, most of them dating from 1940s and 1950s designs, and ranging in size from 57mm through 100mm. Infantry units also are armed with Soviet bloc-derived equipment.

The army has an extensive facility-hardening program. Almost all the forward-deployed artillery can be stored in well-protected underground emplacements. The passive defenses in the forward corps include a large bunker complex to conceal and protect infantry forces, mechanized units, and war matériel stockpiles.

Special Operations Forces

In the early 1990s, the army was made up of a mixture of conventional and unconventional warfare forces. By any consideration, however, North Korea has one of the world's largest special operations forces. Estimates of the size of the army's special operations forces ranged from 60,000 persons to over 100,000 persons. The uncertainty over the number derives from both the lack of information and the varying definitions of special operations forces. Organized into twenty-two brigades and at least seven independent battalions, the special operations forces are believed to be the best trained and to have the highest morale of all North Korean ground forces.

Special operations forces were developed to meet three basic requirements: to breach the flankless fixed defense of South Korea; to create a "second front" in the enemy's rear area, disrupting in-depth South Korean or United States reinforcements and logistical support during a conflict; and to conduct battlefield and strategic reconnaissance. The ultimate goal was to create strategic dislocation. The additional missions of countering opposing forces and internal security were added over time.

The Ministry of the People's Armed Forces controls the bulk of the special operations forces through one of two commands, the Reconnaissance Bureau and the Light Infantry Training Guidance Bureau. The Reconnaissance Bureau is the primary organization within the Ministry of People's Armed Forces for the collection of strategic and tactical intelligence. It also exercises operational control over agents engaged in collecting military intelligence and in the training and dispatch of unconventional warfare teams. The Light Infantry Training Guidance Bureau is directly subordinate to the General Staff Department. The party directly controls approximately 1,500 agents.

Operations are categorized on the basis of the echelon supported. Strategic special operations forces support national or Ministry of People's Armed Forces objectives, operational-supported corps operations, and tactical-supported maneuver divisions and brigades. Strategic missions of special operations forces in support of national and Ministry of People's Armed Forces objectives involve reconnaissance, sniper, and agent operations, but not light infantry operations, which are primarily tactical operations. The main objectives of these units are to secure information that cannot be achieved by other means, neutralize targets, and disrupt rear areas. In executing these operations, special operations troops may be disguised either as South Korean military personnel or as civilians.

Strategic missions require deep insertions either in advance of hostilities or in the initial stages by naval or air platforms. Based on available insertion platforms, North Korea has a one-time lift capability of 12,000 persons by sea and 6,000 persons by air. Most North Korean special operations forces infiltrate overland and are dedicated to operational and tactical missions, that is, reconnaissance and combat operations in concert with conventional operations in the forward corps. Although it is unknown how forces will be allocated, limits on North Korea's insertion capabilities constrain operational flexibility and determine the allocation of strategic, operational, and tactical missions.

North Korean army special operations forces units are broken down into three categories based on mission and mode of operation: agent operations, reconnaissance, and light infantry and sniper. The Reconnaissance Bureau has four sniper brigades and at least seven independent reconnaissance battalions. The Light Infantry Training Guidance Bureau controls fourteen light infantry/sniper brigades: six "straight-leg" brigades, six airborne brigades, and two amphibious brigades. Four light infantry brigades of unknown subordination are under the operational control of the forward corps. In addition, each regular infantry division and mechanized brigade has a special operations forces battalion.

Reconnaissance units are employed in rear area, strategic intelligence collection, and target information acquisition. Light infantry units operate in company- or battalion-sized units against military, political, or economic targets. Sniper units are distinguished from light infantry units in that their basic operational unit is the team, rather than the larger company or battalion of the light infantry unit.

A reconnaissance brigade consists of between 3,600 and 4,200 personnel. It is organized into a headquarters, rear support units, a communications company, and ten reconnaissance battalions. The basic unit of operation is the reconnaissance team, which has from two to ten men. A light infantry brigade has between 3,300 and 3,600 personnel organized into between five and ten battalions. The brigade can fight as a unit or disperse its battalions for independent operations. A sniper brigade's organization parallels that of the light infantry brigade.

The unique special operations forces dedicated to strategic operations are the two amphibious light infantry/sniper brigades subordinate to the Light Infantry Guidance Bureau. These brigades are believed deployed to Wŏnsan on the east coast and Namp'o and Tasa-ri on the west coast. In organization and manpower, they are reduced versions of the regular light infantry brigades. The two brigades have a total strength of approximately 5,000 men in ten battalions. Each battalion has about 400 men organized into five companies each. Some amphibious brigade personnel are trained as frogmen.

In the 1970s, in support of overland insertion, North Korea began clandestine tunneling operations along the entire DMZ, with two tunnels per forward division. By 1990 four tunnels dug on historical invasion routes from the north had been discovered by South Korean and United States tunnel neutralization teams: three in the mid-1970s and the fourth in March 1990. The South Koreans suspect there were as many as twenty-five tunnels in the early 1990s, but the level of ongoing tunneling is unknown.

At the operational and tactical level, infiltration tactics are designed for the leading special operations forces brigades to probe and penetrate the weak points of the defense; disrupt the command, control, and communications nodes; and threaten lines of communication and supply. To achieve its goal of near-term distraction and dislocation of the defender, at least one special operations forces brigade is assigned to each of the four regular army corps deployed along the DMZ.

Military Capability, Readiness, Training, and Recent Trends

Beginning in the late 1970s, North Korea began a major reorganization and modernization of its ground forces. Between 1984 and 1992, the army added about 1,000 tanks, over 2,500 APC/infantry fighting vehicles (IFVs), and about 6,000 artillery tubes or rocket launchers. In 1992 North Korea had about twice the advantage in numbers of tanks and artillery, and a 1.5-to-1 advantage in personnel over its potential adversaries, the United States-Republic of Korea defenses to the south. Over 60 percent of the army was located within 100 kilometers of the DMZ in mid-1993.

North Korea conducts exercises at the division, corps, and Ministry of People's Armed Forces levels, but almost no information was available on their size, scope, frequency, or duration as of mid-1993. Province-level defensive training measures are more common than large-scale training exercises. Exercises involving units that consume scarce resources such as fuel, oil, and lubricants occur even less frequently, inhibiting the readiness of exploitation forces. Most training occurs at the regimental level or below, mainly at the company and platoon levels. There may be integration difficulties at division- and corps-level operations.

During the 1980s, doctrine and organization were revamped to increase the lethality, speed, and combat power of the attack. The shifting of the majority of the North Korean ground forces closer to the DMZ offers the potential for a more rapid advance. The reorganization of P'yŏngyang's exploitation forces in the 1980s suggests that initial attacking forces will be reinforced by heavier and more mobile units to exploit any breakthroughs.

Observation post at Kukhwa-ri, not far from Kaesŏng
Courtesy Tracy Woodward

The North Korean army was not uniformly successful in its 1980s efforts to modernize its forces in support of a high-speed offensive strategy; more needs to be done to update the army's mobility, artillery, and air defense elements. North Korea has increased its tank fleet, but incomplete information suggests that it remains based largely on dated Soviet technology with retrofitted indigenous improvements. Although the quality and quantity of mobile anti-aircraft gun systems remain unknown, there is no indication of any mobile surface-to-air missile (SAM) systems other than man-portable systems such as the SA–7 and SA–14 or SA–16 (based on parade photographs) entering the inventory to augment North Korea's static air defense umbrella. Lack of SAM systems could be a major deficiency in the army's tactical air defense capability during mobile offensive operations. However, in artillery systems the army appears to have made the most of its limited technological base. It has increased the artillery force while maintaining relative quantitative and range superiorities over its potential southern adversary and improving force mobility.

In mid-1993 the chances that North Korea will further modernize its forces appear limited. The technological level of P'yŏngyang's industrial base appears to ensure that, with the possible exception of narrow areas of special interest, built-in obsolescence will be unavoidable, regardless of how undesirable.

227

The Navy

The navy, a separate branch of the KPA, is headquartered at P'yŏngyang. In 1992 the 40,000- to 60,000-person brown-water navy was primarily a coastal defense force. The navy is capable of conducting inshore defensive operations, submarine operations against merchant shipping and unsophisticated naval combatants, offensive and defensive mining operations, and conventional raids. Because of the general imbalance of ship types, the navy has a limited capability to carry out missions such as sea control or denial and antisubmarine operations.

The primary offensive mission of the navy is supporting army actions against South Korea, particularly by inserting small-scale amphibious operations—special operations units—along the coast. The navy also has a limited capability to conduct rocket and shore bombardment raids against selected coastal targets. However, any North Korean force attempting to engage in these operations would be at risk from both air and surface combatants because of limited air defense and detection capabilities.

In mid-1993 the navy seldom operated outside the North Korean military exclusion zone, a zone extending some fifty kilometers off North Korea's coast from which it sought to exclude operations by any other navy. Although seaborne infiltration attempts into South Korea are believed to have been stopped by the 1990s, testimony of North Korean spies apprehended by South Korea in early 1992 indicated successful infiltration continues. Clashes with the South Korean navy and harassment of South Korean fishing boats once occurred with regularity, but such incidents were rare as of mid-1993.

Organization and Disposition

The Naval Command has two separate fleets: the East Sea Fleet and Yellow Sea Fleet. The fleets do not exchange vessels, and their areas of operations and missions determine their organizational structure; mutual support is difficult at best. The Yellow Sea Fleet, made up of five squadrons and approximately 300 vessels, is headquartered at Namp'o, with major bases at Pip'a-got and Sagot and smaller bases at Ch'o-do and Tasa-ri. The East Sea Fleet, with nine squadrons and approximately 400 vessels, is headquartered at T'oejo-dong, with major bases at Najin and Wŏnsan and lesser bases at Ch'aho, Ch'angjŏn, Mayang-do, and Puam-ni near the DMZ. There are many smaller bases along both coasts. The submarine force is decentralized. Submarines are stationed at Ch'aho, Mayang-do, Namp'o, and Pip'a-got naval bases.

In addition to naval units, there also are noncombatants in the North Korean merchant marine, including ten cargo ships operating directly under the KWP and the Ministry of People's Armed Forces. There are sixty-six other oceangoing vessels in the merchant marine operating under the flag of the Ministry of Sea Transportation.

Weapons and Equipment

The naval inventory varies widely (see table 10, Appendix). North Korean surface combatants have dual missions of coastal defense and limited offensive missions under a ''small navy'' doctrine. Aside from special craft and submarines, most other North Korean naval vessels are small combatants; they include torpedo boats, patrol boats and ships, and fast attack craft. North Korea has a variety of special craft. There are a number of steel-hulled high-speed, semisubmersible infiltration craft, several of which have been engaged by South Korean naval forces during the 1970s and 1980s; one has been recovered. A class of air cushioned vehicles (ACVs) derived from technology most probably acquired from Britain also is believed dedicated to amphibious operations. These craft will be well suited to use on the mud flats, seasonal frozen coastal waters, and areas of great tidal variance prevalent along Korea's west coast. Hovercraft are credited with being able to carry about a platoon each. The extent and pace of the hovercraft production program is unknown but more than 100 vessels had been built by mid-1993. Reflecting Soviet influence, most surface craft and submarines are capable of laying mines, and some vessels probably are dedicated to mine detection and sweeping. Approximately twenty-three ships are dedicated to mine warfare.

In addition to conventional submarines, North Korea has between thirty and sixty minisubmarines in service. Details of the minisubmarine fleet are sketchy. North Korea apparently has acquired minisubmarine technology from both Yugoslavia and the Federal Republic of Germany (West Germany). In the early 1970s, China helped North Korea start its own Romeo construction program, which produced new units into the early 1990s. The Romeo and Whiskey classes of conventional diesel-electric attack submarines employ technology, weapons, and sonar dating from the 1950s and 1960s. Their relatively high noise levels make them, by modern submarine standards, relatively easy to detect. This liability is mitigated to some degree by the South Korean navy's use of similar-era systems for detection and attack.

229

Military Capability and Coastal Defense

The navy's main strengths are a modest number of cruise-missile-equipped vessels, large numbers of fast patrol craft, a mine warfare potential, and a large number of small, fast transports for special operations forces. Its weaknesses include inadequate air defense, a low level of technology, and aging platforms. Logistical support is complicated by the variety of Soviet and Chinese designs of its equipment and the inability of the force to conduct sustained operations. In the early 1990s, overall fleet strength was probably on the decline inasmuch as obsolete vessels were not being replaced on a one-for-one basis.

The quality of the navy remains unknown. Joint exercises are not common. Although the navy conducted a few rudimentary exercises with Soviet naval forces in the late 1980s and is believed to have conducted a number of exercises related to command, control, and communications, there is little by which to judge the force's overall performance.

Despite its size, the submarine force also is an unknown quantity. It is difficult to ascertain whether the submarine force is intended primarily for coastal barrier defense or for offensive operations. Some submarines are assigned defensive patrols. The submarines dedicated to offensive operations probably are targeted along South Korea's coastlines near its harbors, in the Yellow Sea, and in the Sea of Japan to interdict sea lines of communication. Offensive mining is another possible mission for some of the minisubmarines.

The surface force is suited for inshore defense and harassment. The smaller craft, although dated, are capable of using Korea's rough coastal topography to mount harassing attacks against larger naval craft. Operations are limited to within fifty nautical miles of the coast.

Many North Korean navy bases have hardened berths and other passive defenses. There is an extensive antiship missile and gun defense network along the coastline. Antiship cruise missile sites were installed in the late 1960s using Soviet-supplied SSC-2b (Samlet) SSMs. Newer and longer-range SSMs entered the inventory in the mid-1980s, most probably the HY-2 (Silkworm), a modification of the Styx system. In all, some six sites are reported, covering both coasts with overlapping antiship cruise missile systems.

The Air Force

The air force became a separate service in 1948. The air force adapted Soviet and Chinese tactics and doctrine to reflect North

Major General Kim Yong-chol, vice minister, Ministry of
People's Armed Forces
Courtesy Tracy Woodward

Korea's situation, requirements, and available resources. Its
primary mission is air defense of the homeland. Secondary missions include tactical air support to the army and the navy, transportation and logistic support, and insertion of special operations
forces. A large force, the air force also can provide limited support
to ground forces.

Organization and Disposition

In 1992 the air force comprised about 1,620 aircraft and 70,000
personnel (see table 11, Appendix). There are three air combat
commands under the direct control of the Air Command at
Chunghwa, one air division (the Eighth Air Division, probably
headquartered at Ŏrang) in the northeast, and the Civil Aviation
Bureau under the State Administration Council. The air combat
commands, consisting of different mixes of fighters, bombers, transports, helicopters, reconnaissance aircraft, and surface-to-air missile (SAM) regiments, were created by integrating and reorganizing

231

existing air divisions during the mid- to late 1980s. Decentralized command and control gave more authority to regional commands.

North Korea has approximately seventy air bases, including jet and non-jet capable bases and emergency landing strips, with aircraft deployed to about twenty of them. The majority of tactical aircraft are concentrated at air bases around P'yŏngyang and in the southern provinces. P'yŏngyang can place almost all its military aircraft in hardened—mostly underground—shelters. In 1990–91 North Korea activated four forward air bases near the DMZ, which increased its initial southward reach and decreased warning and reaction times for Seoul.

Weapons and Equipment

North Korea produces no aircraft itself, although it does produce spare parts for many of its aircraft. Its aircraft fleet of Soviet and Chinese manufacture is primarily of 1950s and 1960s technology, with rudimentary avionics and limited weapons systems capability. In the mid- to late 1980s, the Soviet Union supplied a variety of a limited number of more modern all-weather air-defense and ground-attack aircraft. Most ground-attack regiments have older model Soviet and Chinese light bombers and fighters with limited range and combat payloads.

P'yŏngyang was rather late in recognizing the full potential of the helicopter. During the 1980s, the North Korean armed forces increased their helicopter inventory from about forty to about 300. In 1985 North Korea circumvented United States export controls to indirectly buy eighty-seven United States-manufactured civilian versions of the Hughes MD–500 helicopters before the United States government stopped further deliveries. Reports indicate that at least sixty of the helicopters delivered were modified as gunships. Because South Korea licenses and produces the MD–500 for use in its armed forces, the modified helicopters were useful in North Korea's covert or deceptive operations. The transport fleet has some Soviet transports from the 1950s and 1960s.

Trends, Training, Readiness, and Military Capability

The air force has a marginal capability for defending North Korean airspace and a limited ability to conduct air operations against South Korea. Its strengths are its large numbers of aircraft, a system of well-dispersed and well-protected air facilities, and an effective, if rudimentary, command-and-control system. Its weaknesses include limited flight training; forced reliance on outside sources for aircraft, most of its missiles, radars, and associated equipment; and maintenance problems associated with older aircraft. The effectiveness of ground training—on which the pilots heavily depend—is difficult to judge because there is no information on P'yŏngyang's acquisition or use of sophisticated flight simulators.

Pilot proficiency is difficult to evaluate because it is crudely proportionate to hours and quality of flight time. Although the Republic of Korea Ministry of National Defense's *Defense White Paper, 1990* states that flight training levels are 60 percent of South Korea's, other sources believe the figure is closer to 20 to 30 percent. Lower flight times are attributed to fuel shortages, a more conservative training philosophy, and perhaps a concern for older airframe life expectancies or maintenance infrastructure capacity.

Air Defense

Operational thinking reflects both Soviet doctrine and the North Korean experience of heavy bombing during the Korean War. The result has been a reliance on air defense. Military industries, aircraft hangars, repair facilities, ammunition, fuel stores, and even air-defense missile systems are placed underground or in hardened shelters. North Korea has an extensive interlocking, redundant nationwide air-defense system that includes interceptor aircraft, early-warning and ground-controlled intercept radars, SAMs, a large number of air-defense artillery weapons, and barrage balloons.

At the national level, air defense was once the responsibility of the Air Defense Command, a separate entity from the air force, but which probably was collocated with the Air Force Headquarters in P'yŏngyang. However, that function probably was transferred to the air force in the late 1980s.

The air combat commands appear to have primary responsibility for integrated air defense and are organized with semiautomated warning and interception systems to control SAMs, interceptor aircraft, and air defense artillery units. The First Air Combat Command, in the northwest, probably headquartered at Kaech'ŏn, is responsible for the west coast to the border with China, including P'yŏngyang. The Second Air Combat Command, headquartered at Toksan, covers the northeast and extends up the east coast to the Soviet border. The Third Air Combat Command, headquartered at Hwangju in the south, is responsible for the border with South Korea and the southernmost areas along the east and west coasts.

Important military and industrial complexes are defended by antiaircraft artillery. Point defenses are supplemented by barrage balloons. North Korea has an exceptionally large number of antiaircraft sites. The largest concentration is along the DMZ and around major cities, military installations, and factories.

The bulk of North Korean radars are older Soviet and Chinese models with vacuum-tube technology, which limits continuous operations. The overall early-warning and ground-controlled intercept system is susceptible to saturation and jamming by a sophisticated foe with state-of-the-art electronic warfare capabilities. Nevertheless, the multilayered, coordinated, mutually supporting air-defense structure is a formidable deterrent to air attack. Overlapping coverage and redundancy make penetration of North Korean air defenses a challenge.

Civil Aviation

Civil aviation is subordinate to the air force. Since joining the International Civil Aviation Organization in 1977, the Civil Aviation Bureau has operated as a public airline, although public access by the North Korean citizenry is, like all travel, restricted. The bureau operates international and domestic flights and operations supporting conventional civil aviation, military airlift, and logistic support. Although the Civil Aviation Bureau is not a military organization, its subordination to the air force command makes its equipment, facilities, and personnel readily available for military use in the event of a national emergency or mobilization.

Officer Corps: Recruitment and Education

The first military training school, the P'yŏngyang Military Academy, was established in North Korea in 1945. The Security Cadres School was founded in 1946 and was later renamed the First Officer Candidate School.

The military education and training system for officers is quite elaborate. The officer education system includes approximately seventeen universities, colleges, schools, and academies. Among them are officer candidate schools for each service; basic and advanced branch schools for armor, artillery, rear services, and other branches; mid-career staff colleges; senior war colleges; and special schools, including medical and veterinary service schools.

Officer candidates, typically selected from enlisted men who have served three to four years in the military, receive their initial cadet training at a service academy. The Kang Kon Military Academy near P'yŏngyang is North Korea's equivalent of the United States Military Academy at West Point. The academy offers a two-year course for infantry and rear service; a three-year course for engineering, communications, chemical, and other services; and a six- to twelve-month "short course" refresher for all branches of service.

Two schools are of particular importance. The Man'gyŏngdae Revolutionary Institute, founded in 1947 for children of the party

elite, provides a seven-year quasi-military training program. Kim
Il Sung Military College, the most prestigious military school for
training senior officers and ranking party cadre, has a three-year
course designed for senior company and field-grade officers. Graduation is a prerequisite for promotion to general. A one-year
"refresher" course is offered for senior field-grade and general
officers of all services and for senior party officials.

The Air Academy in Ch'ŏngjin, founded in 1961 when it separated from Kim Il Sung Military College, offers a four-year course
for regular cadets, a three-year mid-career staff college course, and
a one-year refresher course. Senior officer training courses and
refresher courses also are offered. Cadets become pilots or maintenance officers upon graduation from the academy. The Naval
Academy, located at Najin, offers a four-year training program
and a mid-career staff college course of unknown length.

Mid-career staff, or "refresher," training is offered at all the
service academies and at various branch schools. Courses taught
at the service colleges run six months to a year, whereas branch
and other courses tend to be limited to six months.

Recruitment and selection of political officers vary with rank.
Stringent selection requirements include prior military service, a
family with a politically reliable background, and proven party
loyalty. Political officers are trained at Kim Il Sung Political College and Kumsong Political College, among other institutions.
Training focuses on politics, economics, party history, *chuch'e* (see
Glossary) philosophy, and party loyalty. Upon graduating, students
are appointed second lieutenants in political or political security
positions in KPA units. Advanced political officer training also is
provided.

Political officers for field-grade positions are selected by the political department at the corps level from party members in the corps
headquarters. Supplemental training can include a six-month course
at a political college. Candidates for positions at the division or
higher level are identified by the Organization Department of the
General Political Bureau of the KPA. They are then screened by
the party committee and approved by the Secretariat of the party
Central Committee before appointment as head of a political department at the division or higher level.

College Reserve Military Training Units at colleges and universities provide most of the training for reserve officers. Information available about the training does not differentiate between the
officer selection process and other reserve military training. There
may be two separate tracks or a selection process at the end of
training.

	SOWI	CHUNGWI	SANGWI	TAEWI	SOJWA	CHUNGJWA	SANGJWA	TAEJWA	NO RANK	SOJANG	CHUNGJANG	SANGJANG	TAEJANG	CH'ASU	WONSU	TAEWONSU
NORTH KOREAN RANK — ARMY[1]	SOWI	CHUNGWI	SANGWI	TAEWI	SOJWA	CHUNGJWA	SANGJWA	TAEJWA	NO RANK	SOJANG	CHUNGJANG	SANG-JANG	TAEJANG	[2]	[2]	[2]
U.S. RANK TITLE	2D LIEUTENANT		1ST LIEUTENANT	CAPTAIN	MAJOR	LIEUTENANT COLONEL	COLONEL		BRIGADIER GENERAL	MAJOR GENERAL	LIEUTENANT GENERAL	GENERAL				
NORTH KOREAN RANK — AIR FORCE[1]	SOWI	CHUNGWI	SANGWI	TAEWI	SOJWA	CHUNGJWA	SANGJWA	TAEJWA	NO RANK	SOJANG	CHUNGJANG	SANG-JANG	TAEJANG	[2]	[2]	[2]
U.S. RANK TITLE	2D LIEUTENANT		1ST LIEUTENANT	CAPTAIN	MAJOR	LIEUTENANT COLONEL	COLONEL		BRIGADIER GENERAL	MAJOR GENERAL	LIEUTENANT GENERAL	GENERAL				
NORTH KOREAN RANK — NAVY[1]	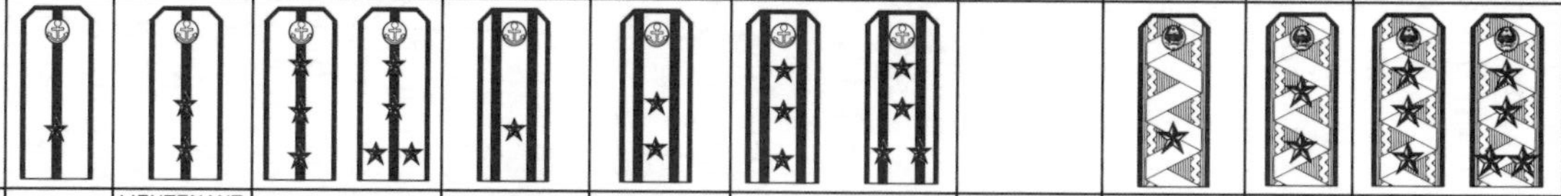 SOWI	CHUNGWI	SANGWI	TAEWI	SOJWA	CHUNGJWA	SANGJWA	TAEJWA	NO RANK	SOJANG	CHUNGJANG	SANG-JANG	TAEJANG	[2]	[2]	[2]
U.S. RANK TITLE	ENSIGN	LIEUTENANT JUNIOR GRADE	LIEUTENANT		LIEUTENANT COMMANDER	COMMANDER	CAPTAIN		REAR ADMIRAL LOWER HALF	REAR ADMIRAL UPPER HALF	VICE ADMIRAL	ADMIRAL				

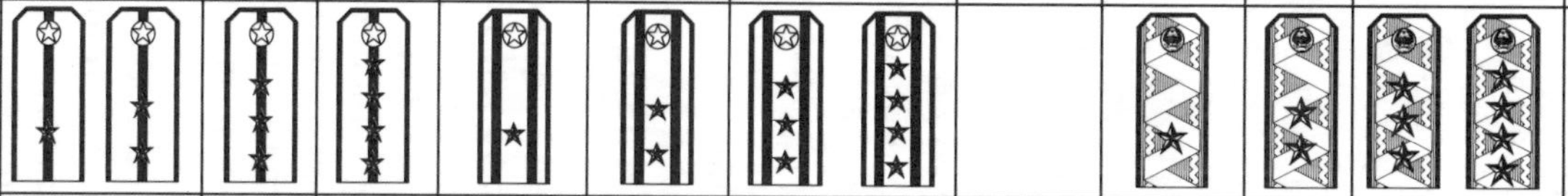

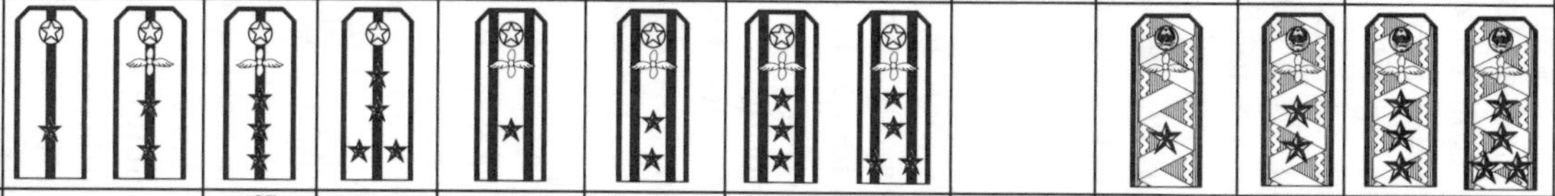

[1] All officer insignia have a gold background, but the color of stripes and borders varies by service: army, red; air force, blue; navy, black. Stars are silver.

[2] No insignia available: Korean ranks translate as vice marshal, marshal, and grand marshal (generalissimo), respectively.

Figure 12. Officer Ranks and Insignia, 1993

Officer rank structure is divided into company-grade, field-grade, and general officers. The army and air force have the same ranks, but the navy has a different nomenclature (see fig. 12). Company-grade officer ranks are four-tiered for the army and air force and three-tiered for the navy.

Promotion is a slow process. There is a minimum period of two years between basic private and private first class (airman basic and airman first class in the air force, or seaman recruit and seaman in the navy) and four or five years between private first class and consideration for noncommissioned officer (NCO) training and sergeant or petty officer status (see fig. 13). NCO training is conducted at an NCO school and lasts between six and ten months.

Until December 1991, Kim Il Sung alone held the rank of marshal in his position as supreme commander of the KPA. In December 1991, Kim Jong Il was named supreme commander of the KPA; and on April 20, 1992, Kim Il Sung was given the title Grand Marshal and Kim Jong Il and Minister of People's Armed Forces O Chin-u were named marshal. The title of vice marshal was also awarded to eight other military leaders. These promotions were followed by a massive wave of senior officer promotions that involved as many as 664 generals.

Military Conscription and Terms of Service

As of mid-1993, North Korea had national conscription for males that included significant pre-induction and post-enlistment obligations. Initial draft registration is at age fourteen, and two pre-induction physicals are conducted at age sixteen. Pre-induction student training includes both high school and college training corps. Senior middle-school students are enlisted in the Red Guard Youth and receive about 300 hours of rudimentary military training annually. Approximately 160 hours of this training takes place at school; the remainder is conducted during a one-time, week-long summer camp. College students are organized into College Training Units. They train for 160 hours annually on campus and participate in a one-time, six-month training camp.

The typical draft age is seventeen—after high school graduation. Some youths are able to postpone entering the military through temporary deferments based on college attendance or civilian occupation skills. The maximum legal draft age is believed to be twenty-five. Eligibility for the draft is based on economic and political factors as well as physical condition. Technicians, skilled workers, members of special government organizations, and children of the politically influential often are excluded from the draft. Most service personnel are single.

Figure 13. Enlisted Ranks and Insignia, 1993

	PYŎNGSA	NO RANK	SANTŬNGBYŎNG	NO RANK	HASA	CHUNGSA	SANGSA	T'UKMUSANGSA
NORTH KOREAN RANK — ARMY[1]	PYŎNGSA	NO RANK	SANTŬNGBYŎNG	NO RANK	HASA	CHUNGSA	SANGSA	T'UKMUSANGSA
U.S. RANK TITLE	BASIC PRIVATE	PRIVATE	PRIVATE 1ST CLASS	CORPORAL/SPECIALIST	SERGEANT / STAFF SERGEANT	SERGEANT 1ST CLASS	MASTER SERGEANT / FIRST SERGEANT	SERGEANT MAJOR / COMMAND SERGEANT MAJOR
NORTH KOREAN RANK — AIR FORCE[2]	PYŎNGSA	NO RANK	SANTŬNGBYŎNG	NO RANK	HASA	CHUNGSA	SANGSA	T'UKMUSANGSA
U.S. RANK TITLE	AIRMAN BASIC	AIRMAN	AIRMAN 1ST CLASS	SENIOR AIRMAN / SERGEANT	STAFF SERGEANT / TECHNICAL SERGEANT	MASTER SERGEANT	SENIOR MASTER SERGEANT	CHIEF MASTER SERGEANT
NORTH KOREAN RANK — NAVY[3]	PYŎNGSA	NO RANK	SANTŬNGBYŎNG	NO RANK	HASA	CHUNGSA	SANGSA	T'UKMUSANGSA
U.S. RANK TITLE	SEAMAN RECRUIT	SEAMAN APPRENTICE	SEAMAN	PETTY OFFICER 3D CLASS	PETTY OFFICER 2D CLASS / PETTY OFFICER 1ST CLASS	CHIEF PETTY OFFICER	SENIOR CHIEF PETTY OFFICER	MASTER CHIEF PETTY OFFICER

[1]Army enlisted insignia are gold on a red background. [2]Air Force enlisted insignia are gold on a blue background. [3]Navy enlisted insignia are gold on a black background.

Women are recruited on a limited scale for rear-area duties: psychological-warfare units, hospitals, administration, and anti-aircraft units. Most women are assigned to units defending fixed installations near their workplaces.

In mid-1993 the legal term of service for enlisted army draftees was believed to be forty-two months. The term of service for draftees in the navy and air force was forty-eight months. However, legal limits regularly are extended. Draftees in regular army units typically are discharged at age twenty-six, regardless of the time of entry into service. Those assigned to special operations forces or the air force often are not discharged until age thirty. Terms of service for draftees, therefore, range from less than four to more than ten years.

Recruits undergo initial military familiarization before being sent to a basic training center. Induction and a month-long basic training program for conscripts are held between March and August. New recruit training is conducted by a training company at the regiment or division level depending on the service. Advanced training varies according to service and branch: infantry and armor training is for one month, artillery training for three months, and communications training for six months. Once assigned to a unit, the individual soldier receives further training, most of which is conducted at the company or platoon level.

Training is conducted under constant supervision and essentially emphasizes memorization and repetition but also includes a heavy emphasis on technical skills and vocational training. Lack of a technical base is another reason for the emphasis on repetitive training drills. Night training is extensive, and physical and mental conditioning also are stressed. Remedial training for initially substandard performances is not uncommon. Such training methods produce soldiers well versed in the basics even under adverse conditions. The degree to which they are prepared to respond rapidly to changing circumstances is less certain.

The quality of life of the enlisted soldier is difficult to evaluate. Conditions are harsh; rations are 650 to 750 grams per day (80 to 90 percent of the South Korean ration), depending on branch and service. Leave and passes are limited and strictly controlled. A two-week leave is allowed only once or twice during an enlistment. A ten-day leave normally is granted for marriage or parental death. Passes for enlisted men are even rarer; neither day nor overnight passes are granted. During tours of duty, day passes are granted for public affairs duties or KWP-related activities. There is conflicting information about the frequency of corporal punishment and the harshness of military justice.

239

A typical daily routine can run from 5:00 A.M. to 10:00 P.M., with at least ten hours devoted to training and only three hours of free or rest time, excluding meals. In addition, soldiers perform many duties not related to their basic mission. Units are expected, for example, to grow crops and to raise livestock or fish to supplement their rations.

Reserves and Paramilitary Forces

Lessons learned from the Korean War still shaped military planning in mid-1993. Because P'yŏngyang has determined that inadequate reserve forces are a critical deficiency, Kim Il Sung has decided to arm the entire population. The Four Military Guidelines formulated in 1962 created a non-active-duty force of between 5 million and 6 million persons.

All soldiers serve in the reserves; there were an estimated 1.2 million reservists in mid-1993. The primary reserve forces pool consists of persons who either have finished their active military service or are exempted and are attached to the reserve forces until age forty (age thirty for single women). Reserve training totals approximately 500 hours annually. Afterward, reservists, along with unmarried women, join the paramilitary Worker-Peasant Red Guards and receive approximately 160 hours of training annually until age sixty.

There are four general categories of reserve forces: reserve military training units, Red Guard Youth, College Training Units, and Worker-Peasant Red Guards. Unit organizations essentially parallel active-duty forces. Some military training units are organized around factories or administrative organizations.

In 1990 the reserve military training units had approximately 720,000 men and women and included as many as 48,000 active-duty troops assigned to between twenty-two and twenty-six divisions, at least eighteen independent brigades, and many smaller units. All maneuver units are believed to have individual weapons for all troops and about 80 percent of the needed crew-served weapons (those requiring a team for operation), including artillery. Transportation assets probably are much lower.

Approximately 480,000 college students have been organized into College Training Units. These units have individual weapons and some crew-served weapons. Training is geared toward individual replacement, and soldiers called to active duty are parcelled out as needed as a manpower pool rather than as organized forces.

Red Guard Youth units are composed of some 850,000 students between the ages of fourteen and seventeen at the senior middle-school level. Emphasis is on pre-induction military familiarization.

The Worker-Peasant Red Guard is composed of some 3.89 million persons between the ages of forty and sixty. They receive 160 hours of military training annually. Unit structure is small, decentralized, and focuses on homeland defense. Units are equipped with individual small arms and have a limited number of crew-served weapons and antiaircraft guns.

The overall quality of the North Korean reserve structure is difficult to evaluate. Through strong societal controls, P'yŏngyang is able to regulate forces and maintain unit cohesion to a greater degree than is possible in more open societies. Reserve military training units probably are good quality forces with the ability to take on limited regular-force responsibilities during wartime.

The reserve force structure apparently was fleshed out in the 1980s, when many older weapons were phased out of the regular forces and passed on to the reserves. Weapons refitting led to restructuring and the development of the Military District Command system. Turning over the homeland defense mission to the command system has allowed North Korean force planners the freedom to forward deploy a greater proportion of the regular forces toward the DMZ.

Role in National Life

The United States Department of Defense estimated that North Korea had a million troops under arms for most of the 1980s, although P'yŏngyang regularly claimed that it maintained its armed forces at around 400,000 persons (see fig. 14). Given the closed nature of North Korean society, there was little publicly available evidence to validate either claim until the research conducted in 1991 by Nicholas Eberstadt and Judith Banister at the Harvard University Center for Population and Development Studies. Their estimates, derived from DPRK population data given to the UN, suggest that the number of males in the North Korean armed forces had increased from at least 740,000 in 1975 to over 900,000 in 1980 and 1.2 million in 1986. The estimates also suggest that more than one out of every five North Korean men between the ages of sixteen and fifty-four was in the military as of 1986. If all military men are of the ages conscripts were thought to serve, that is, ages seventeen to twenty-six, they would constitute almost half the age-group. The armed forces would have accounted for at least 12 percent of the entire male population and at least 6 percent of the total population. As a result of estimated decreases in that age-group over the 1990s, the same size military force will constitute 59 percent of the conscript age-group in the year 2000, and 57 percent in 2005.

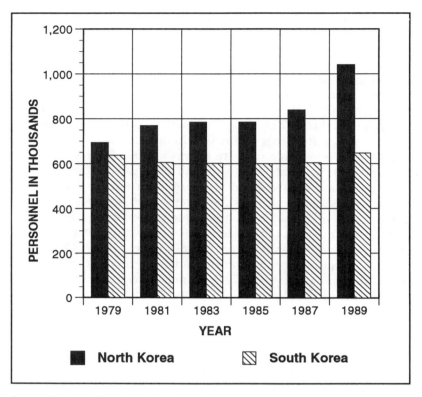

Source: Based on information from United States, Arms Control and Disarmament Agency, *World Military Expenditures and Arms Transfers, 1990*, Washington, 1991, 69.

Figure 14. Comparison of North Korean and South Korean Armed Forces, Selected Years, 1979–89

Although difficult to quantify, the economic consequences of such a massive military establishment are staggering. North Korea's published budget figures, however, are of little use in estimating the impact of the massive military buildup. Many analysts dismiss North Korea's military budget figures completely, while others assume that significant costs related to defense expenditures are hidden under nondefense budget headings. Most estimates put the total for military expenditures in the range of 20 to 25 percent of the gross national product (GNP—see Glossary) (see fig. 15).

Military personnel sometimes are assigned to civilian duty. For example, troops may be assigned to factories to alleviate labor shortages. Training seldom is held during planting or harvesting seasons to allow troops to assist farmers. Much of the construction of major infrastructure projects is completed by military engineering units or regular military personnel mobilized in support of special projects. Military-associated construction since the 1950s includes such diverse projects as the Namhŭng chemical complex, the Sunch'ŏn synthetic fiber complexes, the P'yŏngyang-Wŏnsan and P'yŏngyang-Kaesŏng expressways, the sports complexes for the games of the Thirteenth World Festival of Youth and Students, various barrages and lockgates, the Taech'ŏn power station, the 800-kilometer west coast waterway project, coal mines, cement factories, public housing and government buildings, tramways, and dams.

The number of troops used for construction projects at any one time is unknown. During the 1980s, however, construction became nearly a full-time activity for selected units as result of civilian labor shortages. In 1986 North Korea announced that some 150,000 troops had been transferred to domestic construction projects. A 1987 announcement indicated that 100,000 troops were active in civilian construction projects. These troops were not discharged, and some were merely assigned to the projects. Other troops may have been reassigned to engineering bureaus while they participated in various projects.

At no time did reassignment to construction work represent a real reduction in military strength. However, it undoubtedly had a negative impact on military readiness and capability. Basic individual skills were maintained, but large unit training was more likely to deteriorate.

Relations Between the Military and the Korean Workers' Party

Over the years, Kim Il Sung and the political leadership clearly paid close attention to the military's political role. The military's participation in politics has been co-opted in rough proportion to the share of the country's resources it commands. The military has a dual command structure, and the party has its own organization in the military separate from the Ministry of People's Armed Forces. The senior military leadership is part of the political elite. However, disputes over policy direction and poor performance assessments by the party leadership periodically result in purges of senior military leaders. Because the causes of intrafactional struggles are policy oriented, the impact of these purges on party-military relations is both limited and temporary, and it is not uncommon for purged individuals to return to positions of responsibility. Since the 1960s, relations between the KWP and KPA have been highly cooperative

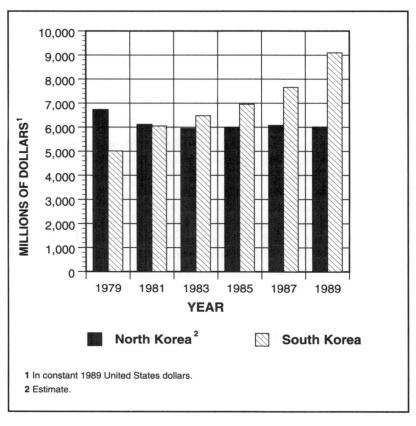

Source: Based on information from United States, Arms Control and Disarmament Agency, *World Military Expenditures and Arms Transfers, 1990*, Washington, 1991, 69.

Figure 15. Comparison of North Korean and South Korean Military Expenditures, Selected Years, 1979–89

and seem to reflect a stable party control system within the military.

Since 1948 the party work and political control system in the KPA has changed dramatically. At that time, the KWP had neither a separate organization dedicated to military affairs nor an organization in the KPA. During the Korean War, a party structure was introduced in order to strengthen ideological indoctrination. After the purges of the late 1950s, the control system was intensified by the creation of the army-party committee system.

In 1969 the party work system was strengthened and centralized with the adoption of a political officer system supervised by the

Secretariat of the Central Committee. Since the adoption of the system, all orders and directives of commanders have required the signature of a political officer. In addition, the activities of political cadres are reported on by the Organization and Guidance Department of the party Central Committee. The political department and party committee reports are submitted through separate channels to the party Secretariat. The Socialist Working Youth League (SWYL) manages nonparty members under party leadership. Above the battalion level, there are Socialist Working Youth League committees. Under the leadership of the political department, there are youth league elements down to the platoon level.

In mid-1993 the KPA and the KWP had overlapping memberships, which strengthened the party's role in the military. With the exceptions of Kim Il Sung and Kim Jong Il, all members of the KWP Military Affairs Committee selected at the Sixth Party Congress in 1980 are active-duty military. Ten of the members also are members of the General Political Bureau. Military representation in the General Political Bureau and the Central Committee is considerable. The average rate of military participation on the Central Committee is 21 percent, ranging from a low of 17 percent in 1948, to a high of 23 percent in 1970. There was 19 percent participation at the Sixth Party Congress in 1980, the most recent congress. The turnover rate of the military in the two committees is lower than that of civilians.

All officers are members of the KWP. Military duty is one of the most common ways of gaining party membership, and approximately 20 to 25 percent of the military are party members. The membership rates of key forward-deployed units may have been as high as 60 to 70 percent.

The party has dual access into the military: directly through the committee system and indirectly through the KWP Secretariat and political-officer system. In effect, the military is allowed its own party organization, but that party organization is supervised through the KWP Secretariat. Theoretically, there is a clear functional separation between the commanding and political officers. The unit commander is responsible for all administrative and military matters while the political officer executes party policies.

Units have political officers down to the company level. Within platoons, political activities are handled by the assistant platoon leader. The tasks of the political officer are twofold: propaganda and organizational work. The political officer is responsible for all ideological training for the unit, selects the party committee, and runs all political meetings of the military units. The power of political officers derives from their ability to attend and comment on all staff meetings, to subject the commander to political criticism, to influence promotions, to inspect units, and to countersign the unit commander's orders.

Military Doctrine and Strategy

As of mid-1993, North Korea had no open forum for propounding official views on military doctrine and strategy. Interpretation and discussion of North Korean military doctrine rely upon analysis of speeches by high-ranking military officers or detectable changes in military organization, structure, and equipment.

The Evolution of North Korean Military Thought

North Korean military doctrine has evolved through as many as four stages since the founding of the KPA in February 1948. North Korean military writings derive from Marxism-Leninism through the conduit of "Kim Il Sung Thought." Kim Il Sung is credited with virtually everything in North Korean military thought, from Lenin's reformulation of Clausewitz's classic definition of war to basic squad tactics.

North Korean military thinking began as a mixture of Soviet strategic and Chinese tactical influences. At the Third Plenum of the Second KWP Central Committee in December 1950, Kim Il Sung's report, "The Present Condition and the Confronting Task," for the first time interjected North Korean combat experience into military doctrine and thought. From 1951 to December 1962, North Korean military orthodoxy was a conventional warfare doctrine based on Soviet military doctrine and operational art modified on the basis of the Korean War experience. This duality is readily acknowledged in official publications such as the KWP journal, *Kŭlloja* (The Worker). Stalin's five "permanently operating factors," factors that determine the course and outcome of war, were directly incorporated into North Korean military doctrine. The factors are the stability of the rear, the morale of the army, the quantity and quality of divisions, the armament of the army, and the organizing ability of the command personnel. The importance of combined arms operations (armor, infantry, and artillery operating in close coordination) also reflects strong Soviet influence.

North Korean military doctrine shifted dramatically in December 1962 away from the doctrine of regular warfare to a doctrine that embraced people's war. At the Fifth Plenum of the Fourth KWP Central Committee in December 1962, Kim Il Sung espoused the Four Military Guidelines: to arm the entire population; to fortify the entire country; to train the entire army as a "cadre army";

Soldiers participate in civilian industrial and agricultural work. Courtesy Democratic People's Republic of Korea Mission to the United Nations

and to modernize weaponry, doctrine, and tactics under the principle of self-reliance in national defense. The adoption of this military line signaled a shift from a Soviet-style strategy to a Maoist protracted war of attrition. Conventional warfare strategy was incorporated into and subordinated to the overall concept of people's war and the mobilization of the entire people through reinforcement of ideological training. These principles are formally adopted in Article 60 of the 1992 constitution.

The shift supplies the doctrinal basis for North Korea's strategy of covert infiltrations into South Korea, assassinations, and attempts at fostering insurgencies in South Korea during the late 1960s. During this period, doctrine also began to stress the need to adapt these concepts to the North Korean situation. Military thinking emphasized the necessity of light weapons, high-angle indirect fire, and night fighting. Renewed emphasis was given to sea denial and coastal defense during this period.

Emergence of the New Doctrine

Through the late 1960s and into the early 1970s, Kim Il Sung continued to favor the political-ideological dimension of warfare over technology or military science. A transformation began in the 1970s, when renewed emphasis was placed on conventional warfare and the modernization of the KPA.

In the August 1976 issue of *Kŭlloja,* an article by Kim Chol Man entitled ''Scientific Features of Modern War and Factors of Victory'' reexamines and reinterprets military doctrine. Kim dwells at length on the importance of economic development and the impact of new weapons on military strategy. Victory in war requires economic development and complete mobilization of a nation's economic potential, including a strong self-supporting munitions industry and material reserves. Military factors are considered in absolute terms rather than on the basis of North Korea's stage of development. Kim argues that the quality of arms and the level of military technology define the characteristics of war.

After some initial debate, Kim Chol Man's argument apparently was accepted and became the new orthodoxy. The primacy of conventional warfare again became doctrine. Kim's article contains several concepts that continue to influence North Korean operational art in the early 1990s; particularly influential are the concepts that emphasize the importance of operational and tactical mobility through the employment of mechanized forces, the importance of firepower throughout the depth of the battlefield, the importance of deep strikes, and the importance of command and control. Kim also stresses that each operational plan and campaign should aim at a lightning war for a quick decision.

Operational Practice in the 1980s and 1990s

The Korean People's Army (KPA) is structured and deployed on the primacy of the offense. Doctrine stresses that decisive results can be obtained only through offensive operations. The offense has three objectives: the destruction of enemy forces, the seizure and control of territory, and the destruction of the enemy's will to fight.

Strategy and tactics are built on the key concepts of combined-arms offensive operations, battlefield mobility, flexibility, and the integration of conventional and unconventional warfare. Mass, mobility, and firepower are the three reinforcing elements of a strategy that, when combined with speed and security at a critical point, will produce a decisive offensive strike.

Changes in force development reflect changes in doctrine and strategy. The military problem facing P'yŏngyang is encountering difficult terrain crossed by the multiple defensive lines, extensive barrier systems, and hardened defensive positions of a determined defender. A heavy emphasis on special forces is the first solution.

After the mid-1970s, the emphasis shifted to firepower. The artillery force, both active and reserve, grew steadily, and self-propelled artillery was deployed. Most North Korean artillery has a greater standoff range than comparable South Korea-United States systems. Hardened artillery positions and a forward-based logistics system of underground facilities for ammunition stockpiles, petroleum, oil, lubricants, and other war supplies appeared to be designed to sustain an initial offensive despite a lack of air superiority. These initiatives only partially addressed the problem, however, because North Korean artillery cannot fire from its hardened artillery sites.

In the 1980s, the emphasis shifted to firepower and mobility as a solution. Some experts believe that maneuver received new emphasis when larger-scale mobile units were created beginning in the early 1980s. Force deployment suggests that P'yŏngyang intends to employ both second-echelon and strategic/exploitation forces.

Employment in Offensive Scenario

The basic goal of a North Korean southern offensive is destruction of allied defenses either before South Korea can fully mobilize its national power or before significant reinforcement from the United States can arrive and be deployed. Final war preparations most likely would not involve a noticeable surge in military-related activity because almost two-thirds of the ground forces and a significant amount of logistical support already are concentrated in the forward area between P'yŏngyang and the DMZ. Immediately preceding the initial infantry assault, North Korean artillery units would attempt to saturate the first-echelon South Korean defense with preparatory and continuous suppressive fire. North Korean infantry and armor elements of the first-echelon divisions of the forward conventional corps would attack selected narrow fronts to create gaps for the follow-on echelons. The penetration would be supported by North Korean special operations forces. At the same time, the KPA would launch several diversionary attacks in order to confuse and disperse the defensive effort. The mechanized corps would attempt to push through any gaps, bypass and isolate defenders, and penetrate as deeply as possible into the strategic rear.

The overall objective of the breakout would be to disturb the coherence of South Korea defenses in depth—including its key command, control, communications, and intelligence infrastructure (C^3I)—so as to disrupt any significant counterattacks. In support of what would be primarily a ground war, the navy might attempt to insert amphibious-trained special operations forces on each coast or to secure the northern islands or support operations against the Kimp'o Peninsula, across the Han River estuary near Seoul. In addition, Scud and FROG missiles would be used during the assault to disrupt rear areas and C^3I. After initial naval support and supply, however, the navy's limited capability to control the sea would leave embarked forces on their own. Both the navy and the air force would be hard pressed to sustain a level of offensive operations and would revert to a largely defensive role.

In order for the KPA's military strategy to succeed on the battlefield, the KPA would have to achieve initial strategic surprise and execute its operations quickly. The most critical period would probably be choosing when and where to commit the mobile exploitation forces.

Defense Industry and Infrastructure

The *chuch'e* ideology's emphasis on a self-sufficient state also extends to military industry and sustainability. The Four Military Guidelines calls for a military force capable of operating for an extended period without external support or intervention.

For its level of technological and economic development, North Korea has developed an impressive military-industrial complex and is nearly self-sufficient in military production. However, because overall technological levels are low, the military is incapable of producing aircraft, sophisticated radars, or electronic equipment. But P'yŏnyang has been successful when it assigns priority resources to specific projects.

North Korea is believed to have stockpiled enough ammunition, food, and petroleum, oil, and lubricants in hardened, underground facilities to sustain combat for several months without outside aid. According to Seoul, by 1989 P'yŏnyang had stockpiled some 990,000 tons of ammunition—an amount sufficient for four months of combat. It is also believed that despite food and energy shortages in the late 1980s and early 1990s, North Korea maintains significant national stockpiles for emergency military use.

Military Industry

North Korea's extensive defense production capability reflects its commitment to self-reliance. Although most equipment is of Soviet or Chinese design, P'yŏnyang has modified the original designs and produces both derivatives and indigenously designed versions of armored personnel carriers, self-propelled artillery, light tanks, and high-speed landing craft (see Relations with the Third World, this ch.).

In mid-1993 North Korea had an impressive, if technologically dated, military production capacity. Ground systems production included a complete line of armored vehicles, field artillery, including a new turreted self-propelled artillery piece first seen in April 1992, and crew- and individual-served weapons. Naval construction included surface combatants up to 1,400 tons, Romeo class submarines, air-cushioned vehicles, and a wide range of specialized infiltration craft. Missile production included antitank guided missiles (AT-3), SA-7 Grails (Soviet surface-to-air missiles produced at the Chongyul Arms Plant), and possibly SA-14 or SA-16 follow-ons, possibly SA-2s, and Scud-derived surface-to-surface missiles. Aircraft production was limited to a partial spare parts and assembly capacity, assembly or coproduction of the Mi-2 helicopter, and production of small trainers. Since the mid-1980s, there has been speculation that North Korea's aircraft-related facility at Panghyŏn would begin production of a jet combat aircraft—possibly a MiG-21 derivative—but as of 1992 no production had occurred. In 1991 South Korean sources believed North Korea might be able to produce its own fighters by 1995. In 1993 two MiG-29s were assembled at the Panghyŏn plant from kits supplied by Russia. Assembly was halted because of North Korea's inability to pay for more parts.

In 1990 North Korea had some 134 arms factories, many of them completely or partially concealed underground. These facilities produce ground service arms, ammunition, armored vehicles, naval craft, aircraft (spares and subassemblies), missiles, electronics, and possibly chemical-related materials. In addition, some 115 non-military factories have a dedicated wartime matériel production mission.

North Korea's arms and munitions industry predates the Korean War. After the war, North Korea began to expand its arms production base through licensing agreements with the Soviet Union. North Korea initially depended on the Soviet Union and China for licensed technology and complete industrial plants. In the 1970s, North Korea was developing variants of standard Soviet and Chinese equipment. Acquisitions from these two sources were augmented beginning in the early 1970s by an outreach program aimed at acquiring Western dual-use technology and equipment. This program included a wide range of initiatives, from acquiring Japanese trucks and electronic gear to obtaining Austrian forging equipment with gun barrel applications, to purchasing United States-manufactured helicopters. North Korea compensates for its limited research and development base by producing a range of more basic systems in quantity.

The defense industrial base is difficult to assess accurately. P'yŏng-yang desires state-of-the-art technology, but is unable to obtain it. Older weapons systems are obtainable, however, and North Korea is able to reverse engineer major systems and to modify and improve on them. Nevertheless, it still lags dramatically behind military state of the art because the systems remain dated. Because of its uneven technological base, North Korea apparently places the highest priority on quantity to make up for a lack of quality.

Special Weapons

Chemical Weapons

The Chemical Directorate, Ministry of People's Armed Forces, is believed to have been established immediately after the end of the Korean War. In the 1950s and 1960s, chemical staffs and units were established in the army down through the division level. In the 1980s, the chemical unit attached to each level was upgraded, from platoon to company, company to battalion, and so on.

Although little information is available regarding the army's offensive chemical doctrine, and an offensive chemical warfare capability was not unequivocally confirmed as deployed as of mid-1993, North Korea has the ability to produce and employ a wide range of chemical weapons. Those weapons are deliverable by a variety of potential launch and delivery vehicles, including most of the military's artillery pieces, multiple rocket launchers, and mortars. The air force can deliver chemical bombs and warheads, as can FROG or Scud missiles. As of mid-1993, the production, rate, and types of chemical agents had not been confirmed, but by the late 1980s as many as eight industrial facilities capable of producing chemical agents had been identified; they were located at Anju, Aoji, Ch'ŏngjin, Hamhŭng, Manp'o, Sinhung, Sinŭiju, and Sunch'ŏn. There were three research institutes; they were located at Kanggye, Sinŭiju, and near Hamhŭng (see Industry, ch. 3). North Korea is credited with the capability to produce nerve agents, blood agents, blistering agents, and choking agents. Some estimates place North Korea's chemical stockpiles at around 250 tons.

The acquisition of defensive chemical warfare is not confined to the army. Each airfield has a chemical platoon equipped with decontamination equipment and detection systems derived from Soviet or Chinese designs. Their missions include training personnel in the use of chemical protective gear and the detection of chemical agents. Chemical training is combined with all types of combat training to develop mission capability under chemical warfare conditions. Army personnel are equipped with protective masks and rudimentary suits or capes, but on a severely constricted basis to conserve equipment stocks. Emergency procedures and the use of gas masks are taught as part of basic training.

Missile Developments

North Korea's battlefield missile program probably began with the reverse engineering of the FROG–5 and the mid-1970s acquisition of local production of China's Samlet antiship missile, a result of a long history of bilateral cooperation. Egypt also has a long-standing bilateral relationship with North Korea and became involved in the missile program as an outgrowth of military and defense industry cooperation that dates back to 1973.

Between 1981 and 1985, North Korea is believed to have reverse engineered the Scud-B using several Egyptian-supplied, Soviet-made Scud-Bs. Production facilities are located on the outskirts of P'yŏngyang, and missile test facilities are concentrated at a few bases along the eastern coast north of Wŏnsan. North Korea first test-launched the Scud-B in 1984 and, with the help of Iranian capital investments, began production by 1987. During the Iran-Iraq War (1980–88), North Korea provided Iran with as great an amount of military supplies as the latter was able to pay for. North Korea also is believed involved in sales or technology-transfer agreements associated with ballistic missile developments with Egypt, Iran, Syria, and Libya. Development of a follow-on, longer-range Scud-C is believed to have commenced around the same time; the first test launches occurred in 1989.

In 1991 North Korea was developing a new type of ballistic missile with a range in excess of 900 kilometers. The new missile was tentatively called the Nodong 1 by Western sources after the name of its test facility. The initial tests failed, but on the basis of North Korea's development pace for the Scud series, deployment would be possible by mid-decade. North Korea successfully test-fired the Nodong 1 in May 1993. A follow-on missile called the Taepodong 1 and the Taepodong 2 by the foreign press, is being developed with a range of up to 6,000 kilometers.

The Nuclear Option

In the early 1990s, there was growing international concern that North Korea was seeking to produce nuclear weapons. In 1991, despite North Korea's repeated denials of a nuclear weapons program, United States policy experts generally agreed that P'yŏngyang was engaged in a nuclear weapons program. The debate has centered on when, rather than whether, North Korea will have a nuclear capability. Estimates range from 1993 to several years later.

North Korean nuclear-related activities began in 1955, when representatives of the Academy of Sciences participated in an East European conference on the peaceful uses of nuclear energy. In 1956 North Korea signed two agreements with the Soviet Union covering joint nuclear research. In 1959 additional agreements on the peaceful uses of nuclear energy were signed with the Soviet Union and China. The 1959 Soviet agreement apparently included setting up a nuclear research facility under the Academy of Sciences near Yŏngbyŏn and developing a nuclear-related curriculum at Kim Il Sung University. Chinese and Soviet assistance with training of nuclear scientists and technicians, although not continuous, is the major source of North Korean nuclear expertise. In the 1980s, P'yŏngyang had a rather eclectic if low-key web of nuclear connections that included Cuba, Czechoslovakia, and the former Democratic Republic of Germany (East Germany). North Korea also is believed to have nuclear-related connections with Egypt, Iran, Libya, Romania, and Syria.

The Yŏngbyŏn center was established in early 1962 at Yong Dong on the Kuryong River, approximately 100 kilometers north of P'yŏngyang and southwest of the city of Yŏngbyŏn. Construction began in 1965 on a Soviet-supplied two-kilowatt nuclear research reactor (IRT2000) that is believed to have become operational in 1967. The reactor was brought under International Atomic Energy

Armistice Hall, North Korean side of the Demilitarized Zone.
Marker commemorates site of armistice negotiations.
Observation post at Demilitarized Zone, looking from
North Korea to South Korea
Courtesy Tracy Woodward

Agency (IAEA—see Glossary) controls in July 1977 and was modified over time to increase its power to approximately eight kilowatts.

During the mid-1970s, North Korea began expanding its nuclear infrastructure. In 1980 construction began on an indigenously designed, graphite-moderated, gas-cooled thirty-megawatt reactor, which probably is primarily for plutonium production. The use of graphite and natural uranium allowed North Korea to avoid foreign involvement and constraints. The reactor apparently became operational in 1987, but its existence has not been formally acknowledged by North Korea.

According to many sources, United States satellites detected additional nuclear-related facilities under construction in the Yŏngbyŏn area during 1989. When completed, the facilities will give North Korea the complete nuclear fuel cycle needed for weapons production. These facilities consist of a high explosives testing site, a reprocessing facility, a third reactor in the fifty-megawatt to 200-megawatt range, and associated support facilities. According to sources, construction began on a third reactor in 1984–85 and on a reprocessing facility in 1988–89; the former was scheduled to be operational by the end of 1992 but was not on-line as of mid-1993. Neither the thirty-megawatt reactor nor the third reactor are said to be connected to a power grid for power generation. In 1990 these reports were substantiated by satellite photography read by Japanese scientists. According to South Korean sources, if all the facilities come online, North Korea will be capable of producing enough plutonium for two to four twenty-kiloton nuclear weapons a year. The facilities, however, are contaminated and not operational.

P'yŏngyang signed the Nuclear Nonproliferation Treaty in July 1985 but delayed signing the IAEA Full Scope Safeguards Agreement. The IAEA granted an eighteen-month extension of the usual eighteen months necessary to administer and sign such agreements. North Korea agreed in principle to the agreement in July 1991, but delayed signing until January 30, 1992; implementation was not to take place until after ratification of the agreement. In a series of agreements with South Korea at the end of 1991, North Korea agreed to set up a Joint Nuclear Control Committee (JNCC) to ensure that there are no nuclear weapons in either country. The committee will develop procedures for additional inspections to encompass facilities normally outside IAEA jurisdiction, such as military facilities.

Foreign Military Relations

Relations with China and the Soviet Union

P'yŏngyang's relations with Beijing and Moscow have changed significantly over time as the result of the changing domestic environment, emerging disparities in the strategic interests of the three countries, and key events such as the Sino-Soviet split, the collapse of communism, and the replacement of the Soviet Union with Russia and the Commonwealth of Independent States (CIS) (see China and the Soviet Union, ch. 4). Data on Chinese and Soviet arms transfers to North Korea are scarce and unreliable.

General trends in post-Korean War assistance can be grouped into six phases. During the first period (1953–56), the Soviet Union supplied assistance unilaterally, and China maintained troops in North Korea. In the second period (1957–60), Soviet de-Stalinization measures led to tension in Soviet-North Korean relations (see Foreign Policy, ch. 4). As China pulled its troops out of Korea, however, it increased military assistance. During the third phase (1961–64, the beginning of the Sino-Soviet split), both China and the Soviet Union gave little assistance. The fourth period (1965–72) was characterized by renewed Soviet assistance and a drop in Chinese assistance. In the fifth period (1973–84), China's support for North Korea increased steadily while the delivery of major equipment from the Soviet Union declined significantly. In the sixth period (1984–89), especially after Kim Il Sung's visit to Moscow in May 1984, Soviet military assistance to North Korea grew dramatically as Chinese military assistance declined. The Soviet Union supplied North Korea with major weapons systems, including late-model jet aircraft, SA–2D, SA–3, and SA–5 SAM systems, and significant support equipment. Cooperation intensified in other military areas. There were yearly joint naval and air force exercises from 1986 to 1990, exchanges of high-ranking military personnel, reciprocal aircraft and warship visits, and exchanges of military intelligence. North Korea permits overflights by Soviet reconnaissance aircraft and bombers, and grants warships access to ports.

The economic and political reforms taking place in Eastern Europe and the Soviet Union in 1989 produced a shift in relations with North Korea. Naval exercises with the Soviet Union were stopped in 1990. As of mid-1993, North Korea's security relations with the CIS and Russia were in flux. North Korea's military relations with Russia have cooled considerably, although there are indications that both countries are attempting to reestablish relations on a pragmatic basis. Press accounts indicate that Russia has assumed its treaty obligations with North Korea. In March 1992, the CIS chief of staff General Viktor Samonov visited North Korea and signed an "annual plan for the exchange of manpower" and an agreement on mutual cooperation. General Samonov indicated that CIS military logistic support is being supplied on a commercial basis and that North Korea is having difficulty meeting the payments.

P'yŏngyang supported Beijing's response to the Tiananmen Square incident in 1989. By the early 1990s, Chinese-North Korean relations had grown warmer, although cooperation apparently has not involved the transfers of major weapons systems. China's relations with South Korea do not appear to negatively affect its relations with North Korea.

Relations with the Third World

Since the mid-1960s, North Korea has been an ardent and increasingly resourceful supplier of military equipment and expertise to governments and resistance movements throughout the Third World. Military assistance has been provided in the form of equipment transfers, in-country training, and advisory groups (see table 12, Appendix).

Beginning in the early 1970s, P'yŏngyang decided to use military assistance programs as an instrument of foreign policy. Ideological concerns incline North Korea to extend military and financial aid to national liberation movements, guerrilla forces, and terrorist groups. Although its small economic base limits the scale of its involvement in external military assistance, North Korea is nevertheless relatively active. Foreign military assistance efforts concentrate on comparatively inexpensive training programs. The true extent of North Korea's involvement in providing military assistance may never be known, however, because of its obsessive secrecy and the inherently covert nature of radical and revolutionary groups.

By 1990 North Korea had provided military training to groups in sixty-two countries—twenty-five in Africa, nineteen in Central and South America, nine in Asia, seven in the Middle East, and two in Europe. A cumulative total of more than 5,000 foreign personnel have been trained in North Korea, and over 7,000 military advisers, primarily from the Reconnaissance Bureau, have been dispatched to some forty-seven countries. As of mid-1993, military advisers from North Korea were in approximately twelve African countries. North Korea is a convenient alternative to the superpowers for military assistance.

External military assistance also includes weapons agreements. Equipment transfers in the 1980s alone totaled nearly US$4 billion.

In Asia economic, technical, and military aid was channeled to Hanoi during the Vietnam War, but the level of aid, and whether it included any manpower support, is open to speculation. North Korea also offered strong verbal support to the "struggle of the Vietnamese people against imperialism." In 1971 the entire North Korean diplomatic mission to Sri Lanka was expelled for giving financial support to the revolutionary People's Liberation Front (Janatha Vimukthi Peramuna). Members of the Thai Communist Party received military training in North Korea in 1976. Pakistan was sold basic ground forces equipment in the late 1970s and early 1980s.

In Africa support was provided to the Popular Front for the Liberation of Saguia el-Hamra and Río de Oro (Polisario) guerrillas operating in the Western Sahara against Morocco and to those in Algeria and Chad. Support came in the form of training and small arms supplied in modest quantities. In the mid-1970s, modest amounts of military equipment were supplied, and training was provided to governments or revolutionary groups operating in Angola, Benin, Burkina, Congo, Ethiopia, Ghana, Madagascar, Mozambique, Seychelles, Tanzania, Uganda, Zambia, and Zimbabwe.

In the 1980s, North Korea's highest-profile military-advisory activity was in Zimbabwe. Beginning in 1981, North Korea equipped and trained the Zimbabwean army's Fifth Brigade for counterinsurgency and internal security duties. P'yŏngyang provided almost all the equipment and about US$18 million worth of small arms and ammunition. The mission was not successful, however, and by 1986 the Zimbabwean government had the unit retrained by British military instructors.

In South America and Central America, P'yŏngyang provided financial aid, military training, and small arms in modest quantities to antigovernment groups operating in Argentina, Bolivia, Brazil, Chile, Guatemala, Mexico, Nicaragua, Paraguay, Peru, and Venezuela during the 1970s. Documents seized during the United States 1983 military intervention in Grenada also revealed plans for North Korean military assistance there, to include small arms, two patrol boats, and ammunition. Military relations with the Sandinista government in Nicaragua included the transfer of patrol boats and other unconfirmed aid. In April 1986, North Korea sold rifles to the government of Peru.

There are indications that North Korean advisers were involved in actual military operations in the Middle East, including reports that North Korean pilots flew Egyptian aircraft during the October 1973 War. North Koreans also are alleged to have operated Libyan tanks during the 1977 Egyptian-Libyan conflict, although North

Korea has never admitted that its advisers participated in combat overseas. Reliable reports suggest that as many as 100 North Korean pilots and air crews were in Libya training pilots on Soviet-supplied aircraft beginning in 1979 and continuing for several years and in some cases were actually involved in operational activities. Support to the Palestine Liberation Organization (PLO) began in the late 1970s and included military training in North Korea and the supply of small amounts of arms. PLO support still may have been continuing in mid-1993.

By the 1980s, many of North Korea's defense industry limitations had been overcome, and by the early 1990s North Korea was capable of supplying a much wider range of weapons and training. Although ideology remains a significant component of military assistance, economic considerations have become increasingly important in weapons transfers. Arms sales to the Middle East garner North Korea hard currency, alternative oil sources, and access to restricted technology. Military equipment transfers have been expanded to include high value-added military equipment such as Scud missiles, antitank guided missiles, tanks and armored vehicles, self-propelled and towed heavy field artillery, and naval vessels.

For the decade ending in 1987, the United States Arms Control and Disarmament Agency estimated that North Korea earned US$3.9 billion from arms transfers to over thirty countries in Africa, the Middle East, and Central America, and spent some US$2.8 billion on arms imports from China and the Soviet Union. Purchases included aircraft, missiles, trucks, radars, and command, control, communications, and intelligence equipment. Exports to Iran of approximately US$2.8 million constituted 71 percent of total weapons exports. Arms sales during the peak year 1982 represented 38 percent of North Korea's total exports. Arms exports between 1981 and 1987 averaged around 27 percent of exports annually, with a 1981 high of 40 percent and a 1986 low of 14 percent.

The Middle East is the major market for North Korean arms, with most sales going to Iran and Libya. Other Middle East clients include Syria, the former People's Democratic Republic of Yemen, the PLO, and the Popular Front for the Liberation of Palestine. Sales to Iran peaked in the first three years of the Iran-Iraq War when Iran ordered almost US$1 billion worth of arms from North Korea; by the end of the war, some US$2.8 billion worth of arms had been purchased. The first Iranian arms agreement in late 1980 covered light infantry weapons and ammunition. Follow-on orders, however, quickly expanded the scope of purchases. These arms transfers also became the basis for cooperation in military production, particularly in short-range ballistic missiles. North Korea also trained the Iranians on Chinese mobile surface-to-air missiles and the Iranian Revolutionary Guards in unconventional warfare. After the end of the Iran-Iraq war, continuing cooperation indicated that technology transfers were still going on.

North Korean-Egyptian cooperation continues to grow. The two nations are believed to have cooperated on each other's battlefield ballistic missile programs. Agreements with Egypt involve replacement parts for Soviet equipment and cooperative efforts in missile technology. In 1980 Egypt signed a US$40 million arms agreement for various ground systems. In 1984 the two countries signed a joint agreement for the development of the Egyptian variant of the SA-2b/Guideline missile. The two countries also may have cooperated on the Egyptian Eagle/SAKR–80 and the BADR–2000/Condor II missile programs.

Training and advisory groups remain an important part of the military assistance policy. In 1988 South Korean sources estimated that North Korea was offering a wide range of military and unconventional warfare training at thirty facilities for anywhere from three to eighteen months. Advisory groups were active in thirty-four countries in 1988, mostly in Asia and Africa. The size of the advisory groups ranges from as few as twenty to over 100 persons.

In the early 1990s, opportunities for North Korean military assistance programs began declining because of the disintegration of the Soviet Union and its hard-line Marxist-Leninist bloc, and the end of several long-running military disputes such as the Iran-Iraq War and conflicts in Yemen, Ethiopia, and Cambodia. Arms exports remain technologically backward, but by offering systems at comparatively low prices and showing little concern about the buyer, P'yŏngyang has gained a niche in markets where compatible Soviet equipment dominates. North Korea's motivation has increasingly shifted from a revolutionary ideological underpinning to cooperative activity with other states that are uncomfortable with the emerging constraints on arms transfers and the dominance of the United States in the new world order.

Incidents and Infiltrations: Targeting South Korea

Since the division of the peninsula, North Korea has used subversion and sabotage against South Korea as part of its effort at reunification. Historically, the military part of this effort has centered on military infiltration, border incidents designed to raise tensions, and psychological warfare operations aimed at the South Korean armed forces. Infiltration by North Korean military agents was commonplace in South Korea after the armistice in 1953.

Over time, however, there were clear shifts in emphasis, method, and apparent goals. P'yŏngyang initially sent agents to gather intelligence and to build a revolutionary base in South Korea.

The 1960s saw a dramatic shift to violent attempts to destabilize South Korea, including commando raids and incidents along the DMZ that occasionally escalated into firefights involving artillery. The raids peaked in 1968, when more than 600 infiltrations were reported, including an unsuccessful commando attack on the South Korean presidential mansion by thirty-one members of North Korea's 124th Army Unit. The unit came within 500 meters of the president's residence before being stopped. During this incident, twenty-eight infiltrators and thirty-seven South Koreans were killed. That same year, 120 commandos infiltrated two east coast provinces in an unsuccessful attempt to organize a Vietnamese-type guerrilla war. In 1969 over 150 infiltrations were attempted, involving almost 400 agents. Thereafter, P'yŏngyang's infiltration efforts abated somewhat, and the emphasis reverted to intelligence gathering, covert networks, and terrorism.

Subsequent incidents of North Korean terrorism focused on the assassination of the South Korean president or other high officials. In November 1970, an infiltrator was killed while planting a bomb intended to kill South Korean president Park Chung Hee at the Seoul National Cemetery. In 1974 a Korean resident of Japan visiting Seoul killed Park's wife in another unsuccessful presidential assassination attempt.

From the mid-1970s to the early 1980s, most North Korean infiltration was conducted by heavily armed reconnaissance teams. These were increasingly intercepted and neutralized by South Korean security forces.

After shifting to sea infiltration for a brief period in the 1980s, P'yŏngyang apparently discarded military reconnaissance in favor of inserting agents into third countries. For example, on October 9, 1983, a three-man team from North Korea's intelligence services attempted to assassinate South Korean president Chun Doo Hwan while he was on a state visit to Rangoon, Burma. The remote-controlled bomb exploded prematurely. Chun was unharmed, but eighteen South Korean officials, including four cabinet ministers, were killed, and fourteen other persons were injured. One of the North Korean agents was killed, two were captured, and one confessed to the incident. On November 29, 1987, a bomb exploded aboard a Korean Air jetliner returning from the Middle East, killing 135 passengers on board. The bomb was placed by two North Korean agents. The male agent committed suicide after being apprehended. The female agent was turned over to South

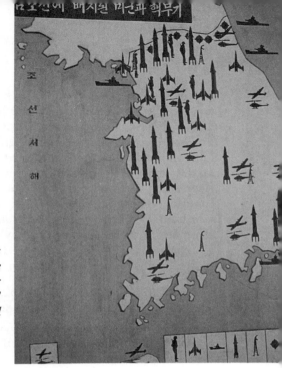

Map at Armistice Hall,
Demilitarized Zone,
depicting North Korea's
view of the deployment of the
"American Army and nuclear
weapons in South Korea"
Courtesy Tracy Woodward

Korean authorities; she confessed to being a North Korean intelligence agent and revealed that the mission was directed by Kim Jong Il as part of a campaign to discredit South Korea before the 1988 Seoul Olympics. In the airliner bombing, North Korea broke from its pattern of chiefly targeting South Korean government officials, particularly the president, and targeted ordinary citizens.

Geopolitical Changes: New World Order and North Korean Security

The demise of communist systems in the Soviet Union and Eastern Europe was a profound shock to North Korea. Although relations with the Soviet Union had cooled in the late 1980s, North Korea was ill prepared for the dramatic devaluation of its strategic value to Russia and the CIS. The ramifications for North Korea's military were unclear in mid-1993, but some aspects are known. North Korea has lost its military alliance with the former Soviet Union, its access to military hardware and expertise at socialist concessionary rates, and the ability to exploit Soviet-United States competition to its advantage. Despite North Korea's strenuous efforts at military independence, in the long term these events will make it increasingly difficult for North Korea to maintain a large, modernizing military and, as well, leave the country increasingly isolated.

Official North-South dialogue was reestablished in late 1984, twelve years after the first series of talks in 1972 had been suspended.

It was not until December 1991, however, that any progress was made on military confidence-building measures or arms control. The North-South Agreement on Reconciliation, Nonaggression, Exchanges, and Cooperation, signed in December 1991, potentially marks initial progress toward a reduction in military tension on the peninsula. The two sides renounced the use of force against each other and pledged to pursue as yet undetermined military confidence-building measures. Little real progress has been made as of mid-1993, however, other than further institutionalizing the structure of their talks. As a show of good faith, the Republic of Korea announced on January 7, 1992, that it was cancelling the United States-South Korea Team Spirit military exercise for that year.

The Declaration on the Denuclearization of the Korean Peninsula initialed on December 31, 1991, bans the testing, manufacture, production, possession, storage, deployment, receipt, and use of nuclear weapons on the peninsula. It also stipulates that neither Korea will possess nuclear reprocessing or uranium enrichment facilities. It requires that the JNCC be organized within thirty days of the exchange of ratified declarations on February 19, 1992. The JNCC has responsibility for implementing the non-nuclear declaration, including bilateral inspections, but in actuality exists only on paper (see Inter-Korean Affairs, ch. 4).

P'yŏngyang is a regime under tremendous pressure, with forces for change in the region threatening its existence. Seoul, which has won the political and economic competition, threatens to absorb North Korea in the same manner as West Germany has absorbed East Germany. Only in military strength, with over 1 million men under arms, does North Korea have an edge over South Korea. Its long-term commitment to a massive force-improvement program has crippled economic growth. Barring an unforeseen turn of events during its inevitable political succession, North Korea gives little sign of a willingness to abandon its painfully acquired military capability. In fact, it might view its military force as the only deterrent to absorption by South Korea.

Nonetheless, P'yŏngyang's leaders are restrained from war by a complex set of military and political factors: the large, well-trained, and well-equipped South Korean military and the increasing political stability in South Korea; the United States security commitment to South Korea and the forward military presence supporting it; and the uncertainty of China's support for military action. As long as the North Korean leadership remains stable, the likelihood of full-scale attack by North Korea remains low.

However, if instability becomes a part of the succession process, the outlook is more problematic. North Korea will be under growing pressure, which will increase the possibility of miscalculation. The potential for political instability in the final stages of the leadership succession further reinforces this concern.

Internal Security

Social Control

The forty-five years since the founding of the DPRK have witnessed the construction of a system of totalitarian control unique even when compared to the communist systems in the former Soviet Union and Eastern Europe. The population of North Korea is rigidly controlled. Individual rights are subordinate to the rights of the state and party. The regime uses education, mass mobilization, persuasion, and coercion to guarantee political and social conformity (see *Chuch'e* and Contemporary Social Values, ch. 2; Political Ideology: The Role of *Chuch'e,* ch. 4). Massive propaganda and political indoctrination are reinforced by extensive police and public security forces.

The regime's control mechanisms are quite extensive. Security ratings are established for individuals and influence access to employment, schools, medical facilities, stores, admission to the KWP, and so on. The system in its most elaborate form consists of three general groupings and fifty-one subcategories. Over time, however, the use of subcategories has diminished.

The population is divided into a core class, the basic masses, and the "impure class." The core class, which includes those with revolutionary lineage, makes up approximately 20 to 25 percent of the population. The basic masses—primarily workers and peasants—account for around 50 percent. The impure class consists of descendants of pro-Japanese collaborators, landowners, or those with relatives who have defected. In the past, restraints on the impure class were strict, but as time has passed they have been relaxed, although the core class continues to receive preferential treatment. Nonetheless, by the 1980s even a member of the impure class could become a party member (see The Korean Workers' Party, ch. 4).

Since the late 1950s, all households have been organized into people's neighborhood units. The units, originally called the five-family system, consist of about 100 individuals living in close proximity. The ward people's committee selects the people's neighborhood unit chief, generally from pensioners in the unit. Meetings are held once a month or as necessary. The primary function of the ward people's committee is social control and propagation of the *chuch'e* ideology.

There are five categories of social control: residence, travel, employment, clothing and food, and family life. Change of residence is possible only with party approval. Those who move without a permit are not eligible for food rations or housing allotments and are subject to criminal prosecution. Travel is controlled by the Ministry of Public Security, and a travel pass is necessary. Travel on other than official business is limited strictly to attending family functions, and obtaining approval normally is a long and complicated process. The ration system does not recognize individuals while they are traveling, which further curtails movement. Employment is governed by the party, with assignments made on the basis of political reliability and family background. A change in employment is made at the party's convenience.

The Public Security Apparatus

The Ministry of Public Security and the State Security Department are responsible for internal security. Although both are government organs, they are tightly controlled by the party apparatus through the Justice and Security Commission and the penetration of their structures by the party apparatus at all levels. The formal public security structure is augmented by a pervasive system of informers throughout the society. Surveillance of citizens, both physical and electronic, also is routine.

The Ministry of Public Security, responsible for internal security, social control, and basic police functions, is one of the most powerful organizations in North Korea and controls an estimated 144,000 public security personnel. It maintains law and order; investigates common criminal cases; manages the prison system and traffic control; monitors citizens' political attitudes; conducts background investigations, census, and civil registrations; controls individual travel; manages the government's classified documents; protects government and party officials; and patrols government buildings and some government and party construction activities.

The ministry has vice ministers for personnel, political affairs, legal counseling, security, surveillance, internal affairs, rear services, and engineering. There are approximately twenty-seven bureaus, but the functional responsibilities of only some of the bureaus are known. The Security Bureau is responsible for ordinary law enforcement and most police functions. The Investigation Bureau handles investigations of criminal and economic crimes. The Protection Bureau is responsible for fire protection, traffic control, public health, and customs. The Registration Bureau issues citizen identification cards and maintains public records on births, deaths, marriages, residence registration, and passports.

Below the ministry level, there are public security bureaus for each province and directly administered city. These bureaus are headed by either a senior colonel or a lieutenant colonel of police, depending on the size of the population. Public security departments at each city or county and smaller substations through the country are staffed by about 100 personnel. They are organized roughly parallel to the ministry itself and have several divisions responsible for carrying out various functions.

In 1973 political security responsibilities were transferred from the Ministry of Public Security to the State Security Department, an autonomous agency reporting directly to Kim Il Sung. The State Security Department carries out a wide range of counterintelligence and internal security functions normally associated with "secret police." It is charged with searching out antistate criminals—a general category that includes those accused of antigovernment and dissident activities, economic crimes, and slander of the political leadership. Camps for political prisoners are under its jurisdiction. It has counterintelligence responsibilities at home and abroad, and runs overseas intelligence collection operations. It monitors political attitudes and maintains surveillance of returnees. Ministry personnel escort high-ranking officials. The ministry also guards national borders and monitors international entry points. The degree of control it exercises over the Political Security Bureaus of the KPA—which has representatives at all levels of command—is unclear.

The Border Guards are the paramilitary force of the Ministry of Public Security. They are primarily concerned with monitoring the border and with internal security. The latter activities include physical protection of government buildings and facilities. During a conflict, they would probably be used in border and rear area security missions.

The Judicial System
Historical Influences

Foreign laws have repeatedly influenced Korea. Korea assimilated the codes of various Chinese dynasties through the close of the Chosŏn Dynasty and Western law (Continental Law) during the Japanese occupation (1910–45). Although Confucian legal culture exerts strong influence on North Korea's legal attitudes, the modern legal system initially was patterned after the Soviet model imposed during the period of Soviet occupation (1945–48).

Neo-Confucian thought does not distinguish among politics, morality, and law. Law in traditional Korea was concerned with the control and punishment of deviance by the centralized bureaucratic political system rather than by private relationships or contracts. The elite viewed law as a last resort against a morally intractable person. The rule of law was little understood by the general population, which often saw it manifested only as an autocratic decree or as a tool of rigid political regimentation. These notions persist as part of the legal culture of North Korea.

No concepts in the Chosŏn Dynasty corresponded to the Western concept of right. Although in principle all classes were guaranteed property rights and the rights to act and initiate legal proceedings, the class nature of society meant that those rights were virtually meaningless for all but the elite. Social stratification was paralleled by de facto legal stratification. Noblemen, or *yangban,* had full exercise of their "rights." The theoretical rights of the middle class and lesser bureaucrats had practical limits, and the commoners and the lowest classes basically had no legal rights.

Morality and politics were reflected in the administration of justice; and structural differentiation among adjudicative, legislative, and administrative functions was contrary to Confucian substantive justice. The magistrate, a generalist scholar-official, was charged with both governing and adjudicating. Legal specialists, who were not from the *yangban* class, never developed into a professional group.

Korea's traditional legal system outwardly disappeared with the incorporation of modern Western law beginning with the Kabo Reforms of 1894 and ending with the imposition of Japanese legal concepts during the Japanese colonial period (see The Legacy of Japanese Colonialism, ch. 1). Traditional legal thought, however, continued to influence North Korean attitudes toward the purpose and function of legal institutions.

With the end of the Chosŏn Dynasty in 1910, decisive changes occurred in Korean law. Traditional Korean institutions suddenly were replaced. The imposition of institutions by the Japanese and their post-1910 use for repressive colonial control constituted a sharp break with the past. Because of the nature of Japanese colonial rule, there was no constitutional law, guarantee of rights, or judicial review of the exercise of political power. The legal system of Korea under Japanese rule was composed essentially of rules, duties, and obligations. However, there was no institutional or procedural separation of powers. The Japanese governor general had unrestrained executive and legislative power, the latter exercised by decree.

With the end of World War II came Soviet occupation. During this period, Soviet legal concepts and codes, as well as the court and procurator structure, were embraced. Soviet legal concepts were the basis for the Court Organization Law of March 1, 1950, and the Criminal Code and Code of Criminal Procedure, both issued on March 3, 1950. In December 1974, a new Criminal Code (five parts, 215 articles) was issued, but few details were revealed to the general public, and its promulgation was not known to outside sources until the late 1980s. The Penal Code (eight chapters, 161 articles) was adopted by the Supreme People's Assembly on February 5, 1987.

The Judiciary

Under the guidance of the Justice and Security Commission of the Central People's Committee, the two main components of the post-1945 judicial system are the Central Court and Central Procurator systems. These organizations perform their functions as "powerful weapons of the proletariat dictatorship, which execute the judicial policies of the Korean Workers' Party." North Korea has a three-tiered court system with a Central Court, provincial courts, and people's courts at the county level. The appeal process is based on the principle of a single appeal to the next highest court.

The Central Court is the final court of appeal for criminal and civil cases and has initial jurisdiction for grievous crimes against the state. According to the 1992 constitution, the Supreme People's Assembly has the power to elect and recall the president of the Central Court and to appoint or remove the president of the Central Procurator's Office (Article 91, items 12–13). The Standing Committee of the Supreme People's Assembly interprets the laws and ordinances in force and elects and recalls judges and people's assessors of the Central Court (Article 101, items 3, 9). The Central Court supervises all lower courts and the training of judges. It does not exercise the power of judicial review over the constitutionality of executive or legislative actions nor does it have an activist role in protecting the constitutionally guaranteed rights of individuals against state actions. The Central Court is staffed by a chief judge or president, two associate chief judges or vice presidents, and an unknown number of regular judges.

The Central Court also arbitrates matters involving the non-fulfillment of contracts between state enterprises and cases involving injuries and compensation demands. These administrative decisions always reflect party policies.

Below the Central Court are the courts of the provinces and cities under central authority—courts that serve as the courts of first and only appeal for decisions made by the People's Courts. They are staffed in the same manner as the Central Court. Like the Central Court, provincial courts have initial jurisdiction for certain serious crimes. In addition, provincial courts supervise the People's Courts.

The people's courts are at the lowest level of the judicial system. They are organized at the county (*gun,* or *kun*) level even though they may have jurisdiction over more than one county or smaller city. They have initial jurisdiction for most criminal and civil cases. Unlike the high courts, they are staffed with a single judge, who is assisted by two "people's assessors," laymen who are temporarily selected for the judiciary. An initial trial typically is presided over by one judge and two people's assessors. If the case is appealed, three judges preside, and a decision is made by consultation.

The constitution does not require legal education as a qualification for being elected as a judge or people's assessor. Over time, however, legal training has received more emphasis, although political reliability remains the prime criterion for holding office.

The Central Procurator's Office parallels the court system. In accordance with Article 162 of the 1992 constitution, "Investigation and prosecution are conducted by the Central Procurator's Office, the procurator's offices of the province (or municipality directly under central authority), city (or district) and county and special procurator's office." The office supervises or conducts investigations, arrests, preparation of indictments, criminal prosecutions, and criminal trial proceedings. It has the right to initiate court appeals. This supervisory function over the judiciary includes ensuring that the court system interprets the law in accordance with the KWP's wishes. As of July 1992, the procurator general of the Central Procurator's Office was Han Sang-kyu; there are three deputy procurators general.

Socialist law-abiding life-guidance committees were established in 1977 in the Central People's Committee and in the people's committees at the provincial, city, and county levels. These ad hoc committees meet once a month and are chaired by the president of the people's committee. The committees are a control measure for ensuring respect for public authority and conformity to the dictates of socialist society. The committees are empowered to implement state power, monitor the observance of law by state and economic institutions, and prevent the abuse of power by the leading cadre of these institutions. To this end, they have oversight of state

*A soldier and
his child by the Tower
of Chuch'e, P'yŏngyang
Courtesy Tracy Woodward*

inspection agencies, the procuracy, and the police; they also have supervision and control of all organizations, workplaces, social groups, and citizens in their jurisdiction. The committees can apply strict legal sanctions to all violations short of crimes.

Little reliable information is available on specific criminal justice procedures and practices as of mid-1993. Although North Korea refuses outside observation of its legal system, it is clear that the limited guarantees legally in place often are not followed in practice. There is reliable information of summary executions in the case of political crimes.

The 1992 constitution guarantees judicial independence and requires that court proceedings be carried out in accordance with laws containing elaborate procedural guarantees. Article 157 of the constitution states that ''cases are heard in public, and the accused is guaranteed the right to a defense; hearings may be closed to the public as stipulated by law.'' According to the United States Department of State's *Country Report on Human Rights Practices for 1990* and a 1988 report by Asia Watch and the Minnesota Lawyers International Human Rights Committee, however, practice is another matter. Additionally, according to the Criminal Code, defense attorneys are not proxies for the defendant but are charged with ensuring that the accused takes full responsibility for his or her actions.

North Korean law limits incarceration during investigation and interrogation to a period not to exceed two months. The period of incarceration, however, can be extended indefinitely with the approval of the Central Procurator's Office. The approval apparently is given quite freely. It is not uncommon for individuals to be detained for a year or longer without trial or charge. During interrogation, at least through the early 1980s, there was strong evidence that prisoners were routinely tortured or ill treated. Habeas corpus or its equivalent is not recognized in theory or practice. In addition, information about detainees is restricted, and it is often very difficult, if not impossible, for concerned family members to obtain any data about someone being detained.

Party influence is pervasive in both criminal and political cases. In criminal cases, the government assigns lawyers for the defense. Defense lawyers are not considered advocates for the defendant so much as independent parties to help persuade the accused to admit his guilt, although they apparently present facts to mitigate punishment. In political cases, trials often are dispensed with, and the Ministry of Public Security refers the cases directly to the State Security Department for the imposition of punishment.

The penal code is draconian in nature and apparently does not accept the principles of modern criminal law that state that there is no crime unless so specified by law, that law may not be applied retroactively, and that the law cannot be extended by analogy. Article 10 of the North Korean Criminal Code states that "in the case of an offense that does not fall under any expressed clause of the criminal law, the basis, scope, and punishment for it shall be determined according to the clause on acts that resemble it most in terms of its type and danger to society."

The penal code adopted in 1987 simplifies the 1974 code without making substantial changes in the definitions of crimes or penalties. The entire section entitled Military Crimes, contained in Part 5 of the previous code, has been deleted. It is likely that military crimes still are treated as a criminal category, and are covered by another, separate code.

The 1987 code generally covers fewer types of crimes. Crimes eliminated from the general heading of treason include armed incursions, hostile crimes against the socialist state, and antirevolutionary sabotage. Penalties also have been relaxed. The number of crimes for which the death penalty can be applied has been reduced from twenty civil crimes to five offenses in addition to those offenses covered under the Military Crimes section. Retained as capital offenses are plots against national sovereignty (Article 44), terrorism (Article 45), treason against the Motherland by citizens (Article 47), treason against the people (Article 52), and murder (Article 141). The death penalty no longer applies to propaganda

and sedition against the government; espionage; armed intervention and instigating the severance of foreign relations; antirevolutionary disturbances; theft of government or public property;
violation of railway, water, or air transportation regulations; mob
violence; unauthorized disclosure of or loss of official secrets; rape;
and robbery of personal property. The maximum sentence has been
reduced from twenty to fifteen years.

In May 1992, the chairman of the criminal law department at
Kim Il Sung University published an address on misinterpreta-
tions of the North Korean Criminal Code. He pointed out that
the code bans death sentences for minors under seventeen years
of age when the crime was committed and for pregnant women.
The code has no penalty of confinement; all noncapital punishment is in the form of forced labor. The code also stipulates that
revisions to it cannot be applied retroactively to define an act as
criminal that was not so at the time of commission or to raise the
maximum penalty. Reductions of penalties, however, apply retroactively. The code also redefines several of the provisions related to
contact with South Korea in a manner apparently aimed at drawing attention to the strict limits of South Korea's National Security Law on unauthorized North/South contacts.

The definition of the most serious political crimes—reforms
notwithstanding—is ambiguous and includes both counterrevolutionary crimes and more general political offenses. Punishment for
counterrevolutionary crimes is severe, it involves capital punishment, loss of property, and even summary execution for almost
any dissident activity. Furthermore, these cases are often decided
without recourse to the appropriate legal procedures. Most political offenses do not go through the criminal justice system, but are
handled by the State Security Department. Trials are closed, and
there is no provision for appeal. Punishment is often broadened
to include the offender's immediate and extended family.

Punishment and the Penal System

Punishment for criminal behavior is determined by both the type
of crime—political or nonpolitical—and the status of the individual.
The underlying philosophy of punishment reflects both Marxist
influences and Confucian moral precepts. According to the 1950
penal code, the purpose of punishment is explicitly Marxist: to sup-
press class enemies, educate the population in the spirit of "socialist patriotism," and reeducate and punish individuals for crimes
stemming from "capitalist" thinking. However, the code's am-
biguity, the clear official preference for rehabilitating individuals
through a combination of punishment and reeducation, and

273

additional severity for crimes against the state or family reflect the lack of distinction among politics, morality, and law in neo-Confucian thought.

Penalties for various types of crimes range from imprisonment, forced labor, banishment to remote areas, forfeiture of property, fines, loss of privileges or work status, and reeducation, to death. With the exception of political criminals, the objective is to return a reformed individual to an active societal role.

There are indications that criminal law is applied differentially. An accused person's class and category can have a substantial effect on treatment meted out by the justice system. The severity of punishment for common crimes such as rape, robbery, and homicide apparently is influenced by such considerations. There also is considerable leeway in the classification of crime; a robbery can be classified as either a common crime with minor punishment or a political-economic crime with far harsher punishment. The classification of crimes also is open to political considerations.

There apparently are several types of detention camps for convicted prisoners. Political criminals are sent to separate concentration camps managed by the State Security Department. Twelve such camps were reported to exist in 1991, holding between 100,000 and 150,000 prisoners and covering some 1,200 square kilometers. They are located in remote, isolated areas at Tongsin and Hŭich'ŏn in Chagang Province; Onsŏng, Hoeryŏng, and Kyŏngsŏng in North Hamgyŏng Province; Tŏksŏng, Chongpyŏng, and Yodŏk in South Hamgyŏng Province; Yŏngbyŏn and Yongch'ŏn in North P'yŏngan Province, and Kaech'ŏn and Pukch'ang in South P'yŏngan Province. Convicted prisoners and their families are sent to these camps, where they are prohibited from marrying, required to grow their own food, and cut off from external communication (which was apparently once allowed). Detainees are classified as antiparty factionalists, antirevolutionary elements, or those opposed to Kim Jong Il's succession. There is conflicting information concerning whether individuals sent to these camps ever reenter society.

A second set of prisons, or camps, is concerned with more traditional punishment and rehabilitation. Prisoners sent to these camps can reenter society after serving their sentences. Among such camps are prisons, prison labor centers, travel violation centers, and sanatoriums. The basic prison is located at the city or province level; some seventeen of these prisons were identified in 1991. They are managed by the Ministry of Public Security for the incarceration of "normal" criminals.

Other types of prisons also exist. Labor prisons are found at the city or province level. Adult and youth centers house those convicted of normal criminal violations. There apparently are separate facilities for the incarceration of those who have attempted to violate travel restrictions or leave the country illegally. It is unclear, however, if these are in fact separate centers, or if those convicted of travel violations are placed in normal prisons. Lastly, minor political or ideological offenders or persons with religious convictions may be sent to sanatoriums where the offenses are treated as symptoms of mental disease. North Korean officials deny the existence of these camps, although they do admit to the existence of "education centers" for people who "commit crimes by mistake."

Prospects for Stability

On the surface, P'yŏngyang appears to have the capability to maintain public order. As North Korea opens to the outside world, it will be necessary, however, to control the impact of external influences. The leadership apparently is well aware of the potential dangers from "foreign pollution." Although reports of economic unrest increased in mid-1993, they remain infrequent, despite North Korea's poor economic performance in the late 1980s and early 1990s.

A number of stabilizing elements assist the regime's efforts to maintain internal order. The society seems united in popular support for the party, and the people have a strong sense of national pride. Kim Il Sung, by all indications, truly is admired and supported by the general population.

Although P'yŏngyang has gone to extreme lengths to quarantine its citizens from information about and the influences of the outside world, and uses its monopoly of the means of socialization to promote one party line, it is fighting a battle it cannot win. Outside information, particularly about South Korea's economic progress and the collapse of communism, is increasingly reaching North Korean society. The massive network of citizen surveillance suppresses overt deviance, although there are growing signs that ordinary North Koreans are not putting much effort or commitment into their work. There also is evidence that the visible privileges of the party elite are well known and resented. This fact suggests that when the post-Kim Il Sung period arrives, it may become apparent that many North Koreans have maintained only a formalistic commitment to the regime and have reserved judgment until given the opportunity to put their preferences into political action.

* * *

Given the closed nature of North Korea, much of the available information on that country comes from the two governments that consider North Korea a potential security threat—the Republic of Korea and the United States. The Republic of Korea Ministry of National Defense's annual *Defense White Paper* series (published in both Korean and English) and the United States Defense Intelligence Agency's 1991 publication, *North Korea: The Foundations for Military Strength,* are particularly noteworthy.

Relatively few book-length studies addressing North Korea's national security posture, the role of its military in society, or its internal security situation are available. Robert A. Scalapino and Chong-Sik Lee's two-volume *Communism in Korea* is increasingly dated, but remains a basic resource for research on all issues dealing with North Korea.

Two publications by the Seoul-based Research Center for Peace and Unification of Korea merit attention. Lee Suck-Ho's *Party-Military Relations in North Korea: A Comparative Analysis* and Suh Dae-Sook's article on the rise of partisan generals, ''Arms and the Hammer and Sickle,'' are insightful, as is Lee Chung Min's *The Emerging Strategic Balance in Northeast Asia: Implications for Korea's Defense Strategy and Planning for the 1990s.*

Other useful sources for general military information include the *Military Balance,* the Stockholm International Peace Research Institute *Yearbook,* and United States Arms Control and Disarmament Agency publications. Occasional articles in *Asian Defence Journal,* often by Gordon Jacobs, and in the various *Jane's* publications, often by Joseph S. Bermudez, also are invaluable. Jacobs and Bermudez have produced interesting insights into parts of the North Korean military through careful analysis of available information.

The value of journal articles on North Korean security affairs varies widely. *Asian Survey, Far Eastern Economic Review, Korea and World Affairs,* and *The Korean Journal of Defense Analysis* are generally useful and relatively free of bias. On the whole, however, journal articles often present contradictory information and use inconsistent terminology. It is also difficult to determine the continued validity of information over time, given the evolution of the North Korean defense establishment.

South Korean investigative journalism, particularly monthlies such as *Wŏlgan Chosŏn,* is increasingly producing the insights of defectors and travelers to North Korea. These pieces offer interesting insights into daily life and public order in North Korea.

Materials in English on public order, internal security, and domestic stability are uncommon because the closed nature of North Korea has inhibited scholarly inquiry into its legal system. Cho Sung-Yoon and Kang Koo-chin are among the few scholars who have studied North Korea's constitution and legal system. Details of the February 1, 1975, revision of North Korea's Criminal Code were only becoming known outside North Korea beginning in 1992.

Source materials in English on most issues in North Korea are uncommon, aside from the translations published by the Joint Publications Research Service and the Foreign Broadcast Information Service. Japan's *Kita Chōsen, Kita Chōsen Mondai,* and *Genji Kenkyū* and the periodic publications of South Korea's Pukhan Yŏn'guso and Kuktong Munje Yŏn'guso are valuable resources for information on domestic dissent or national security matters. An annotated version of the revised 1987 DPRK Criminal Code was published in the March 1992 *Hōritsu jihō* [Legal Review] (Tokyo). A translation of the revised 1992 constitution was released by the South Korean government-affiliated Naewoe Tongsin in November 1992. (For further information and complete citations, see Bibliography.)

Appendix

Table 1. Metric Conversion Coefficients and Factors

When you know	Multiply by	To find
Millimeters	0.04	inches
Centimeters	0.39	inches
Meters	3.3	feet
Kilometers	0.62	miles
Hectares (10,000 m²)	2.47	acres
Square kilometers	0.39	square miles
Cubic meters	35.3	cubic feet
Liters	0.26	gallons
Kilograms	2.2	pounds
Metric tons	0.98	long tons
....	1.1	short tons
....	2,204	pounds
Degrees Celsius	1.8	degrees Fahrenheit
(Centigrade)	and add 32	

Table 2. Ten Major Targets and Interim Results for Third Seven-Year Plan (1987–93) by Sector
(in millions of tons unless otherwise indicated)

Sector	Target for 1989	Results by 1989	Target for 1993
Electricity [1]	100.0	60.0	100.0
Coal	120.0	70.0	120.0
Steel	15.0	10.0	7.4
Nonferrous metals	1.5	1.5	1.7
Cement	20.0	12.0	22.0
Chemical fertilizers	7.0	5.0	7.2
Textiles [2]	1.5	0.8	1.5
Marine products	5.0	3.1	11.0
Grains	15.0	10.0	15.0
Tideland cultivation [3]	300.0	n.a.	300.0

n.a.—not available.
[1] In billions of kilowatt-hours.
[2] In billions of meters.
[3] In hectares.

Source: Based on information from *Kita Chōsen no keizai to bōeki no tenbō* (North Korean Economic and Trade Prospects), Tokyo, 1991, 131–79; and *Pukhan kyŏngje ŭi chŏngae kwajŏng* (The Development Process of the North Korean Economy), Seoul, 1990, 246–48.

Table 3. *Government Budget, Selected Years, 1975–91*
(in billions of wŏn) [1]

	1975		1980		1987		1991 [2]	
	Value	Percentage	Value	Percentage	Value	Percentage	Value	Percentage
Revenues	11.6	100.0	19.1	100.0	30.3	100.0	37.1	100.0
Expenditures								
National economy	6.7	58.8	11.4	60.3	20.0	66.4	25.2	67.9
Social and cultural	2.6	22.8	4.2	22.2	5.7	18.9	6.9	18.7
Military	1.9	16.4	2.8	14.6	4.0	13.2	4.6	12.3
Administration	0.2	1.8	0.5	2.6	0.5	1.7	0.4	1.0
Total expenditures [3] ...	11.4	100.0	18.9	100.0	30.2	100.0	37.1	100.0

[1] For value of the wŏn—see Glossary.
[2] Planned.
[3] Figures may not add to totals because of rounding.

Source: Based on information from Economist Intelligence Unit, *Country Profile: China, North Korea, 1990–91*, London, 1991, 76–77; *Kita Chōsen no keizai to bōeki no tenbō* (North Korean Economic and Trade Prospects), Tokyo, 1991, 7–9; and *Pukhan kyŏngje ŭi chŏngae kwajŏng* (The Development Process of the North Korean Economy), Seoul, 1990, 188–202.

Table 4. *Planned and Actual Production of Selected Industrial and Agricultural Products by Economic Plan, 1961–93*

(in millions of tons unless otherwise indicated)

Product	1961–70		1971–76		1978–84		1987–93	
	Planned	Actual	Planned	Actual	Planned	Actual	Planned	Actual[1]
Electricity[2]	17.0	16.5	28–30	29.7	50–60	50.0	100.0	54.0
Coal	25.0	27.5	50–53	55.0	70–80	70.0	120.0	83.0
Steel	2.3	2.2	4.8	3.8–4.0	7.4–8.0	7.4–8.0	10.0	6.9
Cement	4.3	4.0	7.5–8.0	8.0	12–13	12–13	22.0	13.0
Chemical fertilizers	1.7	1.5	2.8–3.0	3.0	5.0	5.0	7.2	n.a.
Textiles[3]	500.0	400.0	500–600	580.0	800.0	800.0	1,500.0	850.0
Marine products	1.2	1.1	1.6–1.8	1.6	3.5	3.5	11.0	3.7
Grains	6.6	5.0	7.0–7.5	8.0	10.0	10.0	15.0	10.0

n.a.—not available.
[1] 1988 figures.
[2] In billions of kilowatt-hours.
[3] In millions of meters.

Source: Based on information from Joseph S. Chung, "Economic Planning in North Korea," in Robert A. Scalapino and Kim Jun-yop (eds.), *North Korea Today*, Berkeley, 1983, 170–71; and *Kita Chōsen no keizai to bōeki no tenbō* (North Korean Economic and Trade Prospects), Tokyo, 1991, 34–35.

Table 5. Economic Assistance from Communist Countries and the Organisation for Economic Co-operation and Development (OECD), 1945-84
(in hundreds of thousands of United States dollars)

Source of Assistance	1945-49		1950-60		1961-69		1970-76		1978-84	
	Grants	Loans	Grants	Loans	Grants	Loans	Grants	Loans	Grants	Loans
Communist countries										
Soviet Union	0	530	5,148	1,985	0	1,967	0	9,060	0	2,962
China	0	0	3,360	1,725	0	1,050	0	16	2,587	0
East Germany	0	0	1,014	0	0	350	0	0	0	0
Other Eastern Europe	0	0	3,263	39	0	0	0	0	0	0
Total communist countries	0	530	12,785	3,749	0	3,367	0	9,076	2,587	2,962
OECD	0	0	0	0	0	0	0	0	0	12,420

Source: Based on information from Jung Mo Kang, "North Korea's Trade and Economic Cooperation," Seoul, January 1992; and Republic of Korea National Unification Board, Statistics of North Korean Economy, Seoul, 1986, various pages.

Table 6. Value of Exports to Communist and Noncommunist Countries, Selected Years, 1984-90
(in millions of United States dollars)

	1984	1986	1988	1990
Communist countries				
Soviet Union	447.9	642.0	887.3	1,047.4
China	247.5	255.2	212.3	141.5
Other	51.4	56.4	85.2	67.7
Total communist countries	746.8	953.6	1,184.8	1,256.6
Noncommunist countries				
Industrial countries				
Japan	131.1	154.3	293.3	271.2
West Germany	135.1	64.1	41.0	50.7
Other	16.1	15.0	39.7	39.0
Total industrial countries	282.3	233.4	374.0	360.9
Developing countries				
Africa	3.4	13.8	15.1	17.1
Asia	62.6	87.3	173.6	175.2
Middle East	13.4	4.6	3.9	2.5
Western Hemisphere	2.1	4.5	36.6	44.9
Total developing countries	81.5	110.2	229.2	239.7
Total noncommunist countries	363.8	343.6	603.2	600.6
TOTAL	1,110.6	1,297.2	1,788.0	1,857.2

Source: Based on information from *Kita Chōsen no keizai to bōeki no tenbō* (North Korean Economic and Trade Prospects), Tokyo, 1991, 92-93.

Table 7. Value of Imports from Communist and Noncommunist Countries, Selected Years, 1984-90
(in millions of United States dollars)

	1984	1986	1988	1990
Communist countries				
Soviet Union	467.9	1,186.5	1,921.7	1,667.9
China	248.8	280.8	379.7	403.4
Other	53.6	55.1	78.6	84.5
Total communist countries	770.3	1,522.4	2,380.0	2,155.8
Noncommunist countries				
Industrial countries				
Japan	279.4	203.7	262.7	193.7
West Germany	24.9	42.7	44.1	68.7
Other	81.0	84.4	160.1	210.7
Total industrial countries	385.3	330.8	466.9	473.1

Table 7.—Continued

	1984	1986	1988	1990
Developing countries				
Africa	1.8	2.3	11.2	2.5
Asia	128.2	143.8	258.4	259.1
Middle East	2.5	14.5	6.1	3.1
Western Hemisphere	1.7	8.3	44.2	26.2
Total developing countries	134.2	168.9	319.9	290.9
Total noncommunist countries .	519.5	499.7	786.8	764.0
TOTAL	1,289.8	2,022.1	3,166.8	2,919.8

Source: Based on information from *Kita Chōsen no keizai to bōeki no tenbō* (North Korean Economic and Trade Prospects), Tokyo, 1991, 92–93.

Table 8. Chronology of Meetings Between North Korean and South Korean Prime Ministers, September 1990–December 1992

Date	Location
September 1990	Seoul
October 1990	P'yŏngyang
December 1990	Seoul
October 1991 [1]	P'yŏngyang
December 1991 [2]	Seoul
February 1992 [3]	P'yŏngyang
May 1992 [4]	Seoul
September 1992	P'yŏngyang
December 1992 [5]	Seoul

[1] Originally scheduled for February 1991.
[2] Agreement on Reconciliation, Nonaggression, Exchanges, and Cooperation between the North and South signed December 13. Meeting led to December 31, 1991, initialing of Declaration on the Denuclearization of the Korean Peninsula and decision to establish a Joint Nuclear Control Committee after ratification of the declaration.
[3] Exchanged ratified copies of the two December 1991 agreements. Agreed on composition of the membership of three subcommittees—Exchanges and Cooperation Committee, Military Committee, and North–South Political Committee.
[4] Signed a series of protocols for the subcommittees established by treaty in the February agreement; later in May set up the North–South liaison offices in P'anmunjŏm. Agreed to allow at least 100 separated families to have brief reunion visits in August.
[5] Scheduled, but not held.

Table 9. Ground Forces Order of Battle, 1992

	Number
Strength	1,100,000 +
Organization	
Corps	
Conventional	8
Mechanized	4
Armor	1
Artillery	2
Geographic	1
Military district commands	9
Infantry divisions	26–30
Reserve and pacification divisions	22–26
Infantry brigades	3–6
Reserve and pacification brigades	18 +
Mechanized and mobile brigades	23–30
Armor brigades	14–15
Artillery brigades	20–30
Special operations forces brigades	22
Special operations forces battalions	7
Equipment	
Total medium and light tanks	3,600
T–54/55/59	2,200 +
T–62	600 +
T–34	n.a.
APCs	2,500
Other light tanks (PT–76/China's	
T–62/63 and North Korea's M–1985)	n.a.
Artillery	
Self-propelled	5,500 +
Towed	3,000 +
Multiple rocket launchers	2,400
Mortars	
60–160mm	9,000 +

n.a.—not available.

Table 10. Navy Order of Battle, 1992

	Number
Strength	40,000–60,000
Organization	
Fleets	2
Squadrons	
East Sea	9
Yellow Sea	5
Equipment	
Frigate	1
Corvettes	2
Submarines	
Whiskey class	4
Romeo class	19
Missile attack boats (PTG)	39
Coastal patrol boats	
PT	200
PC/PCS/PB	120
PCFS	60
Unspecified	20
Amphibious craft	
Nampo	100
AVC	40 +
LCM/LCU	32 +
Unspecified	23
Mine warfare craft	23

Table 11. Air Force Order of Battle, 1992

	Number
Strength	70,000
Organization	
Air combat commands	3
Air division	1
Interceptor regiments	12
Ground attack regiments	
Il-28	3
Su-25/7	1
MiG-19/A-5	2
MiG-15/17	2
Transport regiments	
An-2	6
Unspecified	6
Helicopter regiments	6
Equipment	
Total aircraft	
Jets	760
Bombers	82
Transports	480
Helicopters	300

Table 11. —Continued

	Number
MiG-15/17, air-to-air and ground attack	310
MiG-19, air-to-air	60 +
MiG-19/A–5, primarily ground attack	100 +
MiG-21, air-to-air	160 +
MiG-23, air-to-air	46
MiG-29, air-to-air	14
Su-7, primarily ground attack	20
Su-25, primarily ground attack	20
Il-28, primarily ground attack	82
An-2, transport	250 +
An-24, transport	10
Unspecified transports and trainers	200 +
Mi-2/4/8/17 helicopters	210 +
MD–500 helicopters	87

Table 12. Arms Trade, Selected Years, 1979–89
(in millions of United States dollars) [1]

	Imports		Exports	
Year	Value [2]	Percentage of Total Imports [3]	Value [2]	Percentage of Total Exports [3]
1979	338	16.2	145	6.8
1981	269	12.2	672	35.5
1983	231	12.7	268	15.7
1985	433	22.1	398	25.4
1987	452	n.a.	430	n.a.
1989	525	n.a.	400	n.a.

n.a.—not available.

[1] In constant 1989 dollars.

[2] To avoid the appearance of excessive accuracy, arms transfer data have been independently rounded, with greater severity for large numbers. Because of this rounding and the fact that they are obtained from different sources, world arms exports do not equal world arms imports.

[3] Because some countries exclude arms imports or exports from their trade statistics and their "total" imports and exports are therefore understated and because arms transfers may be estimated independently of trade data, the resulting ratios of arms to total imports or exports may be overstated and may even exceed 100 percent.

Source: Based on information from United States, Arms Control and Disarmament Agency, *World Military Expenditures and Arms Transfers, 1990,* Washington, 1991, 111.

Bibliography

Chapter 1

Baik, Bong. *Minjok ŭi t'aeyang Kim Il Sung Changgun* (General Kim Il Sung: The Sun of Our Nation), 1 and 2. P'yŏngyang: Inmin Ch'ulp'ansa, 1968.

_____. *Minjok ŭi t'aeyang Kim Il Sung Changgun* (General Kim Il Sung: The Sun of Our Nation), 3. P'yŏngyang: Inmin Kwahaksa, 1971.

Bradbury, John. "Sino-Soviet Competition in North Korea," *China Quarterly* [London], No. 6, April–June 1961, 15–28.

Brun, Ellen, and Jacques Hersh. *Socialist Korea: A Case Study in the Strategy of Economic Development*. New York: Monthly Review Press, 1977.

Carrier, Fred J. *North Korean Journey: The Revolution Against Colonialism*. New York: International, 1975.

Chosŏn Minjujuŭi Inmin Konghwaguk Kwahagwŏn Yŏksa Yŏn'-guso. *Chosŏn t'ongsa*. P'yŏngyang: Kwahagwŏn Ch'ulp'ansa, 1962.

Chosŏn Nodongdang Chungang Wiwŏnhoe. Tang Yŏksa Ton'guso. *Chosŏn Nodongdang Yŏksa Kyojae*. P'yŏngyang: Chosŏn Nodongdang Ch'ulp'ansa, 1964.

Choy, Bong-Youn. *Korea: A History*. Tokyo: Charles E. Tuttle, 1971.

Conroy, Francis Hilary. *The Japanese Seizure of Korea, 1868–1910: A Study of Realism and Idealism in International Relations*. Philadelphia: University of Pennsylvania Press, 1960.

Cumings, Bruce. "Corporatism in North Korea," *Journal of Korean Studies*, 4, 1982–83, 269–94.

_____. "Ending the Cold War in Korea," *World Policy Journal*, 1, Summer 1984, 769–91.

_____. "Kim's Korean Communism," *Problems of Communism*, 23, No. 2, March–April 1974, 27–41.

_____. "North Korea: Security in the Crucible of Great-Power Confrontations." Pages 153–72 in Raju G.C. Thomas (ed.), *The Great Power Triangle and Asian Security*. Lexington, Massachusetts: Lexington Books, 1983.

_____. "The Origins and Development of the Northeast Asian Political Economy: Industrial Sectors, Product Cycles, and Political Consequences," *International Organization*, 38, Winter 1984, 1–40.

_____. *The Origins of the Korean War: Liberation and the Emergence of Separate Regimes, 1945–1947,* 1. (Studies of the East Asian Institute.) New York: Columbia University Press, 1981.

_____. *The Origins of the Korean War: The Roaring of the Cataract, 1947–1950,* 2. Princeton: Princeton University Press, 1990.

_____. "Spring Thaw for Korea's Cold War?" *Bulletin of the Atomic Scientists,* 48, April 1992, 14–23.

_____. "Trilateralism and the New World Order," *World Policy Journal,* 8, Spring 1991, 195–222.

_____. "The Two Koreas: On the Road to Reunification?" *Foreign Policy Association,* No. 294, Fall 1990.

Cumings, Bruce (ed.). *Child of Conflict: The Korean-American Relationship, 1943–1953.* Seattle: University of Washington Press, 1983.

Eckert, Carter J. *Offspring of Empire: The Koch'ang Kims and the Colonial Origins of Korean Capitalism, 1876–1945.* Seattle: University of Washington Press, 1991.

Eckert, Carter J., Ki-baik Lee, Young Ick Lew, Michael Robinson, and Edward W. Wagner. *Korea Old and New: A History.* Seoul: Ilchokak for Korea Institute, Harvard University, 1990.

Foote, Rosemary. *The Wrong War.* Ithaca: Cornell University Press, 1986.

Grajdanzev, Andrew J. *Modern Korea.* New York: Institute of Pacific Relations, 1944.

Halliday, Jon, and Bruce Cumings. *Korea: The Unknown War.* New York: Pantheon, 1988.

Han, Woo-Keun. *The History of Korea.* Honolulu: East-West Center Press, 1972.

Harrison, Selig S. (ed.). *Dialogue with North Korea.* Washington: Carnegie Endowment, 1991.

Hatada, Takashi. *A History of Korea.* (Trans. and eds., Warren W. Smith, Jr. and Benjamin H. Hazard.) Santa Barbara: American Bibliographical Center-Clio Press, 1969.

Henderson, Gregory, and Key P. Yang. "An Outline History of Korean Confucianism, Pt. 1: The Early Period and Yi Factionalism," *Journal of Asian Studies,* 18, No. 1, November 1958, 81–101.

Kim, Han-Kyo. *Studies on Korea: A Scholar's Guide.* Honolulu: University Press of Hawaii, 1980.

Kim, Ilpyong J. *Communist Politics in North Korea.* New York: Praeger, 1975.

Kim, San, with Nym Wales. *Song of Ariran: A Korean Communist in the Chinese Revolution.* San Francisco: Ramparts Press, 1973.

Kim Il Sung. "On the Elimination of Formalism and Bureaucracy in Party Work and the Revolutionization of Functionaries.'' Pages 421–58 in Kim Il Sung, *Kim Il Sung: Selected Works,* 4. P'yŏngyang: Foreign Languages Publishing House, 1974.

Koh, B.C. ''North Korea, 1976: Under Stress,'' *Asian Survey,* 17, No. 1, January 1977, 61–70.

Lee, Chae-Jin (ed.). *The Korean War: 40-Year Perspectives.* (Monograph Series, No. 1.) Claremont, California: Keck Center for International and Strategic Studies, Claremont McKenna College, 1991.

Lee, Chong-Sik. *Korean Workers' Party: A Short History.* (Histories of Ruling Communist Parties, No. 185.) Stanford, California: Hoover Institution Press, 1978.

_____. ''Land Reform, Collectivization, and the Peasants in North Korea,'' *China Quarterly* [London], 32, No. 14, April–June 1963, 65–81.

_____. ''New Paths for North Korea,'' *Problems of Communism,* 26, No. 2, March–April 1977, 55–66.

_____. ''The 1972 Constitution and Top Communist Leaders.'' Pages 192–220 in Dae-Sook Suh and Chae-Jin Lee (eds.), *Political Leadership in Korea.* Seattle: University of Washington, 1976.

_____. *The Politics of Korean Nationalism.* Berkeley: University of California Press, 1963.

_____. ''Stalinism in the East: Communism in North Korea.'' Pages 114–39 in Robert A. Scalapino (ed.), *Communist Revolution in Asia.* Englewood Cliffs, New Jersey: Prentice-Hall, 1965.

Lee, Mun Woong. *Rural North Korea under Communism.* Houston: Rice University, 1976.

Lowe, Peter. *The Origins of the Korean War.* New York: Longman, 1986.

Nelson, Frederick M. *Korea and the Old Orders in Eastern Asia.* Baton Rouge: Louisiana State University Press, 1945.

An Outline of Korean Culture. P'yŏngyang: Foreign Languages Publishing House, 1979.

Palais, James B. *Politics and Policy in Traditional Korea.* (Harvard East Asian Series, No. 82.) Cambridge: Harvard University Press, 1975.

Robinson, Michael. *Cultural Nationalism in Korea, 1920–25.* Seattle: University of Washington Press, 1985.

Scalapino, Robert A., and Chong-Sik Lee. *Communism in Korea.* (2 vols.) Berkeley: University of California Press, 1972.

Shabshina, Fania I. *Ocherki Noveishei Istorii Korei, 1918–45.* Moscow: Izdatel'stvo Vostochnoi Literatury, 1959.

Sohn, Pow-key, Kim Chol-choon, and Hong I-sup. *History of Korea.* Seoul: Korean National Commission, United Nations

Educational, Scientific, and Cultural Organization, 1970.

Suh, Dae-Sook. *Kim Il Sung: A Biography.* Honolulu: University of Hawaii Press, 1989.

_____. *The Korean Communist Movement, 1918–1948.* Princeton: Princeton University Press, 1968.

Suh, Sang Chul. *Growth and Structural Changes in the Korean Economy, 1910–1940.* Cambridge: Council on East Asian Studies, Harvard University Press, 1978.

Tsubo, Senji. *Chōsen minzoku dokuritsu undo hishi* (Secret History of the Korean National Independence Movement). Tokyo: Nikkan Rōdo Tsūshinsha, 1959.

United States. Department of State. *The Foreign Relations of the United States: Conferences at Malta and Yalta, 1945.* Washington: GPO, 1955.

_____. Department of State. *North Korea: A Case Study in the Technique of Takeover.* Washington: GPO, 1961.

Washburn, John N. "Notes and Comment: Soviet Russia and the Korean Communist Party," *Pacific Affairs* [Vancouver], 23, No. 1, March 1950, 59–65.

Chapter 2

"Another Street Built in P'yŏngyang," *P'yŏngyang Times* [P'yŏngyang], April 14, 1992, 6, 7.

Beasley, W.G. *Japanese Imperialism, 1894–1945.* Oxford: Clarendon Press, 1987.

"Buddhism and Translation of Buddhist Scriptures," *North Korea Quarterly* [Hamburg], No. 55, Winter 1989, 43–46.

"Centenary of Kang Ban Sok, Mother of Korea," *P'yŏngyang Times* [P'yŏngyang], April 23, 1992, 8.

Chan, Wing-tsit. *A Source Book in Chinese Philosophy.* Princeton: Princeton University Press, 1963.

Chang, Dae-hung. "A Study of Korean Cultural Minority: The Paekchong." Pages 55–88 in Andrew C. Nahm (ed.), *Traditional Korea: Theory and Practice.* Kalamazoo: Center for Korean Studies, Western Michigan University, 1974.

Chang Yunshik. "Colonization as Planned Change: The Korean Case," *Modern Asian Studies* [London], 5, No. 2, April 1971, 161–86.

Ch'oe, Yong-ho. "Commoners in Early Yi Dynasty Examinations: An Aspect of Korean Social Structure, 1392–1600," *Journal of Asian Studies,* 33, No. 4, August 1974, 611–32.

"Chōsen Shimpō Sha" (The Korean Tiger), *Chōsen kankō annai* (Tourist Guide to North Korea). Tokyo: 1990.

"Chōsen Shimpō Sha" (The Korean Tiger), *Chōsen gahō* (The Korean Pictorial) [Tokyo], No. 6, 1992, 21.

"Churches Revived in the DPRK," *North Korea Quarterly* [Hamburg], No. 55, Winter 1989, 38–42.

Cumings, Bruce. "The Legacy of Japanese Colonialism in Korea." Pages 478–96 in Ramon Myers and Mark R. Peattie (eds.), *The Japanese Colonial Empire, 1895–1945*. Princeton: Princeton University Press, 1984.

Dix, Griffin. "How to Do Things with Ritual: The Logic of Ancestor Worship and Other Offerings in Rural Korea." Pages 57–88 in David R. McCann, John Middleton, and Edward Schultz (eds.), *Studies on Korea in Transition*. Honolulu: Center for Korean Studies, University of Hawaii, 1979.

Do You Know about Korea? Questions and Answers. P'yŏngyang: Foreign Languages Publishing House, 1989.

Eberstadt, Nicholas, and Judith Banister. "Military Buildup in the DPRK: Some New Indications from North Korean Data," *Asian Survey*, 31, No. 11, November 1991, 1095–1115.

_____. *The Population of North Korea*. (Korea Research Monograph No. 17.) Berkeley: Center for Korean Studies, Institute of East Asian Studies, University of California, 1992.

Etō Miyōko. "P'yŏngyang: Juche shisō to ni fuku kaze" (P'yŏngyang: The Wind Which Blows Around the Tower of Juche Thought), *Asahi janaru* [Tokyo], June 7, 1991, 7–10.

The Far East and Australasia, 1991. London: Europa, 1991.

Gekkan Chōsen. *Kita Chōsen: Sono shōgeki no jitsuzō* (North Korea: Views of a Country in a State of Shock). Tokyo: Kodansha, 1991.

"Grand Plan for Construction of P'yŏngyang," *P'yŏngyang Times* [P'yŏngyang], May 23, 1992, 4.

"Ground Broken for 'Kim Il Sung Hall' in Peru," *P'yŏngyang Times* [P'yŏngyang], April 4, 1992, 2.

Ho, Samuel Pao-San. "Colonialism and Development: Korea, Taiwan, and Kwantung." Pages 347–98 in Ramon H. Myers and Mark R. Peattie (eds.), *The Japanese Colonial Empire, 1895–1945*. Princeton: Princeton University Press, 1984.

"In Celebration of Dear Comrade Kim Jong Il's 50th Birthday," *Democratic People's Republic of Korea* [P'yŏngyang], April 1992, 14–19.

"The Indigenous System of Medicine," *P'yŏngyang Times* [P'yŏngyang], March 30, 1991, 4.

Inoue, Shūhachi. *Gendai Chōsen to Kin Shōnichi* (Modern Korea and Kim Jong Il). (Trans., Masaru Tayama.) Tokyo: Yuzankaku, 1984.

International Monetary Fund. *Direction of Trade Annual, 1970-76,* 12. Washington: 1980.

————. *Direction of Trade Yearbook, 1978.* Washington: 1980.

Juhn, Daniel Sungil. "The North Korean Managerial System at the Factory Level," *Journal of Korean Affairs* [Seoul], 2, No. 1, April 1972, 16-21.

Kankoku Kita Chōsen sōren (South Korea/North Korea Handbook). Tokyo: Hara Shobō, 1987.

Kim, Eugene C. "Education in Korea under Japanese Colonial Rule." Pages 137-45 in Andrew C. Nahm (ed.), *Korea under Japanese Colonial Rule.* Kalamazoo: Center for Korean Studies, Western Michigan University, 1973.

Kim, Hyung-chan. "Play as Method for Political Education in North Korean Preschools," *Journal of Korean Affairs,* 3, No. 2, July 1973, 33-41.

Kim, Ilpyong J. "The Mobilization System in North Korean Politics," *Journal of Korean Affairs,* 2, No. 1, April 1972, 3-15.

Kim Il Sung. *Kim Il Sung: Selected Works,* 2. P'yŏngyang: Foreign Languages Publishing House, 1964.

————. "Some Problems Related to the Development of the Korean Language." Pages 346-92 in Kim Il Sung, *Kim Il Sung: Selected Works,* 4. P'yŏngyang: Foreign Languages Publishing House, 1971.

————. "Theses on Socialist Education." Pages 346-92 in Kim Il Sung, *Kim Il Sung: Selected Works,* 7. P'yŏngyang: Foreign Languages Publishing House, 1979.

"Kim Il Sung Awarded Title of 'Generalissimo,' " *Japan Times* [Tokyo], April 14, 1992.

"Kim Il Sung Encyclopedia," *P'yŏngyang Times* [P'yŏngyang], March 14, 1992, 1.

"Kim Il Sung Termed Model for Revering Elders," *Korean Affairs Report,* Joint Publications Research Service, No. 76367, September 4, 1980, 11-15.

"Kim Jong Il Cult Worship System Now Rivals Kim Il Sung's in Intensity," *North Korea News* [Seoul], No. 619, February 24, 1992, 1, 2.

Kŭktong Munje Yŏn'guso. *Pukhan Chŏnsŏ, 1945-1980.* (A Complete North Korean Handbook). Seoul: 1980.

Kwon Youngmin. "Literature and Art in North Korea: Theory and Policy," *Korea Journal* [Seoul], 31, No. 2, Summer 1992, 56-70.

"Law on Protection of Environment," *North Korea Quarterly* [Hamburg], Nos. 44-45, Spring-Summer 1986, 67-69.

"The Leader and the People: Story about Vinalon," *Democratic*

People's Republic of Korea [P'yŏngyang], April 1992, 10.

Lee, Ki-baik. *A New History of Korea*. (Trans., Edward W. Wagner with Edward J. Shultz.) Seoul: Ilchokak, 1984.

Lee Kwang-kyu. *Kinship System in Korea*. (2 vols.) (HRAFlex Series.) New Haven: Human Relations Area Files, 1975.

Lee Mun Woong. *Rural North Korea under Communism*. Houston: Rice University, 1976.

"Let Nonaligned and Developing Countries Build National Culture under the Banner of Independence and Sovereignty." (Kim Ilsong's Official Banquet Speech at First Conference of Ministers of Education and Culture of Nonaligned and Other Developing Countries, September 6, 1983.) *North Korea Quarterly* [Hamburg], Nos. 34–35, Fall–Winter 1983, 80–83.

McCune, Shannon. *Korea's Heritage: A Regional and Social Geography*. Rutland, Vermont: Charles E. Tuttle, 1956.

"Nihon de hajime no kokusai seminā: Genjidai to Juche shisō" (First International Seminar in Japan on Juche Thought and the Contemporary Age), *Chōsen gahō* [Tokyo], No. 6, 1992, 30–35.

"No Medical Fees," *P'yŏngyang Times* [P'yŏngyang], August 17, 1991, 7.

"North Korea's President Writing 'Heroic Epic,' " *Japan Times* [Tokyo], April 11, 1992, 1.

"North Korea Touts Tourism," *Japan Times* [Tokyo], June 24, 1992, 5.

Palais, James B. *Politics and Policy in Traditional Korea*. (Harvard East Asian Series, No. 82.) Cambridge: Harvard University Press, 1975.

Pang Hwan Ju. *Korean Review*. P'yŏngyang: Foreign Languages Publishing House, 1987.

Park, Youngsoon. "Language Policy and Language Education in North Korea," *Korea Journal* [Seoul], 31, No. 1, Spring 1991, 28–40.

Park Myung-jin. "Motion Pictures in North Korea," *Korea Journal* [Seoul], 31, No. 3, Autumn 1991, 95–103.

"Public Education System of the DPRK." In *Do You Know About Korea? Questions and Answers*. P'yŏngyang: Foreign Languages Publishing House, 1989.

Republic of Korea. Ministry of Culture and Information. Korean Overseas Information Service. *A Handbook of Korea*. Seoul: 1978.

Shaw, Warren, and David Price. *Encyclopedia of the USSR: 1905 to the Present, Lenin to Gorbachev*. London: Cassel, 1990.

Sik, Chai Sin, and Hyon Jong Hun. *Cultural Policy in the Democratic People's Republic of Korea*. (Studies and Documents on Cultural

Policies.) Paris: United Nations Educational, Scientific, and Cultural Organization, 1980.

Suh Yon-Ho. "The Revolutionary Operas and Plays in North Korea," *Korea Journal* [Seoul], 31, No. 3, Autumn 1991, 85–94.

Taylor, Robert H. (ed.). *Asia and the Pacific.* (Handbooks to the Modern World.) New York: Facts on File, 1991.

United Nations. Department of International Economic and Social Affairs. Statistical Office. *1988 Demographic Yearbook.* New York: 1990.

_____. Food and Agriculture Organization. *Production Yearbook, 1978.* Rome: 1979.

_____. Food and Agriculture Organization. *Production Yearbook, 1979.* Rome: 1980.

United States. Central Intelligence Agency. *The World Factbook, 1991.* Washington: 1991.

_____. Central Intelligence Agency. *The World Factbook, 1992.* Washington: 1992.

_____. Department of State. *Background Notes: North Korea.* Washington: GPO, July 1989.

"Universities 'Meaningfully' Renamed," *North Korea Quarterly* [Hamburg], Nos. 58–59, Fall–Winter 1990, 55–59.

Vriens, Hans. "North Korea: Road to Nowhere," *Far Eastern Economic Review* [Hong Kong], April 30, 1992, 22.

Wagner, E.W. "The Civil Service Exam Process as Social Leaven—The Case of the Northern Provinces in the Yi Dynasty," *Korea Journal* [Seoul], 17, No. 1, January 1977, 22–27.

"Wonsan University of Agriculture," *P'yŏngyang Times* [P'yŏngyang], December 29, 1990, 5.

"Workers' Houses," *Democratic People's Republic of Korea* [P'yŏngyang], December 29, 1990, 12–13.

The World of Learning, 1991. London: Europa, 1990.

Youngsoon, Park. "Language Policy and Language Education in North Korea," *Korea Journal* [Seoul], 31, No. 1, Spring 1991, 28–40.

(Various issues of the following publications also were used in the preparation of this chapter: *Democratic People's Republic of Korea* [P'yŏngyang], 1987–93, *Korea Today* [P'yŏngyang], 1987–93, and *P'yŏngyang Times* [P'yŏngyang], 1987–93.)

Chapter 3

Aoki, Kazuo. "Japan-North Korea Trade in 1990." Pages 94–108 in *Kita Chōsen no keizai to bōeki no tenbō* (North Korean Economic and Trade Prospects). Tokyo: Japan External Trade Organization, 1991.

Australia. Ministry of Defence. Joint Intelligence Organisation. *North and South Korea Economic Activities*. Canberra: 1975.

Atlas of North Korea. Seoul: Ujin Map Publishing, 1992.

Bazhanov, Eugene, and Natasha Bazhanov. "Soviet Views on North Korea," *Asian Survey*, 31, No. 12, December 1991, 1123–38.

Brun, Ellen, and Jacques Hersh. *Socialist Korea: A Case Study in the Strategy of Economic Development*. New York: Monthly Review Press, 1977.

Cho, Sung Yoon. *Law and Legal Literature of North Korea: A Guide*. Washington: Library of Congress, Law Library, 1988.

Choe, In Duk. "Our Local Party Committee's Political Organization Works for the Increased Production of People's Consumer Goods Through a Mass Movement," *Kŭlloja* (The Worker) [P'yŏngyang], No. 1, January 1990, 80–85.

Choe Hyong-Sik. "Promoting Highly the Might of the Chuch'e Industry Is Important Struggling Task of Present Economic Construction," *Kŭlloja* (The Worker) [P'yŏngyang], No. 1, January 1991, 59–68.

Chong, Son Nam. "Joint Venture Is an Important Form of Economic Contacts with Foreign Countries." Pages 162–68 in *Kita Chōsen no keizai to bōeki no tenbō* (North Korean Economic and Trade Prospects). Tokyo: Japan External Trade Organization, 1989.

Chosŏn chungang yŏngam, 1989 (Korean Central Yearbook). P'yŏngyang: Korean Central News Agency, 1989.

Chun, Hongtack. "Estimating North Korean GNP by Physical Indicators Method." (Paper presented at Korean-American Economics Association Meeting, New Orleans, January 1992.) New Orleans: 1992.

Chung, Joseph S. "Economic Cooperation Between South and North Korea: Problems and Possibilities," *Korea Observer* [Seoul], 20, No. 1, Spring 1989, 1–20.

_____. "Economic Performance and Economic System: The North Korean Case," *Korea and World Affairs* [Seoul], 1, No. 1, Spring 1977, 67–86.

_____. "Economic Planning in North Korea." Pages 164–96 in Robert A. Scalapino and Kim Jun-yop (eds.), *North Korea Today: Strategic and Domestic Issues*. Berkeley: Center for Korean Studies, Institute of East Asian Studies, University of California, 1983.

_____. "The Economic System." Pages 274–300 in Han-Kyo

Kim (ed.), *Studies on Korea: A Scholar's Guide.* Honolulu: University Press of Hawaii, 1980.

————. "Foreign Trade of North Korea: Performance, Policy, and Prospects." Pages 78–113 in Robert A. Scalapino and Hong-koo Lee (eds.), *North Korea in a Regional and Global Context.* Berkeley: Center for Korean Studies, Institute of East Asian Studies, University of California, 1986.

————. *The North Korean Economy: Structure and Development.* Stanford, California: Hoover Institution Press, 1974.

————. "The North Korean Industrial Enterprise: Size, Concentration, and Managerial Functions." Pages 165–85 in Robert K. Sakai (ed.), *Studies on Asia, 1966.* Lincoln: University of Nebraska Press, 1966.

————. "North Korea's Economic Development and Capabilities." Pages 107–35 in Jae Kyo Park, Byung Chul Koh, and Tae-Hwan Kwak (eds.), *The Foreign Relations of North Korea: New Perspectives.* Boulder, Colorado: Westview Press, 1987.

————. "North Korea's Seven Year Plan (1961–70): Economic Performance and Reforms," *Asian Survey,* 12, No. 6, June 1972, 527–45.

————. "The Six Year Plan (1971–76) of North Korea: Targets, Problems, and Prospects," *Journal of Korean Affairs,* 1, No. 2, July 1971, 15–26.

————. "Studying the North Korean Economy: Some Methodological Notes." In *Pukhan kyŏngje ŭi chŏngae kwajong* (The Development Process of the North Korean Economy). Seoul: Institute for Far Eastern Studies, Kyungnam University, 1990.

Clifford, Mark, and Sophie Qaim-Judge. "Caught in a Vice: Economy on Hard Times, as Aid Dries Up," *Far Eastern Economic Review* [Hong Kong], November 29, 1990, 30–32.

Clifford, Mark, and Louise do Rosario. "Trade and Trade-offs," *Far Eastern Economic Review* [Hong Kong], January 16, 1992, 18–19.

"Completion of the Second Seven-Year Plan (1978–84)." Pages 150–62 in *Kita Chōsen no keizai to bōeki no tenbō* (North Korean Economic and Trade Prospects). Tokyo: Japan External Trade Organization, 1985.

Democratic People's Republic of Korea. *First Five-Year Plan for the Development of National Economy of the DPRK (1957–1961).* P'yŏngyang: Foreign Languages Publishing House, 1958.

————. Central Statistical Board. "On the Preschedule Fulfillment of the Six-Year Plan (1971–76) for the Development of the National Economy of the DPRK," *Korea Today* [P'yŏngyang], No. 12, 1975, 32–38.

_____. Central Statistical Board. *Statistical Returns of National Economy of the DPRK (1946–1960)*. P'yŏngyang: Foreign Languages Publishing House, 1981.

"DPRK Premier Yi Gunmo's Report on Third Seven-Year Economic Development Plan (1987–1993) at the Second Session of the Eighth Supreme People's Assembly, April 21, 1987," *North Korea Quarterly* [Hamburg], Nos. 49–50, Summer–Fall 1978, 110–47.

Eberstadt, Nicholas, and Judith Banister. "Military Buildup in the DPRK: Some New Indications from North Korea Data," *Asian Survey*, 31, No. 11, November 1991, 1095–1115.

Economist Intelligence Unit. *Country Profile: China, North Korea* [London], 1985–91.

_____. *Country Report: China, North Korea* [London], 1985–91.

The Far East and Australasia, 1992. London: Europa, 1991.

Foreign Broadcast Information Service—FBIS (Washington). The following items are from the FBIS series:

Daily Report: Asia and Pacific

"Full Text of Report on the Work of the KWP Central Committee Delivered by Its General Secretary Kim Il Sung to the Sixth KWP Congress in P'yŏngyang on October 10," 4, No. 200. (FBIS–APA–200, October 14, 1980, D1–D29.).

Daily Report: East Asia.

"DPRK Moves to Special Economic Zones Viewed," *Chungang ilbo* [Seoul], April 10, 1991. (FBIS–EAS–91–072, April 15, 1991, 21–23.).

"North Korea's Currency, Exchange, Banking Systems," *Tonga ilbo* [Seoul], October 15, 1991. (FBIS–EAS–92–024, February 5, 1992, 27–28.).

"North Korea Increases Economic Cooperation," *Mal* [Seoul], June 1991. (FBIS–EAS–91–178, September 13, 1991, 28–32.).

"UNDP Issues Advisory Notes on North's Economy," *Yonhap* [Seoul], July 31, 1991. (FBIS–EAS–91–147, July 31, 1991, 21–22.).

Han, Bong Chan. "Steady Growth of Agricultural Production," *Korea Today* [P'yŏngyang], 287, No. 8, August 1980, 19–21.

"Hard Sell," *Economist* [London], March 21, 1992, 40.

Hwang, Eui-Gak. *The Korean Economies: A Comparison of North and South*. New York: Oxford University Press, 1993.

Institute of Economic and Legal Research. Academy of Science. *Haebanghu Uri Nara ŭi Inmin Kyŏngje Palchŏn* (Our Nation's Economic Expansion after Liberation). P'yŏngyang: Academy of Sciences Publishing House, 1960.

"Joint Venture Law of the Democratic People's Republic of Korea: Operational Rules." Pages 80–87 in *Kita Chōsen no keizai to bōeki no tenbō* (North Korean Economic and Trade Prospects). Tokyo: Japan External Trade Organization, 1986.

Kang, Jung Mo. "North Korea's Trade and Economic Cooperation." Seoul: Kyung Hee University, January 1992.

Kawai, Hiroko. "North Korean 'Open Policies' and Trade with Japan: The Effects and Function of Japan-DPRK Trade." Pages 147–60 in Masao Okinogi (ed.), *North Korea at the Crossroads.* Tokyo: Japan Institute of International Affairs, 1988.

Kaye, Lincoln. "Hinterland of Hope," *Far Eastern Economic Review* [Hong Kong], January 16, 1992, 16–17.

Kazuhiko Shimizu. "Zone of Dreams," *Far Eastern Economic Review* [Hong Kong], May 28, 1992, 30.

Kim, Youn-soo (ed.). *The Economy of the Korean Democratic People's Republic, 1945–1977: Economic Policy and Foreign Trade Relations with Europe.* Kiel, West Germany: German-Korea Studies Group, 1979.

Kim Il Sung. "For Strengthening South–South Cooperation and the External Economic Work and Further Developing of Trade." Pages 144–54 in *Kita Chōsen no keizai to bōeki no tenbō* (North Korean Economic and Trade Prospects). Tokyo: Japan External Trade Organization, 1984.

_____. *Kim Il Sung: Selected Works,* 2. P'yŏngyang: Foreign Languages Publishing House, 1964.

_____. *Kim Il Sung: Selected Works,* 5. P'yŏngyang: Foreign Languages Publishing House, 1972.

_____. *Kim Il Sung: Selected Works,* 7. P'yŏngyang: Foreign Languages Publishing House, 1979.

Kita Chōsen no keizai to bōeki no tenbō (North Korean Economic and Trade Prospects). Tokyo: Japan External Trade Organization, 1991.

Kloth, Edward W. "The Korean Path to Socialism: The Taean Industrial Management System," *Occasional Papers on Korea,* No. 3, June 1975.

Komaki, Teruo. "Current Status and Prospects of the North Korean Economy." Pages 45–63 in Masao Okonogi (ed.), *North Korea at the Crossroads.* Japan: Institute of International Affairs, 1988.

Koo, Bon-Hak. *Political Economy of Self-Reliance: Juche and Economic Development in North Korea, 1961–1990.* Seoul: Research Center for Peace and Unification of Korea, 1992.

Korea. (Länderkarte.) Gotha, Germany: Hermann Haack, 1990 [map].

Korean Affairs Institute. *Chōsen no keizai* (Korean Economics). Tokyo: Oriental Economist Press, 1956.

Kŭktong Munje Yŏn'guso (Institute for Far Eastern Studies). *Pukhan Chŏnsŏ, 1945–1980* (A Complete North Korean Handbook). Seoul: 1980.

Kuo, Chin S. "The Mineral Industry of North Korea, 1989." Washington: Department of the Interior, Bureau of Mines, 1991.

_____. "The Mineral Industry of North Korea, 1990." Washington: Department of the Interior, Bureau of Mines, 1991.

Lee, Chong-Sik, and Se-Hee Yoo (eds.). *North Korea in Transition.* (Korea Research Monograph No. 16.) Berkeley: Center for Korean Studies, Institute of East Asian Studies, University of California, 1991.

Lee, Hy-Sang. "The August Third Program of North Korea: A Partial Rollback of Central Planning," *Korea Observer* [Seoul], 21, No. 4, Winter 1990, 457–74.

_____. "The Economic Reforms of North Korea: The Strategy of Hidden and Assimilable Reforms," *Korea Observer* [Seoul], 23, No. 1, Spring 1992, 45–78.

_____. "North Korea's Closed Economy: The Hidden Organization," *Asian Survey,* 28, No. 12, December 1988, 1271–79.

_____. "Patterns of North Korea's Economic Transactions with the South," *Asian Pacific Review* [Seoul], 1, No. 1, Spring 1989, 119–23.

Lee, Kun-Mo. "Concerning the Third Seven-year Plan (1987–1993) for the Development of the People's Economy of the DPRK." Pages 131–79 in *Kita Chōsen no keizai to bōeki no tenbō* (North Korean Economic and Trade Prospects). Tokyo: Japan External Trade Organization, 1987.

Lee, Pong S. "The Economy and Foreign Trade of North Korea." Pages 36–54 in Young C. Kim and Abraham M. Halpern (eds.), *The Future of the Korean Peninsula.* New York: Praeger, 1977.

_____. "An Estimate of North Korea's National Income," *Asian Survey,* 12, No. 6, June 1972, 518–26.

_____. "Overstatement of North Korean Industrial Growth, 1946–1963," *Journal of Korean Affairs,* 1, No. 2, July 1971, 3–14.

Lee, Seungkoon. "North Korea's Economic Crisis and the Possibility of Inter-Korean Cooperation," *East Asian Review* [Seoul], 3, No. 2, Summer 1991, 24–40.

Miyatsuka, Toshio. "North Korea's Joint Venture and Special Economic Zones." Pages 124–52 in *Kita Chōsen no keizai to bōeki no tenbō* (North Korean Economic and Trade Prospects). Tokyo: Japan External Trade Organization, 1991.

Murooka, Tetsuo. "North Korea's External Trade." Pages 22–93 in *Kita Chōsen no keizai to bōeki no tenbō* (North Korean Economic and Trade Prospects). Tokyo: Japan External Trade Organization, 1991.

Oh Kwan-Chi. "Chuch'e Versus Economic Interdependence: The Impact of Socialist Economic Reforms on North Korea." Pages 101–13 in Chong-Sik Lee and Se-Hee Yoo (eds.), *North Korea in Transition.* (Korea Research Monograph No. 16.) Berkeley: Center for Korean Studies, Institute of East Asian Studies, University of California, 1991.

Pak, Ky-hyuk. "Agricultural Policy and Development in North Korea." Pages 214–29 in Robert A. Scalapino and Kim Jun-yop (eds.), *North Korea Today: Strategic and Domestic Issues.* Berkeley: Center for Korean Studies, Institute of East Asian Studies, University of California, 1983.

Park, Kyung Ae. "Prospects for Social Change in North Korea and the Relationship Between North and South in the 1990s," *Kusimnyŏndae Pukhan ŭi Pyonhwa wa Nambukhan Kwangye* [Seoul], 1991, 92–96.

Pukhan kyŏngje ŭi chŏngae kwajŏng (The Development Process of the North Korean Economy). (North Korean Study Series, No. 11.) Seoul: Institute for Far Eastern Studies, Kyungnam University, 1990.

Pukhan muyŏkron (North Korean Trade). (North Korean Study Series, No. 1.) Seoul: Institute for Far Eastern Studies, Kyungnam University, 1979.

Republic of Korea. National Unification Board. *Statistics of North Korean Economy.* Seoul: 1986.

Rosario, Louise do. "Passing the Hat: North Korea Taps Supporters in Japan for Aid," *Far Eastern Economic Review* [Hong Kong], October 10, 1991, 75.

Scalapino, Robert A., and Dalchoong Kim (eds.). *Asian Communism: Continuity and Transition.* (Korea Research Monograph No. 15.) Berkeley: Center for Korean Studies, Institute of East Asian Studies, University of California, 1988.

Scalapino, Robert A., and Chong-Sik Lee. *Communism in Korea.* (2 vols.) Berkeley: University of California Press, 1972.

Shim, Jae Hoon. "The Inevitable Burden," *Far Eastern Economic Review* [Hong Kong], August 22, 1991, 21–24.

"A Statistical Appraisal of North Korea's Economic Performance in 1990," *East Asian Review* [Seoul], 3, No. 3, Autumn 1991, 103–10.

Suh, Nam-won. *Pukhan ŭi kyŏngje chŏngch'aek kwa Saengsan kwalli* (North Korean Economic Policy and Production Management). Seoul: Institute for Asian Studies, Korea University, 1964.

Suh, Sang Chul. *Growth and Structural Changes in the Korean Economy,*

1910–1940. Cambridge: Council on East Asian Studies, Harvard University Press, 1978.

_____. "North Korean Industrial Policy and Trade." Pages 197–213 in Robert A. Scalapino and Kim Jun-Yop (eds.), *North Korea Trade: Strategic and Domestic Issues.* Berkeley: Center for Korean Studies, Institute of East Asian Studies, University of California, 1983.

Tamaki, Motai. "Japan's Economic Cooperation with North Korea." Pages 108–23 in *Kita Chōsen no keizai to bōeki no tenbō* (North Korean Economic and Trade Prospects). Tokyo: Japan External Trade Organization, 1991.

_____. "The North Korean Economy During 1990–91." Pages 1–21 in *Kita Chōsen no keizai to bōeki no tenbō* (North Korean Economic and Trade Prospects). Tokyo: Japan External Trade Organization, 1991.

United States. Central Intelligence Agency. *Handbook of Economic Statistics, 1980.* (ER 80–10452.) Washington: 1980.

Wang, K.P., et al. *Mineral Industries of the Far East and South Asia.* Washington: Department of the Interior, Bureau of Mines, 1988.

Woo, Sik Lee. "The Path Towards a Unified Korean Economy," *Korea and World Affairs* [Seoul], 15, No. 1, Spring 1991, 21–38.

World Bank. *World Development Report, 1980.* Washington: 1980.

Yeon Hacheong. "Prospects for North Korea's Opening and Inter-Korean Economic Cooperation," *East Asian Review* [Seoul], 3, No. 4, Winter 1991–92, 49–68.

Yi, Hang-gu. "Pukhan ŭi sangŏp hyŏnhwang," (The Present Business Situation of North Korea) *Pukhan* [Seoul], No. 101, May 1980, 253–61.

Yoon, Suk Bum. "Macroeconomic Interaction Between Domestic and Foreign Sectors in the North Korean Economy: A Schematic Interpretation." Pages 55–77 in Robert A. Scalapino and Hongkoo Lee (eds.), *North Korea in a Regional and Global Context.* Berkeley: Center for Korean Studies, Institute of East Asian Studies, University of California, 1986.

(Various issues of the following publications also were used in the preparation of this chapter: *Asia Yearbook* [Hong Kong], 1987–93; *Asian Perspective* [Seoul], 1987–93; *Direction of Trade Statistics,* 1987–93; *Far Eastern Economic Review* [Hong Kong], 1987–93; *Foreign Trade of the Democratic People's Republic of Korea* [P'yŏngyang], 1987–93; Joint Publications Research Service, *Korean Affairs Report,* 1987–93; *Kita Chōsen kenkyū* (Studies on North Korea) [Tokyo], 1987–93; *Korea Today* [P'yŏngyang], 1987–93; *Nodong simmun* (Workers' Daily) [P'yŏngyang], 1987–93; *Pukhan* (North Korea)

[Seoul], 1987–93; *Vantage Point* [Seoul], 1987–93; and *Yearbook of International Trade Statistics,* 1987–93.)

Chapter 4

An, Tai Sung. "Korea: Democratic People's Republic of Korea." Pages 168–73 in Richard F. Staar (ed.), *Yearbook on International Communist Affairs.* Stanford, California: Hoover Institution Press, 1981.

———. *North Korea: A Political Handbook.* Wilmington, Delaware: Scholarly Resources, 1983.

Barnds, William J. (ed.). *The Two Koreas in East Asian Affairs.* New York: New York University Press, 1976.

Blodgett, John Q. "Korea: Exploring Paths of Peace and Reunification," *Washington Quarterly,* 15, Summer 1992, 171–81.

Brun, Ellen, and Jacques Hersh. *Socialist Korea: A Case Study in the Strategy of Economic Development.* New York: Monthly Review Press, 1977.

Carnegie Endowment for International Peace. *Dialogue with North Korea: Report of a Seminar on Tension Reduction in Korea.* Washington: 1989.

Chang, Jun Ik. *Pukhan Inmin Kundaesa* (History of North Korean People's Armed Forces). Seoul: Somundang, 1991.

Cho, Sung Yoon. *Law and Legal Literature of North Korea: A Guide.* Washington: Library of Congress, Law Library, 1988.

Clough, Ralph N. *East Asia and U.S. Security.* Washington: Brookings Institution, 1975.

Cumings, Bruce. *The Origins of the Korean War: The Roaring of the Cataract, 1947–1950,* 2. Princeton: Princeton University Press, 1990.

Delury, George E. (ed.). *World Encyclopedia of Political Systems and Parties.* New York: Facts on File, 1983.

Democratic People's Republic of Korea. *Kim Il Sung: Prodigy of Human Thinking.* P'yŏngyang: Foreign Languages Publishing House, 1979.

Do You Know about Korea? Questions and Answers. Pyŏngyang: Foreign Languages Publishing House, 1989.

Easton, Lloyd D., and Kurt H. Guddat (eds. and trans.). *Writings of the Young Marx on Philosophy and Society.* Garden City, New York: Doubleday, 1967.

Eberstadt, Nicholas, and Judith Banister. *The Population of North Korea.* (Korea Research Monograph No. 17.) Berkeley: Center for Korean Studies, Institute of East Asian Studies, University of California, 1992.

Han, Sung-Joo. "The Korean Triangle: The United States and the Two Koreas." Pages 43–54 in Chong Sik-Lee and Se-Hee Yoo (eds.), *North Korea in Transition.* (Korea Research Monograph No. 16.) Berkeley: Center for Korean Studies, Institute of East Asian Studies, University of California, 1991.

Jordan, Amos A. (ed.). *Korean Unification: Implications for Northeast Asia.* Washington: Center for Strategic and International Studies, 1993.

Kang-nyeong Kim. "Prospects for the Improvement of North Korea-Japan Relations and Its Impact on Inter-Korean Relations," *East Asian Review,* 4, Summer 1992, 67–86.

Kihl, Young Whan. "North Korea's Foreign Relations: Diplomacy of Promotive Adaptation," *Journal of Northeast Asian Studies,* 10, No. 3, Fall 1991, 30–45.

――――. *Politics and Policies in Divided Korea: Regimes in Contest.* Boulder, Colorado: Westview Press, 1984.

Kim, Chong-won. *Divided Korea: The Politics of Development, 1945–1972.* Cambridge: East Asia Research Center, Harvard University Press, 1975.

Kim, Ilpyong J. *Communist Politics in North Korea.* New York: Praeger, 1975.

Kim, Un-yong. "Constitution and Political System of North Korea," *Vantage Point* [Seoul], 2, No. 4, April 1979, 1–13.

Kim, Young C., and Abraham M. Halpern (eds.). *The Future of the Korean Peninsula.* New York: Praeger, 1977.

Kim Il Sung. *Kim Il Sung: Selected Works,* 7. P'yŏngyang: Foreign Languages Publishing House, 1979.

――――. *Let Us Reunify the Country Independently and Peacefully.* New York: World View, 1981.

――――. *On the Juche Idea: Excerpts.* P'yŏngyang: Foreign Languages Publishing House, 1979.

Koh, B.C. "The Impact of the Chinese Model on North Korea," *Asian Survey,* 28, No. 6, June 1978, 626–43.

――――. "Political Change in North Korea." Pages 1–16 in Chong-Sik Lee and Se-Hee Yoo (eds.), *North Korea in Transition.* (Korea Research Monograph No. 16.) Berkeley: Center for Korean Studies, Institute of East Asian Studies, University of California, 1991.

――――. "Political Succession in North Korea: Problems and Prospects." (Paper presented at Research Institute for Unification Conference, Seoul, October 1991.) Seoul: 1991.

Korean Workers' Party. Party History Institute. *For the Freedom and Liberation of the People.* P'yŏngyang: Foreign Languages Publishing House, 1979.

Kuktong Munje Yŏn'guso (Institute for Far Eastern Studies). *Pukhan Chŏnsŏ, 1945-1980* (A Complete North Korean Handbook). Seoul: 1980.

Lee, Chan Sam. *P'yŏngyang Tŭkp'awon* (P'yŏngyang Correspondent). Seoul: Chungang Ilbosa, 1990.

Lee, Charles S. "North Korea: Country Background Report," *CRS Report for Congress.* (90-475F.) Washington: Library of Congress, Congressional Research Service, September 27, 1990.

Lee, Chong-Sik. "Whither North Korea." (Paper presented at Research Institute for Unification Conference, Seoul, October 1991.) Seoul: 1991.

Lee, Chong-Sik (ed.). *Korea Briefing, 1990.* Boulder, Colorado: Westview Press, 1991.

Lee, Chong-Sik, and Se-Hee Yoo (eds.). *North Korea in Transition.* (Korea Research Monograph No. 16.) Berkeley: Center for Korean Studies, Institute of East Asian Studies, University of California, 1991.

Lee, Sang-du. "On Juche Ideology: A Philosophical Criticism," *Vantage Point* [Seoul], 3, No. 3, March 1980, 1-11.

McCormack, Gavan, and Mark Selden (eds.). *Korea, North and South: The Deepening Crisis.* New York: Monthly Review Press, 1978.

Macdonald, Donald Stone. *The Koreans: Contemporary Politics and Society.* Boulder, Colorado: Westview Press, 1990.

Nahm, Andrew C. *North Korea: Her Past, Reality, and Impression.* Kalamazoo: Center for Korean Studies, Western Michigan University, 1978.

Nam, Koon Woo. *The North Korean Communist Leadership, 1945-1965: A Study of Factionalism and Political Consolidation.* University, Alabama: University of Alabama Press, 1974.

Niksch, Larry A. "North Korea's Nuclear Weapons Program," *CRS Issue Brief.* Washington: Library of Congress, Congressional Research Service, March 11, 1992.

Pang Hwan Ju. *Korean Review.* P'yŏngyang: Foreign Languages Publishing House, 1988.

"Paper Publishes DPRK Constitution," *Naewoe Tongsin* [Seoul], November 26, 1992. Foreign Broadcast Information Service, *Daily Report: East Asia.* (FBIS-EAS-92-241.) December 15, 1992, 38-49.

Porter, Gareth. "Time to Talk with North Korea," *Foreign Policy,* No. 34, Spring 1979, 52-73.

"Pukhan ŭl Umjiginŭn Paegin" (Hundred Persons Who Govern

North Korea), *Wolgan Kyonghyang* (Monthly Journal of the Kyung-hyang Press in Seoul) [Seoul], 1989.

Radio Puresu. *Chōsen Minshu Shugi Jinmin Kyowakoku soshikibetsu jin-meibo* (DPRK Organizational Directory, 1991). Tokyo: 1991.

———. *Chōsen Minshu Shugi Jinmin Kyowakoku soshikibetsu jinmeibo* (DPRK Organizational Directory, 1992). Tokyo: 1992.

Republic of Korea. National Unification Board. *South-North Dialogue in Korea,* No. 54. Seoul: May 1992.

———. National Unification Board. Trends in North Korea. Seoul: November 1991.

Rhee, Sang Woo. ''North Korea in 1991: Struggle to Save Chuch'e amid Signs of Change,'' *Asian Survey,* 32, No. 1, January 1992, 56–63.

Scalapino, Robert A., and Dalchoong Kim (eds.). *Asian Communism: Continuity and Transition.* (Korea Research Monograph No. 15.) Berkeley: Center for Korean Studies, Institute of East Asian Studies, University of California, 1988.

Scalapino, Robert A., and Hongkoo Lee (eds.). *North Korea in a Regional and Global Context.* Berkeley: Center for Korean Studies, Institute of East Asian Studies, University of California, 1986.

Seymour, James (ed.). ''Korean People's Democratic Republic.'' In Albert P. Blaustein and Gisbert H. Flanz (eds.), *Constitutions of the Countries of the World,* 8. Dobbs Ferry, New York: Oceana, July 1973.

Shin, Jung-hyun. ''Changes in Relationship Between the U.S. and North Korea,'' *East Asian Review,* 4, Spring 1992, 3–20.

Shinn, Rinn-Sup. ''North Korea: Squaring Reality with Orthodoxy.'' Pages 85–124 in Donald N. Clark (ed.), *Korea Briefing, 1991.* Boulder, Colorado: Westview Press, 1991.

Storrs, Larry K. ''Communist Holdout States: China, Cuba, Vietnam, and North Korea,'' *CRS Issue Brief.* Washington: Library of Congress, Congressional Research Service, February 11, 1992.

Suh, Dae-Sook. *Kim Il Sung: The North Korean Leader.* New York: Columbia University Press, 1988.

Suh, Dae-Sook, and Chae-Jin Lee (eds.). *Political Leadership in Korea.* Seattle: University of Washington Press, 1976.

Suk Ryul Yu. ''Political Succession in North Korea,'' *Korea and World Affairs* [Seoul], 6, No. 4, Winter 1982, 565–94.

Timmons, Thomas J. (ed.). *U.S. and Asia Statistical Handbook, 1990.* Washington: Heritage Foundation, 1990.

United States. Central Intelligence Agency. *Chiefs of State and Cabinet Members of Foreign Governments.* Washington: 1989–92.

———. Central Intelligence Agency. ''Democratic People's

Republic of Korea: Government Structure.'' Washington: August 1990 [chart].

_____. Central Intelligence Agency. *Directory of Officials of the Democratic People's Republic of Korea.* Washington: 1989–92.

_____. Central Intelligence Agency. *The World Factbook, 1991.* Washington: 1991.

_____. Central Intelligence Agency. *The World Factbook, 1992.* Washington: 1992.

_____. Department of State. *Background Notes: North Korea.* Washington: GPO, July 1989.

_____. Department of State. *Country Reports on Human Rights Practices for 1989.* (Report submitted to United States Congress, 101st, 2d Session, House of Representatives, Committee on Foreign Affairs, and Senate, Committee on Foreign Relations.) Washington: GPO, February 1990.

Weisman, Steven R. ''North Korea Tries to Block Any Effects of Failed Soviet Coup,'' *New York Times,* September 13, 1991, A13.

Wise, Michael Z. ''IAEA Says Agreement Near on Check of North Korean Sites,'' *Washington Post,* February 26, 1992, A20.

Yang, Sung Chul. *Pukhan Chongch'iron* (North Korean Politics). Seoul: Pangyongsa, 1991.

Yum, Hong Chul. ''The Unification Dialogue Between the Two Koreas in the 1990s,'' *Asian Perspective,* 14, No. 2, Fall–Winter 1990, 77–92.

Zagoria, Donald. ''Soviet Policy and Prospects in East Asia,'' *International Security,* 5, No. 2, Fall 1980, 66–78.

(Various issues of the following periodicals were also used in the preparation of this chapter: *Asia Yearbook* [Hong Kong], 1987–93; *Chosŏn ilbo* [P'yŏngyang], 1987–93; *Far Eastern Economic Review* [Hong Kong], 1987–93; Foreign Broadcast Information Service, *Daily Report: East Asia,* 1987–93; Joint Publications Research Service, *Korean Affairs Report,* 1987–93; *Kita Chōsen kenkyū* (Studies on North Korea) [Tokyo], 1987–93; *Kŭlloja* (The Worker) [P'yŏngyang], 1987–93; *Nodong simmun* (Workers' Daily) [P'yŏngyang], 1987–93; *North Korea News* [Seoul], 1987–93; *Pukhan* (North Korea) [Seoul], 1987–93; and *P'yŏngyang Times* [P'yŏngyang], 1987–93.)

Chapter 5

Adelman, Jonathan R. (ed.). *Communist Armies in Politics.* Boulder, Colorado: Westview Press, 1982.

Alves, Dora (ed.). *Change, Interdependence, and Security in the Pacific*

Basin: The 1990 Pacific Symposium. Washington: National Defense University Press, 1991.

Amnesty International. *Amnesty International Report.* London: 1986–92.

An, Tai Sung. *North Korea: A Political Handbook.* Wilmington, Delaware: Scholarly Resources, 1983.

The Anti-Japanese Armed Struggle of the Korean People Organized and Waged under the Personal Leadership of Comrade Kim Il Sung. P'yŏngyang: Foreign Languages Publishing House, 1968.

Atta, Dale Van, and Richard Nations. "Kim's Build-up to Blitzkrieg," *Far Eastern Economic Review* [Hong Kong], March 5, 1982, 26–28.

Bae, Myong-oh. "Development Process of North Korea's Military Strategy," *Vantage Point* [Seoul], May 1982.

Baik, Bong. *Minjok ŭi t'aeyang Kim Il Sung Changgun* (General Kim Il Sung: The Sun of Our Nation), 1 and 2. P'yŏngyang: Inmin Ch'ulp'ansa, 1968.

Bandow, Doug. "Defusing the Korean Bomb." (Foreign Policy Briefing No. 14.) Washington: Cato Institute, December 16, 1991.

Berkley, Gerald W. "Comparisons and Contrasts of the Legal Systems of the Democratic People's Republic of Korea and the People's Republic of China," *Asian Profile,* 19, No. 4, August 1991, 293–302.

Bermudez, Joseph S. "CW: North Korea's Growing Capabilities," *Jane's Defence Weekly* [London], January 14, 1989.

_____. "New North Korean Weapons Systems," *Jane's Defence Weekly* [London], November 7, 1989.

_____. "North Korean Marines," *Marine Corps Gazette,* 71, January 1987, 32–35.

_____. "North Korea's Combined Arms Brigades," *Combat Weapons,* Spring 1986.

_____. "North Korea's Intelligence Agencies and Infiltration Operations," *Jane's Intelligence Review* [London], 3, June 1991, 269–77.

_____. "North Korea's Light Infantry Brigades," *Jane's Defence Weekly* [London] 5, No. 12, March 19, 1986.

_____. "North Korea's Nuclear Programme," *Jane's Intelligence Review* [London], 3, September 1991, 404–11.

Bermudez, Joseph S., and W. Seth Carus. "The North Korean 'SCUD B' Program," *Jane's Soviet Intelligence Review* [London], April 1989.

Bouchard, Joseph F. "The North Korean Naval Balance," *U.S. Naval Institute Proceedings,* March 1988, 128–34.

Cabral, David. "Orders and Decorations of the Democratic People's Republic of Korea." (Monograph on DPRK Awards.) Washington: Orders and Medals Society of America, 1992.

Ch'a, Mun-sop. *Hankuksa* (Korean History), 10. Seoul: Kuksa P'yonch'an Wiwŏnhoe, 1975.

Cha, Young Koo. *Northeast Asian Security: A Korean Perspective.* Washington: Center for Strategic and International Studies, 1988.

Cho, Myung Hyun. *Korea and the Major Powers: An Analysis of Power Structures in East Asia.* Seoul: Research Center for Peace and Unification of Korea, 1989.

Cho, Sung Yoon. *The Constitution of the Democratic People's Republic of Korea.* Washington: Library of Congress, Law Library, 1986.

_____. "Law and Justice in North Korea," *Journal of Korean Affairs,* 2, No. 4, January 1973.

_____. *Law and Legal Literature of North Korea: A Guide.* Washington: Library of Congress, Law Library, 1988.

_____. "Structure and Functions of the North Korean Court System," *Quarterly Journal of the Library of Congress,* 26, No. 4, October 1969, 216–25.

Choi, Chang-yoon. "Korea: Security and Strategic Issues," *Asian Survey,* 25, No. 11, November 1980, 1123–39.

Choi, Young. "The North Korean Military Buildup and Its Impact on North Korean Military Strategy in the 1980s," *Asian Survey,* 25, No. 3, March 1985, 341–55.

Chun Bong Duck, William Shaw, and Dai-kwon Choi. *Traditional Korean Legal Attitudes.* (Korea Research Monograph No. 2.) Berkeley: Center for Korean Studies, Institute of East Asian Studies, University of California, 1980.

Chung, Chin-wee. "The Evolution of a Constitutional Structure in North Korea." Pages 19–42 in *North Korea Today: Strategic and Domestic Issues.* (Korea Research Monograph No. 8.) Berkeley: Center for Korean Studies, Institute of East Asian Studies, University of California, 1983.

Chung, Chong-shik, and Gahb-chol Kim (eds.). *North Korean Communism: A Comparative Analysis.* Seoul: Research Center for Peace and Unification, 1980.

Chung, Kiwon. "The North Korean People's Army and the Party," *China Quarterly* [London] 14, April–June 1963, 105–24.

Clough, Ralph N. *Deterrence and Defense in Korea: The Role of U.S. Forces.* Washington: Brookings Institution, 1976.

_____. *East Asia and U.S. Security.* Washington: Brookings Institution, 1975.

Copper, John F., and Daniel S. Papp (eds.). *Communist Nations'
Military Assistance*. Boulder, Colorado: Westview Press, 1983.

Cordesman, Anthony H. "The Military Balance in Northeast Asia:
The Challenge to Japan and Korea," *Armed Forces Journal International*, 121, No. 4, November 1983, 80-81, 84, 88, 90, 92, 96,
98, 101, 108-9.

_____. "The Military Balance in Northeast Asia: The Challenge
to Japan and Korea," *Armed Forces Journal International*, 121, No.
5, December 1983, 27-28, 30-32, 34-37.

Cotter, Donald R., and N.F. Wikner. "Korea: Force Imbalances
and Remedies," *Strategic Review*, 10, Spring 1982, 63-70.

Council on U.S.-Korean Security Studies. "Emerging Patterns of
Regional Security in Northeast Asia and the Future of the U.S.-
ROK Alliance." (Proceedings of Fourth Annual Conference,
Honolulu, November 15-18, 1988.) Honolulu: 1988.

_____. "ROK-US Security Relations in the 1990s: Problems and
Prospects." (Proceedings of Fifth Annual Conference, Seoul,
November 15-18, 1989.) Seoul: 1989.

_____. "U.S.-Korean Security Relations: New Challenges and
Opportunities." (Proceedings of Third Annual Conference,
Seoul, November 29-December 2, 1987.) Seoul: 1987.

"Criminal Legislation in the People's Democratic Republic of
Korea," *Ungolovnoye Zakono datel'stvo Zarvezhnykh sotsialisticheskikh
gosudarst* (Criminal Legislation in Foreign Socialist States)
[Moscow], 1957. Joint Publications Research Service, *JPRS
Report: East Asia*. (JPRS/DC-406.) 1958.

Cumings, Bruce. *The Origins of the Korean War: Liberation and the
Emergence of Separate Regimes, 1945-57*. Princeton: Princeton
University Press, 1981.

_____. *The Origins of the Korean War: The Roaring of the Cataract,
1947-1950*, 2. Princeton: Princeton University Press, 1990.

Cushman, John H. "The Military Balance in Korea," *Asian Affairs*, 6, July-August 1979, 359-69.

Democratic People's Republic of Korea. Academy of Sciences.
Research Institute of History. *History of the Just Fatherland Liberation War of the Korean People*. P'yŏngyang: Foreign Languages
Publishing House, 1961.

East-West Center and Seoul International Forum. *Issues and Opportunities in U.S.-Korean Relations: A Report of the Committee on
U.S.-ROK Relations*. Honolulu: East-West Center, 1991.

Ebata, Kensuke. "North Korea Receives Ten More MiG-23 Floggers," *Jane's Defence Weekly* [London], 4, No. 7, August 17, 1985,
296.

Eberstadt, Nicholas. "North Korea's Massive Military Machine,"

Asian Wall Street Journal [Hong Kong], December 10, 1991.

Fisher, Richard D., Jr. *Responding to the Looming North Korean Nuclear Threat.* Washington: Heritage Foundation, 1992.

Gelman, Harry, and Norman D. Levin. *The Future of Soviet-North Korean Relations.* (R-3159-AF.) Santa Monica: Rand, 1984.

Gibert, Stephen P. (ed.). *Security in Northeast Asia: Approaching the Pacific Century.* Boulder, Colorado: Westview Press, 1988.

Hahm, Pyong-choon. "Ideology and Criminal Law in North Korea," *American Journal of Comparative Law,* 17, No. 1, 1969.

Harrison, Selig S. "A Chance for Détente in Korea," *World Policy Journal,* 8, Fall 1991, 599-631.

Henderson, Gregory. *Korea: The Politics of the Vortex.* Cambridge: Harvard University Press, 1967.

Ho, Lee Young. "Military Balance and Peace in the Korean Peninsula," *Asian Survey,* 21, No. 8, August 1981, 852-64.

Hong, Jong-Mahn. "Korean Arms Control," *Korea and World Affairs* [Seoul], 12, No. 3, Fall 1988, 485-95.

Hōritsu jihō (Legal Review) [Tokyo], 64, No. 3, March 1, 1992.

Institute for Foreign Policy Analysis. *The U.S.-Korean Security Relationship: Prospects and Challenges for the 1990s.* Washington: Pergamon-Brassey, 1988.

Jacobs, Gordon. "Armed Forces of the Korean Peninsula: A Comparative Study," *Asian Defence Journal* [Kuala Lumpur], November 1982.

_____. "Defector Details Army and Political Moves," *Jane's Defence Weekly* [London], November 7, 1989.

_____. "North Asian Naval Forces," *Asian Defence Journal* [Kuala Lumpur], January 1985, 65-73.

_____. "North Korea: An Offensively-Oriented Navy," *Navy International,* 91, January 1986, 52-55.

_____. "North Korea Looks South: Unconventional Warfare Forces," *Asian Defence Journal* [Kuala Lumpur], December 1985, 10, 12, 14, 16, 18, 20, 22-23.

_____. "North Korea's Arms Industry: Development and Progress," *Asian Defence Journal* [Kuala Lumpur], March 1989, 28, 30-32, 34-35.

_____. "North Korea's Military Command Structure," *Asian Defence Journal* [Kuala Lumpur], February 1986, 4, 6, 10, 12, 14-15.

_____. "USSR, N. Korea: New Relations," *Jane's Defence Weekly* [London], 5, No. 12, March 29, 1986, 581-83.

Jenerette, Vandon E. "The Forgotten DMZ," *Military Review,* 68, May 1988, 32-43.

Jones, Rodney W., and Steven A. Hildreth. *Modern Weapons and*

Third World Powers. Boulder, Colorado: Westview Press, 1984.

Kagan, Richard. *Human Rights in the Democratic People's Republic of Korea (North Korea).* (Prepared by Richard Kagan, Matthew Oh, and David Weissbrodt.) Minneapolis: Minnesota Lawyers International Human Rights Committee; Washington: Asia Watch, 1988.

Kang, In-dok. "Analysis of North Korean Military Policy," *Journal of Communist Studies* [London], 5, No. 1, 1968.

Kang, Koo-chin. "An Analytical Study of Criminal Law in North Korea," *Lawasia* [Sydney], 4, No. 2, December 1973.

————. "An Analytical Study of the North Korean Socialist Constitution," *Korea and World Affairs* [Seoul], 2, No. 1, Spring 1978, 126–62.

Kanin, David B. "North Korea: Institutional and Economic Obstacles to Dynastic Succession," *Journal of Social, Political, and Economic Studies,* 14, Spring 1989, 49–76.

Kihl, Young Whan. "The Korean Peninsula and the Balance of Power: The Limits of Realism," *Korea and World Affairs* [Seoul], 13, No. 4, Winter 1989, 689–707.

Kim, C.I. Eugene. "Civil-Military Relations in the Two Koreas," *Armed Forces and Society,* 11, Fall 1984, 9–34.

Kim, Chong-won. *Divided Korea: The Politics of Development, 1945–1972.* Cambridge: East Asia Research Center, Harvard University Press, 1975.

Kim, Dalchoong, and Cho Doug-Woon (eds.). *Korean Sea Power and the Pacific Era.* Seoul: Institute of East and West Studies, 1990.

Kim, Ilpyong J. *Communist Politics in North Korea.* New York: Praeger, 1975.

Kim, Joonup, and Kim Changsoon. *Han'gkuk Kongsanjuui Undongsa* (A History of the Korean Communist Movement). (2 vols.) Seoul: Asiatic Research Center, Korea University, 1970.

Kim, Tae Hwan. "A General Study of Kim Il Sung's Strategy," *Pukpang Yon'gu Nonch'ong* (Journal of Northern Korean Region Studies), 1, Winter 1975.

Kim, Un-yong. "A Study on the Legal System of North Korea," *Korea Observer* [Seoul], 8, No. 4, Winter 1977, 400–18.

Kim, Young C., and Abraham M. Halpern (eds.). *The Future of the Korean Peninsula.* New York: Praeger, 1977.

Kim, Young Jen. "European Conventional Arms Control Negotiations and the Korean Connection," *Korea and World Affairs* [Seoul], 15, No. 3, Fall 1991, 494–516.

Kim, Yu-Nam (ed.). *Korea, America, and the Soviet Union in the 1990s: Problems and Policies for a Time of Transitions.* Seoul: Dankook University Press, 1991.

Kim Il Sung. *Kim Il Sung: Selected Works,* 7. P'yŏngyang: Foreign Languages Publishing House, 1979.

Koh, B.C. "The Korean War as a Learning Experience for North Korea," *Korea and World Affairs* [Seoul], 3, No. 3, Fall 1979, 366-84.

_____. "North Korea: Profile of a Garrison State," *Problems of Communism,* 18, January-February 1969, 18-27.

_____. "The Pueblo Incident in Perspective," *Asian Survey,* 9, No. 4, April 1969, 264-80.

Kŭktong Munje Yŏn'guso (Institute for Far Eastern Studies). *Pukhan Chŏnso* (A Complete North Korean Handbook), 2. Seoul: 1974.

_____. *Pukkoe Kunsa chŏllyak charyojip* (Collection of Writings on North Korean Military Strategy). Seoul: 1974.

Lee, Chong-Sik, and Oh Ki-wan. "The Russian Faction in North Korea," *Asian Survey,* 8, No. 4, April 1968, 270-88.

Lee, Chung Min. *The Emerging Strategic Balance in Northeast Asia: Implications for Korea's Defense Strategy and Planning for the 1990s.* Seoul: Research Center for Peace and Unification of Korea, 1989.

Lee, Ki-baik. *Present and Future Security Problems of Korea.* Washington: Center for Strategic and International Studies, 1987.

Lee, Suck Bok. *The Impact of US Forces in Korea.* Washington: National Defense University Press, 1987.

Lee, Suck-ho. *Party-Military Relations in North Korea: A Comparative Analysis.* Seoul: Research Center for Peace and Unification of Korea, 1989.

Lee, Young Ho. "Military Balance and Peace in the Korean Peninsula," *Asian Survey,* 21, No. 8, August 1981, 852-64.

Livsey, William J. "Task in Korea: Convince North Attack Is Futile," *Army,* 35, October 1985.

Macdonald, Donald Stone. *The Koreans: Contemporary Politics and Society.* Boulder, Colorado: Westview Press, 1988.

Mack, Andrew. "North Korea and the Bomb," *Foreign Policy,* No. 83, Summer 1991, 87-104.

Marks, Thomas A. "North and South Korean OB," *Military Intelligence,* 7, October-December 1981, 18-24.

Matseulnk, V.A. *Koreyskaya Narodnaya Armiya* (The Korean People's Army). Moscow: Vonnoe Izdvo, 1959.

Mazarr, Michael J. "Orphans of Glasnost: Cuba, North Korea, and U.S. Policy," *Korea and World Affairs* [Seoul], 15, No. 1, Spring 1991, 58-84.

Menetrey, Louis C. "The US Military Posture on the Korean

Peninsula," *Asian Defence Journal* [Kuala Lumpur], August 1988, 12–14, 16–18, 20.

Merrill, John. *Korea: The Peninsular Origins of the War*. Newark: University of Delaware Press, 1989.

The Military Balance, 1990–1991. London: International Institute for Strategic Studies, 1990.

The Military Balance, 1991–1992. London: International Institute for Strategic Studies, 1991.

Nahm, Andrew C. *North Korea: Her Past, Reality, and Impression*. Kalamazoo: Center for Korean Studies, Western Michigan University, 1978.

Nam, Koon Woo. *The North Korean Communist Leadership, 1945–1965: A Study of Factionalism and Political Consolidation*. University, Alabama: University of Alabama Press, 1974.

National Defense University. *Pacific Regional Security: The 1985 Pacific Symposium*. Washington: National Defense University Press, 1988.

Niksch, Larry A. "The Military Balance on the Korean Peninsula," *Korea and World Affairs* [Seoul], 10, No. 2, Summer 1986, 253–77.

Oh, Kong Dan. "North Korea's Response to the World: Is the Door Ajar?" Santa Monica: Rand, 1990.

Okonogi, Masao. *North Korea at the Crossroads*. Tokyo: Japanese Institute of International Affairs, 1988.

Olsen, Edward A. "The Arms Race on the Korean Peninsula," *Asian Survey*, 26, No. 8, August 1986, 851–67.

_____. *U.S. Policy and the Two Koreas*. Boulder, Colorado: Westview Press, 1988.

Olsen, Edward A., and Stephen Jurika, Jr. *The Armed Forces in Contemporary Asian Societies*. Boulder, Colorado: Westview Press, 1986.

Owoeye, Jide. "The Metamorphosis of North Korea's Africa Policy," *Asian Survey*, 31, No. 7, July 1991, 630–45.

"Paper Publishes DPRK Constitution," *Naewoe Tongsin* [Seoul], November 26, 1992. Foreign Broadcast Information Service, *Daily Report: East Asia*. (FBIS-EAS-92-241.) December 15, 1992, 38–49.

Park, Jae Kyu, and Kim Jung Gun (eds.). *The Politics of North Korea*. Seoul: Institute for Far Eastern Studies, 1979.

Park, Tong Whan. "Arms Race: The Korean Implications in the International Politics of Northeast Asia," *Asian Survey*, 20, No. 6, June 1980, 648–60.

_____. "Issues of Arms Control Between the Two Koreas," *Asian Survey*, 32, No. 4, April 1992, 350–65.

Park, Yong-hon. "North Korea's Political Indoctrination Policy and the Sense of Values of Its Youth," *Vantage Point* [Seoul], February 1982.

Pearson, Roger (ed.). *Korea in the World Today.* Washington: Council on American Affairs, 1976.

Polomka, Peter. "The Two Koreas: Catalyst for Conflict in East Asia?" London: International Institute for Strategic Studies, 1986.

Pukhan Yŏn'guso (Institute for North Korean Studies). *Kim Il Sung Kunsaronsŏn* (Collection of Writings on Kim Il Sung's Military Thought). Seoul: 1979.

————. *Pukhan Chŏngch'iron* (Writings on North Korean Politics). Seoul: 1978.

————. *Pukhan Ch'ongnam* (North Korea Handbook). Seoul: 1984.

————. *Pukhan Kunsaron* (Writings on North Korean Military). Seoul: 1978.

Republic of Korea. Army. *Han'guk Kŭnsesa* (The History of the Military System in Korea). Seoul: 1968.

————. Ministry of Culture and Information. Korean Overseas Information Service. *Red Guerrilla Threat in Korea Blunted.* Seoul: 1968.

————. Ministry of Culture and Information. Korean Overseas Information Service. *Tunnel to Aggression,* No. 2. Seoul: 1975.

————. Ministry of National Defense. *Defense White Paper, 1988.* Seoul: 1989.

————. Ministry of National Defense. *Defense White Paper, 1989.* Seoul: 1990.

————. Ministry of National Defense. *Defense White Paper, 1990.* Seoul: 1991.

————. Ministry of National Defense. *Defense White Paper, 1991–1992.* Seoul: 1991.

————. National Unification Board. *A Comparative Study of South and North Korea.* Seoul: 1988.

Research Center for Peace and Unification. *North Korean Political System in Present Perspective.* Seoul: 1976.

————. *Socio-Cultural Comparison Between South and North Korea.* Seoul: 1975.

Rhee, Taek-Hyung. *U.S.-ROK Combined Operations: A Korean Perspective.* Washington: National Defense University Press, 1986.

Scalapino, Robert A., and Dalchoong Kim (eds.). *Asian Communism: Continuity and Transition.* (Korea Research Monograph No. 15.) Berkeley: Center for Korean Studies, Institute of East Asian Studies, University of California, 1988.

Scalapino, Robert A., and Kim Jun-Yop (eds.). *North Korea Today: Strategic and Domestic Issues.* (Korea Research Monograph No. 8.)

Berkeley: Center for Korean Studies, Institute of East Asian Studies, University of California, 1983.

Scalapino, Robert A., and Chong-Sik Lee. *Communism in Korea.* (2 vols.) Berkeley: University of California Press, 1972.

Seiler, Sydney A. "Kim Il-song, 1941–1948: The Creation of a Legend, the Creation of a Regime." (Master's thesis.) Seoul: Graduate School of International Studies, Yonsei University, June 1992.

Shaw, William (ed.). *Human Rights in Korea: Historical and Policy Perspectives.* Cambridge: Council on East Asian Studies and East Asian Legal Studies Program, Harvard Law School, 1991.

Shaw, William, and Choi Dai-kwon (eds.). *Traditional Korean Legal Attitudes.* (Korea Research Monograph No. 2.) Berkeley: Center for Korean Studies, Institute of East Asian Studies, University of California, 1980.

Sohn, Jae Souk. "Factionalism and Party Control of the Military in Communist North Korea," *Koreana Quarterly* [Seoul], 9, Autumn 1967.

Song, Young Sun. "The Korean Nuclear Issue," *Korea and World Affairs* [Seoul], 15, No. 3, Fall 1991, 471–93.

Stockholm International Peace Research Institute. *SIPRI Yearbook 1990: World Armaments and Disarmament.* New York: Oxford University Press, 1990.

_____. *SIPRI Yearbook 1991: World Armaments and Disarmament.* New York: Oxford University Press, 1991.

_____. *SIPRI Yearbook 1992: World Armaments and Disarmament.* New York: Oxford University Press, 1992.

Suh, Dae-Sook. "Arms and the Hammer and Sickle: Kim Il Sung and the Rise of the Partisan Generals in the 1960s," *Korea Journal of Defense Analysis* [Seoul], 1, No. 2, Winter 1989.

_____. *Documents of Korean Communism, 1918–1948.* Princeton: Princeton University Press, 1970.

_____. *Korean Communism, 1945–1980: A Reference Guide to the Political System.* Honolulu: University Press of Hawaii, 1981.

Thomas, Jack. "The Military Situation and Capabilities of North Korea." (Paper presented at Washington Institute for Values in Public Policy Conference on Korean Challenges and American Policy, Washington, December 6–8, 1988.) Washington: 1988.

Tracey, Gene D. "North Korea's Naval Forces," *Asian Defence Journal* [Kuala Lumpur], 7, July 1990, 30–32, 34–36.

United States. Arms Control and Disarmament Agency. *World Military Expenditures and Arms Transfers, 1989.* Washington: GPO, 1990.

_____. Arms Control and Disarmament Agency. *World Military Expenditures and Arms Transfers, 1990.* Washington: GPO, 1991.
United States. Congress. 83d, 1st Session. Senate. Committee on Foreign Relations. *The United States and the Korean Problem: Documents, 1943–1953.* Washington: GPO, 1953. Reprint. New York: AMS Press, 1976.
_____. Congress. 94th, 2d Session. House of Representatives. Committee on International Relations. Subcommittee on International Organizations. *Human Rights in North Korea.* Washington: GPO, 1976.
_____. Congress. 95th, 1st and 2d Sessions. House of Representatives. Committee on Armed Services. Subcommittee on Investigations. *Hearings on Review of the Policy Decision to Withdraw United States Ground Forces from Korea.* Washington: GPO, 1978.
_____. Congress. 96th, 1st Session. House of Representatives. Committee on Armed Services. Subcommittee on Investigations. *Impact of Intelligence Reassessments on Withdrawal of US Troops from Korea.* Washington: GPO, 1979.
_____. Congress. 96th, 1st Session. Senate. Committee on Armed Services. Pacific Study Group. *Korea: The U.S. Troop Withdrawal Program: Report of the Pacific Study Group to the Committee on Armed Services, United States Senate.* Washington: GPO, 1979.
_____. Congress. 100th, 2d Session. House of Representatives. Committee on Foreign Affairs. Subcommitee on Asian and Pacific Affairs. *The Bombing of Korean Airlines Flight KAL-858.* Washington: GPO, 1989.
_____. Congress. 100th, 2d Session. House of Representatives. Committee on Foreign Affairs. Subcommittee on Asian and Pacific Affairs. *Prospects for the Reunification of the Korean Peninsula.* Washington: GPO, 1989.
_____. Congress. 101st, 2d Session. House of Representatives. Committee on Foreign Affairs. Subcommittee on Asian and Pacific Affairs. *Korea: North-South Nuclear Issues.* Washington: GPO, 1991.
_____. Defense Intelligence Agency. *North Korea: The Foundations for Military Strength.* Washington: 1991.
_____. Department of State. *Country Reports on Human Rights Practices for 1990.* (Report submitted to United States Congress, 102d, 1st Session, Senate, Committee on Foreign Relations, and House of Representatives, Committee on Foreign Affairs.) Washington: GPO, February 1991.
_____. Department of State. *Country Reports on Human Rights Practices for 1991.* (Report submitted to United States Congress, 102d, 2d Session, Senate, Committee on Foreign Relations, and House

of Representatives, Committee on Foreign Affairs.) Washington: GPO, February 1992.

_____. Department of the Army. Headquarters. *Handbook on the North Korean Armed Forces.* (DA PAM 30-52.) Washington: 1960.

Urban, Mark L. "The North Korean People's Army," *International Defense Review* [Geneva], 16, July 1983, 927-32.

Wickham, John A., Jr. "U.S. Force Update—Effective Deterrence?" *Jane's Defence Weekly* [London], 7, No. 19, May 16, 1987, 943.

Yi, Ki Baek. *Present and Future Security Problems of Korea.* Washington: Center for Strategic and International Studies, 1987.

Yim, Soon Yim. "Maoism and North Korean Strategic Doctrine," *Journal of East Asian Affairs* [Seoul], 3, No. 2, Fall–Winter 1983, 335-55.

Yim, Yong Soon. "North Korean Military Doctrine," *International Security Review*, 7, No. 2, Summer 1982, 183-204.

_____. "North Korean Strategic Doctrine on the East Asian Regional System," *Korea and World Affairs* [Seoul], 5, No. 2, Summer 1981, 177-202.

Yukkun Sakwan Hakgyo. *Han'guk Kunsa Sasangsa* (The History of Military Thought in Korea). Seoul: 1981.

Yuksa Sahakqwa. *Han'guk ŭi Kunin Chŏngsin* (Military Spirit in Korea). Seoul: Samwhachulpansa, 1978.

(Various issues of the following publications were also used in the preparation of this chapter: Amnesty International Report [London]; *Chosŏn chungyang yŏn'gam* [P'yŏngyang], 1987-93; *Naewoe Tongsin,* [Seoul], 1987-93; *P'yŏngyang Times,* [P'yŏngyang], 1987-93; and *Wŏlgan Chosŏn* [Seoul], 1987-93.

Glossary

cadre—The term for responsible party, government, and economic functionaries; also used for key officials in the educational, cultural, and scientific fields.

chaebŏl—Korean translation of the Japanese word *zaibatsu*, or business conglomerate. A group of specialized (South Korean) companies with interrelated management servicing each other.

chikalsi, or *jikhalsi*—Refers to a major city under the direct administration of the central government rather than a provincial governor. In 1992 there were three *chikalsi:* P'yŏngyang, Kaesŏng, and Namp'o.

chip, or *jip*—The household, i.e., family members under one roof; the term *k'ŭnchip*, or *k'ŭnjip*, meaning "big house," refers to the "main family" of the eldest son, while the term *chagŭnchip*, or *chagŭnjip*, meaning "little house," refers to the "branch family" households of the younger sons.

Choch'ongryŏn—Abbreviation for Chae Ilbon Chŏson In Ch'ong Yonhaphoe, literally General Association of Korean Residents in Japan. Members of this Japan-based association tend to be supportive of North Korea's foreign policy and have kinship and financial ties to North Korea. Known as Chōsen sōren in Japanese.

chokpo—The Korean word for a genealogical record, usually that of an entire clan tracing its ancestry to a common ancestor who lived several hundred years ago.

Ch'ŏllima, or Ch'ŏllima Work Team Movement—Intensive mass campaign to increase economic production inaugurated in 1958; began as Ch'ŏllima Movement (Ch'ŏllima Undong), named after the legendary Flying Horse said to have galloped a 1,000 *li* in a single day; a symbolic term for great speed. Farm and factory workers were exhorted to excel in the manner of Ch'ŏllima riders, and exemplary individuals and work teams were awarded special Ch'ŏllima titles. The labor force was organized into work teams and brigades and competed at increasing production. Superseded in the early 1960s by the Ch'ŏngsanni Method (*q.v.*) and the Taean Work System (*q.v.*), and then in 1973 by the Three Revolutions Team Movement (*q.v.*).

Ch'ŏndogyo—Teachings of the Heavenly Way. This indigenous monotheistic religion was founded in the nineteenth century as a counter to Western influence and Christianity. Its Christian-influenced dogma stresses the equality and unity of man with the universe. Formerly Tonghak (Eastern Learning) Movement (*q.v.*).

chŏngbo—Korean unit of land area measurement. One *chŏngbo* equals about 2.45 acres, or 0.99 hectare.

Ch'ŏngsan-ni Method, or Ch'ŏngsan-ri—A personalized, "on-the-spot" management method or spirit reputedly developed by Kim Il Sung in February 1960 during a visit to the Ch'ŏngsan-ni Cooperative Farm in South P'yŏngan Province. In addition to important material incentives, the method has three main components: party and government functionaries must eschew their bureaucratic tendency of only issuing orders and directives; they must mingle with farmers and uncover and solve their problems through comradely guidance; and they should give solid technological guidance to spur efficient and productive achievement.

chuch'e, or *juche*—Political ideology promulgated by Kim Il Sung. The application of Marxism-Leninism to the North Korean experience. Based on autonomy and self-reliance, *chuch'e* has been popularized since 1955 as an official guideline for independence in politics, economics, national defense, and foreign policy.

corporatism—A political doctrine primarily of Iberian roots; it emphasizes organic, hierarchical politics and analogies with the corporeal body and blood lines.

Demarcation Line—Established under the Korean armistice agreement of 1953; marks the actual cease-fire line between North Korea and South Korea.

Demilitarized Zone (DMZ)—The four-kilometer-wide buffer zone that runs east and west across the waist of the Korean Peninsula for 241 kilometers, dividing it into North Korea and South Korea. The DMZ was created by the Korean armistice in 1953.

do, or *to*—Province, used in combined form, as -do for Kangwŏn-do Province. There are nine provinces in North Korea. *Do* also means island, as in Mayang-do.

exclusionism—Chosŏn Dynasty (1392–1910) foreign policy of isolation adopted after the Japanese invasions in the 1590s.

fiscal year (FY)—Calendar year.

"flunkeyism" (*sadaejuui*)—The opposite of *chuch'e;* excessive dependence on foreign countries—particularly cultural and political dependence on China.

gross domestic product (GDP)—A value measure of the flow of domestic goods and services produced by an economy over a period of time, such as a year. Only output values of goods for final consumption and intermediate production are assumed to be included in the final prices. GDP is sometimes aggregated and shown at market prices, meaning that indirect taxes and subsidies are included; when these indirect taxes and subsidies have been eliminated, the result is GDP at factor cost. The word *gross* indicates that deductions for depreciation of physical assets have not been made. Income arising from investments and possessions owned abroad is not included, only domestic production—hence the use of the word *domestic* to distinguish GDP from gross national product (*q.v.*).

gross national product (GNP)—The gross domestic product (*q.v.*) plus net income or loss stemming from transactions with foreign countries, including income received from abroad by residents and subtracting payments remitted abroad to non-residents. GNP is the broadest measurement of the output of goods and services by an economy. It can be calculated at market prices, which include indirect taxes and subsidies. Because indirect taxes and subsidies are only transfer payments, GNP is often calculated at factor cost by removing indirect taxes and subsidies.

han'gŭl—The Korean phonetic alphabet developed in the fifteenth century by scholars in the court of King Sejong. This alphabet is used in both North Korea and South Korea; in North Korea it is used exclusively, whereas in South Korea a mixture of the alphabet and Chinese characters is used.

International Atomic Energy Agency (IAEA)—Specialized agency of the United Nations established in 1957 to assist member nations with the development and application of atomic energy for peaceful uses and to foster and monitor a universal standard of nuclear safeguards. Through on-site inspections and monitoring, the IAEA ensures that fissile and related nuclear material, equipment, information, and services are not used to produce nuclear weapons as provided for in bilateral nuclear safeguard agreements between the IAEA and individual member nations of the Nuclear Nonproliferation Treaty (NPT), formally the Treaty on the Non-Proliferation of Nuclear Weapons.

International Monetary Fund (IMF)—Established along with the World Bank (*q.v.*) in 1945, the IMF is a specialized agency affiliated with the United Nations and is responsible for stabilizing international exchange rates and payments. The main business of the IMF is the provision of loans to its members (including industrialized and developing countries) when they experience balance of payments difficulties. These loans frequently carry conditions that require substantial internal economic adjustments by the recipients, most of which are developing countries.

national solipsism—Term indicating North Korea's isolationism and its sense that it is the center of the world's attentions.

Nordpolitik, or *pukbang chŏngch'aek*—The name given to the foreign policy pursued by South Korea since 1984 aimed at improving its diplomatic and economic ties with the former communist nations of Eastern Europe and the Soviet Union.

p'a—The lineage, a kinship unit consisting of all descendants of a common male ancestor who, in many cases, was the founder of a village. Some *p'a* contain thousands of households— *chip (q.v.)*—and members conduct ceremonies at the common ancestral gravesite. In some villages or hamlets in traditional Korea, many or most of the people were members of the same *p'a*.

p'ansori—Combine music and literary expression in ballad-form stories, which are both recited and sung by a performer accompanied by a drummer who sets the rhythms—a kind of "one-man opera" in the words of one observer.

suryŏng—Ancient Koguryŏ term for "leader"—Kim Il Sung's highest, and usual, title.

Taean Work System—An industrial management system that grew out of the Ch'ŏngsan-ni Method (*q.v.*). Introduced in December 1961 by Kim Il Sung while on a visit to the Taean Electrical Appliance Plant, the Taean Work System applied and refined agricultural management techniques to industry. Higher level functionaries assist lower level functionaries and workers in a spirit of close consultation and comradery. Party committees control the general management of factories and enterprises and stress political or ideological work as well as technological expertise. The system allows for material incentives to production.

Three Revolutions—Refers to "ideological, technical, and cultural revolutions" that have been stressed since the early 1960s. The term *Three Revolutions* was not used, however, until after 1973.

Three Revolutions Team Movement—Inaugurated February 1973 as "a powerful revolutionary method of guidance" for the Three Revolutions (*q.v.*)—ideological, technical, and cultural— stressed since the early 1960s. Under this method, the Three Revolutions teams are sent to factories, enterprises, and rural and fishing villages for on-the-spot guidance and problem solving in close consultation with local personnel.

Tonghak (Eastern Learning) Movement—Refers to an indigenous religious movement founded by Ch'oe Che-u in the early 1860s that brought together elements of traditional Korean and Christian religious beliefs and was the antecedent of Ch'ŏndogyo (*q.v.*).

wŏn—North Korean currency, also used as a monetary unit in South Korea although its value differs. The North Korean wŏn is divided into 100 chon and has multiple exchange rates—such as for official transactions and for commercial rates in most foreign trade. As of December 1991, US$1 = 97.1 chon.

World Bank—Informal name used to designate a group of four affiliated international institutions that provide advice and assistance on long-term finance and policy issues to developing countries: the International Bank for Reconstruction and Development (IBRD), the International Development Association (IDA), the International Finance Corporation (IFC), and the Multilateral Investment Guarantee Agency (MIGA). The IBRD, established in 1945, has as its primary purpose the provision of loans at market-related rates of interest to developing countries at more advanced stages of development. The IDA, a legally separate loan fund but administered by the staff of the IBRD, was set up in 1960 to furnish credits to the poorest developing countries on much easier terms than those of conventional IBRD loans. The IFC, founded in 1956, supplements the activities of the IBRD through loans and assistance designed specifically to encourage the growth of productive private enterprises in the less developed countries. The president and certain officers of the IBRD hold the same positions in the IFC. The MIGA, which began operating in June 1988, insures private foreign investment in developing countries against various noncommercial risks. The four institutions are owned by the governments of the countries that subscribe their capital. To participate in the World Bank group, member states must first belong to the International Monetary Fund (IMF—*q.v.*).

yangban—The traditional Korean term for the scholar-official gentry who virtually monopolized all official civil and military positions in the bureaucracy of the Chosŏn Dynasty (1392–1910) by competing in a system of civil and military service examinations.

Index

Academy of Agricultural Sciences, 123
Academy of Medical Sciences, 101
Academy of Sciences, 254
acquired immune deficiency syndrome (AIDS), 100
Agreement on Reconciliation, Nonaggression, Exchanges, and Cooperation (1991) (North-South Basic Agreement), xxvii, 162, 200–201, 202, 216, 264
agrarian bureaucracy, 14
agricultural collectives, 41, 76, 107, 139–40
agricultural production, xxiv, xxv, 41, 118, 134, 138, 139, 142, 162; under Japanese rule, 27
agriculture, 6, 8, 134–42; collectivized, 41, 73–76, 112, 139
AIDS. See acquired immune deficiency syndrome
Air Academy, 235
air force, 230–34, 237, 239, 250, 251; term of service in, 239
Algeria, 259
ancestors: veneration of, 64–65, 78, 81
An Chung-gŭn, 25
Angola, 259
Anju District coal mining complex, 129
An Si Fortress, 8
architecture, 86–88
Argentina, 259
armed forces: attitudes toward, 212; commander of, 173, 176, 190, 217; covert operations by, 248; deployment of, 249; factions in, 213–14; and Korean Workers' Party, 243–46; matériel, 249, 251; missions of, 216; mobility of, 249; national command authority, 216, 217; number of personnel in, 241; offensive objectives, 249–50; operational practice, 249; party organization in, 245; percentage of population in, 57; reserves, 235, 240–41; roles of, 168, 241–43
armistice agreement (1953), xxiii, 40, 51, 198, 215–16
army, 220–27, 239, 248, 251; chemical offensive doctrine, 252; Light Infantry

Training Guidance Bureau, 224, 225; Reconnaissance Bureau, 224, 225, 258; special operations forces, 220, 223–26, 249; volunteer, 213
art, xxiv, 84–85; in Chosŏn Dynasty, 14; under Koryŏ, 12; propaganda squads, 85; role of, 84–85; styles of, 85; under Three Kingdoms, 10
Asia Watch, 271
Association for Korean Residents in Japan. See Mindan
August Third People's Consumer Goods Production Movement, 108–9, 133, 134

Banister, Judith, 56, 241
Bank of Korea, 27
base class (ch'ŏmmin), 17
Benin, 259
birth control, 57
Blix, Hans, xxxiii
Bolivia, 259
Border Guards, 267
borders, 4, 50–51
Boxer Uprising (1900), 24
Brazil, 259
Britain, xxxiii, 23
Buddhism, xxiv, 9, 13, 61, 80–81, 82, 83; adoption of, 6, 8; under Chosŏn Dynasty, 13–14, 81; in Koryŏ, 12
Buddhism, Pure Land, 11
budget, 118–20
Bulgaria, 157
bureaucracy, 120; agrarian, 14; attitudes in, 169; under Japanese rule, 27, 31
Burkina, 259
Burning Island, The, 86
Bush, George, 205

Carter, Jimmy, xxxiv, 45
Catholic Church. See Roman Catholic Church
celadon porcelain, 12
Ceaușescu, Nicolae, 68

Contributors

Guy R. Arrigoni is Senior Analyst for Asian Affairs, Department of Defense, Washington, D.C.

Joseph S. Chung is Professor of Economics, Stuart School of Business, Illinois Institute of Technology, Chicago, Illinois.

Bruce G. Cumings is Professor of East Asian and International History, University of Chicago.

Pan Suk Kim is Assistant Professor of Urban Studies and Public Administration, Old Dominion University, Norfolk, Virginia.

Andrea Matles Savada is Supervisor, Asia/West Europe Unit, Federal Research Division, Library of Congress, Washington, D.C.

Donald M. Seekins is Associate Professor of Political Science, College of Law and Letters, University of the Ryukyus, Senbaru, Nishihara, Okinawa, Japan.

Published Country Studies

(Area Handbook Series)

550–65	Afghanistan	550–87	Greece
550–98	Albania	550–78	Guatemala
550–44	Algeria	550–174	Guinea
550–59	Angola	550–82	Guyana and Belize
550–73	Argentina	550–151	Honduras
550–169	Australia	550–165	Hungary
550–176	Austria	550–21	India
550–175	Bangladesh	550–154	Indian Ocean
550–170	Belgium	550–39	Indonesia
550–66	Bolivia	550–68	Iran
550–20	Brazil	550–31	Iraq
550–168	Bulgaria	550–25	Israel
550–61	Burma	550–182	Italy
550–50	Cambodia	550–30	Japan
550–166	Cameroon	550–34	Jordan
550–159	Chad	550–56	Kenya
550–77	Chile	550–81	Korea, North
550–60	China	550–41	Korea, South
550–26	Colombia	550–58	Laos
550–33	Commonwealth Caribbean, Islands of the	550–24	Lebanon
550–91	Congo	550–38	Liberia
550–90	Costa Rica	550–85	Libya
550–69	Côte d'Ivoire (Ivory Coast)	550–172	Malawi
550–152	Cuba	550–45	Malaysia
550–22	Cyprus	550–161	Mauritania
550–158	Czechoslovakia	550–79	Mexico
550–36	Dominican Republic and Haiti	550–76	Mongolia
550–52	Ecuador	550–49	Morocco
550–43	Egypt	550–64	Mozambique
550–150	El Salvador	550–35	Nepal and Bhutan
550–28	Ethiopia	550–88	Nicaragua
550–167	Finland	550–157	Nigeria
550–155	Germany, East	550–94	Oceania
550–173	Germany, Fed. Rep. of	550–48	Pakistan
550–153	Ghana	550–46	Panama

550-156	Paraguay	550-53	Thailand
550-185	Persian Gulf States	550-89	Tunisia
550-42	Peru	550-80	Turkey
550-72	Philippines	550-74	Uganda
550-162	Poland	550-97	Uruguay
550-181	Portugal	550-71	Venezuela
550-160	Romania	550-32	Vietnam
550-37	Rwanda and Burundi	550-183	Yemens, The
550-51	Saudi Arabia	550-99	Yugoslavia
550-70	Senegal	550-67	Zaire
550-180	Sierra Leone	550-75	Zambia
550-184	Singapore	550-171	Zimbabwe
550-86	Somalia		
550-93	South Africa		
550-95	Soviet Union		
550-179	Spain		
550-96	Sri Lanka		
550-27	Sudan		
550-47	Syria		
550-62	Tanzania